D1601362

Cities of the Mind

Images and Themes of the City in the Social Sciences

ENVIRONMENT, DEVELOPMENT, AND PUBLIC POLICY

A series of volumes under the general editorship of
Lawrence Susskind, *Massachusetts Institute of Technoloy, Cambridge, Massachusetts*

CITIES AND DEVELOPMENT

Series Editor: Lloyd Rodwin, *Massachusetts Institute of Technology Cambridge, Massachusetts*

CITIES AND CITY PLANNING
Lloyd Rodwin

THINKING ABOUT DEVELOPMENT
Lisa Peattie

CONSERVING AMERICA'S NEIGHBORHOODS
Robert K. Yin

MAKING WORK
Self-Created Jobs in Participatory Organizations
William Ronco and Lisa Peattie

CITIES OF THE MIND
Images and Themes of the City in the Social Sciences
Lloyd Rodwin and Robert M. Hollister

Other subseries:

ENVIRONMENTAL POLICY AND PLANNING
Series Editor: Lawrence Susskind, *Massachusetts Institute of Technology, Cambridge, Massachusetts*

PUBLIC POLICY AND SOCIAL SERVICES
Series Editor: Gary Marx, *Massachusetts Institute of Technology, Cambridge, Massachusetts*

Cities of the Mind

Images and Themes of the City in the Social Sciences

Edited by

Lloyd Rodwin

Massachusetts Institute of Technology
Cambridge, Massachusetts

and

Robert M. Hollister

Tufts University
Medford, Massachusetts

Plenum Press • *New York and London*

Library of Congress Cataloging in Publication Data

Main entry under title:

Cities of the mind.

(Environment, development, and public policy. Cities and development)
Bibliography: p.
Includes index.
1. Cities and towns — United States — Addresses, essays, lectures. 2. Social sciences — United States — Addresses, essays, lectures. 3. Cities and towns — Addresses, essays, lectures. 4. Social sciences — Addresses, essays, lectures. I. Hollister, Robert M. II. Rodwin, Lloyd. III. Series.
HT123.C4967 1984   307.7'6'0973   84-1991
ISBN 0-306-41426-0

© 1984 Plenum Press, New York
A Division of Plenum Publishing Corporation
233 Spring Street, New York, N.Y. 10013

Printed in the United States of America

To Gyorgy Kepes,
Kevin Lynch, and Gerald Holton,
who sparked our interest in
images and themes

Contributors

Paolo Ceccarelli, Department of Social and Economic Analysis of the Territory, Istituto Universitario di Architettura, Venice, Italy

Michael H. Frisch, Department of History, State University of New York at Buffalo, Buffalo, New York

Gerald E. Frug, Harvard Law School, Cambridge, Massachusetts

Nathan Glazer, Graduate School of Education, Harvard University, Cambridge, Massachusetts

Peter Hall, Department of City and Regional Planning, University of California, Berkeley, California, and Department of Geography, University of Reading, Reading, England

John R. Harris, African Studies Center, Boston University, Boston, Massachusetts

Michael A. Hindery, Department of American Civilization, University of Pennsylvania, Philadelphia, Pennsylvania

Robert M. Hollister, Department of Urban and Environmental Policy, Tufts University, Medford, Massachusetts

Peter Langer, Department of Sociology, Boston University, Boston, Massachusetts

Anthony Leeds, Department of Anthropology, Boston University, Boston, Massachusetts

Kevin Lynch, Carr-Lynch Associates and Professor of City Planning Emeritus, Massachusetts Institute of Technology, Cambridge, Massachusetts

Leo Marx, Program in Science, Technology, and Society, Massachusetts Institute of Technology, Cambridge, Massachusetts

Lisa Redfield Peattie, Department of Urban Studies and Planning, Massachusetts Institute of Technology, Cambridge, Massachusetts

Thomas A. Reiner, Department of Regional Science, University of Pennsylvania, Philadelphia, Pennsylvania

Edward Robbins, Department of Architecture, Massachusetts Institute of Technology, Cambridge, Massachusetts

Lloyd Rodwin, Department of Urban Studies and Planning, Massachusetts Institute of Technology, Cambridge, Massachusetts

Martin Shefter, Department of Government, Cornell University, Ithaca, New York

Charles Tilly, Center for Research on Social Organization, University of Michigan, Ann Arbor, Michigan

Sam Bass Warner, Jr., Department of History, Boston University, Boston, Massachusetts

Preface

Curious about the images of the city that have been evolving in the different social sciences, we did what academics often do in such a situation: we set up a seminar[1] on "Images of the City in the Social Sciences." From the start, we counted on the help of specialists in other fields to pursue their interests. Of the persons who agreed to participate, all but two came from the United States, and their analyses, in the main, reflect the experience of Western countries and the United States.

In our formal instructions to our collaborators, we took for granted that a variety of images of the city could be found or inferred in their fields of expertise. We asked them to identify these images and their functions, to explain how and why they have changed over time, and to relate these images to the distinct intellectual traditions and techniques—analytical or otherwise—in their respective fields. The definition of image was left to the judgment of the participants.

We avoided more detailed instructions for several reasons. We were not sure what to prescribe. We knew that the attention paid to images of the city varied in the different fields: for some, there were clear traditions; for others, it was a novel inquiry. We took for granted that the various disciplines ask somewhat different questions about urban images, and that the meanings in these fields of *urban* and of *image* differ in important ways. We felt, however, that the anticipated variations in the responses might help in the evolution of our thinking. We realized that not everyone would produce the paper we sought, and that some of the images drawn would inescapably reflect the values and special pathways of the person responsible for the sketch. However, the gamble turned out well from our point of view, for the papers we did get surpassed our most sanguine expectations. Strikingly original, they turned out to be provoca-

[1]We are indebted to Philip Shapira and Anthony Mallows for teaching assistance and also to the Charles Abrams Fund for defraying some of the expenses of this Seminar.

tive literature reviews of a nonconventional theme, one that sheds light on the evolution of some of the ideas and methods of the social sciences as well as their urban specializations.

Save for the solicitation of four additional essays (identified in the text), some shifts in the order of presentation, and some editing of materials (in response to the suggestions made in our seminar discussions and to the occasional slips or overlaps), there have been few substantive changes.

The book has three parts. The first is the introduction. It provides an overview—based in part on the subsequent essays—of some of the characteristics of the urban images in the social sciences, as well as the likely directions of future development. The second part examines the evolution of these urban images and themes in specific fields: geography, economics, political science, anthropology, sociology, history, and city planning. The essays in the final part are more general in nature. They provide contextual reviews of several related subjects, for example, an evaluation of the responses to Kevin Lynch's *The Image of the City;* a reappraisal of alleged antiurban images in classic American literature; some reflections on the ideological and symbolic aspects of urban images; a historical case study in urban imagery (focusing on the first United States "urban crisis" in 1890); a critique of the legal concept of the city as the creature of the state; a dissenting view on the conventional distinction between rural and urban in anthropology; and some reflections on the evolution of Marxian and neo-Marxian images of the city.

Far from being a trivial exercise, the study of urban images turns out to be concerned, in the main, with values, assumptions, and policy implications. We are now all the more persuaded that there is much fresh knowledge to be gained by examining the extent to which basic choices are affected by the evolution and strength of these images. No doubt the essays here only begin the exploration of this field. But our aim has been to demonstrate the potential; if we have been successful, others will respond to these efforts.

Lloyd Rodwin
Robert M. Hollister

Contents

PART I

Introduction

Images, Themes, and Urbanography

LLOYD RODWIN AND ROBERT M. HOLLISTER

This collection of essays explores a symbolic realm of urban images and themes. Too frequently, this realm is treated as a backdrop, whereas it deeply influences the plot and characterization. We tend to be only dimly aware of this city of the mind that is the focus of the analyses presented in this book. The thoroughfares and buildings of this invisible city control our movement as much as do the actual streets of New York, Indianapolis, or Bombay. They are tangible to us as metaphors or symbols—the city as a creature of the state, the city as a machine or as an organism, the central city as a jungle or a reservation. Indeed, the concept of the city as a state subdivision or the likening of the city to a machine may presuppose the existence of a body of deeply held ideas—constraining or mechanistic notions whose power is immensely greater than that simply of an apt (or stale) figure of speech.

So far as we know, this is the first systematic examination of the urban images and themes in the various social sciences and some related professional fields. In the course of sifting and comparing these different urban images—and of trying to relate them to some other relevant supportive ideas—we found ourselves increasingly addressing five topics. The first, as might be expected, was the definition of urban images and themes. The second involved the explicitness of their formulation in the different disciplines—and the ways they dealt with the problem of parts

Lloyd Rodwin • Department of Urban Studies and Planning, Massachusetts Institute of Technology, Cambridge, Massachusetts.   *Robert M. Hollister* • Department of Urban and Environmental Policy, Tufts University, Medford, Massachusetts.

and wholes. The third concerned the function of urban images and their patterns of change, especially the factors that have determined their popular or professional acceptance. The fourth involved the relationship of the observer to the urban reality. And the fifth entailed the immediate and long-term prospects of this realm of urban studies.

Although we consider our observations and findings tentative, our hope is that they will provide the reader with an initial orientation, or perhaps an overview, for the more specific essays that follow.

THEMATIC URBAN IMAGES

As might be expected, our thinking about urban images gradually changed in the course of this inquiry. Originally, we dealt with images in the broadest sense. For our purposes, the definition of *image* in the Shorter Oxford Dictionary offered a wide range of possibilities: "a likeness, a mental representation of something, especially a visible object, a mental picture or impression, an idea, conception; a vivid or graphic description; a simile, metaphor, or figure of speech; an optical appearance or counterpart." Any of these terms, we thought, could indicate how people in different fields have viewed or have chosen to characterize the city. There appeared to be little reason to distinguish between images and metaphors.

Perhaps one reason that we clung to this view was that the city has often been summed up attractively in a metaphor. We were struck, too, by the fact that the most trenchant of these metaphors generally reflect Picasso's dictum that "art is a lie to tell a truth." They depict or caricature a condition, a function, a trend, a problem, or an injustice. The idea of the educative city was made unforgettable by the image of a "school without walls"[1]; so too, for the communications view of the city as an efficient switchboard used "to enlarge the range and reduce the cost of individual and social choice"[2]; or the biting view of the inner-core city as a sandbox

---

[1]The forerunner of this concept appears to have been A. Malraux's notion of a "museum without walls." A. Malraux, *The Voices of Silence* (New York: Doubleday, 1954). The idea was later extended to the city by many persons. For one example, see S. Carr and K. Lynch, "Where Learning Happens," *Daedalus* 97 (1968): 1277–1291.

[2]K. Deutsch, "On Social Communication and the Metropolis," in *The Future Metropolis*, ed. L. Rodwin (New York: Braziller, 1961), pp. 129–143.

to occupy people who would be nuisances or otherwise likely to get into trouble[3]; or the comparable characterization of inner cities as the equivalent of (Indian) reservations for the people and their guardians (and those profiting from their presence) who cannot function in the larger society.[4] Powerful, too, is the image of parasitic cities that perform no useful or essential functions[5]; or the neo-Marxian conceptualization of metropolitan (or imperial) power to characterize capitalist urban enclaves that exploit the population of their cities and their hinterlands in behalf of local or expatriate ruling groups[6]; or the shrewd manipulation of tough-minded, realistic, yet basically romanticized conceptions of the life and death of cities.[7]

We ran into difficulties, however, when we tried to assess the value of the numerous images, themes, and metaphors we encountered in the literature and in the papers we received. There was in one sense an *embarras de richesses*. They dealt with different urban subsystems (gravitational, hierarchical, competitive, or economic, social, political, and physical); with different functions (habitat, power, communications, and melting pot); with different roles (educative, legal, exploitative, parasitic, or metropolitan and neocolonial); with different developmental processes (growth, maturity, and decline); with different focuses on physical elements (subjective perceptions and attributed meanings as well as physical form); and with different frames and methods (liberal and Marxist, cross-sectional and historical, descriptive and modeling, quantitative and subjective, parts and wholes). The images also mirrored differences of interpretation of the urban phenomena: changes in ideas—as, for instance, the shift from melting pot to mold; or from an emphasis on managerial to bargaining and then to infighting processes for urban policymaking; or a

[3]G. Sternlieb, "The City as Sandbox," *Public Interest* 25 (1971): 14–21.

[4]N. Long, "The City as Reservation," *Public Interest* 25 (1971): 22–38.

[5]B. F. Hoselitz, "Generative and Parasitic Cities," *Economic Development and Cultural Change* (1955): 278–294.

[6]A. G. Frank, *Latin American Development: Underdevelopment or Revolution* (New York: Monthly Review Press, 1969); M. Castells, *The Urban Question* (Cambridge: M.I.T. Press, 1977), pp. 437–471; M. Harloe, *Captive Cities: Studies in the Political Economy of Cities and Regions* (New York: Wiley, 1977), pp. 1–47; T. G. McGee, *The Urbanization Process in the Third World* (London: G. Bell, 1971), Chapters 1–3.

[7]J. Jacobs, *The Death and Life of Great American Cities* (New York: Random House, 1961); W. Baer, "On the Death of Cities," *Public Interest* 45 (1967): 3–19.

reexamination of the elite versus the nonelite or the self-and-others dichotomy of the city.

What troubled us, in addition, was that all of the images seemed to
have the same value. Each identified some aspect of the city: how persons
or groups behave in this environment; or what a city is, does, or relates to;
or some neglected urban problems or directions for policy. Each image
achieved its effect by stress and sacrifice—by gaining in force what it lost
in scope. Puzzled and dissatisfied, we finally concluded that we were
indeed interested in all kinds of images—technical or political, visual or
analytical, positivistic or normative—*but mainly from the point of view of
the central subject matter of the writer's field.*

These considerations led us to advocate the coupling of images and
themes and to distinguish both from similes and metaphors, which we
now consider specific expressions of the more general *thematic image.*
Combining images and themes prevents overemphasis of the visual. It
links the mental process of visualization with underlying basic ideas. It
helps, also, to identify the different ways of thinking about the city that
have taken root in the scholars' realms.

Our emphasis on the thematic images parallels Gerald Holton's analysis of concepts and themes in the realm of science.[8] We take a cue from,
and share, his interest in questions that are not the core of the scientific
activity of any field, yet are inseparable from it. Holton's focus is on the
meta-aspects of science—on the implicit ideas and presuppositions that
shape or underlie the more specific approaches and research activities of
the practitioners. Characterized as thematic by Holton, they sometimes
involve "unverifiable, unfalsifiable and yet not quite arbitrary hypotheses."[9] Some of the issues cited by Holton in the field of science—such as
holism versus reductionism, mathematics versus materialistic models,
experience versus formalism, and explanatory notions such as teleological
drives and organismic images versus causal mechanistic systems—hold
for the social sciences as well. The substance of these—as well as other—

---

[8]Holton used the notion of *themata* or *theme* to refer to the "dimension of fundamental presuppositions, notions, terms, methodological judgments and decisions . . . which are themselves neither directly evolved from, nor resolvable
into objective observation on the one hand, or logical, mathematical and other
formal ratiocination on the other hand"—*Thematic Origins of Scientific Thought:
Kepler to Einstein* (Cambridge: Harvard University Press, 1974), pp. 28–29 and
Chapter 1.
[9]Holton, *Thematic Origins,* p. 13.

ideas, he shows, "lies hidden at the base of scientific work"; and although not quite part of it, sooner or later, they turn out "to be a central part of (scientific) studies."[10] In any case, the examination of these and related themes is essential for understanding the evolution of the sciences and for developing, Holton hopes, "a wider, more humanistic attitude toward the growth of science itself."[11]

The subject matter of this volume is, in retrospect, an exploration of the meta-aspects of urban studies in the social sciences through the lens of the thematic urban image. Although none of the writers exploring the thematic urban images of particular disciplines may have been aware of Holton's views, each of them has often confronted the kinds of concepts and themes to which Holton has drawn attention. This is so whether the writers were dealing with the theme of the powerlessness of the city as a legal concept; or the evolution of the descriptive and mathematical or the subjective and radical perspectives in urban geography; or the jungle, bazaar, organismic, or machine images in sociology; or the methodological emphasis on parts and wholes in anthropology and history; or the themes of community, business management, market behavior, or ungovernable social forces in political science.

EXPLICITNESS AND SCALE

Not surprisingly, the various fields exhibit distinct differences and common denominators in their handling of thematic urban images. These differences are especially evident with respect to the explicitness of their dominant images and the approach to the unit of analysis, particularly the key issue of parts and wholes.

Some of the fields surveyed have a tradition of attention to urban images, others none at all. Peter Langer, for instance, in his analysis of urban sociology, underlines images that are commonly recognized: the bazaar, the jungle, the machine, and the organism. By contrast, Martin Shefter's discussion of political science masterfully teases out images of the city that have had less distinct recognition or treatment in that field: the city as community, as corporation, and as market (images with readily identifiable parallels in other disciplines). The same holds for "global

[10]Ibid., pp. 17–19.
[11]Ibid., p. 19.

reach," the "space economy," or the city as theater—the thematic images that Charles Tilly discerns in urban history. Even more, the urban images of the geographer and of the social anthropologist, as depicted by Peter Hall, by Lisa Redfield Peattie and Edward Robbins, and by Anthony Leeds, are implicit, reflecting methods and political philosophy. In still another vein, Gerald E. Frug notes our ambivalent attitude toward power and freedom in our appeal to local autonomy to offset the threat of state domination, and our appeal to the state to offset the threat of local domination. And at the end of the spectrum, there is the economist's relative neglect of the theme of the city, although John Harris, too, distills images and themes such as production centers, nodes, agglomerations, innovative seed beds, information and control centers, and externalities, as a more serious tradition develops.

In pondering the common denominators of the images among the disciplines, we found that scale was a critical distinguishing feature; and implicit in the scale of these activities, there is the broader question of parts and wholes. For some purposes, *urban* is a refinement, a disaggregation, a part of a larger whole, such as a region or nation; for other purposes, it stands for the reverse—the integration of components, either of some parts or of some smaller areas—of the city or culture. From the point of view of the field of study, however, the urban elements are only a part of the subject matter covered by the discipline; and in turn, the discipline deals with only a part of the urban from the perspective of a central problem or theme of the discipline.

Thematic urban images, by pointing up the ways in which the urban subject matter—as part of a whole—is viewed by the field of study, identify gaps, insights, and even future problems. The issue of parts and wholes is most explicit in anthropology, which is committed to a focus on the relationships between parts and wholes in cultures. To date, however, anthropology has been able to achieve this aim only in small autonomous societies or in fairly small cities like Middletown. For larger, more complex cultures or cities, anthropologists have studied parts as a way of interpreting, or even serving as an advocate for, the parts in relation to the (urban) whole. Useful as these efforts have been, Peattie and Robbins are now concerned that the unbalanced emphasis on the part is a fundamental shortcoming as well as a distinctive contribution. Moreover, Leeds argues that it is even an error to leave the rural out of the urban, that the rural/urban distinction is an ethnocentric misrepresentation of the functions, institutions, and technologies of rural localities.

Just the opposite situation prevails in economics. There, the urban economic "part" has been invisible and, for all practical purposes, irrelevant to the discipline because it fell in between the macro and micro problems or behavior that economists sought to explain. Only when the urban problem became a serious public issue did economists discover that they had little to say about the subject; and when a tiny minority of the profession turned their attention to the matter, their justification was that it might improve the micro or macro models by illustrating or helping to account for errant behavior associated with externalities or faulty assumptions with regard to mobility, space, knowledge, technology, and perhaps innovation.

Questions of scale also surface in different ways in the other fields. In political science, Shefter notes that the shift in attitudes toward conflict (whether benign or destructive) evidences the breakdown of consensus into what are now perceived as larger and smaller as well as separate and hostile communities, with scholars advocating the views and interests of the different communities. In geography, sociology, and city planning as well, the essays take note of the substantial differences between the total objective, physical, urban reality and the varying, fragmented cognitive images of that reality held by different groups. For the field of urban history, Tilly calls attention to the gaps of understanding that follow from the failures to explore the interactions between two parts of a whole: the processes of change within individual communities and the ongoing changes in national and international processes that have been reshaping the city. And in the field of law, Frug points to the ways in which a more powerful city may serve an increasingly significant intermediary role between persons and the state that can protect our freedom, can help in penetrating the outmoded distinctions between "public" and "private" and can enable us to exert more control on the social decisions that affect our lives.

PATTERNS IN THE DEVELOPMENT AND THE FUNCTIONS OF URBAN IMAGES

In seeking to explain patterns in the development of urban images in their respective fields, our contributors have emphasized the stage of development of each discipline, its methodologies and status, and its shifting theoretical orientations. Although part of the evolution of thematic images in a given field may be explained by reference to factors within the discipline, a second cluster of variables from outside the discipline has been influential as well. These factors include shifts in size and function, changes in population composition, and changes with respect to what is viewed as a problem. Shifting definitions of what constitutes the "urban problem" (and whether or not such a problem exists) have been a large force in shaping the images of several disciplines. Images and themes of the city reflect, and help to mold, the direction and strength of reformist currents.

Put differently, whether explicit or implicit, thematic urban images often reflect a discipline's general research attitudes as well as specific research expectations with regard to urban phenomena. Langer suggests that the shifting popularity of particular themes and images may largely depend on how much theoretical insight they provide and their problem-solving relevance. And he offers the prediction that, "As the 'problem' of the city becomes less its internal composition and more its external predicament, imagery that places the city in its national and international context will be on the resurgence."

As interpreted by Peter Hall, the geographers' way of seeing the city reflects three influences: analytical methods, political philosophy, and trends in the economic system. He suggests that the earlier images of the geographers reflect a period of prosperity and optimism in the United States in the 1950s. Breaking new ground and no longer hobbled by mere description, geographers were confident that their more systematic knowledge would help to fashion policies that would enhance the welfare and the efficiency of the city. The later pessimistic views, according to Hall, reflect the moods prevalent in Britain and the United States in the 1970s—the feeling that the Western and the world economy were in the process of exceptional transformation, and perhaps even in serious trouble. The new images evidence the general pressures for reform as well as a skepticism—in some quarters—about whether the problems can be remedied without more fundamental structural changes in the socioeconomic system.

We see a similar combination of factors at work in determining the development of the urban images in political science. Shefter emphasizes the causal force of the character of city politics at the time the images were formed; the relationships of the political scientists to the various contenders for power in the city; the nature of the conflict; and, in particular, the views of the political scientists on whether the political conflict was destructive or benign. He notes that as political scientists moved from viewing the city as a community to treating the city as a corporation, the profession became more independent and conscious of disciplinary status; and he attributes the emergence in the 1950s of the competitive market as a thematic urban image to the growing influence of behaviorism on the discipline. But the discipline's view of the city as competitive market occurred, he adds, during a period when it was possible to view urban conflicts as essentially benign.

In the case of the anthropologists, however, Peattie and Robbins note that the interest in the city intensified as the number of primitive cultures diminished. The search for new markets for the anthropologists' tools explains the extraordinary interest in the urban theme, the identification of rural and urban images, and some of the new methodological issues of parts and wholes. On the other hand, in Leeds's view, anthropologists' urban images have been determined primarily by adherence to an ethnocentric version of social urbanization that serves to sustain capitalist social forms.

As was noted earlier, when anthropologists turned their attention to the city, they tended to focus on parts in order to interpret the whole. This emphasis on parts rather than the whole in larger and more complex urban societies made it possible for the reformist elements of the discipline to interpret and represent the perspectives of the powerless, the culturally and socially unique, and the ethnic groups—"the world of the little people in large complex places." Although this emphasis typified the U.S. anthropological tradition, it is equally visible in the British tradition—whether in studying the urban environment in changing Africa or contemporary British society. There is, however, concern today among some anthropologists about the price paid for abandoning the former stress on the relationships of both the parts and the whole. The anthropologists' part is often a metaphor for the whole, but it is not the whole, and by stressing what is orderly and functional in the part and slighting the urban as an image of the whole, Peattie and Robbins suggest, anthropologists frustrate not only desirable change but also the achievement of a basic aim of the discipline of understanding the whole culture and society.

The consequences and the functional significance of urban images remain primarily an area of speculation. Yet the guesses and the preliminary hypotheses presented in this volume constitute a powerful argument that this area is a fruitful topic for further inquiry. Just as Peattie and Robbins note that anthropologists' treatment of urban themes may retard change, Sam Bass Warner, Jr., argues that two historical images of the city have had a significant political impact. His analysis suggests that the urban slum as an image has served the cause of social reform, whereas the effect of the city skyline image has been ultimately pacifying and has deflected social change. And in his comparison of the "urban crisis" of the 1960s with that of the 1980s, Michael H. Frisch concludes, "Whereas the urban imagery of our first 'urban crisis' encouraged an engagement with the far broader political and social issues confronting American society, the urban imagery of our more recent version has served to deflect and even finesse such larger political questions."

Not least, Frug shows how the image of the city as the creature of the state has reflected the concerns of liberals, particularly their concern in the nineteenth century with protecting the individual from the power of the state. But the docile acceptance of this image, he demonstrates, leads to uncritical and unrealistic distinctions between public and private corporate behavior and to a failure to perceive the many important ways in which more powerful cities would enhance or protect human freedom.

URBAN REALITY AND THE OBSERVER

Another conspicuous aspect of image research, Boulding says, is that it brings the actors into the act.[12] The concern is inescapably with the correspondence between an urban reality (one that exists or is presumed) and the image of that reality disclosed by the assumptions, the values, the methods, the observations, or the behavior of the actors or organizations interacting with that reality. There are a variety of examples.

One is Kevin Lynch's studies of the images of the physical city held by different people.[13] These differences, never systematically examined before, have helped to transform thinking in the field of urban design and

---

[12]K. Boulding, *The Image* (Ann Arbor: University of Michigan Press, 1956), Chapter 10.

[13]*The Image of the City* (Cambridge: The Technology Press and Harvard University Press, 1960).

produced a whole spate of research by Lynch, Rapaport,[14] and a large number of other people who have been influenced, directly and indirectly, by some of the lines of these investigations—for example, by the differences between the urban images held by professionals and nonprofessionals (such as children, older people, women, and persons in varying occupations); and by the differences in design and in psychological, sociological, anthropological, and other methods of conducting these studies and of interpreting the findings.

Another example is the urban image studies by Anselm Strauss, which traced historically popular images of U.S. cities. Focusing on the images of city officials and chambers of commerce, he documented the ways in which the various parties sought to manipulate and disseminate their views. Later influenced in part by the work of Walter Firey,[15] Strauss explored several other aspects of urban images:[16] the ways they arise and are interpreted by populations with different backgrounds, with different styles of life, and with different roles in the city; the effects of these ways of perceiving on cities as a whole and on the areas within them; and the thoughts of Americans, both past and present, about their cities and the way they have grown.

Still another example is the attitudes that scholars bring to their studies. Although a close look at the history of each discipline moves us well beyond the crude pro- and antiurban terms of discussion, this attitudinal dimension—from positive and enthusiastic to negative and disdainful—remains an essential feature of city images. What scholars in various disciplines see and how they describe that vision are affected by their preferences and aims. This is as true of the anthropologist's hostility to imperialism and sympathy for other cultures as it is of the planner's ideal city or planning process, the economist's efficient workplace and market, the political scientist's attitudes toward conflict, and the Marxist's concern with indicators of the forces illustrating, favoring, or resisting the current transformations in the capitalist system.

One could, of course, veer in the direction of the solipsistic view that the only reality is in the mind of the observer. Indeed, Leo Marx, arguing

[14]For a comprehensive review of research on urban images in this tradition, see A. Rapaport, *Human Aspects of Urban Form* (New York: Pergamon Press, 1977). See also Kevin Lynch's observations in Chapter 9.

[15]*Land Use in Central Boston* (Cambridge: Harvard University Press, 1947).

[16]*Images of the American City* (New Jersey: Transaction Books, 1976).

from the perspective of literary criticism, questions the idea of "citiness." The images of town and country in Hawthorne's *The Scarlet Letter,* he notes, were never intended to be accurate renderings of the New England Puritan town; rather they are symbolic conceptions drawn to reinforce the mood, the atmosphere, and the notions of good and evil Hawthorne sought to depict. Marx simply does not think that it is either possible or meaningful to capture the objective image of the city; and in the seminar discussion, he observes that realism, the nearest equivalent in literature to the objective image, mirrors in retrospect only a limited range of perspectives and values.

Warner's study of slums and skyscrapers in the changing, transient, historically contingent nineteenth- and twentieth-century capitalist cities raises similar questions. Beyond the physical realities, he asks, are they examples of failure and progress or of coping and exploitation? And, to be sure, there are arguments on both sides.

Even if different inferences can be drawn from the same information, we do not believe that the world is a mirage and that the physical city does not exist. On the contrary, we are inclined to think that the more appropriate implication is that varying urban images, when examined with care, will disclose unsuspected interests, feelings, and values that— to vary an observation of Spinoza—will in many ways tell us as much or even more about the authors or users of the image than about the subjects discussed.

It is these subjective features, we think, that turn out to be one of the more distinctive insights produced by these studies. Shefter sensitizes us less to Banfield's unheavenly city than to Banfield's gnawing fear of the disturbing consequences of devising policies that ignore the nonangelic character of its residents. We think about who is drawing the image of the slum and the skyscraper, and why—after reading Warner. Peattie and Robbins provoke us to reexamine more sympathetically the descriptive methods of the anthropologists that could be used "to delegitimize colonialism, missionizing, and the spread of capitalism" or to satirize contemporary urban culture. Hall obliges us to take account of the different images of the city held by descriptive and "scientific" geographers and those held by liberal and Marxist geographers, whose concerns were either to transform the city and benefit particular groups or simply to provide a fresh "bill of particulars" with regard to the behavior of the capitalist system. And Frug forces us to recognize that the current acceptance of the notion of the city as the creature of the state may not be necessary and indeed may turn out to be a positive hindrance to more relevant and imaginative ways of defining the role of the power of cities.

IMMEDIATE AND LONGER TERM PROSPECTS: CONCLUDING REFLECTIONS

Finally, we were surprised to observe the way in which some of our ideas evolved with regard to future activity in the field. Pondering the essays of our contributors led us to two projections of the future: one modest and pragmatic, the other more buoyant and prophetic.

On the modest, pragmatic side, we foresee more research on thematic urban images, replete with provocative hypotheses and refined analytical methods—dealing with such subjects as the evolution, the functions, and the manipulation of urban images. Although we are uncertain which directions will prove most fruitful to explore, at least in relation to the images of the city in the social sciences, a few immediate directions are clear. We have moved from the original question of "What have been the most important images in each discipline?" to a set of identified images. For each field, our inventories constitute a stock of tentative hypotheses that will generate critical discussion and revision—of what is left out, misconstrued, and so forth.

Aside from these reevaluations, we invite attention to the surmise of Gerald Holton that a current need is to look at the way in which images are formed.[17] He thinks that a reason for the neglect of these questions in the past has been the often illogical and sometimes irrational factors involved in what has been called *private* as compared with *public science,* that is, with the ways in which ideas and images are formed and the ways in which they are validated. But what in the past has been regarded as a source of embarrassment, as well as an area not susceptible to analysis, is now deemed important and fruitful, an altogether legitimate subject of inquiry. Holton has suggested three possible leads for exploration: (1) the investigations of perception psychology, particularly the development of concepts in children; (2) the studies of Kurt Lewin and others on the dynamics of personality; and (3) the insights gleaned from the anthropological and folkloric study of recurrent general ideas in the work of individuals and disciplines. These suggestions focus on how ideas are

[17]Holton, *Thematic Origins*, pp. 28–29.

formed and how people try to solve problems. Still other potential leads might be drawn from the investigations of impression management by Erving Goffman or the studies of image manipulation in media communications.

On the buoyant and more risky prophetic side, we expect the exploration of urban thematic images to become at the very least a specialized area of studies in the field of urbanism. Although one could easily argue that work in this area is overdue, it is equally easy to account for the dearth of such research in the past. The most obvious explanation is that it took some time for specialized literature to develop, and until now, it has probably not occurred to anyone to make these exploratory efforts. The subject is also elusive and methodologically frustrating. There is no common definition of *image;* and in some respects, too, prevailing traditions of studying images in different disciplines have sharpened—but may also have limited—the apparent potential of such inquiry by focusing it too narrowly. In urban planning, images of the city involve primarily visual images and environmental design, but in the social sciences, images include themes, concepts, ideas, and symbols. Aside from these difficulties, there is the social scientists' inclination to regard images—and perhaps even themes—as decorative or suggestive but of very limited and possibly even of negative value for analysis and policy.

Despite the difficulties, we think scholars will be increasingly attracted by the uncommon interest of the subject and the likely benefits of greater knowledge of what is sometimes referred to as the "city of the mind," or the invisible city—the not visible constellations of images and themes that help to organize thinking and discourse about the city. And whatever else may account for the previous dearth of interest, the fact is that urban image research is now growing. In addition to the work of Lynch, Rapaport, Strauss, and Morton and Lucia White,[18] there have been important contributions in several other fields. To mention only a few, there are the interpretations by Raymond Williams of the changing English images of town and country—mainly through the lens of literature[19]; the fresh perspectives provided by Ladurie and others on everyday life in medieval and Renaissance cities in Europe[20]; and the

[18]M. and L. White, *The Intellectual Versus the City: From Thomas Jefferson to Frank Lloyd Wright* (Cambridge: Harvard University Press, 1962).
[19]*The Country and the City* (New York: Oxford University Press, 1973).
[20]E. Le Roy Ladurie, *Montaillou* (New York: George Braziller, 1978).

efforts by Henri Lefevre, Manuel Castells, David Harvey, and others to extend Marxist thinking through the reinterpretation of Marxist images of the city.[21]

All of which suggests to us that we are witnessing the emergence of what may well be a new area of specialization within the field of urbanism.

About 25 years ago, Kenneth Boulding coined the word *eionics* to identify the general science of images[22]; but as yet there is no term currently employed—or for that matter even available—to describe this realm of activity in the urban field. Neither *urbanism* nor *urbanology* will do, for both identify the activities of the areas of knowledge covered by specialists in all aspects of urban studies. The subjects we have in mind are more limited: they involve the themes and images that have shaped the perspective of scholars and that are influencing our policies on cities. For convenience, we suggest that this subject matter should be called *urbanography.*

Most likely, developments in urbanography will reflect trends in the fields of urbanism and eionics, and these trends will not always be positive. With the surfacing of the urban issues of the 1950s and 1960s, the problem of cities became a prominent item on the public agenda, leading to the emergence of urban specializations in all the social sciences. With today's concerns focused on energy, stagflation, budget retrenchment, and employment, the interest in cities and social science research is once again on the wane. The prospects in these circumstances for new fields— and perhaps also for urbanography—are far less promising.

Boulding, however, as one might expect from a true believer, is bullish about the prospects of eionics—probably in the intermediate as well as the long run. He declared:

> We are perhaps in the process of organizing a general theory of the empirical world: something which lies between the extreme generality of mathematics and the particularity of particular disciplines. I visualize eionics as occupying a place in this theoretical structure alongside, perhaps, cybernetics. It will be a long time, of course, before the restructuring is in fact underway. It will eventually be recognized

---

[21]Lefevre, *La pensée marxiste et la ville* (Paris, Casterman, 1972), and *La production de l'espace* (Paris: Éditions Anthropos, 1974); Castells, *The Urban Question* (Cambridge: M.I.T. Press, 1972); D. Harvey, *Social Justice in the City* (London: Edward Arnold, 1973); J. Lokjine, *Le Marxisme, l'état et la question urbaine* (Paris: PUF, 1977).

[22]Boulding, *The Image*, Chapter 10.

officially. Until then, the new structures, as new structures always have done, will have to live in an underworld, an underworld of deviant professors, gifted amateurs and moderate crackpots.[23]

To this underworld, Boulding invited his readers. At this stage, we can do no less and, alas, no more!

PART II

Urban Images and Themes in Specific Fields

CHAPTER 2

Geography

Descriptive, Scientific, Subjective, and Radical Images of the City

PETER HALL

Geographers disagree about many things, but on one point, they are unanimous: they study distributions on the earth's surface. The dictionary definition is succinct: "to draw (i.e., describe) the earth." Richard Hartshorne, one of the leading theorists of twentieth-century geography, had an extended definition: "that discipline that seeks to describe and interpret the variable character from place to place as the home of man."[1] That means that human geographers study many phenomena that are identical with those studied by other social scientists. They analyze economies, societies, governmental systems, and states of mind. In doing so, they often use insights and concepts and techniques similar to—or even identical to—those used in these other disciplines. Their first question must always be: Where is this phenomenon to be found? Their second: Why is it found there? Economists and sociologists and political scientists, too, may ask these questions from time to time. But they are not central to these other social scientists' work; to the work of geographers, they are.

Now, cities are nothing if not spatial phenomena; they form a principal part of the subject matter of human geography. So, in a sense, when other social scientists investigate cities, they trespass. Geographers do not by and large mind, because, in turn, they constantly trespass in other

[1]*Perspective on the Nature of Geography* (Chicago: Rand McNally, 1959), p. 47.

Peter Hall • Department of City and Regional Planning, University of California, Berkeley, California, and Department of Geography, University of Reading, Reading, England.

social sciences' fields. But it is important that, in studying the city, the activities of these different workers has become very difficult to distinguish from each other; there is massive overlap and fuzziness.

All this said, during the history of modern geography—a history that, as with many other social sciences, started around 1900—at different times geographers have posed their basic questions in rather different ways, with rather different expectations; and they have sought answers with very different conceptual and technical support. Applied to the subject matter of the city, this fact means that geographers' image of the phenomenon has varied quite sharply from decade to decade—and at no time more so than in the quarter century from 1955 to 1980. These changes logically form the subject matter of this chapter. It draws heavily on the comprehensive analysis of modern geographical thought by R. J. Johnston, and it seeks to extract from that account the features that are relevant in understanding the geographer's changing image of the city.[2]

"TRADITIONAL" GEOGRAPHY, 1900–1955

This period need not detain us long; for it did not contain very much geography that was specifically urban. The reason is that the fundamental aim of geographers at this time was to synthesize separate features into a regional unity. Hartshorne, in his classic *The Nature of Geography*, put it thus: Geography is

> a science that interprets the realities of areal differentiation of the world as they are found, not only in terms of the differences in certain things from place to place, but also in terms of the total combination of phenomena in each place, different from those at every other place.[3]

Commenting on this view in his review of modern human geography, R. J. Johnston pointed out that for Hartshorne the ultimate purpose of geography—the study of the areal differentiation of the world—would be expressed in regional geography. Regions would be identified in terms of their distinctiveness on defined characteristics, and there would be two

[2]See *Geography and Geographers: Anglo-American Human Geography since 1945* (New York: Wiley, 1979), and *City and Society: An Outline for Human Geography* (Harmondsworth, England: Penguin, 1980).
[3]Lancaster, Penn.: Association of American Geographers, 1939, p. 462.

different types of region: first, the *formal or uniform* region, in which the whole area was homogeneous with regard to the phenomenon or phenomena under review, and second, the *nodal or functional* region, in which the unity came from organization around a central node, which could be the core area of a state or a town at the central point of a trade area.[4]

Hartshorne was, of course, trying in part to define what geography ideally should be, but he was also abstracting from what geography then was. In Britain and in the United States, in France and in Germany, for the first half of the twentieth century human geographers saw their chief aim as the definition of regions. In particular, they drew on the work of the great French school of regional geography under Paul Vidal de la Blache, which sought to differentiate natural regions wherein physical differences brought forth different human responses. Significantly, this French work—like most of the studies that derived from it—tended to concentrate on areas dominated by agriculture, where the pace of modern change had been relatively slow and where humanity still lived in close contact with the land. The city, in this kind of region, was the rural market town and administrative seat to which the local farmers brought their produce and which, in turn, supplied them with industrial goods and specialized services.

Doubtless, one of the main reasons for this selectivity was that such regions were easier to handle. Patrick Geddes, the great pioneering Scots biologist-sociologist-planner who well understood the methods of the French regionalists, put it candidly:

> Coming to Civic Survey, where shall we begin? . . . London may naturally claim pre-eminence. Yet even at best, does not the vastest of world cities present a more or less foggy labyrinth, from which surrounding regions with their smaller cities can be but dimly descried. . . . For our more general and comparative study, then, simpler beginnings are preferable . . . the clearer outlook, the more panoramic view of a definite geographic region such, for instance, as lies before us on a mountain holiday.[5]

It was just such an area that Geddes described in his famous Valley Section—in which, significantly, the small market town occupies the central place.

---

[4]*Geography and Geographers*, p. 35.
[5]"Civics: As Applied Sociology," *Sociological Papers* 1 (1905): 104–105.

Geddes, to his everlasting merit and fame, set his sights beyond this. He recognized, as early as 1915, that "the coming World City" was also worthy of study.[6] Around London and Birmingham and Manchester and Glasgow, cities were growing toward each other and were coalescing. To describe this phenomenon, Geddes gave to the English language the word *conurbation*. His Greater London, Lancaston, West Yorkshire, Midlanton, Waleston, and Clyde-Forth regions embraced not only the tightly built-up, coalescent urban areas, but wide hinterlands around them. Twenty years later, when the British geographer C. B. Fawcett rediscovered the term, his resulting definitions were much more sparse. Yet the reality was the same: in Britain, the most highly urbanized nation in the world at that time, the reality for the great majority of the population was not the *pays* of the French geographers, but what one perceptive urbanist later called a "confluent urban pox."[7] As Fawcett described it:

> An observer in an airship hovering above one of these conurbations on a clear dark evening, when all its lamps are lit, would see beneath him a large area covered by a continuous network of lights, glowing here and there in brighter patches where the main roads meet in its nodal shopping districts and elsewhere shading into the darker patches of its less fully urbanized areas—parks, water surfaces, or enclaves of rural land. To such an observer the continuity of the conurbation would be the most salient point about it. If he were high above the Pennines between Leeds and Manchester he could see at least four great conurbations. . . . And it would be easy to imagine an outspreading of all these towards coalescence in one vast urban region covering the whole of this industrialized central area of Britain.[8]

Fawcett thus recognized the existence of a wider urban reality and began systematically—in a way that Geddes never tried to do—to try to define it. This work bore fruit 20 years later, when in the 1951 census the British authorities began to incorporate the conurbation concept into their tabulations. Later still, the geographer T. W. Freeman systematically described the economic and physical structures of these areas.[9] But in the long transition from Geddes to Freeman, the very idea seems to

[6]*Cities in Evolution* (London: Williams and Norgate, 1915), 40–41.
[7]F. Pick, evidence before *Royal Commission on the Geographical Distribution of the Industrial Population, Minutes, 12th Day* (London: H.M.S.O., 1938), Q. 3107.
[8]"Distribution of the Urban Population in Great Britain," *Geographical Journal* 79 (1932): p. 101.
[9]*The Conurbations of Great Britain* (Manchester: Manchester University Press, 1959).

have undergone a transmogrification: starting as a rather wide concept, incorporating the whole sphere of influence of a group of cities, it ended by being defined rather narrowly in terms of urban land uses. In American terminology, it turned from a Standard Metropolitan Statistical Area into an Urbanized Area.

British geographers, perhaps more than any others, were concerned about this phenomenon of the growth and coalescence of cities. In the 1930s, a group of them gave evidence to a Royal Commission on the Distribution of the Industrial Population, which was centrally concerned with the issue.[10] This concern arose from a widespread alarm about the continued sprawl of London into the neighboring Home Counties, which was taking valuable agricultural land and increasing the daily commuter journey. Some like-minded individuals elsewhere had the same concern—especially in New York, where a group including Lewis Mumford and Clarence Stein founded the Regional Plan Association of America to develop an alternative to sprawl. But this group did not include any notable geographers—and it was only 30 years later that a European expatriate geographer, Jean Gottmann, wrote his classic account of Megalopolis.[11] American geography, which flourished especially on the campuses of the Corn Belt and the Prairies, rather saw cities in terms of the older European agricultural-regional model.

THE "QUANTITATIVE REVOLUTION" AND AFTER, 1955–1970

The revolution that overtook geography after 1955—first in the United States, soon afterward in Britain, and more belatedly elsewhere—has been fully described elsewhere.[12] But to understand its significance for the study of the city, it is necessary to summarize its central features. First, from the start, the protagonists of the "new" geography took an explicit philosophical position: they identified themselves with the tenets of logical positivism, a school developed in Vienna during the 1920s.[13]

[10]P. Hall et al., *The Containment of Urban England*, Vol. 1 (London: George Allen and Unwin, 1973), p. 88.

[11]*Megalopolis: The Urbanized Northeastern Seaboard of the United States* (New York: Twentieth Century Fund, 1961).

[12]Johnston, *Geography and Geographers*, Chapter 3.

[13]Ibid., pp. 43–44, 63; M. Los, "Some Reflections on Epistemology, Design and Planning Theory," in *Urbanization and Urban Planning in Capitalist Society*, ed. M. Dear and A. Scott (London and New York: Methuen, 1981).

They argued that the central task of geography was not the differentiation of the earth's surface, as Hartshorne had argued, but the search for underlying laws governing the distribution of certain features on the space of the earth.[14] Second, and following from logical-positivist science, geography must be developed on the basis of good theory, which would subsequently be tested through empirical observation. Third, as far as possible, such theories should be specified in precise quantified form—in a word that became central to the new geography, in the form of *models*. Ideally, these should take a mathematical form; but as few geographers had the necessary training, the central role went to statistics, which were used to test hypotheses.[15]

These were the general underpinnings of the revolution of the 1950s. Strictly, they could have been applied to almost any subject matter. But in practice, the main thrust—particularly in the first decade after 1955— was in economics and in urban geography. Especially was this true of the school at the University of Washington under William L. Garrison, which is often credited with being the birthplace of the quantitative revolution. The main reason for this concentration seems to have been simply that the University of Washington was where most of the available theory was to be found.

In the first place, there was a body of location theory developed by economists and geographers over a long period in Germany—but largely ignored up to that time by both economists and geographers—waiting to be discovered: the agricultural location theory of Johann Heinrich von Thünen (first published in German in 1826 but not translated into English until 1966); the industrial location theory of Alfred Weber (published in 1909, translated in 1929); the central place theory of Walter Christaller (published in 1933, translated only in 1966); and the general location theory of August Lösch (published in 1944, translated in 1954).[16]

---

[14]F. Schaefer, "Exceptionalism in Geography: A Methodological Examination," *Annals, Association of American Geographers* 43 (1953): 227.

[15]Johnston, *Geography and Geographers*, p. 64.

[16]Von Thünen, *Von Thünen's Isolated State*, trans. C. M. Wartenberg, ed. P. Hall (Oxford: Pergamon, 1966); Weber, *Alfred Weber's Theory of the Location of Industries*, trans. C. J. Friedrich (Chicago: Chicago University Press, 1929); Christaller, *The Central Places of Southern Germany*, trans. C. W. Baskin (Englewood Cliffs, N.J.: Prentice-Hall, 1966; Lösch, *The Economics of Location*, trans. W. H. Woglom and W. F. Stolper (New York: Yale University Press, 1954).

Central to this theory, in one way or another, was the mapping of economic costs onto geographic space: the costs of transporting agricultural produce to market, in von Thünen; the costs of shipping raw materials and the final product, in Weber; and the effective "range of a good," related to elasticity of demand, in Christaller and Lösch. Thus, the underlying theory was specifically economic, and it made the usual simplifying assumptions familiar to economists: the presentation of behavior in terms of rational self-interest (the concept of *economic man*); the deliberate removal of complicating factors (the *ceteris paribus* assumption); and the notion that human motives are best studied through actual behavior, rather than through any further investigation of mental states.

The other theoretical underpinning was closely related, though the precise relationship was hard to express. It was the borrowing from Newtonian physics that underlay the gravity model and its later more sophisticated derivatives. In its original formulation, as in the work of the astronomer J. Q. Stewart and the mathematician G. K. Zipf,[17] this theory argued that strong physical principles underlie the distribution of human settlements and human behavior in geographical space. Thus the interaction between any two points on the earth's surface, whether in terms of migration or commuting or other kinds of travel, would be found to be directly proportionate to the size or mass of the places and inversely proportionate to the distance between them—both these terms requiring calibration in a model in order to get precise fit. This relationship which had been identified as of fundamental importance for traffic studies right at the start of the revolution in geography[18] became central to a great deal of work by Garrison and other geographers on intra-urban and inter-urban travel behavior.

These were not the only places where geographers went to find their new theory; among others were statistical biology (whence came the *nearest neighbor* concept) and mathematical graph theory (for the study of networks). But for urban geographers, economic location theory and spatial physics were overwhelmingly the most important. The results, for the geographer's view of the city, were perfectly predictable. Seizing their

[17]Stewart, "Empirical Mathematical Rules concerning the Distribution and Equilibrium of Population," *Geographical Review* 37 (1947): 461–485; Zipf, *Human Behavior and the Principle of Least Effort* (New York: Hafner, 1949).

[18]B. R. Mitchell and C. Rapkin, *Urban Traffic, A Function of Land Use* (New York: Columbia University Press, 1954).

new theoretical and technical tools with enthusiasm, geographers sought
for underlying order in urban behavior. Rational urbanites, in pursuit of
pure economic objectives, whether as producers or consumers, were
confronted with the "friction of distance" in geographical space (a term
coined many years before by the pioneer American urban economist
Robert Murray Haig[19]). In overcoming it, they produced spatial reg-
ularities—in the spacing of cities, in the patterns of land use within those
cities, in the distribution of trips within and between them—that were
the expression of basic, universal laws of spatial arrangement. Human
geography thus appeared to be, quite literally, a social science.

The resulting burst of creative activity produced an enormous
amount of work, much of lasting value. The pioneering central-place work
of Berry, the transportation studies by Garrison, the urban modeling of
Wilson and Batty, and the syntheses of Haggett and Chorley—all add up
to the heroic age of geography.[20]

But it has to be said that the limitations of the work were also its
strength. It achieved so much precisely because it was constrained both
in its assumptions and in its subject matter. Its assumptions of economic
rationality made it good at explaining and even at predicting the kinds of
behavior that were dictated by such a principle: location decisions of firms
or of home buyers, trips by car or by airplane between cities, and the
location of shopping centers in relation to customer populations. It was
less good, and less interested, in explaining urban phenomena where
sociological or psychological or cultural and political factors entered in. It
could not explain, and generally did not try to explain, why identical
houses at identical distances from the city center had very different values, dependent on their social cachet; or why entrepreneurs seemed to
prefer to locate their businesses in small areas or resorts rather than in

[19]"Toward an Understanding of the Metropolis," *Quarterly Journal of Economics*
40 (1926): 422.
[20]Berry, "Cities as Systems within Systems of Cities," *Papers, Regional Science
Association* 13 (1964): 147–163; Garrison, "Spatial Structure of the Economy,"
Annals, Association of American Geographers 49 (1958): 238–239, 471–482;
Wilson, *Entrophy in Urban and Regional Modelling* (London: Pion, 1970), and
Urban and Regional Models in Geography and Planning (London: Pion, 1974);
Batty, *Urban Modelling: Algorithms, Calibrations, Predictions* (London:
Cambridge University Press, 1976); Haggett, *Locational Analysis in Human
Geography* (London: Edward Arnold, 1965); Chorley and Haggett, *Models in
Geography* (London: Methuen, 1967).

run-down industrial cities; or why linguistic groups lived in separate parts of such cities as Brussels or Montreal; or why blacks and whites were still largely segregated in all American cities; or why there were differences in form and function between such pairs as East Berlin and West Berlin, Swiss and French Geneva, Ottawa and Hull, or San Diego and Tijuana.

In other words, the "new" geography did reasonably well what it tried to do, but there were many aspects of the city that it did not even try to study. The result was a view of the city as a piece of optimizing economic machinery, in which individual decision-makers located their factories, offices, homes, schools, parks, and trip patterns according to pure principles of economic advantage as expressed in geographic space. Absent from the picture, almost entirely, was a great deal of the day-to-day reality of the city. The pattern of ownership of factories or offices, which might encourage inertia in one place and sudden transformation in another; the people's perceptions of their city, their desire to conserve and protect some or all of it, and their amount of political muscle in achieving this aim; the power of different groups and individuals in city hall, and the relations of local government with state, federal or central government; racial prejudice and cultural barriers; differences in lifestyle between social and cultural groups, and the resulting desire of some to live among like-minded people—all these were missing, hidden somewhere within the quantifiers' black box. So there was much that this style of geography did not investigate, and even more that it did not explain.

ALTERNATIVE APPROACHES, 1965–1975

Perhaps it was predictable that, in dialectical fashion, the triumph of the logical-positivist quantifiers should eventually produce a counter-movement. More likely, the reaction that did come was prompted in parts by events in the world outside—especially, the trauma of the Vietnam war in the United States and the upheavals of 1968 in Europe. More subtly, there was a general shift in intellectual values at about that time—away from belief in a beneficient science and technology allied to large-scale systems planning, and toward a much more individually oriented, small-scale approach to the study of cities.

This shift found immediate expression in two intellectual developments that proved interesting but that did not produce major traditions. The first was a stress on individual behavior and on individual perceptions as a key to that behavior. It led to some significant work on the "mental maps" of different individuals and groups of individuals, some of it applied at an urban level. Blue-collar blacks in Los Angeles, for instance, were found to have a much more limited geography of the city than middle-class whites; the implication was that their spatial search for jobs and services was more limited than that of the whites. The second intellectual development was a pure stress on the cognition of the individual as a guide to his or her culture; it led virtually to a rediscovery of regional geography, interpreted in terms of individuals' perceptions of time and space. Behind this regional geography was the argument that the positivist thinker imposed his or her own conceptual straitjacket on the subject matter; to avoid this, the researcher needed above all to get inside the mind of the individual actor whom he was studying. Though interesting theoretically, this "phenomenological" approach produced relatively little in the way of empirical research.[21]

THE SECOND REVOLUTION: RADICAL GEOGRAPHY, 1973–1980

More significant by far—and undoubtedly reflecting, in its origins, the ferment of the late 1960s—was a movement that developed strongly in the early 1970s in favor of a "radical" or "socially concerned" geography. It is fair to say that at first this movement was somewhat inchoate and lacking in strong intellectual basis, as Brian Berry alleged in more than one debate.[22] But, as its adherents engaged with their material, two distinct and quite new geographical perceptions of the city emerged.

The first can be broadly described, in the celebrated distinction of David Harvey, as "liberal"; the second as "Marxist." But in practice, the dividing line is a blurred one. Liberals in the radical camp showed considerable interest in—and sympathy with—the Marxist view of urban development[23]; they also contributed to symposia in the Marxist tradition.[24] To a more limited degree, Marxists used work within the liberal

[21]Johnston, *Geography and Geographers*, pp. 136–140.
[22]Ibid., 171–172.
[23]As in Johnston, *City and Society*.
[24]As in K. Cox, "Capitalism and Conflict around the Communal Living Space," in Dear and Scott.

tradition to fit into their theoretical framework.[25] But the two traditions were distinct—and though both have now produced a considerable volume of output, that from the Marxists was becoming almost the standard geographical approach by the early 1980s.

The viewpoint of the liberals was fairly narrowly focused. They asked who got what in the contemporary city (and in other parts and at other levels in geographic space, though the city was predominant in their work). Thus, they studied the distribution of money income, of access to private and public services, of environmental goods, and of any other element that added to the totality of real income.[26] In this process, they might move to the construction of composite territorial social indicators of the "quality of life" in the different areas of a city, as in the work of Richard Webber in England.[27] Then, in seeking to understand how inequalities arose, they looked at the political processes within the city, especially those that affected the location of public services like schools and clinics, as well as those that might bring physical disruption or environmental disamenity in the form of new highways or similar facilities.[28] This latter work, by focusing on the political forces operating in the "local state," helped provide a powerful input to the Marxist school. But insofar as the liberals were concerned about understanding welfare and power as a direct basis for changing the system little by little, their philosophical outlook was fundamentally different from that of the Marxists; it belonged in the broad stream of the liberal left, and it was close to that of the British Fabian Society or to the school of social administration developed by Richard Titmuss at the London School of Economics.

The difference can be seen more closely by focusing on the Marxists

[25]As in the borrowings of D. Massey and R. Meegan, *The Geography of Industrial Reorganization* (Oxford: Pergamon Press, 1979) from D. Keeble, *Industrial Location and Planning in the United Kingdom* (London: Methuen, 1976).

[26]D. M. Smith, *Human Geography: A Welfare Approach* (New York: St. Martin's Press, 1977), and *Where the Grass Is Greener: Geographical Perspectives on Inequality* (Harmondsworth, England: Penguin, 1979).

[27]*Liverpool Social Area Study: 1971 Data: Final Report. PRAG Technical Paper 14* (1977) (London: Centre for Environmental Studies).

[28]A. Mumphrey and J. Wolpert, *Equity Considerations and Concessions in the Siting of Public Facilities (Research on Conflict in Locational Decisions, Discussion Paper* 17) (Philadelphia: Wharton School, 1972); K. M. Cox, *Conflict, Power and Politics in the City: A Geographical View* (New York: McGraw-Hill, 1973), and *Location and Public Problems* (Chicago: Maaroufa Press, 1979).

themselves. It is useful to compare them both with the liberal radicals and
with the quantifiers. First, they have broken with both of these groups
philosophically—because the liberals and the quantifiers share a logical-
positivist philosophy that the Marxists reject. Instead, the Marxists have
adopted the well-known view that all knowledge is the product of a given
socioeconomic formation. Only by understanding the historical laws that
govern the rise and fall of such formations (i.e., by adopting Marxist
analysis) can observers escape from the historical circumstances of their
own time and achieve objective knowledge of reality. From this viewpoint comes the notion that urbanization itself, as well as its manifestations, is the product of given socioeconomic systems; that

> urbanization is decipherable only as a mediated outcome of the social
> dynamics and imperatives of the capitalist mode of production in
> specific conjunctural circumstances . . . urbanization and planning
> can never be effectively treated as objects of theoretical study di-
> vorced from some wider theory of society.[29]

Specifically, the structure of the city is to be explained by the pursuit
of profit, which is the *raison d'être* of capitalist society, modified by the
actions of the State, which has the function of preserving and legitimizing
this society. The specific features of urbanization—the hierarchy of centers, the differentiation of land uses within the city—are seen as necessary
aspects of commodity production through the profit-maximizing process.[30]

Fourth, within this theory the State—both central and local—does
occupy a very specific place. In late capitalism, the form now typical
through most of the world, it is required to perform some functions that
the pure capitalist system cannot any longer achieve. Much of the current
debate within the Marxist camp concerns the precise nature of these
roles, following the alternative formulations of the French Marxists J.
Lokjine (who believed that the State fostered the capitalist accumulation
of capital) and M. Castells (who thought that it existed to provide "collective consumption" in areas where the market had failed—for instance, in
popular housing).[31] The theory of the State is now perhaps the central

---

[29]Dear and Scott, p. 4.
[30]Ibid., 9–10.
[31]Lokjine, *Le Marxisme, l'état et la question urbaine* (Paris: PUF, 1977); Castells,
   The Urban Question (London: Edward Arnold, 1977 [1972]), and *City, Class
   and Power* (New York: St. Martin's Press, 1978).

concern of Marxist urban geographers, as is well seen in the essays in the symposium by Dear and Scott.[32]

The Marxists, like the quantifiers of the mid-1950s, started their "revolution" by an almost exclusive concern with theory building. In the words of David Harvey, from the first major English-language text of this school:

> This kind of empiricism is irrelevant. There is already enough information. . . . The immediate task is nothing more or less than self-conscious and aware construction of a new paradigm for social geographic thought through a deep and profound critique of our existing analytical structures.[33]

The school took these words to heart, and for some years, its writings had an almost exclusively theoretical character—to such an extent, indeed, that, to outsiders, they came increasingly to resemble medieval theological disputations. But more recently, for whatever reason, the output has had a stronger empirical content. The subject matter of this work is significant, for it reveals a new view of the contemporary city. Naturally, because of the economic determinism basic to Marxist thought, this view holds that the city is the product of economic forces—and in this sense, it strangely resembles the mental world of the quantifiers. But at that point, the resemblance stops.

The basic engine driving the Marxist geographers' city is the constantly changing international, national, and regional division of labor. Newly industrializing countries undermine the traditional economic bases of older nations and regions. In the latter, skilled workers in declining industries lose their jobs and end up in unskilled service occupations. Entrepreneurs react to the threat of competition by closing older inner-city plants and concentrating production in rural areas, where unionization is weaker and wages are lower. Multinational enterprises centralize their control functions in a few of the world cities, where they displace other functions to other cities or to suburbs. Because profit seeking and competition are inherent and incessant, this process of change is never-ending.

---

[32]M. Dear and A. Scott, *Urbanization and Urban Planning in Capitalist Society* (New York: Methuen, 1973).

[33]*Social Justice and the City* (Baltimore: Johns Hopkins University Press, 1973), pp. 144–145.

The most interesting feature of this Marxist analysis, perhaps, is what parts it stresses and what parts it underplays. The capitalist economy is said to be in a state of crisis—that is, subject to constant adaptation in the face of competition. But the word *crisis* is given a special potency by the stress on those parts of the spatial system that are failing to adapt and therefore failing to compete, for example, the inner cities of Britain[34] and the textile towns of New England.[35] Less attention so far has been given to the cases of successful innovation and new economic development: the newly industrializing countries themselves, the still-buoyant and prosperous regions of the advanced industrial countries (e.g., Southern England and the American Sunbelt). When it is given, the analysis tends to take a familiar form: the rise of new industrial areas represents a flight of capital out of the older industrial regions with high wages and strong unionization, into places without regulation of industry.[36] What is lacking, save in one or two places, is any deep analysis of the role of innovation and the creation of new industrial enterprises—though the interest of one or two Marxist scholars in the so-called Kondratieff long waves[37] provides a partial exception and a promise for the future.

GEOGRAPHERS' VIEWS OF THE CITY: A COMPARISON

The evolution of geographical thought from 1955 to 1980 represents a quest for progressively deeper levels of explanation. In the 1950s, a new generation of geographers became profoundly dissatisfied by what they saw as the lack of generalization in the old geography. Accordingly, they sought to develop a new kind of human geography that would literally be a social science. It would prescribe general laws that rational men and women would follow in locating their activities in geographical space; it would then attempt to show that, by and large, they actually did follow these laws in their observed behavior. Within its self-set limits, we have

[34]Massey and Meegan; A. Friend and A. Metcalfe, *Slump City: The Politics of Mass Unemployment* (London: Pluto Press, 1981).

[35]B. Bluestone and B. Harrison, *Capital and Communities: The Causes and Consequences of Private Disinvestment* (Washington, D.C.: The Progressive Alliance, 1980).

[36]D. Perry and A. Watkins, *The Rise of the Sunbelt Cities* (*Urban Affairs Annual Reviews*, 14) (Beverly Hills and London: Sage, 1977).

[37]E. Mandel, *Late Capitalism* (Atlantic Highlands, N.J.: Humanities Press, 1973).

seen, this new geography represented a profound advance on the old. But it did leave a large amount of human behavior within its own black box; human motivation was reduced to a desire to minimize the friction of distance. And finally, because of this limitation, the new geography could not pretend to explain all the spatial distributions it found.

In consequence, a new wave of geographers tried to go deeper. After an interesting but not entirely fruitful attempt to go inside the quantifiers' black box through a study of individual behavior, a major group sought a deeper explanation in terms of a historicist approach: the geographical human was no longer an individual free agent but was powerfully constrained by deep historical forces. Just like the quantifiers, this group claimed to hold the keys to a fully "scientific" geography. More satisfactorily than the earlier theory, Marxism would explain key features in the development of the contemporary city: the rise of new headquarters offices in some cities and not in others, the decline of inner-city manufacturing industry, the flight to the suburbs. But there was a key difference: this new theory would not become the servant of planning, as the earlier had tried to be. Planning, like the city itself, was to be seen only as an expression of a certain stage of the evolution of capitalist society: it was therefore to be studied scientifically, but the result was to put the scholar outside the subject matter of the study. Paradoxically, therefore, in comparison with the earlier revolution, Marxism has led to a profound academic quietism.

It is interesting to speculate. The new geography best represented the world in which it arose: America in the 1950s. This was the age of American optimism, of belief in the beneficial effects of science and technology, the feeling that the frontier was again endlessly receding. It was the age of belief in universal mobility, of the multicar family, of suburban sprawl. Almost immediately, some of the new techniques were set to work to plan the development of this world: the gravity model soon became widely employed in metropolitan-area transportation studies, which—following the Interstate Highways Act of 1956—became a principal tool for planning urban freeways and opening up the new suburbs for development. But that, in turn, represented a fact: that the aspirations of this generation—for space, for movement—could actually be represented by the models of the new geography. Those facts that could not be thus represented—the ugly facts of racial segregation and of inner-city decay—would be swept away by the civil rights movement and by urban renewal. Such was the optimistic mood of that age.

In contrast, the Marxist paradigm of the 1970s and the 1980s seems curiously appropriate to the new concerns and perceptions of British and American geographers. (It is significant, perhaps, that in the English-speaking world the movement began in Britain and was exported across the Atlantic by a distinguished émigré.) For this was an age dominated by a feeling that—to a degree unknown since the 1930s—the capitalist economy was in serious trouble. The older industrial economies were facing an unprecedented challenge from the newer economies. In Britain, that challenge was already leading to a serious structural decline of the manufacturing base; in the United States, this phenomenon was more localized, yet it was beginning to affect not only old industrial regions like New England, but also such a pillar of American industrialism as Detroit. So it was relatively easy to see society caught in the grip of relentless economic forces from which it could never escape. Bankruptcies and mass unemployment and takeover were the order of the day. Rational economics, in such circumstances, seemed a less apposite model than Say's "iron laws of capitalism."

In both cases, the city is a kind of cartoon of the major phenomena of the decade: endlessly spreading suburbia, linked by great rivers of freeway traffic, for the first; dying cities, contrasted with multinational headquarter-control megalopolises, for the second. In both, geographers brought to their task philosophical assumptions that were curiously well-suited to their subject matter: the primacy of rationalism and the individual pursuit of enlightened self-interest in the first, the primacy of uncontrollable forces and the helplessness of individual persons or groups of workers or cities in the second. Thus, the filter, through which academics perceive social reality, takes on the color of its age.

CHAPTER 3

Economics

Invisible, Productive, and Problem Cities

JOHN R. HARRIS

When Lloyd Rodwin first asked me to write about the "image of the city" as it has emerged and changed within the discipline of economics, I was taken aback. Although it is quite permissible and even fashionable for architects and planners to talk in terms of "images," we practitioners of the dismal science retreat from such trendy terms and instead pontificate in terms of models. However, a little reflection and encouragement from colleagues persuaded me that most of our models are, in fact, images, even though expressed in abstruse mathematics and turgid prose. After all, an image, too, is an abstraction intended to convey the essence if not the palpable substance of some reality.

THE INVISIBLE CITY

So, reassured that thinking in terms of images would not be totally heretical, I searched the disciplinary scriptures for examples of urban models as they had emerged in the discipline. The standard concordance in the field is Joseph A. Schumpeter's masterfully complete *History of Economic Analysis*,[1] but to my dismay there are no entries under *cities*, *urban*, *agglomeration*, or any obviously related topics. Finally, I found

[1]New York: Oxford University Press, 1954.

John R. Harris • African Studies Center, Boston University, Boston, Massachusetts.

two references to location theory—J. H. von Thünen and A. Weber. Thinking that perhaps Schumpeter had fallen down on the job, I went to the scriptures themselves. Adam Smith had only one short section in *The Wealth of Nations* on Italian cities, and he was pointing out how their enlightened policies of free trade led to wealth, but no reference to what was particularly important about them as cities could be found.[2] I had little more success in looking through the tables of contents and indexes of David Ricardo, John Stuart Mill, and Karl Marx, the other great classical economists.[3]

The next stop was the American Economic Association's encyclopedic *Index of Economic Journals*. Of the 23 main divisions of the discipline, Number 22 is "Regional Planning and Development: Housing," with one of five subdivisions being "Urban-Metropolitan Studies," followed only by Number 23: "unclassified." Volume 1 of the *Index* indicates that from 1886 to 1924 only 12 articles in all were published on urban-metropolitan studies, and most of those are primarily discussions of very specific issues in taxation. Volume 2 of the *Index* covers 1925–1939 and shows 21 entries under urban-metropolitan studies. In the period 1940–1949, the entries in this tiny subfield numbered an even 20, and in 1950–1954, another 22 articles were published. Only in the latter half of the 1950s did much of the tiny amount of literature deal with the overall structure and functioning of cities. Suddenly, in the mid-1950s, the profession discovered the city, and in 1955–1959, 67 articles were published on urban-metropolitan studies. By 1966, 47 articles were published in the single year in this category, and new subcategories in land economics and spatial theory were being added to the *Index*. In later years, the task of the *Index* has been assumed by the *Journal of Economic Literature* and the burgeoning of the literature on urban economics is evident. In fact, it was the formation of the Committee on Urban Economics of Resources for the Future in 1960 that marked the beginning of urban economics as a recognized subdivision of the discipline, and the 1968 publication of *Is-*

---

[2]New York: The Modern Library, 1937. (Originally published, 1776.)

[3]Ricardo, *The Principles of Political Economy and Taxation* (Homewood, Ill.: Richard D. Irwin, 1963) (originally published, 1817); Mill, *Principles of Political Economy*, 6th ed. (London, 1865); Marx, *Capital and Other Writings* (New York: Modern Library edition, 1948) (original in German, 1867–1894; first translation in English, 1905). See M. Blaug, *Economic Theory in Retrospect* (Homewood, Ill.: Richard D. Irwin, 1962), for a lucid and readable account of the development of economic thought.

sues in Urban Economics, edited by Harvey S. Perloff and Lowdon Wingo, Jr., represents the first published stocktaking of the infant field.[4] Even so, it has never attained the status of the older subfields, such as public finance, money, or industrial organization, and one still has to argue the validity of its being offered as a field for Ph.D. comprehensive exams.

It is fair to state that until the past two decades, the image of the city held by most economists was that of the "invisible city." During the years when the discipline was emerging as a response to understanding the transformation of mercantile empires into urbanized industrialized states—from the analysis of free trade and the workings of markets to the institutional analysis of modern monopolies and trade unions—the profession seems to have been strangely blind to the urban transformation that was part and parcel of the economic transformation of the past two centuries. It may nevertheless be illuminating to explore a bit further why the image of the city held by economists was of the city invisible.

Economics as a discipline has developed in response to two imperatives: to provide a scientific description of economic systems and economies; and to provide a basis for solving, or at least taking action intended to ameliorate, specific contemporary problems. Indeed, these two strands have been mutually reinforcing, and most of the seminal work in scientific description has been stimulated by the need to understand contemporary problems. An explanation of why economists ignored the city requires an understanding of the context in which the discipline emerged and the problems that were deemed most pressing.

Again, the starting point must be with Adam Smith, whose *Wealth of Nations*, published in the revolutionary year of 1776, is the wellspring of modern economics. The world that Smith was trying to understand was the world of the twilight years of the mercantilist empires, which were experiencing the birth pangs of the Industrial Revolution. As a scientific describer of phenomena, Smith made his fundamental contribution as an analyst of markets—showing how the relaxation of specific administrative controls over economies did not give rise to disorder but allowed the flowering of a new order governed by impersonal forces. This new order, characterized by Smith as the workings of "an invisible hand," redirected resources from sectors of plenty to sectors of scarcity and simultaneously unleashed entrepreneurial and technological innovations; individual ava-

[4]Baltimore: Johns Hopkins Press for Resources for the Future, 1968.

rice would lead to social benefit. The scientific work of Smith was inspired by the ongoing struggles for relaxation of royal control and administrative direction of economic affairs by the rising industrial and commercial classes. Smith's scientific description provided a justification for and an understanding of the consequences of the specific reforms being advocated.

The categories that were used by Smith to describe economies included the factors of production, land, capital, and labor; the organization of productive units and the technologies they employed; the government as a provider of defense and an arbiter of the rules of the game; and commerce and trade between national units. The processes being studied were those of amassing the factors of production and combining them in organizations to produce goods and services. The geographic distribution of such activities *within* national spaces seemed relatively unimportant and capable of being left to the workings of impersonal markets; the distribution of activities and patterns of specialization between nations was, of course, a topic of concern, and Smith's analysis of the gains from specialization and trade again suggested that the problem was best left to the market to solve.

The next great classical writer, Ricardo, elaborated on the scientific themes of Smith, constructing systematic analytic models of the determination of wages, rents, and profits; the distribution of income; and the working of international trade.[5] The rigor of his models set an example that has been the benchmark of succeeding generations. The policy issues that Ricardo was concerned with centered on the repeal of the corn laws. His scientific description led to predictions that, as population grew, land would become more scarce and the rents accruing to landlords would account for growing proportions of the total output, thereby reducing the incentives for investment in industry. His analysis of international trade led to the proposition that, by allowing England to freely import foodstuffs, the payments to landowners would be moderated, the scarcity of land would cease to be an inhibitor of industrialization, and exporters of food would also be importers of industrial goods. The logical relationship between the scientific description and the advocacy of specific policy measures intended to solve a problem are clear. But the fact that most of the expanding industrial activity would take place in cities was an incidental fact hardly worthy of notice by the analyst concerned with sectoral specialization and factor shares in output.

[5]Ricardo, *Political Economy*.

The other towering classical figure is Marx, whose contributions were immense in terms of scientific description, although it can be argued that his direct concern with solving contemporary problems or taking an advocacy role in the policy arena of his day was slight. The contribution of Marx was the systematic analysis of the processes of capital accumulation as undertaken by the new entrepreneurial capitalist classes and of the way in which such development would lead to a struggle between classes relating to ownership of the means of production. Whereas Ricardo (and Mill) was concerned with the struggle between the owners of land and the owners of capital, and he entered the debate over repeal of the corn laws on the side of the capitalists, Marx concentrated on the eventual struggle between capital and labor. Although he, too, adopted a Malthusian view of population growth leading to the "iron law of wages," the other classical writers took this view to mean that real wages could not rise appreciably, whereas Marx predicted that such a state of affairs would not be passively accepted by the workers forever. Because in Marx's scientific description the evolution of the economic system was completely determined by dynamic laws, there was less reason to engage in problem solving, as the outcome was determinate.[6] Marx's units of analysis were (1) the factors of production of capital and labor and (2) the classes differentiated by their ownership of factors. Although the proletariat and their capitalist antago- nists might be concentrated in urban areas, there was nothing specifically urban about the ways in which capital accumulation and the class struggle would emerge in the analysis of Marx. Therefore, the city as a category of analysis could readily be ignored.

Through the rest of the nineteenth and early twentieth centuries, the analytic apparatus of economics became more systematic, the problem of value was tackled through the successful "marginalist revolution," and the theory of international trade was further refined. This corpus of theo- ry, known as *neoclassical economics*, has been the base of the mainstream of the profession to the present. The thrust of the scientific description was to further the knowledge and understanding of the automatic working of markets—the problem-solving aspect was relatively less important than in earlier and later times, and the main conclusions continued to be that if left to themselves, markets would work in socially desirable ways.

At the turn of the century, the institutionalists, concentrated at the University of Wisconsin, turned their attention to problems of monopoly,

[6]Marx, *Capital*.

antitrust, and labor unions. These radicals disputed the automatic desirability of any market solution and saw an increased role for government in
the regulation of economic affairs. But, again, the categories of analysis for
these scholars were factor owners, enterprises, sectors, and specific national institutions.[7] Less concerned with elegant models of scientific description, these economists saw themselves as advocates of a more humane economic order, and they organized to use government as a positive
influence for protecting the economically weak from the growing power of
monopoly capital that was accountable to no one but its owners. Still, the
fact that many of the problems that these economists were concerned
with were played out in the arena of cities did not cause the city itself to
become noticeable.

With the onset of the Great Depression of the 1930s, when the
reigning neoclassical analysis could not explain the persistence of unemployment and could recommend only patience and an unfettering of the
market, John Maynard Keynes introduced the next revolution in scientific description with a model that showed why aggregate demand could
fail to be sufficient to generate full employment. Not only was the Keyne-
sian model important for scientific understanding, it also provided a justification for policy intervention through government spending that could
affect aggregate demand. Note that the categories used to describe and
analyze the economy were aggregated into national levels and included
income, consumption, investment, government expenditure, aggregate
taxes, the money supply, and the levels of unemployment. The policy
variables of concern were government spending, taxing, and the money
supply—variables that have dominated the exercise of economic policy to
the present.

[7]It is interesting to note that neither Schumpeter nor Blaug mentioned the American institutionalists, although Schumpeter made a brief reference to the resistance of the German institutional and historical school to the marginalist revolution at the turn of the century. The slight was intentional, because it was true
that the institutionalists were in principle opposed to the development of general
economic theory divorced from specific institutional and historical context. The
basic conflict was between inductive and deductive methods. The American
institutionalists were based principally at the University of Wisconsin, and the
leader was John R. Commons. They were, in fact, the dominant founders of the
American Economic Association, but they were eclipsed by the theorists in the
1920s. I have not found a good systematic account of the institutionalist contributions—the whole subject is part of the underground lore absorbed by graduate
students in modern economics programs.

The final main development of the profession up to the mid-1950s was the increasing degree of empirical quantification and the construction and use of statistically-based empirical models. The pioneer was Simon Kuznets, whose Nobel prize was awarded for his development of the system of national accounts and his careful descriptions of the trends of economic growth and change over time.[8]

The categories used in amassing data to describe economies include the output of goods and services classified by sector (agriculture, industry, services, and so on, and the subdivisions thereof); the factors utilized (e.g., employment, capital stock and utilization); factor payments (wages, rents, interest, and profits); and demands by end use (e.g., consumption, investment, and government). All of these data are collected and released at the national level, and the lack of geographic detail is quite startling to anyone who tries to undertake analysis for subparts such as cities or regions.

This categorization of data both reflects the categories that have been deemed important for a scientific analysis of the workings of economies and further directs the attention of succeeding generations of economists to those variables for which data are already available.

EMERGING IMAGES OF THE CITY

Nevertheless, although the city failed to appear as a category of analysis or an object of systematic scientific description up to the 1950s, the fact that structural changes were transforming economies from agrarian to industrial-urban could not be ignored. Kuznets's seminal work on patterns of growth shows clearly the degree to which urbanization, industrialization, and modernization are linked, and from this work gradually emerged the image of the city as a concomitant of structural change.[9] As such, the city cannot and should not be ignored, but it is an epiphenomenon, not an independent driving force. The correlation among economic growth, industrialization, and the share of population residing in urban areas is striking, but one still must ask why is that correlation important for understanding the processes of change.

[8]Kuznets, "Quantitative Aspects of the Economic Growth of Nations," pts. I–III, *Economic Development and Cultural Change* (Oct. 1956, July 1957, and July 1958).

[9]Simon Kuznets, *op. cit.*

In the late 1950s and the 1960s, several economists began to examine the functions of cities in the context of structural change. The obvious questions centered on the reasons that economic activity would concentrate so heavily in cities. Influential articles by Bert F. Hoselitz and Eric E. Lampard examined the functions and emergence of cities in historical perspective. In addition to distinguishing between parasitic and generative cities (the former being a place for the spending of resources extracted from the countryside through coercion, the latter for stimulating the growth and increasing the productivity of the economy), attention was paid to the specific ways in which cities have, in fact, been generative.[10] Following these historical studies, systematic thinking about the functions of cities flourished for a while.[11]

Emerging from this literature was a series of images of the productive city. Within this genre, there were several specific images of the city in its productive role: the nodal city; the incubator of innovation; the center of agglomeration economies; the center of information; and the provider of public goods.

These images flow from the work of economists seeking a scientific description of economic processes. Each image taps another aspect of the productive city, and each image is imprecise because the phenomena to be explained are difficult to observe and impossible to quantify. Why should a city be productive? Indeed, what makes a city a city? The literature is bedeviled with attempts to define what a city is; definitions appear in terms of total population, population density, unification of labor markets, and legal status—none of them particularly satisfactory conceptually, although perhaps serviceable for particular empirical studies. What is clear is that cities represent a spatial concentration of people, assets, and activities. Why might the concentrated location of activities contribute to productivity? The most obvious answer relates to savings on the transportation necessary to accomplish any given degree of specialization of production among economic agents. Although the literature is

[10]Hoselitz, "The Role of Cities in the Economic Growth of Underdeveloped Countries," *Journal of Political Economy* (June 1953); Lampard, "The History of Cities in the Economically Advanced Areas," *Economic Development and Cultural Change* (Jan. 1955).
[11]See particularly Wilbur Thompson, "Internal and External Factors in the Development of Urban Economies," and Eric E. Lampard, "The Evolving System of Cities in the United States: Urbanization and Economic Development," both in Perloff and Wingo, for excellent syntheses and references to the literature on urban growth and function.

quite unclear about the degree to which such specialization takes place within enterprises rather than among them, it remains valid to observe that the coordination of specialized activities is much easier when they are carried out in physical proximity. The scale effects of larger markets are important in the sense that markets can be enlarged only at the cost of transportation and communication which is made easier when the population is concentrated or, at least, when access to the transport net is easy. Taken together, these constitute the image of the nodal city, situated at the confluence of transport networks and well connected internally.[12]

Perhaps more interesting is the concept of the city as incubator of innovation. Jane Jacobs observed that most innovations have taken place in cities and asserted that it must necessarily be so because of the importance of human interaction in stimulating ideas. Raymond Vernon and colleagues identified the specific role of New York in incubating innovation through providing a dense network of specialized suppliers that minimize the initial capital required for an innovator to bring an invention into production. The idea is appealing, and the general evidence is convincing, yet careful statistical studies in recent years have been unable to provide convincing support for the proposition that large cities serve an incubating function.[13] Yet, the image is an important one that taps an idea that is not less valid because it is hard to quantify.

The city as a realization of agglomeration economies is probably the dominant image of urban economists today, yet the concept is circular, and it has proved extremely difficult to quantify and test the idea. The fact

[12]The nodal function has been emphasized by geographers and appears in Alan Pred, *The Spatial Dynamics of U.S. Urban-Industrial Growth 1800–1914: Interpretative and Theoretical Essays* (Cambridge: M.I.T. Press, 1966), and in the basic work in regional science which combined the quantitative aspects of geography and economics by Walter Isard, *Location and Space-Economy* (Cambridge: M.I.T. Press, 1956).

[13]See particularly Jacobs, *The Death and Life of Great American Cities* (New York: Random House, 1961), for an extreme view on the central role of cities. Vernon, *Metropolis 1985* (New York: Doubleday, 1960)—reports on the massive work of a team examining the functions and future of New York, which make explicit for the first time the innovation–incubation effect; Benjamin Chinitz, "Contrasts in Agglomeration: New York and Pittsburgh," *American Economic Review* (May 1961), draws conclusions about urban economic structure and innovation. Robert Leone and Raymond Struyk, "The Incubator Hypothesis: Evidence from Five SMSAs," *Urban Studies* v. 13, no. 3 (Oct. 1976) pp. 325–31 is the most systematic attempt to test these propositions quantitatively—success has been limited, at best.

that cities continue to grow despite increased land costs, congestion, and the like must be explained by some compensating advantages, and in the absence of direct identification of these factors, the name *agglomeration economies* has been given as a substitute for specific knowledge. In trying to explain agglomeration economies, economists have waved their hands at the exploitation of economies of scale within firms, at the presence of specialized labor pools, at the possibilities of further specialization and exchange, at scale economies in infrastructure and services, and at ready access to common pools of information. In the absence of more readily identified variables, John Harris and David Wheeler have tried to measure agglomeration economies as capitalized in land values—an indirect procedure requiring heroic assumptions. Yet, this analysis suggests that the nature of agglomeration economies, and the size of city at which they become exhausted, is quite different for cities performing different economic functions. Manufacturing cities seem to exhaust such economies at much smaller population sizes than do cities playing regional or national headquartering and control functions.[14]

Although obviously related to agglomeration economies, the image of the city as an information and control center is becoming more important. In part, concentrating on information pools in relation to control functions is an articulation of agglomeration; it points specifically to the role of information, which in economic theory has usually been assumed to be perfectly reliable, available to all, and costless. Indeed, analysis of information that is costly and imperfectly obtained is a great complication for economic theory that has been approached only gingerly in recent years—it is not surprising that the city has been ignored within a paradigm that has difficulty in analyzing the factor that may well be the *raison d'être* for the city.[15] Although the image of the city as an information and control center is powerful for the few who have thought systematically about it, it remains fugitive and disturbing to the majority of economists, who think in terms of markets' providing information automatically and costlessly.

[14]Harris and Wheeler, "Agglomeration Economies: Theory and Measurement." University of Keele, England, Center for Environmental Studies. Mimeo, 1971.

[15]See Stephen Hymer, "The Multinational Corporation and the Law of Uneven Development," in J. N. Bhagwati, ed., *Economics and World Order* (New York: The Free Press, 1972), 113–40. Also an excellent treatment is David Wheeler, "An Econometric Analysis of Corporate Headquarters Location Decisions and their Impact on Metropolitan Growth in the United States." Ph.D. dissertation, M.I.T., 1974.

To most economists, the image of the city as a provider of public goods is easily absorbed and comfortable to live with. Because various goods are true public goods (such as police and fire protection and streets) and other goods (such as schools, recreation programs, and public assistance) are conventionally provided through public authorities, it seems natural to identify the city as a political jurisdiction in which are determined both the preferences for the goods to be provided and the means of financing them. In the growing literature on public choice, the city is readily identified as a political mechanism through which public choice is exercised.[16]

Although much remains to be done in constructing a theory that provides a systematic scientific description of the functioning of cities, the best available statement, which weaves these several strands together, is a recent book edited by George Tolley, Phillip Graves, and John Gardner.[17]

Each of these images colors the way in which economists attempt to understand the city and to explain its functions. And it is these images, underlying and being in turn fashioned by scientific description, that provide the base from which economists approach their other principal task, the solution of contemporary problems.

THE CITY AS THE SOURCE AND LOCATION OF CONTEMPORARY PROBLEMS

The flowering of urban economics in the past two decades has been not a response to the imperatives of scientific description but a result of the involvement of economists in analyzing contemporary problems, in response to the growing public consciousness of the racial segregation and the concentrated poverty in the largest cities; of spreading blight in old neighborhoods; of failure of urban renewal to transform the city; of the exodus of industry and of blue-collar jobs from central cities to suburbs; of growing pollution and congestion; and, above all, of the fiscal plight of the major cities, which are faced simultaneously with dwindling revenues and

---

[16]The classic article is by Charles Tiebout, "A Pure Theory of Local Expenditure," *Journal of Political Economy*, 64 (1956). A more recent conceptualization is James Buchanan, "Principles of Urban Fiscal Strategy," *Public Choice* (Fall 1971) 1–16.

[17]Tolley, Graves, and Gardner, *Urban Growth Policy in a Market Economy* (New York: Academic Press, 1979).

increased demands for services. Each of these problems burst on the political scene in the 1960s and clamored for solution. The political process responded with an array of programs intended to solve these urban problems, and economists were prepared to play a major role in fashioning policy solutions. Success in designing macroeconomic policy, particularly the Kennedy tax cut, made the profession confident that with money and the attentive ear of policymakers, urban problems could be solved—the era of social engineering had dawned.

The immediate questions to be asked in each case were: What is the underlying cause of the problem? How can it be affected by policy? And what are instruments through which policy can be exercised? As a new group of economists came forward, claiming that urban economics was the subdiscipline that should have jurisdiction over such problems, and furthermore that the subdiscipline should be given recognition as a field of concentration in terms of graduate training programs, curricula, and faculty staffing, there was some controversy about whether such status was justified. The skeptics asked what were the concepts, corpus of theory, and distinctive tools of analysis that justified such status. To what extent were these problems, which were classed as urban, merely the standard problems that economists were used to looking at, their distinction being merely that they happened to occur in urban areas? The question is important because most of the problems being cited appeared to be relatively standard problems in labor economics, public finance, or cost–benefit analysis, and it was far from clear that more than specific institutional knowledge and rapport with particular policymaking actors was required for any economist to become an urban economist.[18]

In fact, there has emerged a considerable (but hardly universal) recognition that urban problems have a specific, common underlying feature not captured in the core of economic theory. By virtue of the population concentration that makes a city a city and through physical proximity, actions in one sphere have a direct impact on other activities that are not properly reflected in markets—in the jargon, there are pervasive externalities of co-location that cause market failure.

Given the inherent concentration of the profession on market processes and functioning, and given the presupposition, prevailing since Adam Smith, that markets generally give rise to efficient outcomes, it is

[18]See Richard F. Muth, *Urban Economic Problems* (New York: Harper & Row, 1975).

usually assumed by economists that the burden of proof must be placed on the argument that markets are failing to work. And in recent years, the concept of market failure has been influential in guiding policy analysis— a set of conditions have been outlined in which markets will fail to allocate efficiently. One of these conditions (along with such standard cases as monopoly power or discrimination) is externalities.[19] The original idea of externality is conveyed by the bucolic example of the beekeeper and the orchard owner. An abundance of blossoms increases honey production, and the presence of bees going about their business causes the pollination of blossoms and increased fruit production. Yet, the beekeeper does not benefit from the fruit production, and the orchard owner does not benefit from the honey, so that neither has an incentive to produce at the optimal level, because they will fail to capture some of the benefits from their investment. Negative externalities are best illustrated by the owner of a factory that emits large clouds of sulfurous smoke, thereby causing damage to the surrounding area that does not directly impose costs on the factory owner. The surrounding residents have real costs imposed on them that are not mediated by the market, and the polluter has no incentive to reduce pollution because she or he bears only the costs and would not reap the benefits of improved air quality. If property rights are not redefined in ways that would cause markets to arise in which pollination services or pollution discharges would be bought and sold through markets, the existing markets will fail to allocate resources efficiently.[20] On examination, it became clear that urban agglomerations generate a large number of externalities because of spatial proximity. Therefore, a body of theory and analytic tools needed to be developed that specifically take spatial relationships into account, and that body of theory and tools is the core of the speciality of urban economics. To the economic practitioner, the image of the problem city becomes a more specialized image of the externality-generating city.

It may be useful to examine the nature of the externalities bearing on each of the major classes of urban problems that economists have con-

---

[19]Francis Bator, "The Anatomy of Market Failure," *Quarterly Journal of Economics*, 72 (Aug. 1958): 351–79 remains the most lucid general discussion of the concept.

[20]A good discussion is found in Muth, *op. cit.*, chs. 2, 3, 4, and 6. See also Bennet Harrison, *Urban Economic Development* (Washington: The Urban Institute, 1974) and David M. Gordon, *Problems in Political Economy: An Urban Perspective* (Lexington, Mass.: D. C. Heath).

cerned themselves with. Housing deterioration and neighborhood decay are two of the most obvious urban problems to which economists have devoted attention. The key point is that when one purchases a house, it is not only the physical structure that is bought but also the location, the access to services, and the neighborhood surroundings. Yet, the owner of a house cannot control the neighborhood characteristics that enhance or destroy the value of his or her investment. Therefore, if a neighborhood is decaying and others do not maintain their dwellings, it will not pay for an individual to maintain his or her unit because he or she cannot recover the costs if the unit is either rented or sold. In terms of game theory, we have a "prisoner's dilemma," in that, even if all could gain by concerted action in the neighborhood, if any one individual improves his property and others don't, he loses, whereas if others improve their property and he doesn't, he will nevertheless benefit by the free ride. This is the underlying dynamic of blight and its spread: individual actions in response to market incentives contribute to the perpetuation of the problem, and a different level of concerted action and control is required for actions to be taken that could be beneficial to all. Interestingly, in the late 1970s, a process inelegantly dubbed *gentrification* swept parts of many cities—it is, in fact, reverse blight, in which, once a critical mass of upgrading takes place, the neighborhood effects generate gains that can be captured by upgrading adjacent properties, and the process cumulates. Of course, although blight is decried and gentrification clearly optimizes the property values, the latter process is controversial because not only do property values increase, but a replacement of population takes place, so that the individuals who benefit from the change are different from those who are displaced, perhaps to something worse.

The fact that land-use patterns and property values are determined significantly by transportation networks, and that the siting and use of transportation facilities are dependent on land-use patterns, generates another kind of externalities not readily captured by markets. Because transport right-of-ways are public goods that must be sited and built in discrete lumps, there is no reason to believe that markets will automatically lead to the "correct" level of service provision. If there is no subway system but highways and streets are well provided, it is well known that a pattern of low-density dispersed residences will emerge; if a low-density pattern already exists, it will not be economical to construct mass-transit lines because insufficient traffic will be generated. If it is true that in a world of high energy costs cities should be relatively densely settled, with access being provided by mass transit, specific public action will be required in both the siting of transport nets and the control of land use, because markets cannot be depended on to reach the best solutions.

The problems of urban labor markets again display the pervasive problem of spatial externalities. In order for workers to obtain jobs and for employers to tap a labor force, it is necessary for workers to physically reach the workplace each day. The incentives have been such that manufacturing firms have dispersed from the central cities to take advantage of lower land and transport costs, changing to a technology that takes advantage of one-floor layouts. The substitution of clerical and technical workers and machinery for unskilled workers, which has been encouraged by technological changes, has been further stimulated by ready access to such workers in the suburbs—workers who already had access to private automobiles for commuting to work. As a result less skilled jobs have been leaving the cities, and the less skilled workers have been unable to take up the new jobs being generated in the suburbs because they lack access to transportation at a reasonable cost (in both cash and time); at the same time, they have also been barred, by both social and economic forces, from relocating to housing in the suburbs, where they could regain access to work.[21] The spatial interconnections among industrial location, transportation, and residential housing markets are so important that one cannot approach urban employment problems only in terms of aggregating demands and supplies of labor across the metropolitan area to identify imbalances as labor market studies conventionally have done.

Perhaps the most important set of issues that has been addressed is in the area of local public finance. American cities are unique in the degree to which they are fragmented into many political jurisdictions, each with considerable autonomy in levying taxes and providing services. The seminal work of Teibout demonstrated that this fragmentation could lead to the availability of a wider menu of taxes and services, so that individuals could join that unit whose program most suited their tastes. This approach has been further refined through the "theory of clubs."[22]

---

[21]Leon Moses and H. F. Williamson, Jr., "The Location of Economic Activity in Cities," *The American Economic Review* (May 1967): 211–22 provide an explanation in terms of changing relative transport costs of moving freight and moving people; see Harrison, *op. cit.* for a careful treatment of these problems.

[22]Teibout, *op. cit.* and Buchanan, *op. cit.*

The other side of this is that there are systematic incentives for any individual to want to move to a unit with high average income, and for those in a unit to try to keep out anyone with lower-than-average income.[23] It is clear that attempts to redistribute real income within cities through the provision of public services are systematically undone through residential mobility patterns. The final result is that low-income individuals are concentrated in particular political jurisdictions that, by virtue of a low tax base, require a higher burden of taxation on the residents to provide lower levels of services than is true for higher income communities. The crucial analytic point is that another form of externality exists: residential location includes membership in a political jurisdiction, and changes in the tax-service package in a jurisdiction give rise systematically to residential relocation, thereby further changing the tax-service package.

Whereas it is the existence of positive externalities that explains the productive city (the so-called agglomeration economy), it is the negative externalities that characterize the problem city and that make the solutions to the problems particularly difficult.

IMAGES AND THE FUTURE

This chapter has suggested the ways in which economists' images of the city have changed over time in response to the imperatives of the discipline. In turn, these changing images have influenced the ways in which the city has been understood and approached. The scientific descriptive aspects of the discipline emerged from a need to understand the structural changes accompanying the Industrial Revolution. Economies underwent accelerated growth under the control of impersonal market forces, and the imperative of the discipline was to understand how those forces operated. Technological change, capital accumulation, and industrialization, with the associated changes in earnings and income distribution, occupied the attention of most economists, and the image of the city

[23]See Jerome Rothenberg, "Strategic Interactions and Resource Allocation in Metropolitan Intergovernmental Relations," *The American Economic Review*, 59 (1969): 495–504 and "Local Decentralization and the Theory of Optimal Government," in J. Margolis, ed., *The Analysis of Public Output* (New York: Columbia University Press, 1970).

remained the invisible city. Not that the city didn't exist; rather, it seemed unimportant to pay separate attention to an epiphenomenon when the primary phenomenon was not fully understood. The policy problems in which economists engaged were ones of national policy, particularly the degree to which both national and international economic affairs could be left to the direction of markets. The profession was enthralled by the automatic functioning of these impersonal systems, and if cities flourished or fell as a result, it must be in the interest of efficiency.

Explaining the existence of cities only as a concomitant of economic change remained unsatisfying, and some economists began to explore the reasons that cities emerged and to examine their functions with respect to national economies. The image of the productive city began to guide investigation and scientific description. How could the growth of cities in a market framework be explained other than by the fact that they were highly productive? Yet, this task attracted relatively few economists, and for the majority in the profession, the city remained invisible.

It was in response to urgent social and economic problems that urban economics emerged as a subdiscipline, and the dominant image has been that of the problem city. The city became, for most, a center of problems—most of them caused by market failure due to pervasive spatial externalities and remediable through appropriately designed policies. But here social engineering has come on difficult days. What initially appeared to be technocratically-soluble problems have proved to contain intractable social and political dimensions that do not yield to readily imposed policies. The crux of the problem is that spatial externalities impose themselves differentially on different socioeconomic groups. It can be argued that the pattern of externalities has systematically worked to the disadvantage of racial minorities and low-income groups. The effect of political jurisdictioning has been to provide lower levels of real income, in terms of public services, to individuals and families that earn low incomes in the marketplace—thus, the net effect of tax-expenditure policies is to further reinforce the inequalities that emerge in the labor markets. In the existing political structure, attempts to redress these balances result in a systematic flight of the better off to the suburbs or in gentrification and displacement of the poor—either way, central cities and inner suburbs with concentrated low-income populations are made to bear the brunt of adjustment. One cannot look at ways to compensate for externalities without recognizing that these externalities have systematic and not random effects on different groups, each of which has its own means of political mobilization. It is no wonder that the problem city has also been the conflict-ridden city in America in recent years.

With the coming to power of a new political regime that is suspicious of social engineering, is unconcerned with poverty, and has theological faith in the workings of markets, we are seeing a turning away from the image of the problem city, yet it is unlikely that the problems will cure themselves, given the pervasiveness of the externalities that cause market failure. Economists have been interested in the problem city precisely because there were problems to solve. With the turning away from interest in policy solutions (other than letting the market work itself out), it is likely that we will return to the image of the invisible city. Perhaps the natural working of forces will divert population and attention from the problem cities of the already-developed regions to the productive cities of the growing Sunbelt, although one can predict that the problem city will emerge there, too.

CHAPTER 4

Images of the City in Political Science

Communities, Administrative Entities, Competitive Markets, and Seats of Chaos

MARTIN SHEFTER

Political science is a relatively young discipline.[1] It was not until 1880 that an American university first appointed a professor of political science, and it was only in 1903—almost 20 years after the founding of the American Historical Association and the American Economic Association—that there were a large enough number of political scientists, and they were sufficiently conscious of themselves as a distinct discipline, to establish a professional association.[2]

From the discipline's earliest days, however, political scientists have devoted themselves to understanding the city. The most widely used textbook in American government in the late nineteenth century, James Bryce's *The American Commonwealth*, was centrally concerned with the government (and misgovernment) of cities. And the first president of the American Political Science Association, Frank Goodnow, was a specialist in the field of urban government, as well as the author of one of the first textbooks dealing exclusively with this subject.

[1]This paper analyzes some of the major ways in which political scientists have viewed the city over the past century. It does not attempt to discuss all the important works in the field during this period.

[2]A. Somit and J. Tanenhaus, *The Development of American Political Science* (Boston: Allyn and Bacon, 1967), Chapter 2.

Martin Shefter • Department of Government, Cornell University, Ithaca, New York.

From the late nineteenth century through the mid-1960s, three successive images of the city were dominant in the discipline: during the period 1880–1900, political scientists viewed the city as a community; from roughly 1900 until the mid-1950s, they considered municipal governments largely to be administrative entities; and from the mid-1950s through the middle of the following decade, they likened the city to a competitive market. Over the past 15 years, no single image of the city has occupied such a dominant position; rather, political scientists have variously proposed that the cities be regarded as internal colonies of the United States, as the seat of chaos in the American political order, as mechanisms of social control, and as black boxes in input–output models.

The various images of the city formulated by political scientists over the past century differ chiefly in their view of political conflict—whether they regard it as destructive or benign—and how they propose that cities deal with it. In this essay, I will analyze these successive images, and seek to account for why political scientists have viewed the city in these ways. I shall argue that these images are a function of both the structure of city politics during the period when they were formulated and the structure of the profession of political science, in particular the relationship between political scientists and various contenders for power in the city.

THE CITY AS A COMMUNITY

The first image of the city in political science likened the city to a community. This image, as suggested above, was shaped by the orientation of political scientists to the political developments of their day. When James Bryce published *The American Commonwealth* in 1888, the professoriat in the United States had ties to a social stratum—an elite of merchants and allied professionals—that had dominated American cities since the colonial era, but that was in the last stages of being driven from power. The power of that elite had rested on three conditions, which were progressively undermined during the nineteenth century.[3] First, prior to the industrial era, when the economy of American cities was

---

[3]My understanding of the politics of the American city during the colonial and antebellum eras draws heavily upon Amy Bridges's superb study of New York City. See *A City in the Republic: New York and the Origins of Machine Politics* (New York: Cambridge University Press, 1984).

based entirely on commerce, the prosperity of every segment of the city's population depended on the volume of its trade. It was generally recognized that all groups in the city shared such a common interest, and therefore, all were prepared to acquiesce to the leadership of those who conducted this commerce, namely, the city's merchants.

This is not to deny that there were conflicts of interest among different social classes in the commercial city. During the colonial period, municipal governments regulated prices, and the city's artisans and laborers wanted the prices of the goods they consumed to be low, and those of the goods they sold to be high. When faced with such demands, the merchants who ran the municipal government could make concessions— and thereby turn back challenges to their rule—because prior to the Industrial Revolution they did not have to fear that prices set with such political considerations in mind would be upset by competition with goods that were produced elsewhere in large quantities and that were sold at prices determined without regard to such political considerations.

A second condition that sustained the rule of the merchants in the commercial era was the physical and social compactness of the city. Partly as a consequence of primitive transportation technologies (walking was the chief means of getting around the city), and partly as a consequence of the organization of production prior to the development of the factory system (employees characteristically lived as members of their employer's household in rooms above the shops where they worked), there was a great deal of personal interaction between the members of different social classes in the city. This arrangement both personalized relations between the classes, thereby reducing the potential for conflict, and subjected would-be troublemakers from the lower social strata to the scrutiny—and hence the discipline—of those above them.

The final condition buttressing the hegemony of the merchants in the commercial era was more narrowly political. Prior to the emergence and the institutionalization of political parties during the Jacksonian period, those who might wish to challenge the merchant elite simply lacked the organizational means to do so.

In his study of Newburyport, Massachusetts, Stephen Thernstrom provided a striking example of how thoroughly merchants dominated the politics of commercial cities.[4] In 1780, a new state constitution that would tighten suffrage requirements was proposed. The elite of merchants, law-

[4]*Poverty and Progress* (Cambridge: Harvard University Press, 1964), p. 41.

yers, and ministers in Newburyport supported this constitution, and a resolution endorsing it was introduced in the town meeting. This resolution passed unanimously: the city's patriciate was so powerful that it was able to induce many townsmen who had been eligible to vote under the old standards to endorse their own disfranchisement!

Three forces, which gathered strength during the middle decades of the nineteenth century, undermined the political hegemony of this mercantile elite. The first of these was industrialization, which shattered the political unity of the commercial city. It created conflicts of interest within the urban upper class, pitting manufacturers, who sought the enactment of protective tariffs, against merchants, who opposed high tariffs as a hindrance to commerce. Industrialization also heightened conflicts between the working and upper classes because it enabled manufacturers to produce goods at prices that artisans could not possibly meet, forcing them to give up the independence of their former way of life and to work for a wage. The artisans believed that they were the victims of special privileges granted by the government to their competitors; in particular, they blamed their plight on the banks that provided the manufacturers with loans to finance their activities, and they called for an end to the public chartering of such "monopolies." Finally, industrialization fostered conflicts within the working class because it created the unskilled jobs that led immigrants to settle in the cities. In response to this influx, native-born artisans periodically rallied under the leadership of nativist politicians who argued for restrictions on immigration on the grounds that just as the American manufacturer needed tariffs for protection against competition from cheap foreign goods, so too did the American worker need protection against competition from cheap foreign labor. The threat posed by nativists, in turn, led the immigrants to mobilize in self-defense.

A second and related condition that undermined the rule of the mercantile elite was the growing size of the cities and the emergence of residential neighborhoods inhabited predominantly by the members of a single social class. Industrialization fostered these developments because it created the jobs that enabled cities to grow, and through the factory system, it separated workplace from household and thereby made possible the creation of class-homogeneous neighborhoods. These developments posed several threats to the city's mercantile elite. First of all, the separation of home and workplace and the emergence of socially homogeneous neighborhoods removed the political activities of the working classes from the scrutiny of their employers, and it gave them the freedom to act more independently in the political realm. Second, as the cities grew, the people living in outlying areas wanted public services—streets, sewers, water lines—extended into their neighborhoods.[5]

The merchant elite were oriented to the port and the downtown commercial district and did not like being taxed for purposes from which they would not benefit. (This issue also frequently divided industrialists and merchants, because the former wanted new neighborhoods to be opened for residential development so that wages would not have to be raised to cover the high rents that went along with a tight housing market.)

The final condition that undermined the rule of the mercantile elite in American cities was the formation of political parties during the Jacksonian era. Competition between the Democrats and the Whigs mobilized huge numbers of new voters into the electorate, thereby swamping the techniques of political control relied on by the old mercantile elite and turning electoral management into a full-time occupation.[6]

Politicians affiliated with the national parties cemented together coalitions among the various groups mentioned above. They assumed the political leadership of the wage laborers (immigrants generally flocked to the Democrats and the native-born to the Whigs), organizing them through volunteer fire companies and other recreational associations in their neighborhoods. With this political base, they were able to secure election to public office, and then to vote appropriations for extending city services into outlying districts. Finally, they placed their political lieutenants on the public payroll in patronage positions. In other words, these politicians built political machines.

The city's mercantile elite reacted with horror to these developments. They reaped no benefit from the extension of municipal services to outlying neighborhoods, or from the granting of transportation franchises to companies that offered services to these districts, and therefore, they believed that the city's doing so served only private interests rather than the public interest. They thought that it was entirely illegitimate for the city government to spend taxpayers' money—their money—subsidiz-

[5]S. Hays, "The Changing Structure of the City in Industrializing America," *Journal of Urban History* 1 (Nov. 1974): 6–38.

[6]R. McCormick, "Political Development and the Second Party System," in *The American Party Systems: Stages of Development*, ed. William Chambers and Walter D. Burnham (New York: Oxford University Press, 1967), pp. 90–116.

ing the organizations, such as volunteer fire companies, through which machine politicians mobilized their supporters, all the more so because these companies were more adept at mobilizing voters on election day and at fighting with one another than at fighting fires. They did not like the idea of machine politicians' taking over the police department and the police courts because then these agencies of social control enforced the law in ways that served the interests of the machine's constituents rather than in accord with the mercantile elite's own conception of public order.

The merchant elite sought to deal with these problems by establishing the first municipal reform movements. And it was in this context that the discipline of urban political science was established. In the early years of its existence, political science had very little autonomy from the political movements of the day: in their political sympathies and organizational affiliations, American scholars were linked to the so-called Mugwump reform movement. Although a scholarly journal in the field, the *Political Science Quarterly*, was founded in 1886, no professional association of political scientists was organized in the nineteenth century. The closest thing to such an organization was the American Social Science Association (ASSA), whose membership included both scholars and laypeople, and which never settled whether it was devoted to the advocacy of social reforms or the effort to understand society and politics in a rigorous and scholarly way.[7]

The reform movements with which political scientists and the ASSA were linked were led by the "best men" of the city, namely, the members of old mercantile and professional families. It is therefore not surprising that political scientists latched onto James Bryce's analysis of American politics in general, and the politics of American cities in particular. (Anna Haddow, in her history of American political science, reported that "Bryce's work seemed so thorough and satisfactory as a description of the whole system of American government that for a number of years no comparable treatise appeared to rival it as a textbook."[8]) Bryce, whose closest American contacts were leaders of the nineteenth-century reform movement—among them Theodore Roosevelt, E. L. Godkin, and Seth

[7]T. Haskell, *The Emergence of Professional Social Science: The American Social Science Association and the Nineteenth Century Crisis of Authority* (Urbana: University of Illinois Press, 1977).
[8]*Political Science in American Colleges and Universities, 1636–1900* (New York: A. Appleton-Century Co.; 1939), p. 260.

Low—formulated the most theoretically sophisticated statement of that movement's ideology.

Bryce, in the observation most frequently quoted from his book, asserted that the government of cities was the "one conspicuous failure" of American democracy.[9] The source of this failure, he argued, was "the prominence of inferior men in politics and the absence of distinguished figures." These inferior men (i.e., machine politicians) could be overthrown if the "best citizens" (i.e., the members of old mercantile and professional families) would unite across national party lines, under the leadership of "statesmen, journalists, and lecturers" (i.e., the intellectuals linked to this class), and play a sustained role in urban politics. The rule of "rings and bosses" could be ended "were the better citizens to maintain unbroken through a series of elections that unity and vigor of action of which they have at rare moments, and under the impulse of urgent duty, shown themselves capable."[10]

Bryce denied that there were any legitimate conflicts of interest either within the upper class or between the upper and the lower classes in the United States; the lower classes, he asserted, were "generally ready to follow when they are wisely and patriotically led."[11] In other words, Bryce's image of the late-nineteenth-century American city was of a politically homogeneous *community*, fundamentally similar to the mercantile city, in which the artisans were generally prepared to follow the leadership of the merchants, because the well-being of both depended on the volume of the city's commerce. The strategy of dealing with conflicts of interest in the industrializing city adopted by Bryce and the political scientists who found his analysis so persuasive was simply to deny their existence.

In what direction were the "best citizens" to lead the city? Bryce was silent on this point except to say that the opinion leaders must convince all members of the public that their interests lay in "good government." To this extent, the image of the city as a community did not challenge the

---

[9]This and the following two paragraphs draw on Kenneth Fox's analysis of Bryce. See Fox, *Better City Government* (Philadelphia: Temple University Press, 1977), 34–39. Cf. W. Sayre and N. Polsby, "American Political Science and the Study of Urbanization," in *The Study of Urbanization*, ed. P. Hauser and L. Schnore (New York: Wiley, 1965), 115–156.

[10]J. Bryce, *The American Commonwealth*, Vol. 2 (London: Macmillan, 1889), p. 141.

[11]Ibid., p. 141.

rather stringent limits that the state legislatures and the courts placed on the authority of municipal governments at the time. The proponents of this image were quite prepared to have conflicts over what municipal governments should and should not do settled by the simple expedient of the courts' declaring null and void policies opposed by the social forces with which they were allied.

THE CITY AS AN ADMINISTRATIVE ENTITY

The second image of the city—the city as an administrative entity— was formulated by political scientists during the Progressive Era. The political scientists who developed this image resembled their predecessors in one important respect: they, too, were affiliated with the municipal reform movements of their day. However, in contrast to their predecessors, who defended the interests of an established mercantile elite against a rising class of industrialists, the political scientists of the Progressive Era played a far more creative role: they sought to overcome this cleavage within the metropolitan upper class by formulating a "scientific" program of municipal reform that would serve the interests of all groups in the city. Moreover, in contrast to the earlier generation of political scientists, who sought to limit the power of city governments, the political scientists affiliated with the Progressive movement sought to expand those powers. They argued that the interests of everyone in the city could be served by a powerful municipal government, so long as that government was properly organized—organized in a way that would lead it to serve the "public interest" rather than private interests.

Changes in both city politics and the political science profession account for the formulation of this new image and for its ready acceptance by the municipal reform movements of the Progressive Era. As for changes in city politics, the old mercantile elites and the new industrial magnates who had been at loggerheads throughout much of the nineteenth century generally found it prudent to join forces at the turn of the twentieth century. By this time, the political machines of most major cities in the United States had become strong enough organizationally to attain a substantial measure of autonomy from the elements of the business community with which they had initially been allied.[12] In addition,

[12]M. Shefter, "The Emergence of the Political Machine: An Alternative View," in *Theoretical Perspective in Urban Politics*, ed. Willis Hawley and Michael Lipsky (Englewood Cliffs, N.J.: Prentice-Hall, 1976), 14–44.

at the turn of the century, the merchants who formerly had advocated strict economy in government were beginning to propose that municipal governments undertake substantial new tasks. A case in point is the New York Chamber of Commerce, which in the 1890s became the leading force pressing for the construction of a subway system, for substantial improvements in the city's harbor facilities, and for a new municipal water-supply system. No element of the business community wanted the machine to be in charge of the city while these projects were being constructed, for these projects could provide machine politicians with an enormous supply of patronage and thereby strengthen the machine still more.[13] In other words, all segments of the business community now had reason to unite in opposition to the machine, and to be receptive to a program calling for the strengthening of municipal governments.

Changes within the discipline of political science contributed to the formulation of such a program. By the turn of the twentieth century, political scientists were becoming more self-conscious and were gaining in self-confidence. They organized a professional association, the American Political Science Association (APSA), in 1903, and they began publishing a new journal, the *American Political Science Review*, in 1906. These activities bespoke a conviction among political scientists that they were formulating an independent science of politics, that is, that they possessed knowledge about politics that was superior to that of the laity.

Though the founding of the APSA indicated that the political science discipline was becoming more autonomous, the very self-confidence of the discipline's practitioners led them to believe that they could make a distinctive contribution in the world of politics. Rather than relying on an already-existing image of the city as had the previous generation, political scientists during the Progressive Era played a leading role in formulating a new image—the city as an *administrative entity*—and in convincing the municipal reformers of their day to conceive of the city in this way and to support the program of governmental reorganization it implied. Three political scientists sat on the committee that drafted the "municipal program" of the National Municipal League, the leading reform organization of the day. And political scientists regularly contributed to the League's journal, the *National Municipal Review*.

The analysis of urban affairs propounded by political scientists during the early decades of the twentieth century was grounded upon the prem-

---

[13]D. Hammack, *Power and Society: Greater New York at the Turn of the Century* (New York: Russell Sage Foundation, 1982), Chapter 5.

ise that the very nature of cities dictated the most important policies that they should pursue: If large numbers of people were to live in close proximity to one another, steps had to be taken to prevent the spread of communicable diseases, extinguish fires, supply the population with drinking water, preserve law and order, maintain public thoroughfares, and so forth. To say the same thing in different words, they believed that there was relatively unambiguous public interest that individuals could fail to acknowledge only out of selfishness or ignorance. Thus, though progressive political scientists insisted that the task of municipal governments involved both the formulation of policy and its administration—and that policymaking involved the decisions concerning ends over which, in principle, reasonable persons could disagree—they believed that in practice there were few occasions in cities when controversies and conflicts were legitimate. As Frank Goodnow, the leading political scientist of this school, put it,

> In state and national government new questions of policy are continually coming up . . . in municipal government the appearance of such questions is rare. The work of the city and its officers is rather the consistent, continuous administration of policies which have been determined upon and which should remain for a comparatively long time unchanged.[14]

Conflicts and controversies arose in cities largely because party politicians or special interests sought to extract some unwarranted privilege from municipal government.

This understanding of the city had important implications for how municipal governments should be organized. Progressive political scientists and reformers insisted that municipal administration should be separated from politics. What this meant concretely was that the actual services that cities performed—fire protection, public health, and the like—should be conducted by bureaucracies, under the control of a single commissioner, who reported to a chief executive. (Previously, municipal services had been performed by multimembered boards and commissions under the supervision of city council committees.) The bureaucratization of municipal functions would reduce the influence of party politicians

[14]F. Goodnow, "The Place of the Council and the Mayor in the Organization of Municipal Government—The Necessity of Distinguishing Legislation from Administration," in National Municipal League, *A Municipal Program* (New York: Macmillan, 1900), p. 76.

over the distribution of public services and would increase the influence of professionals and experts, like the reformers themselves. Interestingly, the commitment to functionally organized bureaucracies was so deeply ingrained in Progressive political science that, for 50 years, urban government textbooks were organized along precisely these same lines, with chapters on public health, welfare, public safety, education, and so forth.[15]

Progressive political scientists also advocated increasing the power of the chief executive. In large cities, this would be the mayor—the public official of greatest visibility, and consequently the one whose election could most be influenced by respectable newspapers, the Chamber of Commerce, and the like, and over whom the machine was likely to have the least control. The Progressive ideal, however, was the city manager— a professional public administrator, akin to professional business managers, military officers, or officials in the British or German civil service. The antidemocratic implications of this reform are worth noting: The most important official in the city government would not be subject to popular election.

Another ideal of Progressive political science was the city council whose members were elected at large, rather than by wards. This ideal was the institutional manifestation of the notion that there was a unitary public interest of the city as a whole, and consequently that elected officials should not be beholden to partial interests, such as neighborhood interests. Finally, the Progressives called for nonpartisan elections, for similar reasons: "There is no Democratic or Republican way to clean a street," they asserted.

Both in theory and in practice, these reforms restricted democracy as it was traditionally conceived of and practiced in the United States. They reduced the number of officials subject to popular election. They weakened the central institution through which popular participation in politics was organized, namely, the political party; one consequence was to reduce greatly the levels of voting participation in municipal elections. And in place of the political party (or the political machine), these reforms established the bureaucracy as the central institution of municipal government. Schools, welfare departments, and other bureaucracies came to perform functions formerly performed by the machine, and they did so

[15]Fox, 80–86.

under the guidance of professionals and experts, rather than of politicians who were at least partly beholden to the electorate.

In sum, the image of the city as an administrative entity sought to deal with conflicts over who should rule the city by reorganizing the institutions of municipal government in a way that worked to the political advantage of the groups with which the proponents of this image were allied. Moreover, this image denied that there were very many legitimate differences of interest and opinion in municipal affairs, and hence it masked the sleight-of-hand involved in this way of dealing with political conflicts in the city.

THE CITY AS A COMPETITIVE MARKET

The image of the city as an administrative entity persisted for a remarkably long period of time in American political science—roughly from 1900 through 1955. It was challenged during the period 1955–1965 in books and articles written by Edward Banfield, Robert Dahl, Herbert Kaufman, Norton Long, Martin Meyerson, Nelson Polsby, Wallace Sayre, James Q. Wilson, and Raymond Wolfinger.[16]

These scholars formulated an image of the city as a *competitive market,* that is, a multiplicity of independent groups, no one of which was dominant, and whose interaction yielded the common good. In contrast to the images described above, the market model regarded political conflicts in cities as benign.

As before, this new image was formulated and gained adherents in response to changes in city politics and in the discipline of political science. The most important political change that enabled scholars to regard political conflicts as an expression of democracy rather than as a manifestation of pathology was the waning of the long-standing cleavage be-

---

[16]Myerson and Banfield, *Politics, Planning, and the Public Interest* (New York: Free Press, 1955); Banfield, *Political Influence* (New York: Free Press, 1961); Banfield and Wilson, *City Politics* (Cambridge: Harvard Universty Press, 1963); Dahl, *Who Governs?* (New Haven: Yale University Press, 1961); Long, "The Local Community as an Ecology of Games," *American Journal of Sociology* 54 (Nov. 1958): 251–261; Polsby, *Community Power and Political Theory* (New Haven: Yale University Press, 1963); Sayre and Kaufman, *Governing New York City* (New York: Russell Sage, 1960); Wolfinger, "Reputation and Reality in the Study of Community Power," *American Sociological Review* 25 (1960): 636–644.

tween reformers, who drew their support from middle- and upper-class native-born Protestants, and machine politicians, whose votes came from immigrants and their children.[17] In the 1950s, a new generation of politicians came to the fore in American cities. Mayors such as Richard Lee of New Haven, Robert Wagner of New York, John Collins of Boston, James Tate of Philadelphia, and Richard Daley of Chicago were products of the political machines in their cities, but they implemented many of the administrative arrangements favored by reformers, and they put together coalitions of foreign stock voters and small businesspeople, on the one hand, and downtown business leaders, newspaper publishers, and civic elites, on the other hand. The key program around which these mayors assembled their coalitions was urban renewal.[18] The use of public subsidies and of the power of eminent domain to induce developers to construct office buildings, convention centers, department stores, and luxury apartment complexes in and near the central business district was supported by the downtown business community because it provided benefits to its members, and it was endorsed by the press as a way to stem the flight of the middle class (i.e., their subscribers and their advertisers' customers) to the suburbs. Moreover, downtown redevelopment provided mayors with visible accomplishments that they could point to when they campaigned for reelection, and it promised to halt the erosion of the city's tax base—and this halt appealed to marginal homeowners and small businesspeople. The waning of rancorous conflicts between machine politicians and reformers enabled political scientists to view that fight in dispassionate terms—as a conflict between different social groups with different outlooks on politics, rather than as a holy war between the forces of righteousness and the forces of evil.

Changes in the political science discipline after World War II further encouraged students of urban politics to view city politics in these terms. During the 1950s, the behavioral movement was at the intellectual cutting edge of the field. Behavioralists argued that it was possible and desirable to construct a science of politics on the model of the natural sciences: political scientists, they argued, should not permit their person-

[17]R. Salisbury, "Urban Politics: The New Convergence of Power," *Journal of Politics* 26 (Nov. 1964): 775–797.

[18]J. Mollenkopf, "The Postwar Politics of Urban Development," *Politics and Society* 5 (1975): 247–295.

al values to color their scholarly research; rather than taking one or another side in contemporary political disputes, they should search for laws of political behavior that explained why different political groups acted as they did.

The decisive intellectual break with the image of urban politics fashioned by political scientists during the Progressive Era was made by Edward C. Banfield in his appendix to a book he wrote jointly with Martin Meyerson, *Politics, Planning, and the Public Interest.*[19] In this appendix Banfield attacked one of the central concepts of Progressive political science, the public interest; or, rather, Banfield raised questions about the Progressives' interpretation of this concept. He pointed out that there are two ways in which the public interest can be understood. One is the understanding of the Progressives': the public interest is what is common to the public as a whole. However, Banfield noted, there is an equally legitimate interpretation of the public interest; namely, it is the aggregate of the individual interests of the city's residents. In making this latter observation, Banfield was simply reminding political scientists of the existence of the moral philosophy of utilitarianism, which, of course, is the foundation that underlies both classical and neoclassical economics.

A second important break with the image of the city as an administrative entity was Lawrence Herson's 1957 article, "The Lost World of Municipal Government."[20] Herson noted that political scientists who studied the city seemed utterly oblivious of the behavioral movement that was sweeping the rest of the discipline. The field of municipal government was a "lost world," whose residents were still repeating the old-fashioned and discredited doctrines that by now were more than a half-century old. Herson ended his article with a call for a new science of urban politics that would draw its theories and models from other contemporary social sciences.

Herson's call was answered within four years with the almost simultaneous publication of Edward C. Banfield's *Political Influence*, Robert Dahl's *Who Governs?*, and Wallace Sayre and Herbert Kaufman's *Governing New York City.*[21] All three works sought to answer the question that Dahl posed in the title of his book—"Who governs the city?"—and

[19]Meyerson and Banfield, pp. 303–329.
[20]*American Political Science Review*, 51 (June 1957): 330–345.
[21]Banfield, *Political Influence*; Dahl, *Who Governs?*; Sayre and Kaufman, *Governing New York City.*

all answered this question by arguing that the city was not ruled by a cohesive elite; rather, urban governments were responsive to a wide variety of groups. These books—most explicitly, Banfield's and Dahl's—likened the city to a competitive market in which no single firm is able to set the price.

A second facet of this image of the city as a competitive market was an argument that, through political conflict and bargaining, the numerous interests in the city were able to obtain a measure of influence over public policy that was roughly proportional to the number of people who shared that interest and the intensity of their attachment to it. Just as classical and neoclassical economists argued that a hidden hand operated through the market to maximize public welfare, so, too, did "pluralist" political scientists—as this school came to be known—argue that the political processes of the city yielded the public interest. (Indeed, Banfield went so far as to argue that in Chicago, the city he studied, the mayor overcame some of the limitations of the market as a mechanism of social choice—its inability to provide collective goods and to ensure that externalities would be taken into account.)

One final point regarding the image of the city as a competitive market is worth noting: the pluralists borrowed their model from the field of economics. Lawrence Herson had suggested that sociology was the field from which political scientists could most fruitfully draw their models, and at the end of his article, he briefly sketched an image of the city focusing on the (supposed) impersonality, rootlessness, and anomie of urban life. To my knowledge, not a single important work in political science published in the decade following the appearance of Herson's article took up this suggestion. Why did political scientists borrow their image of the city not from sociology but from economics?

I would suggest the following explanation. Politics in most large American cities in the 1950s and the early 1960s was dominated by what Marxists would call a *hegemonic bloc*. The coalitions of politicians, businesspeople, newspaper publishers, and civic leaders in these cities not only dominated mayoral elections, they also were responsible, as indicated above, for the most important public policy—urban renewal—that the cities were pursuing at this time, and for setting the terms of political discourse in their cities. The representatives of these coalitions argued that the major goal of the municipal government should be to revitalize the central business district, so as to attract business firms and the middle class to the city; this goal was widely accepted as the appropriate one for the city to pursue. The existence of such a hegemonic bloc provides fertile ground for the growth of liberal economic and political theories in the national and international arenas[22]; it is plausible to argue that this is also the case in the urban area. Given the private ownership of capital, offering incentives for capital to invest *does* in fact benefit the working class as well as the upper by creating new jobs, and *does* benefit small taxpayers as well as large ones by adding to the city's tax base.[23] Moreover, the very existence of such a dominant political coalition and of a popular consensus behind the policies that it supports makes it unlikely that political competition will get out of hand and turn into violent strife. And the limited boundaries of political contestation—interest groups in Dahl's New Haven and Banfield's Chicago generally confined their activity to a limited sphere of public policy and sought only marginal adjustments in the distribution of public benefits—made it reasonable for proponents of the market model to view political conflict as benign.

RECENT IMAGES OF THE CITY

Over the past decade and a half, no single image has dominated the way political scientists view the city to the same extent as the images of the city as community, administrative entity, and competitive market did in their day. Rather, political scientists over the past 15 years have variously described the city as an input–output system, a mechanism of social control, an internal colony of the United States, and a seat of administrative or political chaos. How can one account for this fragmentation?

This most recent set of changes in the way that political scientists

---

[22]J. Kurth, "The Political Consequences of the Product Cycle: Industrial History and Political Outcomes," *International Organization* 33 (Winter 1979): 1–34; S. Krasner, *Defending the National Interest* (Princeton, N.J.: Princeton University Press, 1978).

[23]Public subsidies to encourage investment benefit other taxpayers only if the firms offered the subsidies would not otherwise have located in the city, and if the cost of these subsidies, and of the additional public services consumed by the firms receiving them, do not exceed the tax revenues generated by these firms. As a matter of fact, urban renewal programs, despite the claims of their proponents, generally failed to meet these standards. See J. Rothenberg, *Economic Evaluation of Urban Renewal* (Washington, D.C.: The Brookings Institution, 1967).

view the city is a consequence, again, of changes in both American cities and the political science profession. As for the first of these, the hegemony of the coalitions of politicians and businesspeople that had played a central role in the governance of American cities since World War II shattered in the mid-1960s. Urban renewal, which formerly had been regarded as beneficial to the city as a whole, came to be called "Negro removal," and, more generally, the issue of race became the central focus of urban politics. This issue generated intense political conflict. Blacks— usually in alliance with upper-middle-class professionals in federal agencies, in universities and foundations, and in the city itself—demanded not only an end to urban renewal programs that destroyed low-cost housing in their neighborhoods, but also greater influence over municipal policymaking and administration, as well as a larger share of the benefits distributed by city governments. These demands were voiced in a number of arenas and in a variety of ways: appeals to federal agencies that distributed federal grants-in-aid to cities, court suits, election campaigns, and protest demonstrations. This political assertiveness, in turn, led to the political mobilization of the groups on which burdens would be imposed if these demands were granted—especially city employees, white parents opposed to school busing, and marginal homeowners sensitive to increases in property taxes.

These developments had some important implications for the way in which many (though not all) political scientists viewed the city. First of all, it led many to question whether it was indeed true, as the proponents of the market model had argued, that the bargaining that occurred through the normal processes and institutions of urban government accorded to each group in the city influence over different public policies that was roughly proportional to the size of the group and the intensity of their views on the policy in question. Writing in 1961, Robert Dahl had found it possible to refer to urban renewal as a "collective benefit," by which he meant a program that benefited everyone in the city.[24] A half dozen years later, when protesters were conducting raucous demonstrations in an effort to save their homes from being destroyed by renewal projects, it was considerably more difficult to maintain this view. Such changes in urban politics also altered the way in which political scientists viewed political conflicts in cities. Because political disputes in American cities had rarely turned violent during the decade and a half following

[24]Dahl, *Who Governs?* pp. 59–62.

World War II, it was possible for proponents of the market model to regard conflict as benign. When threats of violence, and violence itself, became commonplace in American cities, some political scientists drew back in horror and searched for ways to restore civil harmony; others asserted that violence was a legitimate mode of political expression.

At the same time that the politics of American cities was being transformed, changes were occurring in the discipline of political science. The behavioral movement, which had been at the intellectual cutting edge of the discipline in the 1950s, came under attack in the mid-1960s. Many political scientists continue to pursue the goals of the behavioral movement: they seek to create an autonomous discipline of political science that is value-free, and that is neither allied with nor overtly displays sympathy toward any of the contenders for power in the city. However, this understanding of the way to go about studying politics has been challenged from a number of directions during the past 15 years. Each of these challenges rejects one or more tenets of the behavioral movement—as indicated by the character of its institutional base and the journals in which its adherents publish—and each differs from the behaviorists and from the others with respect to the political forces with which it sympathizes and/or the audience to which it appeals. The fragmentation of the political science profession along these various lines, in conjunction with the fragmentation of the urban political order in the mid-1960s, explains why political scientists have not agreed on a common image of the city. On the contrary, each faction within the discipline has formulated its own image, reflecting its distinctive concerns.

The City as a System

A majority of political scientists remain attached to the behavioral movement—if the papers delivered at the annual meetings of the American Political Science Association and the articles published in the leading political science journals can be taken as an indication of where the discipline's center of gravity lies. Like their predecessors in the 1950s, these political scientists strive to model their research on the natural sciences and to avoid taking sides in the political conflict that they study, and they address their writings to other members of the discipline.

The image of the city most commonly employed by this group depicts urban politics as a *system* that converts popular demands into public policies.[25] This image is, if anything, even more scientistic than the market model of the 1950s and the early 1960s. Whereas behaviorally inclined political scientists 20 years ago borrowed their model from the hardest of the social sciences (economics), their counterparts in more recent years have gone one step further and borrowed a model from the softest of the engineering sciences (systems analysis or operations research), which is the branch of engineering that deals with the boundary between the world of people and the world of machines.

Despite this difference, however, the questions addressed by contemporary systems theorists are similar to those posed by the scholars who formulated the market model: Are cities ruled by a small elite, or do their policies reflect the views of other elements of their population? Is it true, as the Progressives assumed, that the structure of governmental institutions in cities substantially influences the policies that they pursue, or are the social characteristics of cities and their residents of greater importance? Moreover, systems theorists have as sanguine a view of political conflict as proponents of the market model: in the language of systems theory, conflicts over the policies that municipal governments should pursue are termed, rather bloodlessly, differing "inputs." Evidently, being closeted in the computer center, systems theorists failed to notice in the late 1960s that there were important (or, at least, vocal) groups outside who, in calling the political institutions of a city (or the nation) "the system," were asserting that these institutions were unresponsive to popular influence and should be overturned. This imperviousness truly is a tribute to how greatly a discipline is able to define its own universe of discourse, without reference to events in the world outside!

The City as a Mechanism of Social Control

The first major challenge to the behaviorists and their images of the city was launched by neo-Marxist scholars, most of whom were graduate students or young faculty members when political turmoil erupted in American cities (and on university campuses) in the 1960s. They denied that political science could be value-free, and they proclaimed their sympathy with insurgent political forces in American cities. One institutional expression of this challenge was the organization of a Caucus for a New

[25]For an overview of this literature, see B. Hawkins, *Politics and Urban Policies* (Indianapolis: Bobbs-Merrill, 1971).

Political Science within the APSA, which sponsors panels at the association's annual meetings; another was the founding of a new academic journal, *Politics and Society*. It should be noted that although the neo-Marxists clearly sympathize with certain contenders for power in the city, their view of politics is not identical to that of the groups with which they sympathize. On the contrary, they draw on an independent intellectual tradition—Marxism—that has never enjoyed widespread support among the lower classes in the United States. And the articles and books written by the neo-Marxists are addressed to other scholars, not to a popular audience.

The central question that neo-Marxists have posed in their writings is this: Why did the insurgent groups of the 1960s not enjoy greater success than they did in advancing their interests through the institutions of urban government? In an effort to answer this question, the neo-Marxists have formulated an image of urban government as a mechanism of *social control*. One of the earliest critiques of the image of the city as a competitive market, Peter Bachrach and Morton Baratz's "The Two Faces of Power," argued that far from faithfully reflecting the opinions of all groups in the city, the institutions of municipal government deflect, defeat, or deny legitimacy to those demands that threaten the interests of powerful political forces.[26] Bachrach and Baratz did not use the phrase "social control," but this is the meaning they intended to convey with the less felicitous term "nondecision" that they coined to describe this process. This meaning is conveyed more explicitly in the work of Frances Fox Piven and Richard Cloward (work that draws more directly on Marxist concepts than that of Bachrach and Baratz). In analyzing the urban programs of the Great Society, Piven and Cloward argued that the function of these programs was the same as that of all social welfare policies, namely, to pacify the unemployed at times of political turmoil, and to compel as many of them as possible to work once political order is restored; that is, these programs "regulate" the poor.[27]

Finally, and most explicitly of all, Ira Katznelson has argued that the advent of universal male suffrage during the Jacksonian era, as well as the mobilization of voters through political parties organized in neighborhoods (rather than at workplaces), encouraged the working class in the

[26]*American Political Science Review* 56 (Dec. 1962): 947–952.

[27]*Regulating the Poor* (New York: Pantheon, 1971); *Poor People's Movements* (New York: Pantheon, 1977); F. Piven, "The Urban Crisis: Who Got What and Why," in *1984 Revisited*, ed. R. P. Wolff (New York: Random House, 1972).

United States to conceive of politics in terms of community and ethnicity, rather than in terms of social class. In the 1960s, black protesters—as well as their allies and their opponents—shared this same view of what urban politics is all about. This understanding of the city and its politics, together with the demands that it implies, the organizations through which it is institutionalized, the coalitions that it encourages, and the cleavages that it fosters, accounts for the failure of all the conflict and turmoil of the 1960s to result in a fundamental alteration of the structure of urban politics. In other words, the institutions of urban politics serve at one and the same time as channels of political incorporation and as mechanisms of social control. Indeed, Katznelson argued that social control should be one of the central concepts in the study of urban politics.[28]

The City as an Internal Colony

A second challenge to the hegemony of behaviorism was launched during the 1960s by black political scientists, who not only denied that the study of politics could be value-free but also rejected the notion that, at least with regard to blacks, there should be an autonomous discipline of political science: black political scientists, they asserted, should be part of the general movement for black liberation.[29] An institutional bastion of this school of thought is the Joint Center for Political Studies, an organization that sponsors conferences and publishes studies of black politics. The center provides a forum for black elected officials and political activists as well as scholars. Similarly, *The Black Scholar*, a journal of black studies, opens its pages to both black academics and black activists. Finally, during the 1960s, at least, black studies programs typically provided students with opportunities to engage in fieldwork under the supervision of community leaders. The permeability of the boundary between the university and "the community"—between the study of politics and activity in the world of politics—resembles the state of affairs that existed in the disci-

[28]"The Crisis of the Capitalist City: Urban Politics and Social Control," in Hawley and Lipsky, 214–229; *City Trenches* (New York: Pantheon, 1980).

[29]Needless to say, not all black political scientists share the views described in this section. The most influential statement of this point of view is Stokely Carmichael and Charles Hamilton's *Black Power: The Politics of Liberation in America* (New York: Random House, 1967). Significantly, this book was the product of collaboration between a political activist (Carmichael) and a political scientist (Hamilton).

pline at large during the Progressive Era: the Joint Center for Political Studies is similar to the National Municipal League, *The Black Scholar* resembles the *National Municipal Review*, and, like political scientists during the Progressive Era, black scholars seek to play a role as an intellectual vanguard in the political movement with which they are allied. Toward this end, they have formulated an image of the city that has distinct implications for the political goals that blacks should pursue.

This image regards the black urban ghetto as an *internal colony* of the United States. As in the relationship between colonies and imperial powers abroad, black ghettos serve as a source of cheap labor, a market for goods more expensive than those it exports, and a source of employment for civil servants from the dominant society. One can hypothesize that this image has considerable appeal to black scholars who regard themselves as part of the black liberation movement because it links together two concerns of that movement: decolonization abroad and the attainment by blacks of greater political and economic power at home. With regard to the question of political conflict, this image both justifies it (it is akin to a war of national liberation) and indicates the goal toward which it should be directed (the municipal equivalent of decolonization, that is, community control of community institutions in black neighborhoods).

The City as a Seat of Administrative Chaos

The final challenge to behaviorism in political science was mounted in the late 1960s and during the 1970s by political scientists engaged in policy analysis. In contrast to the proponents of both the marketplace and the systems models of one city, who pursued knowledge for its own sake,[30] policy analysts seek to influence the formulation and administration of public policies in cities. Within the field of policy analysis, however, it is useful to distinguish between two schools—the insiders and the outsiders—which seek to ally with different political forces and to appeal to different audiences in their efforts to exert such influence. The images of the city formulated by these two schools of policy analysis differ accordingly.

Policy analysts who belong to the first school—the insiders—seek to

[30]For example, in the introduction to *City Politics*, Edward Banfield and James Q. Wilson explicitly stated that the effort to understand politics is "intrinsically satisfying" and provides "its own justification and reward" (p. 4).

ally with mayors and to work through high-level administrators, in order to improve the management of municipal affairs. The institutional base for these policy analysts is provided by the Urban Institute, a federally funded research institute, and by graduate schools of public policy—most notably Harvard's Kennedy School of Government, Berkeley's School of Public Policy, and Yale's School of Organization and Management— schools whose faculty members move back and forth between government service and university teaching, and which train students to work as administrators. The journals in which they publish—*Policy Studies* and the *Journal of Policy Analysis and Management*—have as their audience both academics and public administrators. The orientation of this school of policy analysts is revealed most clearly in Douglas Yates's *The Ungovernable City,* one of the most thoughtful and self-conscious works in this vein.[31] (Yates explicitly distinguished between the "political analysis" of Dahl's *Who Governs?* and Banfield's *Political Influence* and the "policy analysis" of his own book.) A central chapter in Yates's book is entitled "The View from City Hall."

From the vantage point of City Hall, the most important characteristic of the city is how difficult it is to manage; accordingly, the major image that Yates formulated is the city as a locus of *administrative chaos.* The very title of his book refers to the city's ungovernability, and in the course of his argument, Yates proposed two models of urban politics that vividly illustrate his theme that from the vantage point of the policymaker or the administrator, the central characteristic of the city is its chaos. One of these models refers to city politics as "street fighting pluralism." "Pluralism" had been used as a term of praise—as a synonym for "democracy"— by the political scientists of the 1950s and the early 1960s who regarded the political conflict in cities as benign. Yates, by contrast, suggested that urban political conflict is akin to an eye-gouging, knee-in-the-groin street fight. Yates also proposed a "penny arcade" model in which city politics is compared to a shooting gallery, a slot machine, and a pinball machine. The metaphor of city politics as a game had been proposed 20 years earlier in a classic article by Norton Long, "The Local Community as an Ecology of Games," but the connotation that Long had intended was precisely the reverse of Yates's.[32] In referring to an "ecology of games," Long implied that there is an underlying harmony in city politics, just as

[31]Cambridge: M.I.T. Press, 1977.
[32]N. Long, "The Local Community as an Ecology of Games," *American Journal of Sociology* 54 (1958): 251–261.

there is in a natural ecosystem. Yates, by contrast, likened city politics to games whose central features are chance and random motion.

The City as a Seat of Political Chaos

Members of the second school of policy analysts, the outsiders (or neoconservatives, as they are more commonly known), believe that it is necessary to change elite opinion if the most serious problems of the city are to be alleviated. This view follows from their analysis of the basic dynamics of contemporary American politics. The most important change in American politics during the past two decades, they argue, is the rise of a "new class" of professionals who are employed chiefly in government agencies, the news media, and the nonprofit sector (universities, foundations, and public interest groups), and who enjoy considerable influence over public policy by virtue of their influence over elite and popular opinion. The members of this class, in an effort both to solve social problems and to increase their own power, have secured the enactment of policies that expand the domain of government, and that have resulted in serious adverse consequences for the nation's social fabric (by undermining institutions, such as the family, that hold society together), as well as for its political stability. To reverse these trends, it is necessary to get opinion leaders, the public at large, and policymakers to recognize these dangers.

The major institutional base for this school of policy analysts is the American Enterprise Institute, and the leading journal in which its members publish is *The Public Interest*. The most influential statement of this view in the realm of urban affairs is Edward Banfield's *The Unheavenly City*.[33] Banfield argued that the most serious problem in the American

---

[33]E. Banfield, *The Unheavenly City* (Boston: Little, Brown, 1970). It should be emphasized that *The Unheavenly City* is not a work of policy analysis in the narrow sense of containing recommendations for the enactment of specific public policies in cities. Its chief concern is to analyze the political forces that have shaped the response of policymakers to urban problems, and, as Banfield notes in the preface to the book's second edition, "the 'recommendations' in the next-to-the-last chapter were intended . . . merely as a takeoff point for a discussion of the political circumstances that make such recommendations pointless" (*The Unheavenly City Revisited*, p. viii). Nonetheless, the book does end with an expression of hope "that facts, rational analysis, and deliberation about the nature of the public interest will play a somewhat larger part than hitherto in the formation of both opinion and policy" (Ibid., p. 286).

city is the presence of large concentrations of blacks who believe themselves to be—and are considered by influential elites to be—the victims
of racial oppression. Such beliefs can lead to riots, as they did in the
1960s, and, Banfield predicted, as they would continue to do for 20 years
or more. More seriously still, the belief by important segments of the
middle and upper classes that blacks are systematically oppressed by
American society can undermine the stability and alter the character of
the nation's political system. Banfield's central image, then, is that the
city is a potential source of *political chaos* in the United States.

Banfield's concern about the political consequences of urban problems is most evident in his discussion of possible remedies for the social
problems of cities, that is, unemployment, poverty, crime, limited education, and the like. He proposed a number of policies to cope with these
problems and discussed proposals made by others, but he noted that
these present a number of dilemmas and difficulties. The first is that it is
politically impossible to secure the enactment of virtually all the measures
(e.g., permitting children to leave school and go to work at age 14, abolishing the minimum wage) that, he argued, might alleviate these problems. The second, and more serious, is this dilemma: there really is no
reliable way of ascertaining which particular poor people, or unemployed
workers, or criminals are the victims of circumstance, and which are
members of the incorrigible lower class, other than by providing them
with opportunities to better themselves; but this approach means continuing to pursue some of the policies that have contributed to the city's
problems (because they give free rein to the members of the incorrigible
lower class), and it requires abstaining from at least some of the harsh
measures that are necessary to deal with such persons.

Finally, and most seriously of all, the policy proposals that have the
greatest political appeal are quite unlikely to have their intended consequences. The failure of such programs, unfortunately, is taken as a confir-
mation by politically important groups that the American system is inca-
pable of dealing justly with its least fortunate citizens. The spread of such
a belief can threaten the free and democratic character of American society. In the last analysis, it is this threat to free institutions that is the
central problem of the city. And Banfield's conviction that the stakes are
high explains, I suspect, the tone of alarm, and the depiction of chaos, in
Banfield's book: it is a warning to his readers that the dangers at hand are
great. *The Unheavenly City*, though a work of contemporary policy analysis, stands in the oldest tradition of social thought in the United States:

the American jeremiad.[34] The epigraph to Banfield's book is drawn from
Cotton Mather's *Theopolis Americana:*

> Come hither, and I will show you an admirable Spectacle!
> 'Tis an Heavenly CITY. . . . A CITY to be inhabited by an
> Innumerable Company of Angels, and by the Spirits of Just
> Men. . . .
> *Put on thy beautiful Garments,*
> O America, the Holy City![35]

As the title of his book indicates, Edward Banfield has stood Cotton
Mather on his head. Like a Puritan preacher who seeks to set his con-
gregation on the right path by vividly portraying the torments of hell,
Banfield, in his description of the city as a source of chaos in the American
political order, intended, it would appear, to convince his readers that by
ignoring the unpleasant fact that some inhabitants of the city are anything
but angelic and just, we will turn America into an Unheavenly City.

CONCLUSION

   In this chapter, I have argued that the images of the city in political
science are shaped by the structure of urban politics and the relationship
between political scientists and various contenders for power in the city.
By now, it should be clear that I am not claiming that political scientists
merely parrot the opinions of the groups with which they are allied. At
times, causality has flowed in the other direction: political scientists
(among other intellectuals) have influenced the way in which various
groups view the city, as well as the understanding on the part of these
groups of where their interests within it lie. The image of the city as an
administrative entity, formulated by political scientists during the Progressive Era, is the clearest example, and the image of the city as an
internal colony, formulated by black intellectuals, played a similar, albeit
somewhat less important, role in the emergence of the demand among
blacks for community control in the 1960s. At other times, the relationship between political scientists and different contenders for power in the

---

[34]S. Bercovitch, *The American Jeremiad* (Madison: University of Wisconsin Press,
    1978).
[35]Banfield, *The Unheavenly City.*

city has been defined by the doctrine of disciplinary autonomy, and in these cases, the images formulated by academics have not resembled those of any group in the city. The market and systems models are examples.

Despite this last qualification, the extent to which students of urban politics have shared the outlook of one or another of the subjects of their study (that is, have taken a partisan or committed stance) is striking. Such things cannot be precisely measured, but one has the impression that this stance is more common among political scientists who study cities than among those who study American national government, and, relatedly, that the former are more likely than the latter to propose fundamental changes in the structure of the institutions that they study—ranging from proposals for city managers and at-large elections during the Progressive Era to plans for community control in the 1960s.

What accounts for this difference? The explanation, I would suggest, lies on the demand side of the market for political ideas. Americans have been far more willing to make fundamental alterations in the structure of city governments than they have been to tinker with the institutions of national government. Entire city charters are scrapped and new ones adopted with relatively little hesitation, whereas greater caution is exercised in amending—let alone rewriting—the U.S. Constitution; for example, since 1788, New York City has been governed under nine different charters, whereas only five amendments to the U.S. Constitution have been adopted that alter the structure of national political institutions.[36] The reason for this difference, I hypothesize, is that one of the premises on which liberal democracy in the United States was founded (that the ownership of property is widespread, and that therefore mass participation in politics is not threatening to the security of property) was violated in the nation's major cities quite early in the history of the republic. By 1850, at the latest, a solid majority of the voters in large cities were proletarians in the strict sense of the term: they owned no property. Therefore, the meaning of democracy has been far more unsettled in the

---

[36]These amendments are the Eleventh, providing for separate balloting for the president and the vice-president by the electoral college; the Seventeenth, providing for the direct popular election of Senators; the Twentieth, abolishing the lame duck session of Congress; the Twenty-second, limiting the president to two terms; and the Twenty-sixth, providing for presidential succession.

cities than on the national level. The elites in American cities have been open to suggestions about how popular participation in politics can be reorganized—be it through nonpartisan elections or through elections to community school boards—so as to secure their own influence, to preserve public order, and even, at times, to improve the lot of the lower classes.

CHAPTER 5

Anthropological Approaches
to the City

LISA REDFIELD PEATTIE AND EDWARD ROBBINS

Anthropology and sociology have only rather recently become distinct disciplines; they share a common history in nineteenth-century social thought, and joint departments are still not uncommon. Furthermore, they are currently being further entangled by the now-booming field of "urban anthropology," in which a variety of approaches share little with each other besides using the city as a research setting, and being done by people trained in departments of anthropology.

If one had looked at anthropology in 1950, however, it would still have been possible to pick out the "anthropological view" of cities—or rather, to identify two major traditions, within which anthropologists, distinctively, looked at cities.

One part of the anthropological tradition dealing with cities came out of archaeology and prehistory. The archaeological investigation of the ancient cities of the Middle East, of India, and of Middle and South America was the basis of an analysis of the role of cities as centers of accumulation, of trade, and of cultural specialization.[1] The city was the setting in which new institutions (such as the State), new social groupings (such as the specialized priesthood), and new kinds of knowledge (such as written accounting and early astronomy) came into being. These studies

---

[1] V. G. Childe, *What Happened in History* (Baltimore: Penguin, 1942).

Lisa Redfield Peattie • Department of Urban Studies and Planning, Massachusetts Institute of Technology, Cambridge, Massachusetts.   *Edward Robbins* • Department of Architecture, Massachusetts Institute of Technology, Cambridge, Massachusetts.

of the history of the city and of the city in history, in turn, form a link to a strain in anthropological thought coming out of the nineteenth-century social thinker's concern with the evolution of culture.

Redfield's "ideal types" of the "folk society" and "the urban"[2] were an attempt to develop a framework for thinking about human history and about urbanization in the present growing directly out of such polarities as Ferdinand Tönnies's *Gemeinschaft/Gesellschaft,* Maine's status/ contract, and Émile Durkheim's mechanical/organic solidarity. Although in *The Folk Culture of Yucatán*[3] Redfield tried to locate points on his essentially abstract continuum in particular exemplary communities (the isolated bush community of Quintana Roo as most "folk," the city of Mérida as most "urban"), in this way of thinking the city figured not so much as a specific place, or as a community, but as the setting in which new states of mind could come into being. The city has a central historical role in the transformation of culture[4] or is seen in the context of the relations between elite and peasant cultures ("the Great Tradition and the Little Tradition") within single societies, as in Singer's "Anthropological Approach to Indian Civilization."[5]

Horace Miner's account of Timbuctoo[6] and J. Gulick's study of Tripoli,[7] although describing the way the city works internally, also tend to call attention to the roles played by the cities in the societies of which they are a part, and to ask to what degree they represent specifically "urban" cultural forms.

Anthropology was, however, much more strongly identified with the study of primitive or at any rate non-urban societies. The central practice of anthropology, in its classical phase, had four components: the primitive (or, stretching it a bit, the peasant) as subject matter; functionalism as

[2]R. Redfield, "The Folk Society," *The American Journal of Sociology* (1947):293–308.
[3]Chicago: University of Chicago Press, 1941.
[4]R. Redfield and M. Singer, "The Cultural Role of Cities," *Economic Development and Culture Change* 3 (1954):53–73; M. Singer, "The Expansion of Society and Its Cultural Implications," in *City Invincible: A Symposium on Urbanization and Culture, Development in the Ancient Near East,* eds. C. M. Kraeling and R. M. Adams (Chicago: University of Chicago Press, 1960); Redfield, *The Folk Culture.*
[5]M. Singer, *When a Great Tradition Modernizes* (New York: Praeger, 1972).
[6]*The Primitive City of Timbuctoo* (Princeton, N.J.: Princeton University Press, 1953).
[7]*Tripoli: A Modern Arab City* (Cambridge: Harvard University Press, 1967).

analytic framework; cultural relativism as moral mandate; and participant observation as methodology.

Anthropology, until recently, was done within the framework of a colonial system that preempted issues of power and political choice. The separation between rulers and ruled was very sharp, and it created between the two a sort of intellectual no-man's-land, the space on which the anthropologist set up shop to report on the natives to the colonial powers and their universities. The colonial system constituted a taken-for-granted frame within which the "native cultures" sat.

Furthermore, the anthropologist was usually working far from home and alone (or perhaps as part of a husband-and-wife team) and on a small budget. Working in small communities without written histories and statistics, and struggling with the problems of "entry" and "rapport" in one or another exotic and perhaps not cordial group of people, anthropologists came to emphasize participant observation and qualitative description and analysis.

The development of the functionalist perspective, in which any society could be seen as an integrated system of mutually interrelated and functionally interdependent parts, provided both the theoretical underpinnings and the analytic methdology for integrating such qualitative data into a description of a "human whole."

Radcliffe-Brown's *The Andaman Islanders* (1922) provides the classic statement of this position:

> Every custom and belief of a primitive society plays some determinate part in the social life of the community, just as every organ of a living body plays some part in the general life of the organism. The mass of institutions, customs and beliefs forms a single whole or system that determines the life of the society, and the life of the society is not less real, or less subject to natural laws, than the life of an organism.[8]

When Evans Pritchard published his *Social Anthropology* in 1951, he summed it up:

> The social anthropologist studies primitive societies directly, living among them for months or years, whereas sociological research is usually from documents and largely statistical. The social anthropologist studies societies as wholes—he studies their ecologies, their economies, their legal and political institutions, their family and kin-

---

[8]Glencoe, Ill.: Free Press, 1964, 229–230.

ship organizations, their religions, their technologies, their arts, etc.,
as parts of general social systems.[9]

Finally, the practice of anthropology was centered on the concept of
culture and the doctrine of cultural relativism. The assertion that each
culture must be judged in its own terms as a "way of life" gave anthropologists a very strong sense of moral mandate.

Both sociology and anthropology had strong strains of reformism, but
differently focused. Sociologists did stratification studies or investigated
"social problems" in their own societies. Anthropologists were dealing
with colonialism at the ground level and, often with a substantial degree
of naiveté, came to think of themselves as the advocates of the "natives."
Their accounts of native cultures may read like simple description, but
they are also argument: by showing that "primitive" or "uneducated"
people were behaving in an orderly and sensible way, the anthropologists
were implicitly trying to delegitimize colonialism, missionizing, and the
spread of capitalism. "Cultural relativism" may be read as an argument
against racism.

When anthropologists came to study cities, one natural approach was
to apply to cities—not too large ones—the form of description that had
been tried out on the little communities. The result was community
studies.

In taking this approach, anthropologists found that their strategies of
qualitative description had their own unique potential for establishing
distance between describer and described; to describe American institutions in the same terms as primitive behavior was to satirize. This phenomenon is recognizable in the Lynds' *Middletown* study and is highly
developed in Lloyd Warner's descriptions of the strange collective rites of
the tribesmen of Newburyport.

Robert and Helen Lynd apparently had not set out to do a "community study"; they wanted to study religious practice and institutions in a
typical small town. In planning the study, they were attracted by the
ethnographic categories for describing any "culture" that had been developed by the anthropologists Clark Wissler and W. H. Rivers. The result
was the study of Muncie, Indiana, as *Middletown: A Study of Contemporary American Culture.*[10]

---

[9]London: Cohen and West, 1951.

[10]R. S. Lynd and H. M. Lynd, *Middletown: A Study in Contemporary American
Culture* (London: Constable, 1929).

Lloyd Warner, the major figure in the study of the city-as-tribe, held appointments in both anthropology and sociology and never declared himself by taking a Ph.D. in either. He came back from studying an Australian tribe and started in on Newburyport; the result was the five volumes of the "Yankee City" series.[11] Here, there were a big research team, funding, access, and the potential of historical data,[12] but the conceptual approach was the "community," with its mutually interrelated and functionally interdependent parts: its customs and ideas around status ("class"), its beliefs ("culture"), and its rituals. The effect is often very funny, and we may also enjoy J. P. Marquand's commentary on all this in *Point of No Return*.[13]

Warner later took his act to the Midwest and zeroed in on Morris, Illinois, with special attention to the role of the public schools in the class structure.[14] Warner also seems to have been the instigator of the study of Natchez in which a black researcher, Allison Davis, and a couple of white researchers, Burleigh and Mary Gardner, worked opposite sides of the street and came up with *Deep South*.[15] Hortense Powdermaker, before she went to Africa and did a book on "The Human Situation in the Rhodesian Copperbelt,"[16] did a number on Hollywood in *The Dream Factory*.[17]

The "classic period" thus manifested two distinct anthropological approaches to the city: that growing out of the interest in human cultural history, in which the city appears as a center of specialization and change, and that growing out of the study of primitive societies, in which the city appears as another human community.

[11]W. L. Warner and P. S. Lunt, *The Social Life of a Modern Community* (New Haven, Conn.: Yale University Press, 1941); W. L. Warner and P. S. Lunt, *The Status System of a Modern Community* (London: Oxford University Press, 1942); W. L. Warner and L. Srole, *The Social Systems of American Ethnic Groups* (Chicago: University of Chicago Press, 1945); W. L. Warner and J. O. Low, *The Social System of a Modern Factory* (New Haven: Yale University Press, 1947); W. L. Warner, *The Living and the Dead* (New Haven, Conn.: Yale University Press, 1959).
[12]See S. Thernstrom, *Poverty and Progress: Social Mobility in a Nineteenth Century City* (Cambridge: Harvard University Press, 1964).
[13]Boston: Little, Brown, 1949.
[14]*Democracy in Jonesville* (New York: Harper & Row, 1949).
[15]Chicago: University of Chicago Press, 1941.
[16]*Copper Town* (New York: Harper & Row, 1962).
[17]*Hollywood: The Dream Factory* (Boston: Little, Brown, 1950).

We may note in passing that these two strands of anthropological thought on cities, although each reasonable alone, present, when taken together, an extremely odd picture. When anthropologists study cities in the more underdeveloped and slow-changing parts of the world (North Africa, India), the city appears as a center of cultural change. However, when they study cities in the United States, the model of thought is the timeless world of the primitive tribe, and the city appears as the repository of a bundle of functionally linked and generally unchanging cultural traits and social institutions.

A rather different approach to the city is to treat it as a setting for in-migration, adaptation, and the organization of new neighborhood communities.

Here, the theme of the city as a center of cultural and social invention takes a new populist twist; in the slums and shantytowns where others have seen disorganization, the anthropologist discovers positive coping, institution building, and creativity. Here, the classic theme of "not racial or cultural inferiority, but cultural difference" gets modulated into a new key. Where others have seen lack, anthropologists see difference. In the disorderly slum, they find rational striving and social organization. These people, they tell us, are behaving in an orderly, sensible way.

Among anthropologists working in Latin America, especially, a good deal of this research has taken on a strongly mission-oriented character. The anthropologists' mission was to defend the occupants of shantytowns against the efforts of the public authorities to eradicate such settlements as unsightly slums. Again, the anthropologists saw orderly striving and institution building where others had seen disorder and cultural lack. The squatter settlements were interpreted as representing "a process of social reconstruction through popular initiative."[18] Squatter settlements were "not the problem but the solution." The residents were bravely defending their homes. Their shanties were better housing in process, and the incremental building process through which they were being generated proved the most adaptive possibility for people whose incomes were low and irregular. The settlement process itself was seen as social consolidation and progress.[19]

[18]W. Mangin, "Latin American Squatter Settlements: A Problem and a Solution," *Latin American Research Review* 2 (1967):65–98.
[19]W. Mangin, "Squatter Settlements," *Scientific American* 217 (1967):21–29; W.

There has also been an anthropology of urban poverty in which the anthropologist was able to join the social-problems tradition via the participant-observation, enthnographic approach. The old Chicago school of sociology, with its social types and its ecological niches, has risen again, and we have accounts of the life of poor Puerto Ricans in San Juan and New York,[20] alcoholics on skid row in Seattle,[21] and lower-class blacks.[22]

Here, anthropologists repeat again the melodies of the profession's youth, modulated in a new key. These groups, they tell us, are not disordered; they experience another order. They are simply following rules other than ours, rules that we do not see at first. Those black men who seem to be lolling aimlessly on the street corner, refusing to look for work, are actually behaving purposefully, and their purposes are sensible ones. The theme now is a kind of populist affirmation of the creativity of those at the bottom.

The materials are modern and urban, but the story would not surprise Bronislaw Malinowski. It was Malinowski, in his "New Tasks for Anthropology," who scripted the new scenario in his call for an anthropology of the "urban" native.[23] Urban anthropology is precisely a response to that call.

"Urban anthropology" is currently booming. There is a journal by that name, as well as several readers and texts.[24] Courses are taught. A

Mangin, "Latin American Squatter Settlements"; A. Leeds, "The Significant Variables Determining the Character of Squatter Settlements," *America Latina* 12 (1969):44–86; A. Leeds, "Housing Settlement Types, Arrangements for Living, Proletarianization and the Social Structure of the City," *Latin American Urban Research* 4 (1974); A. Leeds and E. Leeds, "Brazil and the Myth of Urban Reality," in *City and Country in the Third World*, ed. A. Field (Cambridge, Mass.: Schenkman, 1971).

[20]O. Lewis, *La Vida: A Puerto Rican Family in the Culture of Poverty—San Juan and New York* (New York: Vantage Books, 1968).

[21]J. P. Spradley, *You Owe Yourself a Drunk: An Ethnography of Urban Nomads* (Boston: Little, Brown, 1970).

[22]E. Liebow, *Tally's Corner: A Study of Negro Streetcorner Men* (Boston: Little, Brown, 1967); U. Hannerz, *Soulside: Inquiries into Ghetto Culture and Community* (New York: Columbia University Press, 1969).

[23]B. Malinowski, "New Tasks for Anthropology," in *Dynamics of Culture Change* (New Haven: Yale University Press, 1945).

[24]Elizabeth Eddy, ed., *Urban Anthropology Research Perspectives and Strategies* (Athens: University of Georgia, 1968); T. Weaver and D. White, eds., *The Anthropology of Urban Environments* (Washington, D.C.: Society for Applied

society for urban anthropology has just formed, has elected officers, and is debating its relationship to the Society for Applied Anthropology and the Society for the Study of Social Problems.

If urban anthropology is new and booming, as a method and as a form of social inquiry urban anthropology is, for the most part, still rooted in functionalism, albeit under new rubrics: holistic descriptions of small groups and microenvironments and naturalistic description.

Malinowski felt that the native needed guidance in the changing circumstances wrought by modernization. Modern "urban anthropologists" have kept the faith in believing that a naturalistic description of the native's *part* in urban society would guide us through the complexity of the urban *whole.* Thus, in both the United States and Britain, where anthropologists have been the most active in describing the problems of urbanism and urban society, the theoretical and methodological terms for the study of urban society have been derived from the study of preurban small-scale and rural societies. The image offered has been one of many small parts practicing their cultural and social predilections in a large undefined whole, be it rural or urban—the latter being only larger and more heterogeneous in population. The focus is on the detail, not the whole canvas.

In Britain, the concern about understanding urbanism[25] was born out of the crises of postcolonial revolt and social unrest wrought by the accelerated pace of Western political, economic, and cultural domination in the Third World in general,[26] and Africa in particular. Industrializa-

---

Anthropology, 1972); A. Southal, ed., *Urban Anthropology: Cross-cultural Studies of Urbanization* (New York: Oxford University Press, 1973); G. M. Foster and R. V. Kemper, *Anthropologists in Cities* (Boston: Little, Brown, 1974); P. C. W. Gutkind, *Urban Anthropology: Perspectives on Third World Urbanization and Urbanism* (New York: Barnes and Noble, 1974); R. F. Fox, *Urban Anthropology: Cities in Their Cultural Setting* (Englewood Cliffs, N.J.: Prentice-Hall, 1977); E. Eames and J. C. Goode, *Anthropology of the City: An Introduction to Urban Anthropology* (Englewood Cliffs, N.J.: Prentice-Hall, 1977); S. D. Uzzell and R. Provencher, *Urban Anthropology* (Dubuque, Iowa: W. C. Brown, 1976); G. Spindler and L. Spindler, eds., *Urban Anthropology in the United States: Four Cases; Chicano Prisoners, Black Families in Chicago, Portland Longshore, Fun City* (New York: Holt, Rinehart and Winston, 1978); R. Basham, *Urban Anthropology: The Cross-Cultural Study of Complex Societies* (Palo Alto, Calif.: Mayfield Publishing, 1978).
[25] A. L. Epstein, "Urbanization and Social Change in Africa," *Current Anthropology* 8 (1967):275–295.
[26] P. Worsley, *The Third World* (Chicago: University of Chicago Press, 1964).

tion, especially mining; a new social geography implying increased racial, ethnic, and class antagonisms; and a new political and cultural environment defined by Western inroads and the world market—all moved British anthropologists to change the locale and the emphasis of their studies. They became and have remained concerned with the increasing shift of "native" populations from rural, cultural, homogeneous habitats to urban, culturally heterogeneous environments. This shift was and still is marked by an increased economic dependence on Western goods and services by what were traditionally—in the British view—self-sufficient peoples, as well as by an increased involvement of these peoples with new administrative, commercial, and industrial centers.

What the British anthropologists wanted to provide was a description and an understanding of ongoing relationships between the pristine traditional Africa and its postcolonial reality. Urbanism, a key symbol of the changing Africa, was chosen as the linchpin and the urban locale as the boundary for the discussion of changing Africa, as well as the Third World.[27] But although urbanism was to be the metaphor for a changing Africa in struggle with itself and its history, the theoretical approach relied not on an understanding of the historical and large-scale structural events but on the naturalistic description of the microenvironments[28] that were delineated by that structure and history. The whole was to be an unexamined and undescribed given, defined through its effects on its parts, that is, the particular racial, tribal, ethnic, or local group under observation.[29]

As the groups under observation varied socially, culturally, and economically, and as their particular circumstances were diverse, the issue of urbanism for British urban anthropologists implied a multiplicity of theoretical problems and perspectives. They argued[30] that as urbanism and urban society were so diverse and as they presented so many faces to different peoples and groups, urbanism should not be viewed as a totality

[27]Gutkind, *Urban Anthropology* (Barnes & Noble, 1974).

[28]V. Pons, *Stanleyville* (Oxford: Oxford University Press, 1969).

[29]P. C. W. Gutkind and D. G. Jongmans, *Anthropologists in the Field* (The Netherlands: Assen, 1967); D. Forde, ed., *Social Implications of Industrialization and Urbanization in Africa South of the Sahara* (Paris: UNESCO, 1956).

[30]J. C. Mitchell, "Theoretical Orientations in African Urban Studies," in *The Social Anthropology of Complex Societies*, ed. Michael Banton (London: Tavistock, 1966); J. C. Mitchell, *Social Networks in Urban Situations: Analyses of Personal Relationships in Central African Towns* (Manchester: Manchester University Press, 1969).

but as a constantly changing set of *situations* into which groups fit and to which various groups responded differently. Thus, urbanism was the study of flux and not structure, the study of an ever-changing ethnographic present rather than a historically and structurally distinct moment in human development.

For every anthropologist who found that the urban situation was defined by the nature of rural change,[31] there were those who argued that urbanism created the opportunity for new forms of rural economic stability and social relations.[32] Some anthropologists saw the urban center as disruptive to social organization for particular elements, although helpful to others,[33] depending on their intentions and dispositions in living in the city. For those who wanted to develop a new way of life, the city offered a potential for growth and stability, whereas for those natives for whom the city was simply an economic necessity, psychological and social dislocation were often the result. Other commentators theorized that urbanism, on the whole, created a greater potential for social unity beyond the traditional tribal groups[34] because of the particular situations defined by urban life. Analysts even disagreed about the nature of urbanism in defining new lifestyles for recent migrants to the urban core. Whereas some saw it as a specific form demanding acculturation,[35] others argued that the urban environment was simply a larger "rural" place, demanding no particular changes with the traditional social organization of culture.[36] Urban social organization has been viewed as a function of tradition,[37] or as a process *sui generis*.[38] Whatever the particular conclusion or theory, it has always been based on the observation of a particular group or locality,

---

[31]K. L. Little, *West African Urbanization: A Study of Voluntary Associations in Social Change* (Cambridge: The University Press, 1965).

[32]W. Watson, *Tribal Cohesion in a Monetary Society* (Manchester: Manchester University Press, 1958).

[33]P. Mayer, *Townsmen and Tribesmen: Conservatism and the Process of Urbanization in a South African City* (Cape Town: Oxford University Press, 1961).

[34]Mitchell, "Theoretical Orientations"; A. L. Epstein, *Politics in an Urban African Community* (Manchester: Manchester University Press); Little, *West African Urbanization*.

[35]E. Hellman, "Rooiyard: A Sociological Survey of an Urban Native Slum Yard," *Rhodes-Livingstone Papers* 13 (1948); Little, *West African Urbanization*.

[36]Mayer, *Townsmen and Tribesmen;* Watson, *Tribal Cohesion*.

[37]Mayer, *Townsmen and Tribesmen;* Forde, *Social Implications*.

[38]Epstein, "Urbanization and Social Change"; D. Parkin, *Neighbors and Nationals in an African City Ward* (Berkeley: University of California Press, 1969).

rather than on a comparative structural or historical perspective about the whole process called *urbanism* or the whole place called the *city*.

Even when dealing with the internal dynamics of the "urban situation," the urban is viewed as a relation between local places[39] or as an expression of a social field[40] or as a collection of individual social networks.[41] Network is the methodological support to the theoretical notion of the situation. If the traditional social group had a social and cultural idiom that defined it, the urban group did not. If the ideology of kinship formed the boundary for the study of the traditional, the network formed the basis for the study of the urban, with its greater social complexity and broader social boundaries. Whatever the case, the whole remains less than the sum of its parts. The net effect is that we have a picture of the actors without a notion of the stage on which they play. We have a sense of order without the logic of its rules.

With few exceptions,[42] we are left without any sense of history (notably, few studies of autochthonous urban centers have been undertaken by anthropologists) of the urban or any sense of what the urban is or will be. Instead, categories such as colonial, administrative, or industrial center are introduced with no relation to either the social reality that they present or the physical fabric that they represent in the quest of a sense of urban Africa. Without a sense of place, the British anthropological notion of urbanism and the urban becomes mystified with a hidden metaphorical boundary through which the observable small groups under study move. There is no image to grasp onto, no place to set with the stuff of the city or the urbane. The concepts are elusive, and the social groups are set *mise-en-scène* for our edification. We are given neighborhoods but no urban map; the ruled without the rulers; socialization and acculturation without a measure of what it is that people are socializing into; an ad hoc and post hoc world of elements without a sense of their logical relations.

[39]Parkin, *Neighbors and Nationals.*
[40]Gutkind, *Urban Anthropology.*
[41]A. L. Epstein, "The Network of Urban Social Organization," *Rhodes-Livingston Journal* 29 (1961):29–62.
[42]P. C. Lloyd, A. L. Maboguinje, and A. L. Awe, eds., *The City of Ibaden: A Symposium on its Structure and Development* (Cambridge: Cambridge University Press, 1967); B. Magubene, "Urban Ethnology in Africa: Some Theoretical Issues," Paper for Ninth International Congress of Anthropological and Ethnological Sciences, Chicago, 1973; L. Kuper, *An African Bourgeoisie: Race, Class and Politics in South Africa* (New Haven, Conn.: Yale University Press, 1965).

Even where British anthropologists have ventured into their own society, their work is most notable for its emphasis on the local groups and the microenvironment.[43] Urban class becomes family network, and neighborhood becomes kinship, when described by the anthropologist. To a greater extent than not, British anthropologists with the methodological limits of naturalism have more often left the complex image of the city to others when observing their own society, preferring, instead, to undertake research in small, clearly boundable communities in rural Britain.[44]

Like their British counterparts, the American urban anthropologists have tended to emphasize the part rather than the whole. Texts—more commonly in the United States than in Britain—refer to some larger category called *city* or *urban,* but there is no greater search for its substance as a form of political economy[45] (as one might find in political geography or sociology[46]) in the United States than in Britain. Instead, American urban anthropology has been described by one of its most active participants as having as its most noticeable aspect at this point in time "very little generalization at any level" and a predilection for the study of groups, not the city.[47]

Urban anthropology in recent American work, as in Britain, has been an anthropology of urban effects rather than an anthropology of what is doing the affecting. Work has been done on a large number of different groups residing in urban places and spaces. Everybody from cocktail waitresses[48] to gypsies[49] has been observed, categorized, and described.

[43]E. Bott, *Family and Social Network* (London: Tavistock, 1957); P. Willmott and M. Young, *Family and Kinship in East London* (London: Routledge and Kegan Paul, 1957).

[44]R. Frankenberg, *Village on the Border* (London: Cohen and West, 1957); C. Bell and H. Newby, *Community Studies: An Introduction to the Sociology of the Local Community* (New York: Praeger, 1972).

[45]D. Harvey, *Social Justice and the City* (Baltimore: Johns Hopkins University Press, 1973).

[46]M. Castells, *The Urban Question* (Cambridge: M.I.T. Press, 1977); J. P. Mellor, *Urban Sociology in an Urbanized Society* (London: Routledge and Kegan Paul, 1977).

[47]J. R. Rollwagen, "Introduction," *Urban Anthropology* 4 (Spring 1975):1–4.

[48]J. P. Spradley and B. Mann, *The Cocktail Waitress: Women's Work in a Man's World* (New York: Wiley, 1975).

[49]R. C. Gropper, *Gypsies in the City: Culture Patterns and Survival* (Princeton, N.J.: Darwin Press, 1975).

Enviable work on underclass groups, racial and cultural minorities, and the socially, economically, and politically oppressed is to be found,[50] but without, for the most part, a sense of how the urban is defined and how urban society relates to the history of the particular groups described. The city, here, substitutes as a metaphor for the economy, but without itself being examined.

Again, as with the British, "urban is as urban does," be it in the United States or the Third World. The key is the methodological necessity of studying the part rather than the whole or the part as a metaphor for the whole rather than in relation to the whole. The general image is sacrificed for specific observable certainty. The synecdoche of the culturally specific hides the reality of the historical and structural whole.[51]

The specific certainty is that of the powerless, the culturally and socially unique, and the ethnic in their quest to respond to forces larger than themselves in order to make a life and a place. In describing this process, American anthropologists, as well as their British counterparts, have done a real service in describing the world of little people in large complex places. Nonetheless, they have done those people a disservice by seeking in their behavior that which is functional, responsive, and adaptive—that is, what is ordered and rational in the small world but that may prevent change of that world. The natives, so well described for others, is not taught or guided through the situation to which he or she is responding. The search for the general, the sense of place, its structure, and the dialectic between its parts and the whole must be undertaken if anthropologists are to take up the challenge of the city.

Instead of imaging the group, anthropologists need to image the whole, that is, the city. With this image and a sense of the small or the part, anthropologists can generate a dialectic that is unique among the social sciences. Naturalism has a place when added to the scene of the totality; an anthropology of urban life has a contribution to make when and if it can image the place, the historical moment, and the structural form urban life defines. Without this image, we have little perspective on the place of the urban in the everyday practice of human culture and society, the very stuff that anthropologists claim to want to understand.

[50]Fox, Urban Anthropology. Basham, Urban Anthropology.
[51]See C. Perin, Everything in Its Place: Social Order and Land Use in America (Princeton, N.J.: Princeton University Press, 1977); and C. Geertz, The Social History of an Indonesian Town (Cambridge: M.I.T. Press, 1955), for an example of this problem.

CHAPTER 6

Sociology-Four Images of Organized Diversity

Bazaar, Jungle, Organism, and Machine

PETER LANGER

> The central problem of the sociologist of the city is to discover the *forms* of social *action* and organization that typically emerge *in* relatively permanent, compact settlements of large numbers of *heterogeneous* individuals.[1]

THE DOMINANT PROBLEM IN URBAN SOCIOLOGY

Although Wirth's statement has been extensively quoted, much of the impact of its imagery of the city has been overlooked. The words that have been italicized in the quotation point to a particular urban imagery that has led to an emphasis on certain types of research and to a deemphasis on other approaches to the city.

The most widely quoted part of Wirth's formulation has to do with his definition of the city in terms of size, density, and the heterogeneity of its population. It is the latter criterion—social heterogeneity—that has been the focus of most urban research. Size and density have always been regarded as defining cities, but the suggestion that it is the diversity of people and not just their number and mass that make the city socio-

[1] Louis Wirth, *On Cities and Social Life*, ed. Albert J. Reiss, Jr. (Chicago: University of Chicago Press, 1964), 68. (Italics added.)

Peter Langer • Department of Sociology, Boston University, Boston, Massachusetts.

logically distinctive was picked up on as the most illuminating aspect of contemporary cities. The heterogeneity of population noted by European writers was greatly magnified in booming industrial cities such as Chicago, and the classic Hobbesian question of order seemed to take on new dimensions when the population in question spoke different languages, came from different continents, and had few traditional models on which to base their relations with one another. As the problem of social order was the core of the new discipline of sociology, the social diversity of the city became the key urban problem to be investigated.[2]

The second critical element in Wirth's statement is his belief that the proper role of the sociologist is to investigate the *forms* that emerge in the city. Here, Wirth was firmly convinced that there is a pattern or an organization that underlies the superficial chaos of the city. This search for form and regularity, which was at the heart of the new discipline of sociology, remains at the center of contemporary sociological analysis. Certain popular images of the city have not been acceptable starting points for sociological study. "Hodgepodge," "jumble," "tangle," "mishmash," "amalgam," and "potpourri" are all images of diversity, but an unordered diversity that flies in the face of the entire sociological enterprise. The sociologist attempts to order her or his subject matter. Images of the city must, therefore, be of *ordered diversity*.

Third, ordering the diversity of the city can be done in many ways. The architect can look at building styles and influences, the transportation planner at the means of conveyance, and the economist at the regularization of retailing practices. For Wirth, the role of the sociologist in the study of the city was to study social *action*. Human social action—what people do, not what they think—was what Wirth thought sociology was about. The images that people carried about in their heads were the proper focus for the psychologist or the urban anthropologist and were of secondary importance to the sociologist. This turning away from the images held by people is particularly curious in light of Robert Park's comments on the city:

> The city is . . . a state of mind, a body of customs and traditions, and of the organized attitudes and sentiments that inhere in these customs and are transmitted with this tradition. The city is not, in other words, merely a physical mechanism and an artificial construc-

---

[2]For a discussion of the importance of the concept of *community* in sociological analysis, see Robert A. Nisbet, *The Sociological Tradition* (New York: Basic Books, 1966).

tion. It is involved in the vital processes of the people who compose it.[3]

Park's concern with how the sentiments and traditions of the people in the city influence the development of the city was overlooked in Wirth's statement, and it has continued to be overlooked by most urban sociologists. In an attempt to establish scientific legitimacy, the "hard-nosed" sociologist has usually been happy to leave the study of "soft" images of the city to colleagues in other fields.

The fourth aspect of Wirth's statement is perhaps the least realized by his followers. The study of the city is the study of what things "emerge *in*" (my italics) the city and thus is focused on the *internal* structure of the city. The most interesting aspect of the city to Louis Wirth was the internal organization of the city, because the most interesting problem at the time was the problem of relationships among the socially heterogeneous populations of the city. As the internal divisions of the city became less novel, if not less of a problem, later sociologists took a more external approach to the city. We will discuss this approach below, but the point to be made here is that this development lies outside the main thrust of urban sociology, as influenced by Wirth and the Chicago school. Images of the city that envision the city in the context of the outside world did not have much attraction for the early sociologists. "The city on a hill" or the city as fortress or as hell or as a reservation or as a garden simply do not provide relevant imagery for the problem of the organization of the population *within* the city itself.

The power of Wirth's statement is thus seen in its ability to set forth an image of the city as a place of *organized diversity*, and to focus research on the internal social organization of the city. Within this broad framework, urban sociologists have developed specific images of the city that reflect tensions within the discipline itself. These images are sometimes explicitly stated but are more often than not unselfconscious orienting devices in the study of the city.

A TYPOLOGY OF URBAN IMAGES

The sociologist shares with the rest of the population the love–hate relationship with the city that has been widely commented on in Ameri-

---

[3]Robert E. Park, Ernest W. Burgess, and Roderick D. McKenzie, *The City* (Chicago: The University of Chicago Press, 1967), 1.

can studies, and that decisively influences one's image of the city. The city may be seen as a place of dirt, disease, crime, pollution, vice, poverty, and other social problems, or it may be seen as a place of culture, art, wealth, employment, vitality, sophistication, and social opportunities. Thus, evaluation of the city in a positive or a negative manner becomes the first defining dimension of sociological approaches to the city.

The second dimension along which sociologists differ in their approach to the city has to do with the analytical unit that they focus on in their work. Many sociologists will argue that groups or institutions are the proper units of analysis, not individuals. This divide over whether a microscopic or a macroscopic approach to the topic is most fruitful is a pervasive argument in all the subject areas of sociology.

When cross-classified these two basic tensions give rise to a typology of urban imagery that summarizes the most important sociological approaches to the city (see Figure 1).

The City as Bazaar

The city as bazaar imagines the city as a place of astonishing richness of activity and diversity unparalleled in nonurban areas. It is a market, a fair, a place of almost infinite exploration and opportunity, a center of exchange. The richness of opportunity of the city exposes each individual to a variety of experiences and fosters the development of unique combinations of social affiliations and lifestyles. There is a liberation from the one-dimensionality of the small town or the countryside.

The City as Jungle

The city as jungle sees the city from the group up as a densely packed, intricately intertwined, potentially dangerous place. Its diverse

		Evaluative Dimension	
		Positive	Negative
Analytic Dimension	Microscopic	City as Bazaar	City as Jungle
	Macroscopic	City as Organism	City as Machine

Figure 1. A typology of urban images.

species crowd each other, search for their own place in the sun, and battle each other for room to develop and reproduce. Niches are cultivated and defended, and it is perilous to stray too far from familiar paths. Paradoxically, this rich, lush growth is precariously based, and it can easily be turned into a wasteland.

The City as Organism

The city as organism sees the diversity of the city as a system of specialized organs functioning for the common good of the corporate body. Each part of the body has a role to perform, and this performance benefits the well-being of the entire body. As in any organism, there are certain organs that control critical bodily functions, but these "hearts" and "brains" are sympathetically connected with the entire organism and serve the common good. There are diseases that harm the organism, but a healthy urban body keeps these diseases under control.

The City as Machine

The city as machine sees the complexity of the city as running as smoothly and as intricately as the organism, but rather than being controlled for the common welfare, the machine is an object controlled by its creators, who are a small group of people. The urban machine is designed to produce products that provide wealth for some people and not for others. There is none of the benign guidance of the organism; instead, a calculating single-mindedness is directed toward the welfare of only one part of the city's population.

These four images of the city can be found in sociological research from the time of the classical nineteenth-century social analysts up to the present day.

The different images of the city rise and fall in popularity because of the changing nature of the problems that the cities seem to face at any particular time. The initial power of the image of the city as an organism lay in its ordering of the superficial chaos of the city. This ordering, however, seemed too benign in nature for scholars writing during periods of intense social unrest, such as the 1930s and the 1960s. During such periods in our intellectual history, organic imagery subsides in importance and machine imagery increases because of its focus on the conflicts inherent in the organization of the city. These two images are thus linked in their opposition to each other, and they rise and fall as the perceived social conflict of the society rises and falls. In a similar way, scholars who use the individual as their unit of analysis have alternately focused on the jungle imagery, with its ideas of scarcity and struggle, or on the bazaar image, with its focus on the problems of affluence, which characterized much of the work of the 1940s and 1950s, and which increased again in the 1970s.

Despite their ideological variance, both the machine and the organism call attention to the critical role that external factors play in the life of a city. They both increase in importance when attention is focused on the role of state, national, and international political and economic decisions in the development of the city. During a time such as the present, when changes in political and economic policies seem to be influencing the cities drastically, both the machine and the organism arise to shed light on these external linkages. The city becomes not a settlement apart from the rest of society but a habitat shaped by the wider society.

Although many examples could be used to illustrate each of these ideal types, we will develop each of these four images by analyzing its classical roots and its most contemporary research expression. The variety of images that evolved within the framework codified by Louis Wirth shows the durability of that conceptualization and its usefulness for the urban researcher. Saying that it has not illuminated all urban issues does not detract from the light that it has shed on a vast array of problems.

THE CITY AS BAZAAR

Bazaar imagery presents the city in its richness of activities and opportunities, as well as in its diversity of individuals. Although the economic marketplace has been seen as the essential element in the creation of cities by such scholars as Max Weber, market imagery refers not to the actual marketplace but to the social richness, the equivalent of a bazaar or fair.[4]

No student of the city has probed the richness of the city as perceptively as Georg Simmel in his two essays "The Metropolis and Mental Life" and "The Web of Group-Affiliations." Simmel is a master, looking at

[4]Max Weber, *The City*, trans. and ed. by Don Martindale and Gertrud Neuwirth (New York: Free Press, 1958).

social life in a dualistic manner, and seeing both the positive imagery of the bazaar and the negative imagery of the jungle.

In "The Web of Group-Affiliations" (1922), Simmel focused on the individual moving through the urban world. In contrast to the rural world, where ascribed statuses restrict individual movement and opportunities, the density and diversity of the city constantly put the individual in touch with myriad possibilities unknown outside the city. The critical issue here is the *potential* richness of the activities that an urbanite can sample. The city is a vast array of goods and delights, an ever-unfolding display of activities, a salad bar of ingredients from which an individual can create his or her particular sustenance. The individual is not enclosed in a "primary" group that provides him or her with social, economic, artistic, recreational, religious, sexual, and political resources; rather, the individual is freed to develop his or her own resources. The key lies in the many different groups to which any individual may belong:

> The number of different social groups in which the individual participates, is one of the earmarks of culture. The modern person belongs first of all to his parental family, then to his family of procreation and thereby also to the family of his wife. Beyond this he belongs to his occupational group, which often involves him in several interest-groups. . . . Then, a person is likely to be aware of his citizenship, of the fact that he belongs to a particular social class. He is, moreover, a reserve officer, he belongs to a few clubs and engages in a social life which puts him in touch with different social groups.[5]

Simmel stated that at all times a person begins her or his life as a member of one group and then comes to participate in a multitude of groups. These multiple group-affiliations may take two distinctly different forms. The first form is a *concentric* pattern, in which a person's affiliations arise from a central status, and all the social circles to which a person belongs rest inside one another like a stack of cups:

> The peculiar character of group-formation in the Middle Ages in contrast with the modern way has been stressed frequently. In the Middle Ages affiliation with a group absorbed the whole man. It served not only a momentary purpose, which was defined objec-

[5]Georg Simmel, *Conflict and the Web of Group Affiliations*, trans. Kurt H. Wolff and Reinhard Bendix (New York: Free Press, 1955), 138. For an excellent discussion of the dualistic nature of Simmel's sociology, see the introduction by Donald N. Levine to Georg Simmel, *On Individuality and Social Forms*, ed. Donald N. Levine (Chicago: University of Chicago Press, 1971).

tively. It was rather an association of all who had combined for the
sake of that purpose while the association absorbed the whole life of
each of them.[6]

Simmel contrasted this all-embracing pattern with the intersecting and
weblike pattern of the market metropolis:

> The modern pattern differs sharply from the concentric pattern
> of group-affiliations as far as a person's achievements are concerned.
> Today someone may belong, aside from his occupational position, to a
> scientific association, he may sit on a board of a corporation and
> occupy an honorific position in the city government. . . . The indi-
> vidual may add affiliations with new groups to the single affiliation
> which has hitherto influenced him in a pervasive and one-sided
> manner.[7]

Clearly, Simmel was referring to an individual who has a great deal of
freedom of movement and a great many resources with which to take
advantage of the many possibilities of the city. Although the city provides
for a release from the "pervasive and one-sided" determinism of the old
order, the assumption in Simmel's analysis is that the urbanite is mobile,
affluent, and resourceful. The urbanite is not restricted to one place. She
or he glides over the urban landscape, picking and choosing the associations that create a particular, individualized social world.

Simmel's imagery of endlessly overlapping and intersecting social
circles flowing across physical space is developed in the currently burgeoning group of studies united under the term *network analysis*. Network analysts treat the interpersonal network as the unit of analysis and
strive for a ground-up portrayal of the structure of networks in the metropolis.[8] Reacting against the notion that social behavior can be under-

[6]Simmel, *Conflict*, 148–149.
[7]Ibid., 150–151.
[8]Major works that have shaped the network perspective are Elizabeth Bott, *Family and Social Network* (London: Tavistock, 1957); and J. Clyde Mitchell, ed.,
Social Networks in Urban Situations (Manchester: Manchester University
Press), 1–50. Two of the best contemporary network analyses are Claude Fischer
et al., *Networks and Places* (New York: Free Press, 1977); and Barry Wellman,
"The Community Question: The Intimate Network of East Yorkers," *American
Journal of Sociology*, 84 (March 1979):1201–1231.

The network analysts extend the concern with the social relations of urbanites that was developed in the work of Morris Axelrod, "Urban Structure and
Social Participation," *American Sociological Review* 21 (Feb. 1956):14–18; Wen-
dell Bell and Marion D. Boat, "Urban Neighborhoods and Informal Social Rela-

stood as the acting out of internalized goals and values, network analysts take a radical structuralist position, attempting to understand social conflict, consensus, and communication in terms of the actual connections between social units, not in terms of people's professed intentions.

In "The Network City," Paul Craven and Barry Wellman presented a Simmelian market of possibilities that gives rise to patterns of allegiance and avoidance among the diverse elements of the population:

> The rich, and often bewildering, complexity of social life in the city is such that the sociologist who would seek to understand it has always had to adopt some strategy of analysis by which to guide his inquiry. . . . [T]he fundamental concern of network analysis [is] to inquire into the nature of interactional and organizational links between social units. . . . Sociologists who take this approach see the city not so much as a conglomeration of people and institutions but rather as a multitude of social networks, overlapping and interacting in various ways. This approach emphasizes such questions as "Who is linked to whom?", "What is the content of their relationship?", and "What is the structure of their relational network?"[9]

Network studies build on the formulations of Wirth but advance that work by focusing on the *links* between social units and the patterning of these links in the organization of the metropolis. These studies make more concrete Simmel's ideas about the intersections of social circles in the metropolis.

There is a bazaar imagery of a richness of opportunities and a diversity of elements underlying the network approach to the formation of intricately connected social patterns. But the bazaar reflects only one way in which the city may be perceived in its diversity. Another part of Simmel's analysis of the city portrays the city in a multifaceted way.

THE CITY AS JUNGLE

The jungle is a strong image for most of us. The jungle is a natural area of extreme lushness and fertility. It is densely populated with an enormous variety of kinds of life, twined together and crawling over each

---

tions," *American Journal of Sociology* 62 (Jan. 1957):391–398; and Jacqueline M. Zito, "Anonymity and Neighboring in an Urban High-Rise Complex," *Urban Life and Culture* 3 (Oct. 1974):243–263.
[9]*Sociological Inquiry* 43 (Dec. 1973):57–88.

other. It is a place where the struggle for survival goes on in a graphic way, with each species fighting for its place in the sun, its part of the sustenance of the soil. The jungle has a specialized place for each species as it finds its niche and jealously guards its territory. The jungle is dangerous for those who don't know how it operates and for those who stray from the pathways that they have developed. The jungle, with all its power and all its majesty, is surprisingly fragile and delicate, living off its own resources, based in infertile soil, always teetering on the brink of a disaster that could turn it into a Sahara.

Diverse, dense, dangerous, and delicate, the jungle has been a strong implicit image for sociologists concerned with the everyday life of the potentially discordant elements of the city. The diversity that, from the market perspective, makes for richness of choice, from the jungle perspective presents each person with constant contact with strangers who are potential problems. The city as jungle has been the most dominant image of the city among sociologists, and the utility of that imagery is evidenced by the diverse body of research that has arisen from this tradition.

The sociological image of the jungle must be contrasted with the popular image of the city as a jungle. When the urbanite says, "It's a jungle out there!" the reference is to the competition in the city, which is clearly a part of the sociological imagery. However, the urbanite also often means, "It's chaos out there!" The sociological image of the jungle shows the order behind that seeming chaos; at the same time, it does not downplay the perceived threats and intense struggles taking place in the environment. The use of imagery derived from plant and animal ecology was picked up by sociologists because this conceptualization allowed them to make sense of the struggles of individuals within the metropolis.

The jungle imagists differ from the bazaar imagists in their explicit concern with competition for space and the confrontations between strangers in the city. Differences in social class and political power are critical for the jungle sociologists because what seems like a market of richness for the wealthy changes into a jungle for people more restricted in resources. The wealthy are able to minimize the problems of competition and confrontation because they have the resources to win these battles. However, on a certain level, they are as much a part of the jungle as everyone else. The presence of the jungle–bazaar duality in urban imagery is reflected in the two-sided approach of Simmel, which we can see in his famous essay "The Metropolis and Mental Life" (1903).

Bazaar sociologists often focus on the *private*, personal aspects of social interaction in the city, whereas the jungle sociologists concentrate on the *public*, impersonal aspects of moving through the diverse population of the city.[10] In his essay, Simmel developed the problems that the urbanite faces while existing in a large, dense, and socially diverse environment. The central problem is that the person is constantly confronted with strangers about whom he or she knows nothing and who overwhelm the person in such a manner that it becomes impossible to learn personal details about any of these people. On urban streets, the only way we can survive is to develop a posture of reserve and impersonality:

> This mental attitude of metropolitans toward one another we may designate as reserve. If so many inner reactions were responses to the continuous external contacts with innumerable people as those in the small town, where one knows almost everybody one meets and where one has a positive relation to almost everyone, one would be completely atomized internally and come to an unimaginable psychic state. Partly this psychological fact, partly the right to distrust which men have in the face of the touch-and-go elements of metropolitan life, necessitates our reserve.[11]

To use the words of a contemporary student of Simmel, the public world of the city is "a world of strangers."[12] As much as the diversity of the city liberates us in our private affairs, this diversity restricts us in our attitudes and our movements through the public world of the metropolis.

Simmel's concern with how the city is organized in order to prevent clashes between strangers has been an ongoing concern in sociology. Although he has much broader interests than the study of the city, the work of Erving Goffman continues the tradition of investigating how trust is maintained in a world of strangers. In his studies of people in public

---

[10]One of the few discussions of this critical distinction is by Hans Paul Bahrdt, "Public Activity and Private Activity as Basic Forms of City Association," in *Perspectives on the American Community*, ed. Roland Warren (Chicago: Rand McNally, 1961), 78–85.

[11]Georg Simmel, *The Sociology of Georg Simmel*, trans. and ed., Kurt H. Wolff (New York: Free Press, 1951), 415. For an attempt to test Simmel's ideas empirically, see Stanley Milgram, "The Experience of Living in Cities," *Science* 167 (March 1970):1461–1468.

[12]Lyn Lofland, *A World of Strangers: Order and Action in Urban Public Space* (New York: Basic Books, 1973), 17–32.

places, Goffman has conceptualized the person as an actor playing out roles, concerned with maintaining face, and searching for cues on the other's social worthiness. This concern with the "presentation of self" is an adaption to life in a jungle, where diverse elements are constantly coming into contact with self-interested others.[13]

One problem with Simmel's and Goffman's analyses of how people adapt to the density and the heterogeneity of the city is that they can delude us into envisioning the city as one large *downtown* area. Simmel wrote about some ways in which people can "privatize public space,"[14] but he did not develop the most essential feature of the urban landscape: the creation of subcommunities in the metropolis. The study of the partitioning of the city into numerous territorial worlds in which the overall diversity of the city is much reduced has been a major aspect of Wirth's Chicago tradition: the city is not one hodgepodge of races, classes, and ethnicities, but a mosaic of different social worlds that touch on one another and overlap at critical points.[15] People carve out their particular territorial niches in the metropolis, over which they come to have some control and within which they are able to develop the sense of identity and comfortableness that one large downtown would make impossible. The development of local neighborhoods, with history, traditions, and customs of their own, has become one way of establishing some control within the city. These smaller worlds reduce the impersonality and arbitrariness of the metropolis, and they demonstrate that, although the city is a world of strangers, it is also a world of personal knowledge and predictability.

The rich growth and complexity of local territorial communities were conceptualized in terms of the ecological imagery of the invasions, accommodations, and successions that are constantly reshaping the face of the city. The city is not disorganized; rather, it is organized by the processes of competition for scarce resources. This struggle is hard, and when it is

[13]Goffman, *The Presentation of Self in Everyday Life* (Garden City, N.Y.: Doubleday, 1959); Goffman, *Behavior in Public Places* (New York: Free Press, 1963).

[14]"Privatizing public space" is a phrase used by Lofland, ibid., 118–157. See also Sherri Cavan, "Interaction in Home Territories," *Berkeley Journal of Sociology* 8 (1963):17–32.

[15]One of the best of the early Chicago studies is Harvey Zorbaugh, *The Gold Coast and the Slum* (Chicago: University of Chicago Press, 1929).

played out in terms of a struggle for particular pieces of territory, it is often dangerous.[16]

The urban jungle emerges as a place in which the continual problem-solving of the population of the city gives rise to an organization of the diversity of the city. This imagery of the city arising from the activities of countless men and women is at the heart of both the jungle and the bazaar images of the city. There is another very different way of conceptualizing the way in which the city has been organized, and that is by focusing on certain properties of the city as a whole, rather than on those of the individuals in the city. This more macroscopic approach is contained in the images we are calling the *city as organism* and the *city as machine*.

THE CITY AS ORGANISM

Equating the society with an organism marked a critical stage in the development of nineteenth-century social theory. The critical juncture in organic imagery was Herbert Spencer's work on social evolution, in which he combined the evolutionary perspective of Auguste Comte with the focus on the division of labor of Adam Smith. The result was a view of social development in terms of ever-increasing social heterogeneity for which the organism seemed a particularly apt image.[17]

As Wilbert E. Moore stated, organic analogies were appealing to the post-Darwinian social evolutionists:

> Particularly in the work of Herbert Spencer, elaborate analogies between specialized units of society and parts of the human body were developed. Evolutionary doctrine provided a ready rationale for differentiation through genetic variability and for the use or function of organic parts by their contribution to the survival of the organism.[18]

---

[16]Jungle imagery has often been connected with a concern about crime in the city, as in Robert Cooley Angell, "The Moral Integration of American Cities, II," *American Journal of Sociology* 80 (Nov. 1974):607–629. The classic work of the Chicago school on crime is Clifford R. Shaw and Henry D. McKay, *Juvenile Delinquency and Urban Areas* (Chicago: University of Chicago Press, 1942).

[17]Herbert Spencer, *On Social Evolution*, ed. J. D. Y. Peel (Chicago: University of Chicago Press, 1972), 57.

[18]"Functionalism," in *A History of Sociological Analysis*, ed. Tom Bottomore and Robert Nisbet (New York: Basic Books, 1978), 327–328.

Moore noted that the fundamental assumptions of organic imagery are social differentiation and a social integration in which all the parts of a social body "must fit the system—that is, must have a function." There was an emergent quality to the entire system, which created a reality of its own and which could best be understood on its own level and not by an analysis of the activities of the parts making up the system:

> The primary key here has been the focus on a whole relatively autonomous social unit, whether called a culture by the anthropologists or a society by the sociologists. This "macro" focus has distinguished functionalism not only from various social-psychological concerns with the transactions between individuals and various social units, but also from various "process" orientations as represented by the German formalists such as Leopold von Wiese or their American counterparts represented by Robert E. Park and Ernest W. Burgess.[19]

On the level of the city, the organic imagery differs from our jungle imagery by focusing less on the processes by which individuals create the city and more on the properties of the emergent system.

The most influential organic imagery was contained in Émile Durkheim's classic *The Division of Labor in Society* (1893), with its analysis of modern society as having an "organic solidarity" based on an adhesion of socially specialized units, as opposed to the "mechanical solidarity" of relatively homogeneous traditional societies. Although Durkheim's ideas on traditional societies have been the focus of revision for almost a century, his emphasis on the diversity of the population in modern society continues to be taken as a given. Durkheim was consumed by the Hobbesian problem of order, and in order to explain how a socially diverse population could exist without falling into a war of all against all, he developed the organic imagery of a body in which each part is dependent on each other part for its own well-being. Through organic imagery, diversity was turned into *specialization*, and the basis for the new social order was laid bare.[20]

Given the widespread importance of organic imagery in sociology as a whole, it is somewhat surprising that this imagery has not fostered more research on the city. Ironically, organic imagery may have been so powerful that it has inhibited its own utility as an orienting characterization of

[19]Ibid., 335.
[20]Durkheim, *The Division of Labor in Society*, trans. George Simpson (New York: Free Press, 1933).

the city. An imagery in which everything fit together perfectly and in which every part necessarily contributed to the whole provided little guidance to the study of the city, in which it seemed manifestly clear that there were tensions, conflicts, and contradictions. In the battle for conceptual dominance, organic imagery provided little problem-solving power for the internal issues of the city that were the focus of the Wirth formulation and that have continued to fascinate problem-oriented urban sociologists. Organic imagery has been most stimulating in the area of the relations between the city and the society at large, but as we have seen above, this external concern has not been well-developed in traditional urban sociology. This lack of concern seems to be changing because the "great change" in communities in the last few decades has been the declining autonomy of the city and its dependence on national and international economic, fiscal, and political policies.[21] As the "problem" of the city becomes less its internal composition and more its external predicament, imagery that places the city in its national and international context will be on the resurgence. The resurgence of organic imagery may, however, be tempered by another perspective, which takes a macroscopic view of the city and which has traditionally been more focused on the problem aspects of the city: Marxist machine imagery of the city.

THE CITY AS MACHINE

The image of the city as a machine combines a macroscopic perspective with an evaluation of the city as a place of social inequality and harm for large parts of the population. As Wilbert Moore noted, both Durkheim and Marx were "antireductionists," and neither man had "any enthusiasm for the vulgar hedonism or utilitarianism of classical economics. . . . Marx and Durkheim differed as to whether the rules are to be regarded as manipulative or consensual, but not as to their superindividual quality."[22] Differ they did, indeed, as is reflected in the following statement of Marx:

> The division of labour offers us the first example of how, as long as man remains in natural society, that is, as long as a cleavage exists

---

[21]Roland L. Warren, *The Community in America*, 3rd ed. (Chicago: Rand McNally, 1978), 52–95.
[22]Pp. 325–326.

between the particular and the common interest; as long, therefore,
as activity is not voluntarily, but naturally, divided, man's act becomes an alien power opposed to him, which enslaves him instead of
being controlled by him.[23]

This enslavement of the ordinary citizen in the metropolis, like that
of Charlie Chaplin in *Modern Times,* is the essence of machine imagery.
Unlike the organism, the machine is organized for the self-interest of the
masters of the machine. The machine is controlled by the powerful and
does not provide for the well-being of its subservient parts. This imagery
is in direct contrast to the imagery of the city as a "dynamo" spinning off
benefits for its entire population.[24]

One of the most recent works in the Marxist urban tradition has
explicitly used the imagery we are developing here. Harvey Molotch, in
"The City as a Growth Machine: Toward a Political Economy of Place,"
disputed the idea that what is good for the urban elite is good for the rest
of the people of the city.[25] Relying on data that suggest that a growing,
expanding city does not create new jobs for its labor force, Molotch
contended that the city is actually a machine controlled by business,
political, and professional elites. These elites prosper by growth in and
of itself, and any suggestion that this growth has "trickle-down" benefits for the rest of the population is either blatant self-promotion or naive
utopianism.

Machine imagists focus on decisions made at the top of the social
structure that critically determine the shape of the metropolis. David
Harvey, Manuel Castells, John Mollenkopf, and Molotch have all focused
on coordinated self-interest and *power* in their studies of the city:

> There has been a continuing tendency to conceive of a place
> quite apart from a crucial dimension of social structure: power and
> social class hierarchy. Consequently, sociological research based on
> the traditional definitions of what an urban place is has had very little
> relevance to the actual day-to-day activities of those at the top of local
> power structure whose priorities set the limits within which decisions

---

[23]*Selected Writings in Sociology and Social Philosophy,* ed. T. B. Bottomore and
Maximilien Rubel (New York: McGraw-Hill, 1956), 97.

[24]Alex Ganz and Thomas O'Brien, "The City: Sandbox, Reservation, or Dynamo?" *Public Policy* 21 (Winter 1973):107–123.

[25]*American Journal of Sociology* 82 (Sept. 1976):309–332.

affecting land use, the public budget, and urban social life come to be
made.[26]

This statement is an accurate assessment of much of urban sociology, but
it ignores the major contribution of Robert and Helen Lynd in their works
on Middletown. Influenced by Marxism, the Lynds combined a concern
with the role of the city in the larger society and a focus on internal power
differences within the city. Although their terms "business class" and
"working class" may be a quiet approach to the issues of social inequality,
the Lynds were second to no one in their emphasis on social class and
economic power in the ordering of the diversity of the city:

> While an effort will be made to make clear at certain points
> variant behavior within these two groups, it is after all this division
> into working class and business class that constitutes the outstanding
> cleavage in Middletown. The mere fact of being born upon one or the
> other side of the watershed roughly formed by these two groups is
> the most significant single cultural factor tending to influence what
> one does all day long throughout one's life; whom one marries, when
> one gets up in the morning, whether one belongs to the Holy Roller
> or Presbyterian Church . . . and so on indefinitely throughout the
> daily comings and goings of a Middletown man, woman, or child.[27]

In *Middletown in Transition*,[28] the Lynds continued their emphasis
on social class and looked at the impact that the Depression was having on
life in the city. The Lynds thus united a concern with the internal diversity of the city's population and an analysis of the position of the city in the
larger social system. The reason that the classic work of the Lynds has
recently been overlooked is that the work was not easily duplicated in
cities larger than Middletown's Muncie, Indiana. To the present day,
there has been a strong tendency to focus either on the internal divisions

---

[26]Ibid., 309. For other works from this perspective see William K. Tabb and
Larry Sawers, eds., *Marxism and the Metropolis* (New York: Oxford University
Press, 1978); David Harvey, *Social Justice and the City* (Baltimore: Johns
Hopkins University Press, 1973); and Manuel Castells, *The Urban Question*
(Cambridge: M.I.T. Press, 1977). For a very different use of machine imagery,
see Christine L. Fry, "The City as a Commodity: The Age-Graded Case,"
Human Organization 36 (Summer 1977):115–123.

[27]*Middletown* (New York: Harcourt Brace and World, 1929), 23–24.

[28]Robert F. Lynd and Helen Merrell Lynd, *Middletown in Transition: A Study in
Cultural Conflicts* (New York: Harcourt Brace, 1937).

of the city or on the place of the city in the wider society because of the enormous work involved in combining the two perspectives in the empirical study of large cities. The work of the new generation of Marxist-oriented urban sociologists is attempting to overcome these obstacles and to proceed with the investigation of the city as a machine controlled by and for particular social groups.

IMAGES OF THE CITY IN FUTURE SOCIOLOGICAL RESEARCH

The images of the market, the jungle, the organism, and the machine continue as orientations to the study of the organized diversity of the city. The relative salience of any imagery is dependent on its ability to provide guidance in two different directions. The first is a theoretical insight into the issues of social *process* as well as insight into social structure. Second, the imagery is helpful to the extent that it has a *problem-solving* relevance. These two criteria of clarification of process and problem-solving relevance have both been met by the jungle imagery of the city. The processes of competition, struggle, accommodation, and manipulation, which give rise to the patterning of the city's diverse elements, have been clearly set forth at the same time that such everyday problems as crime, housing displacement, neighborhood deterioration, and racial conflict have been addressed. The two criteria have also been met by the machine imagery, with its theoretical bases in Marx's notions of control of the means of production and its focus on the problems of social inequality and poverty. As mentioned above, one of the problems in the use of this machine imagery has been the difficulty of simultaneously investigating the internal complexity and the external linkages of large cities. Organic imagery has a strong theoretical base in functionalist theory, but it waned as the original excitement over discovering any pattern in the city gave way to images with a stronger social-problem focus. As the issues of external dependence and systemic linkages reemerge in the study of urban problems, organic imagery may combine with machine imagery in a macroscopic approach to the city that portrays it neither as the "city of vice" or as the "city of virtue." Bazaar imagery is active at the moment, as witnessed by the ever-increasing network studies of the city. However, the future of this line of research is dependent on the development of a stronger concern with the *processes* by which social networks are created, maintained, and dissolved. Without this element, bazaar imagery will be an interesting but theoretically unfocused branch of urban sociology.[29]

We have emphasized that sociologists have rarely taken the images that people have of the city as proper subjects for sociological study. There is, however, an important group of studies that do deal with the images that people have of the city. Growing out of the theoretical school of symbolic interactionism, these studies show how the images that people have of the city affect their social behavior. An analysis of these works is essential in any discussion of urban images.

Earlier, we quoted Robert Park's statement that "the city is a state of mind." The sociological study that has been the most influential in pointing out the importance of these states of mind in the city has been Walter Firey's *Land Use in Central Boston*.[30] Firey convincingly showed that economic forces did not deterministically shape the pattern of land use in the city. Economic issues were influenced by cultural images and historical symbols that played critical roles in directing population into certain areas of the city and in resisting business encroachment on other areas of the city. Firey's work is widely cited, but in a manner similar to the Lynds' contribution, it has been put on a pedestal, and its lessons have been ignored in recent research.

The contemporary sociologist who has renewed interest in images of the city is Gerald Suttles in his work on the social consequences of the "cognitive maps" discussed by Kevin Lynch and his followers.[31] Suttles has a jungle imagery of the city and follows Simmel and Goffman in his concern with the problem of establishing a sense of personal control within the urban environment. Suttles has focused on the local neighborhood as a central structure that minimizes the danger and the uncertainty of the urban jungle. Suttles has contended that the images that people have of different neighborhoods are essential to an understanding of the city:

> Cognitive maps provide a set of social categories for differentiating between those people with whom one can or cannot safely associate and for defining the concrete groupings within which certain

[29]Of the contemporary network analysts, Wellman (*op. cit.*) and Fischer (*op. cit.*) are most aware of the static quality of much network analysis. Wellman's work in progress is developing more dynamic approaches to urban networks.

[30]Cambridge, Mass.: Belknap Press, 1947.

[31]Kevin Lynch, *The Image of the City* (Cambridge: M.I.T. Press, 1960).

levels of social contact and cohesion obtain. These cognitive maps, then, are a creative imposition on the city and useful because they provide a final solution to decision making where there are often no other clear cutoff points for determining how far social contacts should go.[32]

Within the jungle of the city, we create areas in which we feel that "people like us" are located; we give these areas names ("Woodlawn," "Savin Hill," "Indian Village"), and they become safe places in which to shop, work, and play, as well as reside. Within our "home areas," associations develop that transform the city from a Simmelian world of strangers or a Goffmanesque world of "impression management" into a world of predictability and comfortableness.[33]

Recent work by Albert Hunter has shown the importance of neighborhood images in residents' attachment and commitment to areas of the city. Commenting on the views of the residents of one racially integrated inner-city area of Rochester, New York, Hunter wrote:

> This community, like so many other similar areas throughout urban America, is consciously advertising itself as a stable, racially integrated area in an attempt to attract white residents who view this characteristic as a positive ideological value or ideal. Many of the middle-class white residents of the area proclaim the fact that they are living the value of racial integration while many of their "liberal" friends from suburbia hypocritically espouse one ideal and live a different reality.[34]

The image of an area becomes a badge of identification and a symbolic reference point for the residents who live there. This is a critically important aspect of the inner-city rejuvenation that is occurring in most American cities. Areas of the city are not just locations for housing; they are areas that *mean* something to all people conversant with the vocabu-

[32]*The Social Construction of Communities* (Chicago: University of Chicago Press, 1972), 22. Also see Suttles, *The Social Order of the Slum* (Chicago: University of Chicago Press, 1968).

[33]Suttles, *Social Construction*, 233–268. A critical theoretical discussion of these issues is in Herman Schmalenbach, "The Sociological Category of Communion," in *Theories of Society*, ed. Talcott Parsons et al. (New York: Free Press, 1961), Vol. I, pp. 331–347.

[34]"The Loss of Community: An Empirical Test through Replication," *American Sociological Review* 40 (Oct. 1975):546; see also Hunter, *Symbolic Communities* (Chicago: University of Chicago Press, 1974).

lary of that particular city. Careful study of these images is essential to any study of neighborhood change and transition.

Missing in the current literature are studies of the images of entire cities and regions in the manner of Strauss's work on the American city. As cities and states increasingly plan advertising campaigns for (and against) business and residential immigration from other areas of the country, the role of image making in the rise and fall of particular cities is an important area of study. Just as corporations hire specialized agencies to develop their "corporate image," explicit image production and manipulation by cities is a growing occurrence that can be valuably studied within the context of our present discussion. Park's view of the city as a state of mind should continue to be a guide for the study of the city, not as a collection of buildings and streets, houses, and offices, but as a concrete realization of the social values and the cultural ideals that shape the social diversity of the city.

ACKNOWLEDGMENTS

I am indebted to Roslyn Feldberg, Claire Paradiso, and Lloyd Rodwin for their helpful comments.

CHAPTER 7

History

Notes on Urban Images of Historians

CHARLES TILLY

HISTORICAL IMAGES OF THE CITY

History is so porous a subject, and writing history so various an endeavor, that almost any image that anyone—historian or not—has ever held of cities appears somewhere in a historical account. From Herodotus's splendid Athens to Mumford's rotten Rome, the evaluations cover the possible range. A conscientious survey of urban images in history would amount to an inventory of all existing conceptions of the city. That inventory would be charming but useless, like the reproductions of antique mail-order catalogues that appear on gift-book counters toward the end of each year. It would also be many times as bulky. True, one can economize by classifying: the city as a point in space as opposed to the city as the setting of battles and pageants, the city as a storehouse of civilization versus the city as a cesspool, the city as a market or the city as an organization, and so on. Even such a classification results, if faithfully pursued, in an enumeration of all the logical and aesthetic principles that one might employ in sorting cities. An idle task, at best.

Instead of frittering away effort on taxonomy, let us consider the dilemma faced by historians who write about cities: how to portray the textures of individual cities, and yet to connect those cities firmly to general historical processes. The dilemma confronts an urban historian who wants to place the subject in the overall stream of social change, just

Charles Tilly • Center for Research on Social Organization, University of Michigan, Ann Arbor, Michigan.

as surely as it challenges the political or social historian who wants to follow broad processes of change through the lives of particular cities. How shall we fashion a sound analysis of the growth of large-scale manufacturing that permits us to capture the differences in the experiences of people in, say, England's Birmingham and Manchester during nineteenth-century industrialization? How shall we carry out that dual analysis without reducing to bare points on a graph those cities of tenements, alleys, canals, workers, capitalists, widows, brawls, shouts, and stenches?

The problem does not result simply from clashing levels of abstraction, from inconsistency between the general and the particular. Here is the difficulty: cities are, above all, *places*, whose analysis requires a sense of spatial and physical structure; analyses of broad historical processes rarely deal effectively with spatial and physical structure. Working out the implications of broad historical processes for spatial and physical structure is never easy. As a consequence, treatments of urban geography seldom articulate usefully with discussions of the development of national electoral politics, or of the growth of new ideologies. Likewise, historical accounts of revolution or of changes in family organization usually have only the weakest implications for changes in the character of the city as a place. It is as if the text consisted of clusters of microdots, each cluster conveying its own internal message, and also appearing to form part of a larger message—whereas the magnifying glass used to read the text has only two settings, one for the microdots, the other for the whole array, and nothing in between.

Why try to articulate the two? Why not treat the historical development of particular cities and the changes of whole countries, as distinct problems, each requiring its own intellectual frame? Why not wait for the occasional daring synthesizer to join the two problems? Why not? Because urban history itself will be the loser. Without provisional synthesis, urban historians run the risk either of drifting into antiquarianism or of following strong but poorly formulated questions into confusion.

If analysts of large-scale change neglect urban form and reduce the cities they examine to locations in abstract space, they will not only ignore a crucial feature of those cities but also misconstrue the causal links among the features that they do observe. Without an understanding of how people use different parts of a city, for example, students of cities easily fall into thinking of migration as a solvent of social ties and a producer of rootless individuals. That misconception, in its turn, leads easily to the idea that massive in-migration produces crime and conflict.

Once they see the segregation of many cities into "urban villages" formed by migrants from the same origins who are attached to each other by the routines of chain migration, however, students of cities begin to grasp the fact that large-scale migration actually *creates* solidarities and social controls. Only by articulating the connections between long flows of migrants and the fine spatial organization of the city do we acquire a proper sense of migration's impact on the city's social life. Similar relationships hold for many other features of urban experience.

The usual division of labor in urban history makes more difficult that articulation of cities as places with cities as points within large social processes. When, for instance, Leo Schnore assembled papers representing the best current work in the "new urban history," the papers divided as follows[1]:

Cities as Places
Martyn J. Bowden, "Growth of the Central Districts in Large Cities"
Kenneth T. Jackson, "Urban Deconcentration in the Nineteenth Century"
Kathleen Neils Conzen, "Patterns of Residence in Early Milwaukee"
Zane L. Miller, "Urban Blacks in the South, 1865–1920: The Richmond, Savannah, New Orleans, Louisville and Birmingham Experience"

Cities as Points in Large Social Processes
Allan R. Pred, "Large-City Interdependence and the Pre-electronic Diffusion of Innovations in the United States"
Gregory H. Singleton, "Fundamentalism and Urbanization: A Quantitative Critique of Impressionistic Interpretations"
Claudia Dale Goldin, "Urbanization and Slavery: The Issue of Compatibility"
Robert Higgs, "Urbanization and Inventiveness in the United States"
Joseph A. Swanson and Jeffrey G. Williamson, "Firm Location and Optimal City Size in American History"

Cities as Places within Large Social Processes
NONE

---

[1]*The New Urban History: Quantitative Explorations by American Historians*, ed. L. F. Schnore (Princeton, N.J.: Princeton University Press, 1975).

To be sure, the four articles in the first category bear on social processes that crossed the boundaries of any single city, and that depended on changes in the United States as a whole. But the analyses themselves make those links neither explicit nor problematic.

The problem is not simply a matter of the scale at which particular analysts feel comfortable working. When Jane Jacobs wrote her stimulating *Death and Life of Great American Cities*,[2] she showed herself to be a sensitive observer of neighborhood-to-neighborhood variation in the texture of social life. The whole book concerned the effects of spatial patterns and built environment on the quality of social interaction in different parts of cities. Yet, when the same author turned to her *Economy of Cities*,[3] the cities in question collapsed to points on the graph. Implicitly, Jacobs's distinctions among craft production, mass production, and diversified production as successive stages in a city's manufacturing describe places that have—or can have—substantially different internal structures. More so than mass production, diversified production ought to make possible the sort of variety and complexity Jacobs values. Implicitly, then, the distinctions among craft, mass, and diversified production link the two books. Explicitly, nevertheless, Jane Jacobs did not work out the consequences of successive forms of industry for the city as a place.

One more example: Gary Nash's remarkable book, *The Urban Crucible*, compares the eighteenth-century histories of Boston, New York, and Philadelphia up through the American Revolution.[4] A number of earlier students of the period from the Seven Years War' to the Revolution have examined the geography of politics in those cities—delineating, for example, the roles of activists from the South End and the North End of Boston during the Stamp Act crisis. Furthermore, a comparison of Allan Kulikoff's analysis of segregation by wealth in prerevolutionary Boston with Sam Bass Warner's observation of occupational mixing in eighteenth-century Philadelphia suggests the possibility of significant differences in the structures of the two cities: perhaps Boston's exceptional activism depended in part on the mobilization of people in class-homogeneous neighborhoods.[5] Nash did not follow the geographic lead. Instead, he

[2]New York: Random House, 1961.
[3]New York: Random House, 1969.
[4]*The Urban Crucible: Social Change, Political Consciousness, and the Origins of the American Revolution* (Cambridge: Harvard University Press, 1979).
[5]"The Progress of Inequality in Revolutionary Boston," *William and Mary Quarterly*, 3d series, 28 (1971):375–412; Warner, *The Private City: Philadelphia in*

treated each of the cities as the repository of a somewhat different mixture of social classes resulting from its particular economic position, then gave an account of the various class alignments that emerged in the politics of the three cities. The account is fresh and illuminating. But it says nothing about the three cities as places.

One might reasonably complain that urban form has little to do with the problem that Nash set himself. That is exactly the point. The current division of labor in urban history draws the line among problems at city limits: on one side, problems to which the study of spatial organization is obviously relevant, or even crucial; on the other, problems in which it makes eminent sense to treat individual cities as elementary points in space; and practically no problems, recognized as such by the practitioners, that straddle the line. As a result, urban history, for all its occasional brilliance, rarely contributes much to our understanding of the interaction between large social processes and the changing form of cities.

DRAWING A BLANK

Even within the city limits, studies of social processes often ignore the city's spatial structure. Only one case this time: Stephan Thernstrom's masterful *Other Bostonians* traces the life histories of almost 8,000 of Boston's residents from 1880 to 1970.[6] Questions about social mobility and immobility dominate the book. Geographic mobility into and out of the city, furthermore, figures both as a technical problem and as an important phenomenon. But the book pays no attention to mobility from one part of the city to another, or to differences in social mobility among residents of different parts of the city. Not one of the 81 statistical tables treats the city's spatial structure. The book contains nary a map of Boston. Discussions of the relationships—mostly nonexistent—between the extent of a group's residential segregation and its occupational achievement come closest to taking local geography into account. Because the description of residential segregation involved is a single index summed over all areas of the city, even that one concession to spatial organization falls far short of conveying the city's changing internal structure.

Three Periods of Its Growth (Philadelphia: University of Pennsylvania Press, 1968).
[6]*The Other Bostonians: Poverty and Progress in the American Metropolis, 1880–1970* (Cambridge: Harvard University Press, 1973).

In Thernstrom's Boston, people fall into ethnic and occupational categories but otherwise have no local existence. In that Boston, questions about the locality transmute themselves into questions about the nation as a whole: in the United States of the industrial age, how much, and how, did opportunities for mobility vary from time to time and group to group? Pursuit of those questions does not obviously require any attention to urban spatial organization. So long as the object is to fill in the cells of a social-mobility table, one can treat the city's map as a blank.

To some degree, the connections that Thernstrom and other urban historians have made with major historical questions justify the drawing of the city as a blank. Before Thernstrom initiated a series of social-mobility studies in one American city after another, few historians saw that treatments of individual cities could aim beams of light on opportunity and inequality in American life as a whole—and therefore, by reflection, on the apparent lack of class-conscious militancy among American workers, and on the common supposition that in the twentieth century an open society began to close down. Thernstrom deserves credit for an outstanding accomplishment. Nevertheless, his accomplishment contributes little to our sense of Boston and other cities as places with complex internal geographies.

Many other questions that historians have brought to cities likewise encourage them to blank out the spatial pattern. That is especially true of questions imported from the social sciences: questions about demographic changes in industrialization, questions about class structure, questions about organizational life, and so on. As social scientists usually pursue those questions, locations matter little except as evidence about the social categories to which people belong: living in a neighborhood high on the hill marks a family as elite; living in a predominantly Greek neighborhood strengthens the presumption that a family of Greek extraction is "ethnic"; other locations provide information for the placement of other sorts of people. Location within the city dissolves into position within an abstract social space. As a consequence, urban historians look at place after place without contributing to our understanding of the organization of cities as spaces.

Not all urban historians who examine large-scale social processes as they work themselves out in particular cities therefore neglect spatial organization. In a fairly direct reaction to the abstractness of social-mobility analyses, for example, Theodore Hershberg and his fellow researchers of the Philadelphia Social History Project have spent much of their energy pinpointing the locations in the nineteenth-century city occupied by different sorts of people and activities.[7] Attention to space has made it possible for them to investigate how changes in transport, shifts in the location of jobs, and urban growth affected the journey to work; that is only one example of the many problems they have addressed. John Cumbler has organized his history of working-class life and collective action in nineteenth-century Lynn, Massachusetts, around the reshaping of urban neighborhoods and home–work relationships with the decline of small-scale craft production and the concentration of capital in large firms.[8] In exquisitely fine detail, Olivier Zunz has analyzed alterations in the texture of Detroit's neighborhoods—including changes in the structure of racial, ethnic, and class segregation—with the growth of big industry after 1880.[9]

Zunz's study deserves special attention, for he deliberately undertook to make the study of spatial structure and built environment relevant to large questions of social history. For that purpose, he took his observations of land use, building type, and population down to the individual plot and structure. Zunz argued (although with many qualifications and considerable subtlety) that processes relating people to their work dominate the shape of the city, for example, that, in periods when the urban labor force is growing largely through the influx of long-distance migrants via chain migration, the local clusters created by the migration dominate the map of the city. He argued, furthermore, that the scale of production strongly affects the scale of segregation—where workplaces are generally very small, for instance, segregation by class and common origin takes the form of small clusters of similar households. It follows that an observer who looks at changes at the level of relatively large geographic units, such as wards or census tracts, is likely to mistake an increase in the *scale* of segregation for the emergence of segregation in a previously mixed city. In the case of Detroit, these two principles combined to produce a fundamental rearrangement of Detroit's ground plan around World War I. Then, Zunz tells us, the rapid expansion of automobile plants and other

---

[7]*Philadelphia: Work, Space, Family, and Group Experience in the Nineteenth Century,* ed. T. Hershberg (Oxford: Oxford University Press, 1981).

[8]"The City and Community: The Impact of Urban Forces on Working-Class Behavior," *Journal of Urban History* 3 (1977):427–442.

[9]O. Zunz, *The Changing Face of Inequality: Urbanization, Industrial Development, and Immigrants in Detroit, 1880–1920* (Chicago: University of Chicago Press, 1982).

large employers, coupled with the migration of blacks and whites from the South to the city, rapidly created the class- and race-segregated industrial city that we know today. Zunz's analysis takes spatial structure seriously, without forgetting why we might be interested in it as a clue to general social processes. Such analyses are rare.

Urban historians face a real dilemma. Constrained by today's questions, materials, and procedures, they do not easily, or often, examine the relationship between large historical processes and the textures of individual cities. For the most part, they treat the two separately. They bring together historical processes and city textures mainly by broad allusions at the beginnings and ends of studies that remain doggedly on one side of the line or the other. This despite Oscar Handlin's 20-year-old challenge to his colleagues:

> The distinctive feature of the great modern city is its unique pattern of relations to the world within which it is situated. Large enough to have a character of its own, the modern city is yet inextricably linked to, dependent upon, the society outside it; and growth in size has increased rather than diminished the force of that dependence. Out of that relationship spring the central problems of urban history— those of the organization of space within the city, of the creation of order among its people, and of the adjustment to its new conditions by the human personality.
>
> It is, of course, perfectly possible to approach the history of these communities in a purely descriptive fashion—to prepare useful accounts of municipalities, markets and cultural centers on an empirical basis. But such efforts will certainly be more rewarding if they are related to large questions of a common and comparative nature.[10]

What is more, 200 pages farther into the same book, Eric Lampard echoed Oscar Handlin:

> Although there are limits to which [sic] any one discipline could or should treat urban developments in their entirety, it is time surely to frame a broader approach to urban history, one that elucidates concrete local situations in the *same* terms that are used to treat more general transformations in society. Individual cities, for example, can be treated as particular *accommodations* to a many-sided societal process: urbanization. . . . The scope of historical studies should thus be broadened and more systematic effort made to relate the

---

[10]"The Modern City as a Field of Historical Study," in *The Historian and the City*, ed. O. Handlin and J. Burchard (Cambridge: M.I.T. Press and Harvard University Press, 1963), p. 3.

configurations of individual communities to on-going changes that
have been reshaping society.[11]

In the very same volume, ironically, the speculative and theoretical essays spring gracefully from broad social changes to urban form and back,
and the two sustained discussions of a particular city—studies of Philadelphia by Sam Bass Warner and Anthony Garvan—barely mention the
interaction between national or international processes and the reshaping
of the city.[12] Conclusion: bridging the gap is easier to advocate than to
accomplish.

BRIDGES ACROSS THE GAP

Nevertheless, determined students of cities have found a few standard ways to cross the divide between large social changes and alterations
within particular cities. We might call the three most prominent *global
reach, space economy,* and *city-as-theater.*

Global reach consists of evoking a principle that pervades an entire
society or civilization, then treating the internal organization of cities as a
direct expression of that principle. Max Weber, Oswald Spengler, Henri
Pirenne, and Arnold Toynbee all invented global-reach accounts of cities.[13] None of them, however, provided as full a statement as Lewis
Mumford has. In *The City in History* and many other writings, Mumford
has worked out an analysis of cities as expressions of two principles, in
varying combinations.[14] The first principle: accumulation, symbolized by
the Neolithic agricultural village. The second: conquest, symbolized by
the Paleolithic hunter. Neither one in itself, thinks Mumford, leaves
much room for leisured, humane daily life. The initial synthesis of the two
principles, however, produced the first cities—small in scale and heavily

[11]"Urbanization and Social Change: On Broadening the Scope and Relevance of
Urban History," in Handlin and Burchard, p. 233.
[12]Warner; Garvan, "Proprietary Philadelphia as Artifact," in Handlin and
Burchard.
[13]Weber, *The City*, trans. and ed. by D. Martindale and F. Neuwirth (Glencoe,
Ill.: Free Press, 1958); Pirenne, *Medieval Cities* (Princeton, N.J.: Princeton
University Press, 1925); Toynbee, *Cities on the Move* (London: Oxford Univer-
sity Press, 1970).
[14]*The City in History: Its Origins, Its Transformations, and Its Prospects* (New
York: Harcourt, Brace and World, 1961).

dependent on agriculture, but nonetheless combining warrior-kingship with an unprecedented accumulation of goods.

From then on, according to Mumford, the extent and balance of accumulation and conquest determined the internal structure of cities and also limited their viability. In Europe, he says, a relatively modest and balanced advance of the two principles created the harmonies of medieval cities: wall, market, fortress, and cathedral marked out a city in which even people of moderate circumstances could live comfortably. Hypertrophy of conquest and control produced the ostentatious baroque city, with its palaces, monuments, and parade grounds. Exaggeration of accumulation and consumption produced the gritty industrial city, with its tenements, gridwork streets, and smokestacks. Pushed beyond all bounds by the masters of the later industrial city, incessant conquest and (especially) accumulation destroy any possibility of humane existence, indeed any semblance of an urban community. The city destroys itself. We live in the image of Rome:

> From the standpoint of both politics and urbanism, Rome remains a significant lesson of what to avoid: its history presents a series of classic danger signals to warn one when life is moving in the wrong direction. Wherever crowds gather in suffocating numbers, wherever rents rise steeply and housing conditions deteriorate, wherever a one-sided exploitation of distant territories removes the pressure to achieve balance and harmony nearer at hand, there the precedents of Roman building almost automatically revive, as they have come back today: the arena, the tall tenement, the mass contests and exhibitions, the football matches, the international beauty contests, the strip-tease made ubiquitous by advertisement, the constant titillation of the senses by sex, liquor, and violence—all in true Roman style. So, too, the multiplication of bathrooms and the over-expenditure on broadly paved motor roads, and above all, the massive collective concentration on glib ephemeralities of all kinds, performed with supreme technical audacity. These are symptoms of the end: magnifications of demoralized power, minifications of life. When these signs multiply, Necropolis is near, though not a stone has yet crumbled. For the barbarian has already captured the city from within. Come, hangman! Come, vulture![15]

Although Mumford's analysis is contestable in many ways and incomplete in many others, it has the virtue of creating a direct link between large social changes and the spatial organization of cities: the changing priorities of dominant classes produce decisions that dominate the locations

[15]Ibid., p. 242.

and distributions of activities, populations, and structures within the city. That argument matters to Mumford because it suggests the possibility of changing the texture of cities by altering priorities. It matters to us because it indicates one escape from the historian's dilemma. Global reach makes the same principles that inform social life in general reshape the internal structure of cities.

Space economy builds a very different bridge. As Eric Lampard's ever-skeptical but always-hopeful essays have established over the years, economic historians keep alive the idea that the logic of costs (and, to a lesser extent, of benefits) dictates a distinctive spatial pattern for each system of production and distribution.[16] That spatial pattern stretches seamlessly from the scale of a neighborhood to the scale of a continent. Richard Meier, for example, has sketched a "communications theory" of urban growth, in which transaction costs under varying technologies affect the relative feasibility of conveying goods, services, and various sorts of information over long distances or short, and thus shape neighborhoods and continents at the same time.[17] Allan Pred treats "biased information fields" as determining the relative advantages of different locations for the pursuit of major activities, and as thereby constraining the whole pattern of urban growth.[18] Although making less of the formal structure of space economy, Yves Lequin has analyzed nineteenth-century Lyon and its hinterland as a single interdependent site of industrial production.[19] And G. William Skinner has extended a classic treatment of space-economy—the economic geographers' model of nested urban hierarchies built up from the markets for different commodities—into a portrayal of the entire Chinese urban system.[20]

In addition to his imaginative leap from an abstract market region to a concrete Chinese subcontinent and the indefatigable assembly of evidence on Chinese regions, Skinner has added to the interest of the classic model by conceiving of a China characterized by not one but *two* urban

[16]Lampard, *Urbanization and Social Change.*

[17]*A Communications Theory of Urban Growth* (Cambridge: M.I.T. Press, 1962).

[18]*Urban Growth and the Circulation of Information: The U.S. System of Cities 1790–1840* (Cambridge: Harvard University Press, 1973); *Urban Growth and City-Systems in the U.S. 1840–1860* (Cambridge: Harvard University Press, 1980).

[19]*Les Ouvriers de la Région Lyonnaise 1848–1914*, 2 vols. (Lyon: Presses Universitaires de Lyon, 1977).

[20]"Urban Development in Imperial China," in *The City in Late Imperial China,* ed. G. W. Skinner (Stanford, Calif.: Stanford University Press, 1977).

systems: a bottom-up hierarchy created by the unsteady filling in of markets with the growth of production of trade; and a top-down hierarchy created self-consciously by imperial agents intent on conquest and control. The parallels to Mumford's principles of accumulation and control are engaging. But even more engaging is Skinner's proposal that the relative position of any community within the two hierarchies determines its internal structure—with a location that stands "higher" with respect to the market hierarchy than with respect to imperial control tending to give priority of power and space to merchants and marketing rather than to administrators and administration. (The proposal avoids tautology because Skinner's model specifies the expected sizes and geographic positions of places at different levels of the two hierarchies.) Clearly, these models of space economy provide the means, at least in principle, of bridging the gap between urban spatial structure and large-scale social processes.

The third way across is very different. It is to conceive of the city as a theater for the human drama. The main problems and developments of the drama are very general; but they work themselves out in a particular setting, and in response to its particularities. Richard Trexler, for example, has shown us the great families of Florence living out the rivalry among patron–client networks that informed the lives of Italy's Renaissance cities.[21] Trexler portrayed the public display of wealth and following in the great civic processions as a context in which the failure to command deference and envy not only cost a family self-esteem but also decreased its influence in the city's subsequent affairs. In the process, he treated the importance of family palaces and public squares as settings for the ritualized combat among clienteles. Thus, the organization and use of urban space become part of the struggle for power.

Similarly, John Brewer has used the popular movements and electoral struggles of the eighteenth-century London area to examine the emergence of articulated demands for popular sovereignty in Britain and its American colonies.[22] More than a "case study," the analysis of Lon-

[21]R. Trexler, *Public Life in Renaissance Florence* (New York: Academic Press, 1980).

[22]*Party Ideology and Popular Politics at the Accession of George III* (Cambridge: Cambridge University Press, 1976); "The Wilkites and the Law, 1763–74: A Study of Radical Notions of Governance," in *An Ungovernable People,* ed. J. Brewer and J. Styles (New Brunswick, N.J.: Rutgers University Press, 1980); "Theatre and Counter-Theater in Georgian Politics: The Mock Elections at Garrat," *Radical History Review* 22 (1980):7–40.

don's struggles reveals the development of an ideology, a vocabulary, and a repertoire of action that would eventually become dominant in the English-speaking world. Brewer's analysis is an imperfect example of the city-as-theater, for it slights the day-to-day use of the city's space: the ways that file after file of protesters marched through the Strand on the way to petition the king of St. James or Parliament at Westminster; the incorporation of Southwark's King's Bench Prison (site of John Wilkes's imprisonment in 1768) into the Sacred Way of Wilkite processions; the use of local coffeehouses as rallying places for different trades and their interests; the significance of Mansion House and Guildhall as points of reference for civic and corporate power. Yet Brewer's portrayal of the turbulent gatherings on the hustings during the contested elections of the later eighteenth century opens the way to an integration of large political processes, extending far beyond London, with the uses of the city's territory as a stage for the working out of those processes.

WHAT RIME HAS THIS SPACE?

Global reach, space economy, and city-as-theater mitigate the urban historian's dilemma, but they do not resolve it completely. Global-reach accounts beg the question of the mechanisms translating very large social processes into the forms of cities. Space-economy accounts say little about the relations of dominance, subordination, solidarity, and conflict that inform any city's social structure. Presenting the city as theater almost inevitably takes the stage setting for granted, instead of explaining how it changes. Of course, any theory that purports to explain everything probably explains nothing. Nevertheless, we might hope for a more comprehensive analysis of the connections between urban spatial structure and large social processes than any of the three approaches now permits.

At the moment, the problem does not result mainly from our ignorance about cities as such. It lies in the relative weakness of the available accounts of the large social processes impinging on cities. An unduly technological account of industrialization has hidden the role of the accumulation and concentration of capital in the shaping of Western cities. An excessively optimistic account of state making has disguised the importance of coercion, extraction, and surveillance in creating the patrolled metropolis we know today. The conjunction of capitalism and state making created the contemporary Western city, with its extraordinary concatenation of large workplaces, residential segregation by class, high-priced central locations, massive governmental intervention to assure the profitable use of those central locations, huge but shaky systems of transportation, and political struggle over the collection and allocation of municipal revenues. Conceptions of global reach, space economy, and city-as-theater can each contribute to our understanding of the ways in which capitalism and state making performed these dubious wonders. But it will take renewed conceptions of capitalism and state making themselves to surmount the urban historian's dilemma. With those renewed conceptions, urban historians will begin to understand the Western city as the arena in which capitalist power and state power not only set the main themes of the drama but also rearrange the very stage on which its players act.

ACKNOWLEDGMENTS

I have confined most of the paper's discussion to American examples, in order to keep it focused. I am grateful to Dawn Hendricks for help with bibliography, and to Olivier Zunz for several valuable suggestions, including a reminder of the significance to the problem of the paper of Allen Kulikoff's work on Boston.

CHAPTER 8

City Planning

Images of the Ideal and the Existing City

THOMAS A. REINER AND MICHAEL A. HINDERY

Images are, in Kenneth Boulding's words, "subjective knowledge."[1] To add to an understanding of the city-planning profession, close attention should be given to images held and purveyed by planners. The behavior both of planners and of their clients depends on images—not the least that class of behavior called *research*.

Images are clusters of ideas and knowledge: they are holistic and aggregative. They serve as shorthand, akin to metaphor, organizing values as well as information.[2] They are essential parts of the advocate's communication and form part of the discourse between the administrator and the public at large. Images are one form of expressing goals for the environment.

Images of the city exist on three planes. Each class of image has its own structure and its own place in urban planning endeavors, in establishing underlying perceptions of the city. This paper shows that each has been an integral part of the field's development and that planners' writings and activities embrace each type of image.

1. The city serves as an image for the articulation of an encompassing ideal.

[1]*The Image* (Ann Arbor: University of Michigan Press, 1956), 11.
[2]Boulding; D. R. Weimer, *The City as Metaphor* (New York: Random House, 1966).

Thomas A. Reiner • Department of Regional Science, University of Pennsylvania, Philadelphia, Pennsylvania.   *Michael A. Hindery* • Department of American Civilization, University of Pennsylvania, Philadelphia, Pennsylvania.

2. The city is seen as an expression of other constructs, artifacts, and processes.
3. A given city is effectively identified and understood by reference to customs, structure, and the colophons that serve as that city's image bearers.

The city as an image for the expression of an overarching concept has a long history. In classical antiquity, the cosmos was represented by the crossroads within a walled confine. Jerusalem, heaven on earth, called forth the familiar city as a domain expressive of the human potential for holiness.[3] Innumerable works of art and literature, music, film, and theater have seized on the city as the evocative symbol for expression of contemporary conditions, the promise of wealth, the fount of energy, and the source of anxiety or oppression.[4] Within such a cultural milieu, the city planner also works. It would appear to be no accident that utopias have widely (though not universally) been given an urban form, for here, civilization, the civic existence, is at its peak expression.[5]

The contemporary city, in the second use of imagery, is seen by means of a variety of images, often conflicting: as a factory or a market writ large, as an organic entity akin to a plant, or as an all-encompassing structure made of component building blocks. Such images compactly communicate ideology, both by virtue of their affect and by highlighting elements of their content. These images, too, suggestively serve to identify possible relationships within complex urban structures and to provide research agendas.

Each city has over the years seen symbols attached to its very existence. These serve to give identity to the place, to its inhabitants, and to its history and present activities. Some are, as images, accidental, some

[3]See, e.g., A. Rapoport, "On the Cultural Origins of Settlements," in *Introduction to Urban Planning*, ed. A. J. Catanese and J. C. Snyder (New York: McGraw-Hill, 1979). Also, "The City was . . . primarily a symbolic representation of the universe itself . . ." L. Mumford, "Utopia, the City, and the Machine," *Daedelus* 94 (Spring 1965):682.
[4]For example, the collection of excerpts in A. Strauss, *The Image of the City* (Chicago: Aldine, 1968).
[5]D. Riesman, "Some Observations on Community Plans and Utopia," *Yale Law Journal* 58 (Dec. 1947):174–200; G. Kateb, "Utopias and Utopianism," *International Encyclopedia of the Social Sciences* (New York: Macmillan/Free Press, 1968); I. Todd and M. Wheeler, *Utopia* (New York: Harmony, 1978); F. E. Manuel and F. P. Manuel, *Utopian Thought in the Western World* (Cambridge: Belknap, 1979).

contrived. The Eiffel Tower, the Big Apple, and the Kremlin evoke Paris, New York, and Moscow. Pamplona to the outsider is almost synonymous with the running of the bulls, and New Orleans' and Rio's carnivals are similarly linked. On a more homely level, orienting points, structures, and events, as Kevin Lynch's investigations disclosed, all shape the public's knowledge and appreciation of the city and people's orientation within the urban environment.[6]

In brief, images can take three different forms: there are images *of* the city, which use the city, generic, as a metaphor to express some crucial aspects of the human condition; there are images *for* the city, which seek to suggest an idea, an artifact, or a process to symbolize one or a class of cities and thereby to establish its essential qualities and meaning; and there are images *in* the city, which by their very association in the specific give character and identity to place.

Each of these image dimensions has a part to play in the work of city planners. We will give particular attention to the images that shape planners' views of the city, and to the images that planners use to communicate their craft and findings to their clients and to the public at large. In particular, we shall consider three bodies of works. The first are certain ideal community proposals, such as Ebenezer Howard's Garden City and Le Corbusier's plans for the rebuilding of the twentieth-century metropolis as his Ville Radieuse. These have helped give identity to the field as well as serving as representative statements of urban development goals.[7] Second, we shall review a series of planning texts (the so-called LPA volumes) as, over several decades and volumes, these have served to bring to planners and a wider public current knowledge of the planning field.[8] Third, we shall analyze a sequence of plans and development

---

[6]Strauss; K. Lynch, *The Image of the City* (Cambridge: M.I.T. Press, 1960).

[7]These are described and discussed in R. Fishman, *Urban Utopias in the Twentieth Century* (New York: Basic Books, 1977); and by T. A. Reiner, *The Place of the Ideal Community in Urban Planning* (Philadelphia: University of Pennsylvania Press, 1963).

[8]International City Managers' Association (ICMA), *Local Planning Administration*, ed. L. Segoe (Chicago: Author, 1941); 2nd ed., ed. H. K. Menhinick (1948); 3rd ed., ed. M. McLean (1959); ICMA, *Principles and Practices of Urban Planning*, ed. W. Goodman and E. Freund (Chicago: Author, 1968); ICMA, *The Practice of Local Government Planning*, ed. F. So et al. (Washington, D.C.: Author, 1979). Also W. Bair, "Urban Planners: Doctors or Midwives," *Public Administration Review* 37 (Nov. 1977):671; M. G. Scott, *American Planning Since 1890 . . .* (Berkeley: University of California Press, 1969); I. Stollman, "The Values of the City Planners," in ICMA (1979).

strategies for one urban area, Philadelphia, from the perspective of the images that these documents convey.

Ideal communities have many uses and reflect a variety of creators' motivations.[9] They serve as models to test new concepts, or to assess the consequences of a wholehearted commitment to a given goal. They also serve to communicate and propagate certain shared values to those outside the planning profession: procedural values (e.g., the notion of the holistic setting of an ideal, or the concept of control of growth) and substantive values (e.g., the separation of distinct activities). To communicate such values, ideal communities may use the vocabulary of image. The image may be explicitly presented: the city as workplace or as marketplace. Or the image may be more subtle, as an integral part of the proposal. The critic or user of the ideal community is then left with the task of eliciting the image content.

Half a dozen governing images have been repeatedly employed to establish the character of the ideal city: the village, the block, the skyscraper, the marketplace, the factory, and the body. We shall briefly discuss the elements of each and refer to examples in the ideal-communities literature.

The village, with its connotations of stability, integration and solidarity, self-sufficiency, maintenance of traditional ways, and integration of land and capital, represents a challenging reaction to the burdens of industrialization, to the excesses of the industrial city, to "coketown" (Mumford). One finds elements of the village ideal in Howard's Garden City and the host of derivatives or subsequent formulations. The compromises or shortcomings of the ideal reflect the need to accommodate productive enterprise within the scheme: the modern alternative to the farm or in-house craftwork as locus of employment.[10]

The block, or rather the block front, is an urban image carrying ideals of both differentiation (appropriate to contemporary city life) and homogeneity (sufficient to assure mutual support). The block front is particularly the domain of the growing child and the housebound adult, though in everyone's calendar (as shown on the weekend) the block is home. The undifferentiated, alienating city is the foil against which the designer proposes the ideal. Among the ideal communities with this orientation

[9]Reiner, Chapter 3.

[10]L. Mumford, *The City in History* (New York: Harcourt Brace, 1961), Chapter 15; E. Howard, *Garden Cities of Tomorrow*, 2nd ed. (London: Sonnenschein, 1898); Fishman.

are the Goodmans' "paradigm II" and strong elements of the Perry Neighborhood. Of course, the ideology was given strong expression in Jane Jacobs' *The Death and Life of Great American Cities*. There are elements of recollection of the guild-based medieval European town in these image-based ideal communities.[11]

The skyscraper has as its core idea the articulation of modern technology, the notion of ease and comfort, shelter from a basically hostile environment, and the promise of close and more efficient human interaction in a variety of roles. There is the promise of efficiency as distances are sharply reduced. Le Corbusier's models, and more recently Soleri's, have in a variety of political milieux sought to design such an urban world. Variations of such proposals seek the construction of largely self-contained structures for the conducting under one roof of most of the day-to-day activities of all or part of a "city's" population. Generally, communal and other services are provided within the building, with varying degrees of socialization (e.g., early child care and food preparation). Easy communication within the edifice replaces the complex and inefficient circulation in existing urban areas.[12]

If the preceding three images focus on the residential sphere of human existence, the next images turn to other spheres. The city as factory (generically as a workplace) or as marketplace stimulated the imagination of utopists well before the ideal community genre. Economic analysis has been one of the intellectual props that conceive of a vital justification—if not origin—of the city in the spatially proximate juxtaposition of factors of production: capital and labor. The factory has, of course, stratified the work force, and so segregation of the population (in contrast to the integration noted earlier) is to be expected. The logic of land use as well as of other design features is governed by the production imperative. Examples from the socialist (N. A. Miliutin) and the capitalist (T. Garnier) world abound. The Goodmans' third paradigm of ideal community is one that carries company-town ideology to its logical extreme.

[11]Perry, "The Neighborhood Unit," *Regional Survey of New York and Its Environs*, Vol. 7 (New York: Regional Plan Association, 1929); Jacobs, *The Death and Life of Great American Cities* (New York: Random House, 1961); P. Goodman and P. Goodman, *Communitas* (Chicago: University of Chicago Press, 1947); Mumford, *The City in History*, especially Chapter 10; also, e.g., H. Pirenne, *Medieval Cities* (Princeton, N.J.: Princeton University Press, 1925).
[12]LeCorbusier/C. E. Jeanneret-Gris, *La Ville Radieuse* (Paris: Éditions de l'Architecture d'Aujourd'hui, 1933) (and discussion by Fishman); P. Soleri, *Arcology, the City in the Image of Man* (Cambridge: M.I.T. Press, 1969).

The proposed distribution of activities and land uses serves to enhance productive efficiency alone.[13]

The city as market represents an alternative, as the Goodmans themselves constructed their triad of paradigms. Exchange rather than production is the most important form of human intercourse: the aesthetic of display, ease of access, excitement of people, and goods in abundance characterize the models. Whether reflective of the medieval bourg's arcades and stalls or the contemporary shopping center, the market image conveys life, stimulation, creativity, and openness. In addition to the Goodmans' first paradigm, the market image appears to underlie the ecological models of the Chicago school (e.g., Burgess) and a number of other ideal communities.[14]

The city as an organic entity, a plant or an animal, reflects in part the image of the body politic. No portion can survive long without the others. Accretion and retraction in incremental steps characterize change, just as cells continually are born, live, die, and are replaced. Microunits of the acts combine repeatedly in predictable fashion to establish the whole. The entity, the city, has life independent of any component. Design elements replicate natural, rather than machine-made products. Eliel Saarinen was just one of a number of writers who have tried to spell out such a picture.[15]

[13]Milituin, *Sotsgorod: The Problem of Building Socialist Cities*, trans. A. Sprague (Cambridge: M.I.T. Press, 1974); T. Garnier, *Une Cité Industrielle* (Paris: Vincent, 1918); Goodman and Goodman. For works analyzing the socialist city, see R. J. Osborn and T. A. Reiner, "Soviet City Planning . . ." *Journal of the American Institute of Planners* 28 (Nov. 1962):239–250; T. A. Reiner and R. H. Wilson, "Planning and Decision Making in the Soviet City: Rent, Land, and Urban Form," in *The Socialist City: Special Structure and Urban Policy*, ed. R. A. French and F. E. I. Hamilton (New York: Wiley, 1979) (and other papers in the French and Hamilton volume). On the underlying economic justification of cities, see, for example, W. Isard, *Location and Space-Economy* (Cambridge: M.I.T. Press, 1956); E. M. Hoover, *An Introduction to Regional Economics* (New York: Knopf, 1971), Chapter 10; H. W. Richardson, *Urban Economics* (Harmondsworth, England: Penguin, 1971).

[14]Goodman and Goodman; E. W. Burgess and D. J. Bogue, *Urban Sociology* (Chicago: Phoenix-University of Chicago Press, 1968); also W. Christaller, *Central Places in Southern Germany*, trans. C. W. Baskin (Englewood Cliffs, N.J.: Prentice-Hall, 1966).

[15]Saarinen, *The City: Its Growth, Its Decay, Its Future* (New York: Reinhold, 1943); Rapoport; T. A. Reiner, "Policy Planning: Environmental and Utopian Aspects," *Architectural Design*, 45 (June 1975):359–363. Also Mumford, *The City in History*, Chapter 10.

These images reflect discouragement with, doubt about, and disdain for the industrialized modern metropolis.[16] Ideal communities share, in large measure, a search for identity in an undifferentiated mass. Their design also seeks to articulate viable roles for their inhabitants in the belief that city dwellers should function more effectively than they have in the past: as family members, or as consumers, or as producers. The images implicitly carry within them ideals or preferences for a number of structural features. The concern with control of growth or rational adaptation to growth (by means of adding repeatedly integral units) surfaces again and again. We note repeated efforts to link scale to some measure of human experience. And the search for order is a recurrent theme.

Today's planners and the plans that they produce show the relevance and vitality of these images. The planners' works seem to reflect an amalgam of such constructs. We shall now turn to another more prosaic body of writings: texts for the planning professional. Urban images are implicitly embedded in these technical guides, which have kept up with American practice for more than four decades. The series of texts prepared under the auspices of the International City Manager's Association was initially titled *Local Planning Administration*. Now in its fifth edition (1979), and widely distributed, the series had its origins as an adjunct to a correspondence course in the 1930s for "top level administrators."[17]

The first published edition appeared, in 1941, at the end of the Depression and with the start of World War II. The volume was edited in its finished version by the respected planning consultant Ladislas Sego; in fact, parts are credited to his authorship.

The volume's emphasis, as is the avowed emphasis of each volume in the series, is on planning, rather than on the city itself. Yet a number of features of the city emerge from the pages of the text; these help to illuminate the changing perspectives of the field. The city is seen, in the first edition, mainly as a physical artifact. It is a collection of buildings set

[16]These resonate to the same questioning of the industrial city as does Mumford in *The City in History*. U.S. writings in this vein are part of a significant tradition in American thought: see T. Bender, *Toward an Urban Vision: Ideas and Institutions in Nineteenth Century America* (Lexington: University of Kentucky Press, 1975); M. White and L. White, *The Intellectual Versus the City* (Cambridge: M.I.T. Press, 1962). Also note the criticism of this position, as in C. N. Glaab and A. T. Brown, *A History of Urban America* (New York: Macmillan, 1967), and L. Marx, *The Machine and the Garden: Technology and the Pastoral Idea in America* (New York: Oxford University Press, 1964).
[17]See footnote 8 for full citations.

on streets and of activities with clearly defined and emphasized spatial identity. A mapping seems best to communicate the state of the city; surveys generate land maps. Indeed, the street map and plan are held to have enormous impact on city growth. Perhaps, with the benefit of hindsight, it may not be an exaggeration to say that the planner's image of the city was a set of building blocks. Their placement was at stake, though their general attributes and number were largely given. The Depression only slightly dampened the promotional tone of the planner's vision. The volume repeatedly and in several ways notes that the intervention in an essentially *laissez-faire* equilibrating environment is justified by the imperatives of urban growth. The building blocks grew sharply in number. Disorganization and a decline in the quality of the blocks' attributes resulted. The blocks had only dimly identifiable identity and characteristics (other than general land-use designation, bulk, and density—little could be known of the people who live or work in them, for example, or of their income, ethnic origin, etc.). The authors had in mind the search for the good life as a general economic and social purpose that is served by managing the physical structure.

By the time the third edition went to press (1959), the postwar "affluent society" and expansionist set of the nation was well ingrained in the planning domain as well. The volume, edited by Mary McLean, was written as a response to the preceding decade's "population explosion and attendant problems of urban growth." These problems were largely seen in a way that could still be expressed in land use terms; indeed, through much of the volume, the city and urban planning are seen with land use as the unit of analysis. No longer defining planning largely in physical terms, however, the volume calls for integrated economic and demographic studies. These served as basic background materials for the rational analysis that by now had been declared to be central to planning: not an art but an administrative process. Such a process was one that viewed the city as a "unity." There was no sense of underlying conflict. The planner, in fact, was a participant in efforts to channel growth and, in so doing, to search for the appropriate vision.

Perhaps the concept of an image was antithetical to the era, with its confidence in rational and comprehensive solutions with clearly defined propositions. If there was one, it might have been an ordered phalanx forging ahead—the managed solution—in sharp contrast with the inchoate mass of the unplanned city.

The current edition (dated 1979 and edited by Frank So) sees many of these emphases changed. The physical city, though not bypassed, has receded. The volume's first chapters deal with information, values, and management processes. Where the city as a physical entity surfaces, it is in the context of interaction among social, economic, and physical factors. It is, however, interesting that the chapter dedicated to the "Development Plan" looks to the physical plan as the comprehensive long-run instrument of change.

Whereas earlier editions focused on growth—of population and infrastructure, as well as the important component of housing—the 1979 volume self-consciously views the city as stable, and as possibly declining. The tone is one of maturity rather than exuberant adolescence. And whereas earlier editions discussed techniques of clearance or redevelopment in those cases where change was in order, the fifth edition calls for renewal, adaptive reuse, and preservation as the principles governing change. Whereas the earlier volumes spoke of the plan and the planning process as unifying principles, the authors in the most recent book call attention to competing goals and to conflict management. Planners themselves respond to plural values and are themselves actors among contending forces. Perhaps the most apt image underlying the pages is that of a frugally managed estate. No major changes are imminent. Conservation and low-key resource use set the tone. Contending parties seek to exploit the estate, but it is clear that not all will share equally in the frustrating distribution of the fruits of labor.

Philadelphia is the core of a large region characterized by many features of mature industrialization.[18] It originated as a planned town, and in the past decades, the city and the region have been well known for highly professional and innovative city and metropolitan planning. There are parallels between the city's planning initiatives and the imagery presented in the ideal community and professional planning literatures.

William Penn, the City's founder, proposed a "Greene Countrie Towne" for the land between the Delaware and Schuylkill rivers, some

---

[18]P. O. Muller, K. C. Meyer, and R. A. Cybriwsky, *Metropolitan Philadelphia: A Study of Conflicts and Social Cleavages* (Cambridge, Mass.: Ballinger, 1976). The three images of Philadelphia, as the City of Brotherly Love, the Green Country Town, and the Cradle of Liberty, date from the city's early days. They appear continuously and frequently in works about the city: histories, essays, and paintings all rely on this imagery. This reliance was demonstrated in the discussions and writings of a senior seminar in urban studies that the authors taught in the fall semester of 1981 at the University of Pennsylvania.

two miles square. The plan set aside open spaces and unrestricted access to the rivers. These were to provide breathing spaces for the heart of what Penn was sure would increasingly come to be a densely built-up city. The in-town lots were large, with ample space for gardens. The city's surroundings were to remain farmland. The master map of 1683 included a square of 10 acres in the town's center (subsequently moved two blocks) where the City Hall now stands, and four squares of 8 acres in each quarter of the fledgling city; these squares are still among Philadelphia's major form-giving features.[19]

Yet Penn was also concerned with the image that social conditions would give his new town, declaring that not its rare natural advantages but the character of its people would determine its destiny. Convinced that Philadelphia was to be a "holy experiment" providing "an asylum for the good and oppressed of all nations," Penn supplied the city with another image in the name he chose: *Philadelphia*, "City of Brotherly Love." Penn's intent was to people his town with environment-sensitive, hard-working, and considerate folk.[20]

As a setting for certain subsequent events, Philadelphia was destined to take on a third, dominant image. It is the "Cradle of Liberty," with a basis in the founder's notion of religious tolerance as well as the city's associations with the American Revolution and the writing of the Constitution. In Philadelphia, liberty was conceived, a new nation was born, and the first steps were taken toward national economic independence. From the earliest days, when Penn made his commitments to entrepreneurship, economic and political liberties were intertwined, as were the leaders from both domains. The land plan of 1683 was clearly designed to facilitate such an ambience. And to this day, the icons and the images of Philadelphia—given clear articulation in the spatial arrangement, which shows prominence attached to Independence Hall and the Liberty Bell, and in the dominance that, to this day, the statue of William Penn asserts over City Hall—remain as the best known features of the city and the elements of its urban design form.[21]

[19]A. N. B. Garvan, "Proprietary Philadelphia as Artifact," in *The Historian and the City*, ed. O. Handlin and J. Burchard (Cambridge: M.I.T. Press, 1963).

[20]E. D. Baltzell, *Puritan Boston and Quaker Philadelphia* (New York: Free Press, 1979); T. Cochran, *Pennsylvania: A Bicentennial History* (New York: Norton, 1978).

[21]L. D. Lafore and S. L. Lippincott, *Philadelphia, The Unexpected City* (Garden City, N.Y.: Doubleday, 1965); R. S. Wurman and J. A. Gallery, *Man Made Philadelphia* (Cambridge: M.I.T. Press, 1972).

Manufacturing changed Philadelphia in the nineteenth century and created new images for it. As the economic outlook became most strongly linked with industrial development, the perceptions of the city's economy became a microcosm of regional economics, which, in turn, was seen as a smaller scale replica of the national economy. Philadelphia came to serve as the industrial hub for a region of some 3 million people by the end of World War I.[22] The automobile, which changed patterns of settlement, and the challenge of relative affluence and a sense of industrial progress drew the attention of a number of civic leaders, who created the Regional Planning Federation of the Philadelphia Tri-State District. The organization prepared and published a regional plan, with the help of a number of consultants.[23] The document's chief concern was with land use planning, and with determining how the physical needs of a continually growing city (as yet the realities of the Depression had not hit home) could be met.

Philadelphia was viewed as the region's industrial and market center, its well-being basic to the larger area's residents. Projects under the plan were to provide amenities for the workshop, which appeared as Philadelphia's dominant image. The entities worthy of study were the components of industrial progress: primarily transportation and population distribution. Increased production was essential. The plan also reflected the provision that no large city nor any community within the environs would be self-contained. In tune with what was seen as requisite for the well-functioning workshop, the plan stressed the public good not only as "health, comfort, and happiness," but also as, for example, the provision of good rail and highway transportation. The latter was seen as vital for the access required for industrial development. This and other projects meant to strengthen the physical infrastructure constituted the report's planning agenda. The image contained within the plan is that of a workshop that must produce continued growth in population and in the various productive and exchange sectors. Growth and improvement in economic outlook were intimately intertwined. The volume reflects the faith in industry so characteristic of the last decades of the past century and the first half of the present one. The city came to represent the locus of the

[22]*Philadelphia: Work, Space, Family, and Group Experience in the Nineteenth Century,* ed. T. Herschberg (New York: Oxford University Press, 1981); S. B. Warner, *The Private City: Philadelphia in Three Periods of Its Growth* (Philadelphia: University of Pennsylvania Press, 1968).

[23]*Regional Planning: The Region—Past, Present, and Future* (Philadelphia: Author, 1936).

meeting—at times, the collision—of machines with people. Consistent with the then-fledgling scientific management movement, a plan was seen as a reflection of an exact science. The diagnosis of ills and the establishment of the "facts" would generate the proper prescription. The authors emphasized the physical city, for what was visible, three-dimensional, could be manipulated. Altered spatial relationships would achieve the practical ends of efficiency and convenience, and the physical environment would shape peoples' lives. The ideal Greater Philadelphia, like all contemporary ideal-community designs, had a strong architectonic, engineering foundation.[24]

World War II and the immediately following years witnessed a change in Philadelphia's role. Declines in the significance of manufacturing and industry in the city, along with the lessened importance of the central business district relative to suburban shopping, yielded a subtle change in the policy image. Between 1947 and 1952, the City Planning Commission, under the direction of Edmund Bacon, prepared a series of plans for Philadelphia. These correctly anticipated the city's new role as a provider of services and as a place of exchange. Whereas industry in the earlier era was quite widely distributed over the city, the new functions resulted in a sharp focus on Philadelphia's core. The plans called for the removal of industrial railroad yards, the produce market, and other such uses from the center city. These were to be replaced with office towers and retail centers, with some attention given to the housing generated by the demands of the new work force. The downtown of the city became well engineered and a true "center." The image of the city can perhaps best be expressed as that of the marketplace, hopefully for a large region.[25]

The 1950s saw a new form of home rule in place and the installation of reform government. An important facet of each was the commitment to rational management and, specifically, to the most forward-looking and technically competent urban planning.[26] Out of this commitment came a

[24]Ibid., Scott.
[25]E. Bacon, *The Design of Cities*, rev. ed. (New York: Viking, 1974); *Journal of the American Institute of Planners*, "Special Issue: Planning and Development in Philadelphia," ed. R. B. Mitchell, Vol. 26 (Aug. 1960).
[26]*Journal of the American Institute of Planners*; J. Reichly, *The Art of Government: Reform of Organization Politics in Philadelphia* (New York: Fund for the Republic, 1959).

series of proposals designed to implement the center-city "market"—and in 1960 came a citywide comprehensive plan.[27]

The comprehensive plan was built on the premise that the city is the means for bringing together people and the facilities that serve them. As in all plans, there was concern with improving the economic base: through increasing the vitality of the productive and exchange base, and through strengthening the tax base. Such improvement can result from establishing a strong central business district, which sits atop a hierarchy of communities and service centers, which, in turn, are based on shared interests in a sense of place. Efficient communication is provided within a system essentially in equilibrium: land use that generates traffic and transit routes equal to demand; industrial and commercial space equal to the needs for land to keep the labor force occupied; and income of the workers that generates rents for various densities of residential land.

The Comprehensive Plan of 1960, written perhaps at the apogee of the acceptance of scientific planning in the United States, exudes the confidence that a comprehensive analysis of the many facets of urban existence, as well as a consistent development of various elements of the city's structure, could yield an urban future at once balanced and satisfying for many interests. The plan does recognize a competitive world— between cities. Capital improvements are justified as the price that must be paid for the maintenance of economic standing in a national urban system. There is thus a consistency with the call in planning texts to give increasing emphasis to economic factors in planning analyses. The strategy of development is largely expressed in terms of economic aims.[28]

---

[27]Philadelphia City Planning Commission, *Comprehensive Plan: Physical Development Plan for the City of Philadelphia* (Philadelphia: Author, 1960); also Delaware Valley Regional Planning Commission, *The Delaware Valley Plan* (Philadelphia: Author, 1966).

[28]Within a decade, the confidence expressed (for example, in the ICMA manual, 1959 edition) became muted. See, for example, *Urban Planning in Transition*, ed. E. Erber (New York: Grossman, 1970); *Planning in America: Learning from Turbulence*, ed. D. R. Godschalk (Washington, D.C.: American Institute of Planners, 1974); R. Goodman, *After the Planners* (New York: Simon and Schuster, 1971). The questioning of planning decisions and the growth of advocate organizations in Philadelphia sparked conflict and challenged established institutions: see, for example, P. Levy, *Queens Village: The Eclipse of Community* (Philadelphia: Institute for the Study of Civic Values, 1978); T. A. Reiner, R. J. Sugarman, and J. S. Reiner, *The Crosstown Controversy, A Case Study*, Transporation Study Center of the University of Pennsylvania (1970).

Efforts to focus on the problems of the city have become more broad and integrated in the intervening years, in part as social concerns have come to dominate urban agendas. Pragmatism and incrementalism have become the dominant approach, and the greatest resource the city has is now identified as its people. Rather than talking about needed facilities, as had earlier plans, the Mayor's Urban Strategy of 1978 identified a planning process that would facilitate active participation by neighborhood-based organizations and public-private partnerships, and that would emphasize fiscal realism and management; a rational and systematic approach to long-term development priorities would necessitate decisions and commitments.[29] It is as if the image of the city is given by a multitude of round tables, where discussions among conflicting neighborhoods and contending interest groups is held with the hope of identifying common ground and commitments. Such an image—although consistent with the view of many organizations at the neighborhood level at the same time that these questioned the city's commitments—suggests looking at the city from street level rather than from the skyline, with its offices and boardrooms. People—not machines, not abstractions—are the focus. Differentiations within the population are valued, not transcended or suppressed. Conflict is recognized as inevitable, even welcome. The interactability of many problems is recognized. Within a year, a national policy document gave legitimacy to the needs of cities like Philadelphia, and its neighborhoods, as communities in distress.[30]

These comments can hardly do justice to the scope and the technical competence of the series of documents; and, of course, there are numerous other planning initiatives associated with Philadelphia's development. We do wish to note, however, that the planner's image—whether the workshop, the marketplace, or another—seems to reflect the times as well as the essential background of the imager and his or her ideological and professional position. The postwar decades saw a succession of specialists take on a dominant role in urban planning. Bacon's training in and commitment to civic design have an impact to this day; his presence was intensely felt in the first stages. Economists, together with land use analysts and modelers, left their mark on the middle years of the city's and

[29]Philadelphia Mayor, *The City of Philadelphia: An Urban Strategy* (Philadelphia: Mayor's Office, 1978).
[30]U.S. President, *The President's 1978 National Urban Policy Report* (Washington, D.C.: U.S. Dept. of Housing and Urban Development, 1978).

the metropolitan planning bodies. The policy managers, public entrepreneurs, and developers have been perhaps the most influential figures of the past decade. The map, the model, and the decision matrix
have in succession come to stand as images of the planners' tools.[31]

---

[31]It would be unjust to ignore totally local planners' activism and concern with
distributive justice. A period in the 1960s, roughly equivalent with the years of
the War on Poverty, saw an institutionalized decentralization of resource allocation, a commitment (if only partial) to social goals, and a recognition that distinct
constituencies had distinct needs. To achieve such a commitment, a strong
locality or neighborhood presence was built into the planning system consistent
with a view of the city as composed of separate communities. To some degree,
formal planning structure reflects these areas' interests to this day.

PART III

Reflections on Context and the Interpretation of Urban Images

CHAPTER 9

Reconsidering The Image of the City

KEVIN LYNCH

The Image of the City was published over 20 years ago, and it is still listed in bibliographies.[1] It is time to wonder what it led to. The research was done by a small group with no training in the methods they used, and no literature to guide them. Several motives led them to the study:

1. An interest in the possible connection between psychology and the urban environment, at a time when most psychologists—at least, those in the field of perception—preferred controlled experiments in the laboratory to the wandering variables of the complicated, real environment. We hoped to tempt some of them out into the light of day.

2. Fascination with the aesthetics of the city landscape, at a time when most U.S. planners shied away from the subject, because it was "a matter of taste" and had a low priority.

3. Persistent wonder about how to evaluate a city, as architects do so automatically when presented with a building design. Shown a city plan, planners would look for technical flaws, estimate quantities, or analyze trends, as if they were contractors about to bid on the job. We hoped to think about what a city should be, and we were looking for possibilities of designing directly at that scale.

4. Hope of influencing planners to pay more attention to those who live in a place—to the actual human experience of a city, and how it should affect city policy.

[1] K. Lynch (Cambridge: M.I.T. Press, 1960).

Kevin Lynch • Carr-Lynch Associates, and Professor of City Planning Emeritus, Massachusetts Institute of Technology, Cambridge, Massachusetts.

These motives found an early outlet in an erratic seminar on the aesthetics of the city in 1952, which considered, among several other similar themes, the question of how people actually found their way about the streets of big cities. Various other unconnected ideas sprouted during a subsequent fellowship year spent walking the streets of Florence, which were recorded in some brief and unpublished "Notes on City Satisfactions." These ideas matured during 1954, when I had the opportunity of working with Gyorgy Kepes on a Rockefeller grant devoted to the "perceptual form of the city." As we walked the Boston streets and wrote notes to each other, and as I listened to his torrent of ideas on perception and daily experience, the minor theme of city orientation grew into the major theme of the mental image of the environment.

Undoubtedly, there were many other less explicit influences: from John Dewey, with his emphasis on experience, to ideas of the "transactional" psychologists, with their view of perception as an active transaction between person and place. I had done fairly extensive reading in psychology, without finding much that was helpful. I had always learned much more from stories, memoirs, and the accounts of anthropologists. We were not then aware of K. E. Boulding's key study, *The Image*,[2] which was published at the same time as our own work and became an important theoretical underpinning of it. The role of the environmental image was an idea in the air, however.

The first study was too simple to be quite respectable. We interviewed 30 people about their mental picture of the inner city of Boston, and then we repeated the exercise in Jersey City (which we guessed might be characterless) and Los Angeles (booked as the motorized city). We took Boston because it was there, and we knew it and liked it. We asked people what came to their mind about the city, and to make a sketch map of it, and to take imaginary trips through it. We asked them to describe its distinctive elements, to recognize and place various photographs, and (with a smaller sample) to go on actual walks with us. Later, we stopped people in the streets and asked for directions to places. Meanwhile, other members of the team, uncontaminated by all this interview work, surveyed the town, in order to make some guesses about what a typical image would be, given the physical form.

This small group of informants produced an astonishing flood of perceptions. At times, as we listened to their tapes and studied their draw-

[2]Ann Arbor: University of Michigan Press, 1956.

ings, we seemed to be moving down the same imaginary streets with them, watching the pavements rise and turn, the buildings and open spaces appear, feeling the same pleasant shock of recognition, or being puzzled by some mental gray hole, where there should have been some piece of the city. Our conclusion—or perhaps the hardening of our pre-conceived notion—was that people had a relatively coherent and detailed mental image of their city, which had been created in an interaction between self and place, and that this image was both essential to their actual function, and also important to their emotional well-being. These individual images had many common features—similarities that arose from common human strategies of cognition, common culture and experi-ence, and the particular physical form of the place that they lived in. Thus, an observer, familiar with the local culture and with the general nature of city images, could, after a careful study of the town, make predictions about likely common features and patterns of organization in the mental images of that place. We developed methods for eliciting these mental images from people, as well as a way of classifying and presenting them. We asserted that the quality of that city image was important to well-being and should be considered in designing or modify-ing any locality. Thus, orientation had been expanded into a general method of analyzing place, and a vivid and coherent mental image had been elevated to a general principle of city design. Later, this idea was expanded further, to include a vivid image of time as well as place.[3]

All of this from talking to 30 people! It was not surprising that there were sharp criticisms. The obvious remark was that the sample of people was far too small, and too biased, to permit of such sweeping assertions. Our handful of interviewees were all young, middle-class people, and most of them were professionals. The attack was well mounted; and yet it failed. The original work has by now been replicated in many commu-nities, large and small, in North and South America, Europe, and Asia, because the method is cheap and rather fun to do. In every case, the basic ideas have held, with the important proviso that images are much modi-fied by culture and familiarity, as was predicted in our original specula-tions. But the existence and role of the place image, its basic elements, and the techniques of eliciting and analyzing it seem astonishingly similar in some very diverse cultures and places. We were lucky.

A second criticism was that the techniques of office and field inter-

---

[3]K. Lynch, *What Time Is This Place?* (Cambridge: M.I.T. Press, 1972).

view, of photo recognition, and of map drawing were inadequate to get at the true mental image, so deeply lodged in the mind. Map drawing, in particular, is too difficult for most people, and thus it is a very misleading index of what they known. Even just talking may be an exercise in pleasing the interviewer more than a revelation of inner patterns, many of which may be inaccessible to the person.

In principle, the comment is just. What is in the mind is an elusive thing. Environmental psychologists are busy debating the relative merits of various tricks for entering that fascinating realm. But one can reply that, although each method may elicit only a piece of the internal picture, and that may be distorted as well as partial, yet, if a sufficient array of probes is employed, a composite picture develops that is not very far from the truth. Of course, it may only be the tip of the iceberg, whose base is hidden far below, but the tip is the tip of a real iceberg, nonetheless. Luckily for us, the environmental image is usually not a painful subject for most people, something to be defended by unconscious barriers. People like to talk about it.

The possibility remains that the image brought forth for discussion in an interview is not the same one that is used in actually operating in a city. This possibility can be checked only by working with people as they actually move about, as we did in our street interviews. But even if the two images were disjunctive (which does not seem to be the case), the interview image can still have an important social and emotional role.

A method war erupted over map drawing, which was one of the techniques we used that seemed at first to take everyone's fancy. Drawing is indeed an unfamiliar act, as compared with talking, not only for most interviewees, but also (which may be the real problem) for most interviewers as well. Yet I cling to the value of drawing as a means of expression, especially of spatial ideas, despite our cultural downgrading of visual communication (a downgrading that may now be reversed, at least in a passive sense, for the current TV generation). Much can be read from amateur maps, in supplement to verbal comments, if one allows for common drafting difficulties. Drawings convey emotional tone as well as substance, just as actual speech does.

Whereas researchers worried over our methods, designers were fearful that these same methods might usurp their central creative skill—that a "science of design" might suddenly seize their territory. Image analysis would then lead automatically to form decisions, untouched by the free imagination. But their fears were quite unfounded. Analysis can describe a present situation and its consequences, and even—much more uncertainly—predict the consequences of some altered arrangement, but it is powerless to generate new possibilities. This is the irreplaceable power of the creative mind. Image studies, although they may threaten designer pretenses about how other people feel about places, are no more threatening to the central act of design than is an analysis of structure or of climate. On the contrary, perception studies could support and enrich design.

The most critical attack of all was that the study was overblown, if it meant to identify a basic principle of place quality. It focused on way finding, which was surely a secondary problem for most people. If lost in a city, one can always ask the way or consult a map. The study may have analyzed the nature of the way-finding image accurately enough. But it only assumed its importance and never demonstrated it. What do people care if they have a vivid image of their locality? And aren't they delighted by surprise and mystery?

This was a more direct hit. The study never proved its basic assumption, except indirectly, via the emotional tone of the interviews: the repeated remarks about the pleasure of recognition and knowledge, the satisfaction of identification with a distinctive home place, and the displeasure of being lost or of being consigned to a drab environment. Succeeding studies have continued to collect this indirect evidence. The idea can be linked to the role of self-identity in psychological development, in the belief that self-identity is reinforced by a strong identity of place and time. A powerful place image can be presumed to buttress group identity. The pleasures of perceiving a complex, vivid landscape are frequently experienced and recorded. Mature, self-confident people can cope with drab or confused surroundings, but such places are crucial difficulties for those internally disoriented, or for those at some critical stage of their development.[4] It is reasonable to think that a featureless environment deprives us of some very important emotional satisfactions. These convictions have been reinforced by many expressions of popular culture, as well as findings in psychology, art, and the sociology of small groups. (As to the role of surprise and disorder, I return to that below.) Nevertheless, it is true that this central assumption remains an assumption, however it may be shored up by anecdote, personal experience, or its connection to the structure of other ideas.

If these four criticisms—of sample size, method, design usurpation,

---

[4]H. F. Searles, *The Non-Human Environment* (New York: International University Press, 1960).

and basic relevance—were the important ones made at the time, there were also other unremarked cracks in our structure, which only opened up later. The first, and most immediately dangerous, was the neglect of observer variation, which we passed over in order to show the effect of physical variation. This neglect was deliberate and explicit, as the role of visual form had been widely ignored, and it was also important to show that a given physical reality produces some common images of place, at least within one culture. Image variation among observers—due to class, age, gender, familiarity, role, and other such factors—was expected to be a finding of subsequent studies. Indeed, it was. Broader samples, such as those interviewed by Appleyard in Ciudad Guayana,[5] made clear how social class and habitual use cause people to see a city with very different eyes.

What was not foreseen, however, was that this study, whose principal aim was to urge on designers the necessity of consulting those who live in a place, had at first a diametrically opposite result. It seemed to many planners that here was a new technique—complete with the magical classifications of node, landmark, district, edge, and path—that allowed a designer to predict the public image of any existing city or new proposal. For a time, plans were fashionably decked out with nodes and all the rest. There was no attempt to reach out to actual inhabitants, because that effort would waste time and might be upsetting. As before, professionals were imposing their own views and values on those they served. The new jargon was appropriated to that old end, and its moral was stood on its head. Instead of opening a channel by which citizens might influence design, the new words became another means of distancing them from it. Indeed, the words were dangerous precisely because they were useful. They afforded a new way of talking about the qualities of large-scale form, for which designers had previously had only inarticulate feelings. Thus, the words seemed true in themselves.

Fortunately, designers have gone on to other fashions, and accumulating studies have made it evident how differently a low-income teenager thinks of a city from a middle-class professional (just as both see a compact, labyrinthine city very differently from one that sprawls over an extensive grid). The perception of a city is a transaction between person and place, which varies with variations in each factor, but which has

[5]D. Appleyard, *Planning a Pluralist City: Conflicting Realities in Ciudad Guyana* (Cambridge: M.I.T. Press, 1976).

stable rules and strategies. Armed with a sense of those strategies, and a set of analytical methods, a designer can help citizens to understand what they see and value and can thus help them to judge proposed changes. In their work in Cambridgeport, Carr and Herr[6] showed how these same image techniques could be used as a means of participation. In a few cases, image studies are now used in that way, but the first effect on city design was often pernicious.

Our second omission, less easy to repair, was that we elicited a static image, a momentary pattern. There was no sense of *development* in it—of how that pattern came to be, nor of how it might change in the future, as the person matured, her or his function changed, her or his experience enlarged, or the city itself was modified. The dynamic nature of perception was denied. Once again, the study unwittingly fed a designer illusion: that a building or a city is something that is created in one act, then to endure forever.

It is far more exhausting to analyze how an image develops, because this requires a longitudinal analysis. Yet that will be a necessity, if we mean to get a true understanding of this dynamic process and to link these studies to fundamental research in developmental and cognitive psychology. Some starts have been made: Denis Wood on the growth of the image of London among teenage visitors[7]; Banerjee's comparison of the images of newcomers and old inhabitants[8]; and Smith's replication of the original Boston studies[9] which showed how 10 years of physical change had affected the public image of that place. The track of image development in the maturing person and also the path of change as one becomes familiar with a place are both progressions (or regressions) that stand in need of close analysis.

The static view is mistaken not only as a matter of understanding, but also as a matter of value. We are pattern makers, not pattern worshipers.

[6]P. B. Herr et al., *Ecologue/Cambridgeport Project* (Cambridge: M.I.T. Department of Urban Studies and Planning, 1972).

[7]D. Wood and R. Beck, "Talking with Environmental A, an Experimental Mapping Language," in *Environmental Knowing: Theories, Research, and Methods*, ed. G. T. Moore and R. G. Golledge (Stroudsburg, Pa.: Dowden, Hutchinson and Ross, 1976).

[8]T. K. Banerjee, "Urban Experience and the Development of the City Image" (Ph.D. dissertation, M.I.T. Department of Urban Studies and Planning, 1971).

[9]B. A. Smith, "The Image of the City 10 Years Later" (Master's thesis, M.I.T. Department of Urban Studies and Planning, 1971).

Unless we are mentally at risk, our great pleasure is to *create* order, in an ascending scale of complexity as we mature. This is the pleasure that designers so enjoy—and so often deny to others. The valuable city is not an ordered one, but one that can be ordered—a complexity whose pattern unfolds the more one experiences it. Some overarching, patent order is necessary for the bewildered newcomer. Beyond that, the order of a city should be an unfolding order, a pattern that one progressively grasps, making deeper and richer connections. Hence our delight (if we are internally secure) in ambiguity, mystery, and surprise, as long as they are contained within a basic order, and as long as we can be confident of weaving the puzzle into some new, more intricate pattern. Unfortunately, we do not have any models for an unfolding order.

Third, the original study set the meaning of places aside and dealt only with their identity and their structuring into larger wholes. It did not succeed, of course. Meaning always crept in, in every sketch and comment. People could not help connecting their surroundings with the rest of their lives. But wherever possible, those meanings were brushed off the replies, because we thought that a study of meaning would be far more complicated than a study of mere identity. This original renunciation is now itself being renounced, particularly in the studies of environmental semiotics, in which the technical analysis of meaning in language is applied to the meaning of place. Interesting as this work is, it labors under the difficulty that places are not languages: their primary function is not the communication of meaning, nor can their elements be so neatly parsed into discrete signifiers. Nevertheless, if it can free itself of that analogy—if places can be considered in their own nature, and not as silent speech—the study of environmental meaning will undoubtedly bring rich results for city designers. Some promising advances have been made, by Appleyard just before his death,[10] Rapoport,[11] and others. If only it were not so difficult!

Last, perhaps, I would criticize our original studies because they have proved so difficult to apply to actual public policy. This difficulty is strange, because the principal motive of the whole affair was to change the way in which cities were shaped: to make them more responsive to their inhabitants. To my chagrin, the work seems to have had very little real effect of that kind, except for the first flurry of misuse, now so happily faded away.

[10]In his incomplete and unpublished manuscript "Identity, Power, and Place."
[11]A. Rapoport, "The Meaning of the Built Environment," (1983).

To my surprise, on the contrary, the work led to a long line of research in other fields: in anthropology and sociology to some extent, and to a larger degree in geography and environmental psychology. Golledge and Moore's *Environmental Knowing*,[12] and Evan's review article, "Environmental Cognition,"[13] summarize this extensive work and lay out the current debates and preoccupations. The original findings have been extended, corrected, built upon, and superseded. In that sense, the work has fulfilled its function. That function was largely unforeseen, except for our hope of attracting perceptual psychologists to an interest in the urban environment. The work has become a small part of a much larger, and intellectually more fascinating, study of the nature of human cognition. Environmental psychology and cognitive geography are now well-established areas of concern in their general fields. Cognitive anthropology is maturing. The function of the human brain is the central mystery, and the study of humankind's perception of its environment has a valid place in it.

On the other hand—ironically—the early work has had only a minor impact on actual city design. Although researchers were quick to take up the idea, and many amateur city-lovers as well, fewer professionals have done so, saving only that early spurt, cited above. Those that have tried it in real situations report that the results are interesting, but hard to put to use. A soil survey or an analysis of a housing market leads quite easily into city design. Why should an analysis of the image of place, first motivated by design preoccupations, fail to do so?

One reason is that there are many mental images of the city. If one is concerned with an area used by many diverse people, it may be difficult to set out the common problems, and these problems may not be central to the concerns of any one group. Therefore, these techniques are more telling in smaller, more homogeneous communities, or in dealing with tourists, who are more dependent on overt visible clues. Yet, even in complex metropolitan areas, certain images are apparently very widely held.

I think that a deeper reason for this lack of application lies in the special place of esthetics in our culture. Esthetics is thought to be something separate from the rest of life (which it is not), and the perceptual form of something is believed to be solely an aesthetic issue (which it is not, either). Esthetics can be considered a sacred issue—the highest goal

---

[12]Moore and Golledge, *op. cit.*

[13]G. Evans, "Environmental Cognition," *Psychological Bulletin* 88, no. 2 (1980):259–287.

of human activity once basic wants are satisfied. Or it may seem to be a secondary affair, subordinate to more fundamental needs. In either case, it is thought special, idiosyncratic, and not subject to rational debate. Thus, it is not an appropriate concern for public policy, or at least, it must be dealt with separately, gingerly, and at a late stage of decision. Urban design, which tries to deal with public aesthetic issues in conjunction with other "functional" issues (as if seeing were not functional!), holds only an uneasy position in this country. By custom and by institution, public policy at larger scales deals with economic and social ends, whereas perceptual questions are addressed at the level of small territories, or of single buildings. Decision makers often base their choices on a strong personal image of the environment, but this image is implicit and is not tested against others. Politicians do not base their campaigns on explicit sensuous issues, although such questions are often hidden motives in political battle, and even though there is the pervasive, inarticulate public response to the way localities look. What is usually called *urban design* today is more often large-scale architecture, which aims to make an object in one sustained operation, according to the will of a gifted professional. It may even be no more than a visible gloss, applied to a development "package" to help it glide along the rails of decision. True city design— dealing directly with the ongoing sensed environment of the city, in collaboration with the people who sense it—hardly exists today.

This quirk in our view of the world limits what we do. A public agency is unlikely to support a costly piece of analysis that deals with "mere aesthetics," and it is also unlikely to see how the results might fit into its decisions. The agency will be cautious about deciding anything on what seem to be such arbitrary grounds. The professional, in his or her turn, may prefer to cloak aesthetic judgments in the more dignified mantle of other criteria, and so keep his or her aesthetic underbody as safe as possible from defiling amateur hands.

Some attempts have been made to apply image surveys to city policy in this country, notably in San Francisco,[14] Dallas,[15] and Minneapolis.[16] These attempts are dissected in Yata's "City Wide Urban Design Pol-

[14]San Francisco Department of City Planning, *San Francisco Urban Design Study,* 8 vols., and *Urban Design Plan* (San Francisco, 1969–1971).
[15]Dallas Department of Urban Planning, *The Visual Form of Dallas* (Dallas, 1974).
[16]Minneapolis Planning Commission, *Toward a New City* (Community Renewal Plan, Minneapolis, 1965).

icies."[17] They are not convincing examples of the effectiveness of this particular technique. More work has been done in other countries, notably in Japan, in Israel, and in Scandinavia. In this country, again, there is some application of the method in tourist areas, where images may equate with dollars, or at the local neighborhood level, where a settled and vocal group have an explicit stake in the quality of their surroundings.

But decision makers—and many professionals—still find the technique peculiar. Despite the continuing notoriety of the early study, it has been an enthusiasm of researchers in other fields, or of amateurs and contemplatives, or of beginners in the profession. I tried, in *Managing the Sense of a Region*,[18] to show how such studies and issues could actually be applied to public management decisions in complicated urban regions. For the most part, however, these were speculations, rather than actual experiences.

It may be that there is some characteristic of the analysis that adapts it for research, but not for policy. This characteristic is not yet apparent to me. It is ironic that a study launched with the primary aim of affecting policy seems to have missed its target and hit another one. I remain in hope that the flight is not yet over.

[17]T. Yata, "City-Wide Urban Design Policies" (Ph.D. dissertation, M.I.T. Department of Urban Studies and Planning, 1979).
[18]K. Lynch (Cambridge: M.I.T. Press, 1976).

CHAPTER 10

The Puzzle of Antiurbanism in Classic American Literature

LEO MARX

Whenever American attitudes toward the city are under discussion we are likely to hear a familiar note of puzzlement. We hear it, for instance, near the end of the influential study by Morton and Lucia White, *The Intellectual versus the City: From Thomas Jefferson to Frank Lloyd Wright.* After making their case for the centrality of antiurban motives in American thought and expression, the Whites invite us to share their perplexity. "How shall we explain this persistent distrust of the American city?" they ask. "Surely it is puzzling, or should be."[1]

But should it be? My aim here is to reconsider the bias against the city that allegedly makes itself felt in our classic American literature. At the outset, it must be admitted that many of our greatest writers have not displayed anything like a fondness for or even, for that matter, much interest in the actualities of the urban experience in America—far from it. To recognize just how far, we need only try to recall the way city life is depicted in the work of the poets in the main line that leads from Emerson to Whitman, Frost, and Stevens, or in the central tradition in prose that includes Cooper, Emerson, Thoreau, Hawthorne, Melville, James, Twain, Fitzgerald, Hemingway, and Faulkner. Which of these writers

---

This chapter was read at the Conference on Literature and the Urban Experience, Rutgers University, Newark, New Jersey, April 19, 1980.

[1]Cambridge: Harvard University Press, 1962, p. 221.

Leo Marx • Program in Science, Technology, and Society, Massachusetts Institute of Technology, Cambridge, Massachusetts.

may be said to have given us an adequate specification of city life in this country? Which is not vulnerable to the charge of neglect, whether benign or malign, of urban reality? The two who at first thought may seem most deserving of exemption from that charge are Whitman and James. But only at first. For though it is true that New York is the setting for much of Whitman's poetry, his New York is less like a city anyone ever inhabited than it is, in Richard Chase's apt words, "a paradoxically urban-pastoral world of primeval novelty."[2] As for James, it is true that he also set his most important work in cities, but he made a sharp point of the fact that they were *not* American cities. His explanation could hardly be more pertinent to my argument. Invoking a musical analogy, James observed that the major key of urban life in the United States is "absolutely, exclusively," the key of "down-town." Only by writing in that key, he admitted, could a novelist hope to attune himself to what really mattered in the American city, but to the key of "down-town," he nonetheless confessed to being incurably deaf.[3] A further inference of James's remark is that in London, Paris, and Rome—the sites he chose for his most ambitious novels—the key of "up-town" still had resonance enough to yield novelistic significance. On second thought, then, neither James nor Whitman is an exception. Their work manifests no more concern that that of the other writers mentioned for the exact rendering of urban reality in America.

Should we be puzzled by this fact? I think not, but even if I am correct in suggesting that much of the puzzle can be dispelled by ridding ourselves of the false assumptions that underlie it, the puzzle's very existence is an interesting, perhaps even significant, datum of our cultural history, and it calls for some explanation. Why is it that our writers, artists, and intellectuals are *expected* to convey a fond approval of the modern city? If we can account for this largely misguided expectation, we will be in a better position, I think, to address the more important issue: how to understand the implicit attitude toward the city in the work of so many of our most gifted writers. Let me say at once that I do not think it makes sense to interpret their neglect of urban reality as evidence of a deep bias against "the city" as such. In imaginative literature, indeed, the concept of the "city" must be understood as in large measure an abstract

[2]R. Chase, *Walt Whitman Reconsidered* (London: Victor Gollancz Ltd., 1955), p. 95.
[3]Preface to "Daisy Miller," in *The Art of the Novel: Critical Prefaces*, ed. R. P. Blackmur (New York: Charles Scribner's Sons, 1955), pp. 272–274.

receptacle for displaced feelings about other things. I shall be arguing that the attitude that the Whites and others have mistaken for antiurbanism is better understood as an expression of something else: a far more inclusive if indirect and often equivocal attitude toward the transformation of society and of culture, of which the emerging industrial city is but one manifestation.

First, however, let us consider a few of the more compelling reasons for expecting American writers to convey an affirmative attitude toward city life. Behind this expectation, there is a view of history, and its starting point is the ineluctable fact that we have been a city-building people. From the very beginning, indeed, the European occupation of North America has been a process of relentless urbanization. During the Atlantic crossing in 1630, John Winthrop envisaged the colony that the Puritans were about to establish as "a city upon a hill." The trope was conventional, to be sure, but it nonetheless expressed an important attribute of the Calvinist mentality. Though many of these migrating English were of rural origin, they were carriers of an essentially bourgeois culture, or what Max Weber was to call "the Protestant ethic." They were burghers in spirit, and like most other European settlers, they conceived of the colonizing enterprise as an affair of organized communities. Their aim was to set up villages, towns, and potential cities in the wilderness. During the colonial period, settlement by the unaffiliated was discouraged, and historians have long since discarded the beguiling notion of a westward-moving frontier comprised of individual "pioneers" like Daniel Boone or Natty Bumppo. The effective cutting edge of population until the end of the nineteenth century was a chain of small communities that often, as in the dramatic instance of Chicago, became cities overnight. Demographers have shown us that for many people the movement of population from east to west was a movement from one city to another, and it was accompanied by a simultaneous movement, throughout the nation, from country to city. When the Republic was founded, roughly 9 out of 10 Americans lived in a rural environment; by now, that fraction is less than 3 out of 10. In this view of the past, we are a city-building, city-dwelling people, and so it would seem reasonable to expect our high culture to "reflect" that ostensible preference for an urban way of life.

To this conception of the American past, it is necessary to add the received wisdom concerning the ancient and virtually timeless affinity between city life and the life of the mind. Cities, after all, are the places where scholars, artists, and writers naturally congregate. They do so because, for one thing, most of the vital institutions of mental production—universities, libraries, theaters, museums, galleries, publishers, printers—have almost invariably been located in cities. (Monasteries, perhaps, are the outstanding exception.) Cities are the places where ideas travel most quickly, where one can most readily become knowing or, so to say, urbane. The origins of civilization itself are thought to have been closely bound up with the invention of settled agriculture and cities, and historians of early man often cite the relative size and prosperity of a people's cities as a more-or-less reliable index of the level of culture to which it has attained. The long history of cities as the environment most conducive to thought lends credence to the claim that city life has been held in special favor by most intellectuals in the West. More often than not, they have chosen urban settings for their literary accounts of utopia, and by the same token, many influential thinkers, from Socrates to Karl Marx, have looked on the countryside as a region of mindlessness, not to say idiocy. All of which would seem to justify the notion that the antiurban motives that make themselves felt in American literature—if that, indeed, is what they are—constitute a puzzle in need of explanation.

Now, the first thing to be said about this argument is that it posits a banal and finally misleading conception of the relations between that urbanizing America out there in reality and the imagined world we encounter in literature. It assumes that a national literature invariably should "lend expression to," or "reflect" (as in a sort of copy image), the dominant features of national experience. But to make that assumption is to universalize the specific aesthetic program of certain writers, especially the modern realistic novelists, whose chief aim, indeed, has been to create a fictive illusion of social actuality. Think of all those important American writers, not yet mentioned, who in fact did make an effort to render the concrete particulars of urban experience in the United States. I have in mind, for example, Howells, Wharton, Norris, Crane, Dreiser, Dos Passos, Wright, Farrell, Baldwin, Ellison, and Bellow. It is significant that these names, often assigned to the categories of *realism* or *naturalism*, seldom appear in the roster of "classic" American writers. When we stop to think about the tacit criteria for membership in that amorphous literary society, as roughly defined in the work of several modern critics and scholars, notably D. H. Lawrence, Van Wyck Brooks, F. O. Matthiessen, Charles Feidelson, Jr., and Richard Chase, we soon realize that a chief criterion has been a commitment to an essentially nonrepresentational and often expressly *anti*realistic method of composition.[4] Nathaniel Hawthorne might have been speaking for most of the other classic American writers when he explicitly repudiated realism or, as he described it, that "form of composition . . . presumed to aim at a very minute fidelity, not merely to the possible, but to the probable and ordinary course of man's experience." Instead, he claimed for himself the artist's privilege of rearranging everyday experience and presenting it, as he put it, "under circumstances, to a great extent, of the writer's own choosing or creation."[5]

The distinction between these two forms of composition is absolutely vital for anyone concerned about discriminating among the various literary treatments of urban life. Granted that no verbal composition can actually provide a mirror image of anything, much less a whole city, there still is an immense difference between a realistic novel aimed at creating some such illusion and an avowed "romance" of the sort Hawthorne defines. As he surely realized, the line between those two compositional types can become terribly fuzzy or can disappear entirely, and yet the usefulness of the distinction, where it is discernible, cannot be exaggerated. In *Sister Carrie*, for example, Dreiser immediately reveals his documentary purpose. It is apparent in the opening pages that he wants his readers to respond by saying, in effect, "Yes, of course, this is a perfect picture of Chicago, just the way it must have been when Carrie Meeber got off the train on that day in August 1889." When a writer

---

[4]Consider, especially, D. H. Lawrence, *Studies in Classic American Literature* (1923; New York: Viking Press, 1961); Van Wyck Brooks, *Emerson and Others* (New York: E. P. Dutton, 1927) and *The Flowering of New England* (1936; New York: E. P. Dutton, 1952); F. O. Matthiessen, *American Renaissance* (New York: Oxford University Press, 1941); Charles Feidelson, *Symbolism in American Literature* (Chicago: University of Chicago Press, 1953); and Richard Chase, *The American Novel and Its Tradition* (New York: Doubleday, 1957).

The privileged status accorded to the "classic" writers by this honorific label is of course open to question. That the label carries with it a burden of class, ethnic, regional, and other unacknowledged assumptions seems obvious enough. For present purposes, however, the existence of this subcategory within the prevailing conception of American literature may be taken for granted. A certain academic legitimacy has been conferred on it by the standard anthologies and course syllabi of our schools and universities, and by the mutually supporting judgments of writers, critics, teachers, and audiences that created the entire canon. However skewed, in other words, it is in a sense an authentic product of the dominant culture.

[5]Preface, *The House of the Seven Gables* (1851).

manifestly sets out to present us with an exact, detailed, seemingly comprehensive imitation of urban reality, then it certainly makes sense to ask
whether he has selected truly significant details and has got them right.
But such a test is beside the point in reading the work of a writer like
Hawthorne, who immediately signals his unconcern with any such accurate, solidly specified rendering of the environment.

Hawthorne's practice in *The Scarlet Letter* exemplifies the way a
writer's concept of form—in this case, an explicitly nonrepresentational
form—governs his or her treatment of the city. Because this romance is
set in seventeenth-century New England, moreover, we can assume that
it will not provide us with any *direct* evidence (the sort we might expect
to derive, for instance, from descriptive imagery) of Hawthorne's attitude
toward American cities of his own time. The nearest thing to a city here is
Boston, and though it is only a small outpost of civilization on the edge of
a vast continental wilderness, we may think of it as a city because we
know it is going to become one, and also because it already is the Puritan
capital, the center of power and authority, as well as the most densely
populated place in Massachusetts Bay. At the outset, Hawthorne exer-
cises his romancer's privilege by singling out three visible features of the
town—the prison, the cemetery, and the scaffold—and by casting a high-
light on them. He is not in the least interested in conveying a literal
image of the way Boston looked at the time, a fact whose significance was
lost, unfortunately, on the makers of the recent television production,
who went to such disconcertingly great lengths to create a historically
accurate and detailed naturalistic set. On the contrary, Hawthorne deliberately focuses all of our attention on three tangible manifestations of the
hard, reality-oriented, authoritarian spirit of the Calvinists whose power
is concentrated there.

As decreed by the characteristically American moral geography, the
original source of that iron-hearted spirit lies to the east, in Europe, and it
is only natural that the deepest yearnings of someone like Hester Prynne,
a victim of Puritan repression, are identified with the untrammeled forest
that stretches out to the west. On the quotidian plane of the action, of
course, the forest is the only place where she and Dimmesdale can risk
any gestures of intimacy. Nature, the wild territory beyond the confines
of Boston, is Hester's true orbit, the locus of the freedom and self-fulfill-
ment of which she dreams. The moment she is released from prison,
accordingly, she moves out of Boston to a comparatively remote cottage
facing the forest toward the west:

> On the outskirts of the town, within the verge of the peninsula, but not in close vicinity to any other habitation, there was a small thatched cottage. It had been built by an earlier settler, and abandoned because the soil about it was too sterile for cultivation, while its comparative remoteness put it out of the sphere of that social activity which already marked the habits of the emigrants. It stood on the shore, looking across a basin of the sea at the forest covered hills towards the west. . . . In this little, lonesome dwelling, . . . Hester established herself, with her infant child.[6]

To live on the outskirts of Boston proper is important to Hester. Her choice of this half-in, half-out relation to the town is one of the first signs we get of her concealed but obdurate resistance to the dominant culture. As it turns out, of course, she is anything but your typical have-it-both-ways suburbanite, and her peninsula home proves to be only a way station on the spiritual route to the great climactic forest episode. There, in the moral wilderness, she finally discloses to Dimmesdale the heretical extremism of her ruminations and her bold plan to gain freedom for them both. It entails nothing less than his willingness to join with her in a public repudiation of everything for which Boston stands. "'Doth the universe lie within the compass of yonder town?'" she asks him. "'And what hast thou to do with all these iron men, and their opinions? They have kept thy better part in bondage too long already.'"[7]

On its face, admittedly, this is an unlikely choice of a text to exemplify the way the city is represented in our classic American literature. The animus that Hester directs against the Puritan town obviously is not evoked by its comparatively urban character. Boston is made to seem grim and repressive, it is true, but we are given no reason to suspect that Hawthorne (or Hester) considers those qualities intrinsic to urban life. It is not Boston's cityness, realized or potential, that she would repudiate, it is the kind of society whose power is concentrated there. Express attitudes toward the city *qua* city, in short, have little or nothing to do with the matter, and that is just the point I am trying to make. To Hawthorne, the significant attributes of this place—its essential qualities as a human habitat—are part of something else: the Puritan way of life. His judgment of that culture, not his personal feelings about cities as places to live, is what governs the way he writes about Boston in *The Scarlet Letter*.

The point would be too obvious to mention if it were not so often

---

[6]*The Scarlet Letter* (1850), Chapter 5, "Hester at Her Needle."
[7]Ibid., Chapter 13, "The Pastor and His Parishioner."

ignored. It is chiefly ignored by academicians who regard the literary treatment of cities as a question, at bottom, of representational accuracy. I have in mind the kind of investigation of the "image of the city" in art or literature that is conducted in American studies these days. The investigator proceeds on the assumption that literature "reflects" reality. In spite of frequent denunciations by critics, incidentally, the metaphor of *reflection* still seems to be the most popular figure available for conveying a sense of the relationship between art and life. In any case, a corollary of the representational theory of literature is the assumption that passages dealing with a particular subject, such as the city, have inherent significance when detached, more or less arbitrarily, from their immediate literary context and compared with each other and with what we know about those real cities out there in the writer's society.

But of course no work of art, including the work of the most literal-minded, programmatic, realistic novelist, bears any such direct, unmediated relation with raw experience. There are significant differences, however, between the planes of abstraction on which the relationship—that mediation of form—may be established. Hence, the first problem for a critic is to identify that plane or, to put it differently, to grasp the principles, explicit or implied, governing the way in which literary form mediates the transmutation of experience in a particular piece of writing. It makes no sense to approach the work of the classic American writers in search of "responses" to the city on the plane of direct sensory experience, as if the writers were attempting to convey exact images of the real thing. Hawthorne's conception of Boston is formed on that relatively high plane of abstraction where his most general ideas about art converge with his most general understanding of society and its history. That conjunction is apparent, for example, in his choice of the scaffold as a focal point of Boston life in *The Scarlet Letter*. It is at once an expression of his theory of fiction, or romance, as a symbolic reconstruction of reality, and of his recognition of the centrality, in our collective experience, of those large, organizing symbol systems we now refer to, in the anthropological sense, as *cultures*. His ambivalent attitude toward Puritan culture, rather than an effort to imitate the character of daily life in seventeenth-century Boston, is what governs his treatment of that town in *The Scarlet Letter*.

In opting for a nonrepresentational method, Hawthorne had no intention of cutting all ties between his kind of fiction and social reality. He did not want to create a free-floating world of pure imagination, but rather a "neutral territory," as he put it, "somewhere between the real world and fairyland, where the Actual and the Imaginary may meet, and each imbue itself with the nature of the other."[8] Hawthorne believed that in fiction, to cite Melville's cogent formulation of their shared understanding, we should look for "even more reality" than in "real life." Like religion, Melville said, fiction "should present another world, and yet one to which we feel the tie."[9] As Melville understood, I believe, Hawthorne had dismissed the too literal program of the realistic novel in the service of what Dostoevski would call a higher realism. That is the meaning of Hawthorne's famous stricture to the effect that a "romance" must "rigidly subject itself to laws, and . . . sins unpardonably so far as it may swerve from the truth of the human heart."[10] This statement has usually been taken as a brief for "psychological realism," but its implications reach far beyond the sphere of individual motives. Judging by his best work, the "laws" of mental life to which he refers apply to collective as well as individual, public as well as private, experience. Indeed, Hawthorne is propounding a more ample method of literary representation designed with a view to the particularly complex conception of reality it aims to convey. Because this reality includes the mental set of those who experience and, in a measure, create it, it cannot be apprehended by any merely pictorial "reflection" of the external world, or by any rendering, however detailed, of individual sense experience. To represent the shared mentalities through which the experience of Hawthorne's characters have been screened, only a symbolic rearrangement of "real life" will suffice.

All of this enables us to account for the seeming antiurbanism in Hawthorne's work. The tacit key to any one of his characters' attitudes toward the city is the degree of that person's identification with the dominant culture. The Puritans in *The Scarlet Letter* presided over the building of Boston, it is their town; hence, the ruling elect and those who most nearly identify with them understandably exhibit the most affirmative attitude toward the place. At the other extreme, comporting with her embrace of a radical antinomian, or separatist, viewpoint, is Hester's alienation and her scheme for getting away. Between these polar viewpoints, presumably, a hypothetical spectrum of attitudes may be imagined, and a vital aspect of this dialectical concept of culture—dialectical in

[8]Ibid., "The Custom House, Introductory to *The Scarlet Letter.*"
[9]*The Confidence Man* (1857), Chapter 33.
[10]Preface, *The House of the Seven Gables.*

the sense that Hawthorne posits a conflict of value as its essence—is continuity over time. Thus, each of the opposed attitudes toward Puritan life (including the Puritan city) has its nineteenth-century equivalent, and much of the power of *The Scarlet Letter* derives from Hawthorne's skill in suggesting how the conflict it dramatizes is being replayed in his own day.

T. S. Eliot once observed that Hawthorne had "a very acute historical sense,"[11] and in truth he had recognized, long before Max Weber or Perry Miller, that the first settlers had brought with them, embedded in their theology, the seeds of the narrowly utilitarian, acquisitive ethos that had burst into full secular bloom two centuries later. In the self-righteous saints who had persecuted Hester Prynne, Hawthorne would have us recognize the ideological forebears of Judge Pyncheon of *The House of the Seven Gables*; he is the kind of successful man of affairs who dominated the nineteenth-century New England city, and who is described at one point as "subtle, worldly, selfish, iron-hearted, and hypocritical."[12] The epithet *iron-hearted* here helps to convey Hawthorne's sense of the historical continuity of culture; indeed, the image of iron is the nucleus of a recurrent cluster of images in his work that includes rust, fire, smoke, and blackness, and it serves to make graphic the connection between the hell-fired mentality of the first generation and the prevailing belief system in that society in the era of emerging industrial capitalism. Iron connotes the practical and specifically technological bent that was to become a distinguishing feature of the new industrial order, and it accords with the Puritan view of nature and the natural as the sphere of the satanic: a fallen world redeemable only by the elect. In a deft satirical sketch, "The Celestial Railroad," Hawthorne depicts Calvinism as the incubator of that belief in material and technological progress that had replaced Christianity as the dominant American faith; it was an ideological transformation closely bound up with the metamorphosis of the Puritan town into the modern Vanity Fair or capitalist city.

But it would be wrong to imply that the critical attitude toward the American city implicit in Hawthorne's work derives only—or even chiefly—from a negative view of the dominant culture. In the forest, when Hester disdainfully refers to "yonder town" as a place that she and her lover ought to leave forever, she is not merely impelled by her contempt for its iron-hearted ruling class. As important in hardening her

11"Henry James," in *The Shock of Recognition*, ed. Edmund Wilson (New York: Modern Library, 1955), 861.
12Chapter 18, "Governor Pyncheon."

will is her impassioned belief in the attainability of an alternative way of life. In imploring Dimmesdale to forget the past and begin a new life elsewhere, she repeatedly refers to the presence of nature, repre-sented—initially and most tangibly, at least—by the forest that surrounds them, as evidence that the necessary conditions for a new beginning are accessible to them. She perceives untrammeled nature as the embodi-ment of a moral and metaphysical as well as a literal (physical) sanction for her extravagant conception of the freedom and happiness she and Dimmesdale might gain by leaving Boston. " 'Doth the universe lie with-in the compass of yonder town,' " she asks,

> which only a little time ago was but a leaf-strewn desert, as lonely as this around us? Whither leads yon forest track? Backwards to the settlement, thou sayest! Yes; but onward, too! Deeper it goes, and deeper into the wilderness, less plainly to be seen at every step! until, some few miles hence, the yellow leaves will show no vestige of the white man's tread. There thou art free! So brief a journey would bring thee from a world where thou has been most wretched, to one where thou mayest still be happy![13]

Hester's language, like the natural setting, conveys the continuing ideological force of her visionary individualism two centuries later—in Hawthorne's own time. At the outset, to be sure, he had taken pains to associate her with "the sainted Ann Hutchinson," the antinomian heretic banned by the Puritan orthodoxy. The honorific epithet indicates that Hawthorne's "narrator" is sympathetic with this native strain of radical nonconformism, and the doctrine Hester espouses in her effort to strengthen Dimmesdale's will ("'What we did had a consecration of its own. We felt it so!'") closely approximates the root theological assump-tions of antinomianism. But Hawthorne also describes Hester's secret reflections in a way calculated to evoke the largely secularized radicalism of his dissenting contemporaries, the Transcendentalists. When he says, in Chapter 13, that Hester's repudiation of authority had reached the extremity at which "the world's law was no law for her mind," he man-ifestly is echoing Emerson (in "Self-Reliance"): "No law can be sacred to me but that of my nature." A constant feature of this protestant viewpoint is that degree of assurance, or self-trust, consonant with a nondeferential attitude toward received modes of thought and behavior. But whereas Ann Hutchinson would have attributed a "consecration" like that claimed by Hester to the intervention of a transcendent deity, Hester's language

---

[13]Chapter 17, "The Pastor and his Parishoner."

places her closer to Emerson and his belief in nature as "the present expositor of the divine mind."[14]

Hester's susceptibility to an Emersonian feeling for nature is what lends her views a seeming antiurban bias. In pleading with Dimmesdale to leave Boston, she does sound, it must be admitted, as if she were asking him to reject all forms of social habitation—whether village, town, or city—in favor of some other sort of life "closer to nature." She urges him to contemplate the happiness that awaits them in the trackless forest ("'There thou art free'"), as if she took literally the metaphor of a journey into the deep heart of nature. Given the tone of the duplicitous narrator, moreover, a careless or gullible reader might be led to suppose that Hawthorne was ratifying Hester's belief. But as the subsequent action reveals, she had been carried away by the rapture of the moment, and it seems evident that the entire forest episode is meant to expose what Hawthorne regards as the large element of projection, or wish-fulfillment fantasy, in transcendental pastoralism.

Hawthorne's skeptical attitude becomes clear in the chapter of virtual parody in which Hawthorne "so manages his atmospherical medium" as to have the clouds reciprocate the lovers' mood.[15] When they are completely intoxicated by the prospect of their imminent liberation, the gloomy forest ("Such was the sympathy of Nature . . . with the bliss of these two spirits!") suddenly is lit by a burst of sunshine. But of course, this is not much more ridiculous than Hester's notion that she and Dimmesdale have only to plunge off into the forest to be free and happy. That idea is of a piece with the rest of Hester's extravagantly utopian expectations. It has nothing whatever to do with a bias against "the city" as such, a fact that becomes evident when we learn that the lovers actually had decided not to escape into nature after all. "It had been determined," Hawthorne casually reveals in Chapter 20, after the aura of the forest idyll has been dispelled, "that the Old World, with its crowds and cities, offered them a more eligible shelter and concealment than the wilds of New England, or all America."

I want to suggest that Hawthorne's theory and practice will serve as an almost paradigmatic example of the way the classic American writers treat the environment. Their work is nonrealistic in the sense that they

[14]*Nature* (1836), Chapter 7, "Spirit."
[15]Chapter 18, "A Flood of Sunshine."

represent place not chiefly for what it is, but for what it means. The meanings they attach to forests, oceans, mountains, prairies, villages, towns, cities, etc., are dialectical, not univocal: they derive from a play of conflicting ideas and feelings represented in the narrative. (The town and the forest in *The Scarlet Letter* have diametrically opposed significance for the orthodox and for Hester.) This enacted conflict of values and meaning within the text usually can be aligned with a similar conflict in that extraliterary realm we call, for shorthand purposes, American society or culture.

A distinguishing feature of this body of writing is its domination by protagonists, like Hester, whose deepest yearnings are expressed in numinous visions of the natural landscape. She might be speaking for any one of them when she urges Dimmesdale, in the forest, to "'Begin all anew! Hast thou exhausted possibility in the failure of this one trial?'" I am thinking of that familiar roster of pastoral figures: Natty Bumppo, the "I" of Emerson's *Nature* and Thoreau's *Walden*, Ishmael, Christopher Newman,[16] Huckleberry Finn, Jay Gatsby, Nick Adams, and Ike Mc-Caslin. All of these characters enact the ideal life of the American self journeying away from the established order of things into an unexplored territory that we tend to think of as "nature." The object of the journey, implied or avowed, is the nearest possible approximation to the situation of the autonomous, unencumbered self.

The entire canon might be described, in other words, as a continuous replaying or testing of the Emersonian doctrine of self-reliance as the epitome of the "natural." (It is interesting that Lawrence, who evidently was fascinated by Emerson but for some reason ended up not writing about him, had initially called his *Studies in Classic American Literature* "The Transcendental Element in American Literature."[17]) To realize that ideal condition of the self is to disengage from ordinary social reality, but to describe this omnipresent pastoral motive as an expression of a bias against cities is grossly reductive and misleading. The topography here—place in a literal sense—is a vitally important but nonetheless secondary

---

[16]Although Newman, like the protagonists of James's later international theme novels, finally goes to Europe, his idea of disengagement from his business vocation initially comes to him when he impulsively leaves Wall Street and drives out to Long Island to contemplate the rustic landscape.

[17]*The Symbolic Meaning, The Uncollected Versions of "Studies in Classic American Literature,"* ed. A. Arnold (New York: Centaur Press, 1962).

subject, or vehicle, of the great central figurative conception whose primary subject, or tenor, is the search for inner freedom and fulfillment. As Thoreau said about his ardent cultivation of the bean field, these repeated moves away from "society"—or "the city"—are undertaken chiefly for the sake of tropes and expression. To call *Walden* "a bible of anti-urbanism," as the Whites do, is a grand impertinence.[18]

That antiurbanism is largely beside the point is further indicated by the fact that the pastoral impulse enacted in these typical American fictions is seldom rewarded with success. The outcome of the action in *The Scarlet Letter* reinforces Hawthorne's judgment of Hester's vision, implicit in the ironic rigging of the forest episode, as magnificently extravagant and infeasible. The truth is that not one of the works in question can be finally described as an unqualified "pastoral of success."[19] *Walden* comes as close as any to being that, but the more carefully one reads the book, the more narrowly personal and limited Thoreau's triumph seems. Since Thoreau's time, in any event, our best writers working in this mode have tended increasingly to compose pastoral romances of manifest failure; they continue to enact the retreat/quest, but it would seem that they do so chiefly in order to deny it, and the resulting state of mind is one of structured ambivalence.

Perhaps the most revealing twentieth-century instance of this mode of rendering the modern industrial city by an American writer is *The Great Gatsby*. Fitzgerald's fable is particularly useful for our purposes because he has Gatsby (and, to a lesser extent, Nick Carraway) assimilate their conceptions of New York to an illusionary pastoral viewpoint. That that is Gatsby's mode of perception becomes evident to Nick, in his role as narrator, in the famous ending when he finally discovers the clue to Gatsby's character. Lying on the beach, looking across the Long Island Sound at dusk, Nick suddenly recognizes that all of the incongruities of Gatsby's behavior can be explained by his characteristically American propensity to credit the pastoral hope. It is a view of life that had initially been fostered in Europeans by the image of the beautiful, rich, vast, seemingly unclaimed continent. The physical reality of the place, all that it promised in the way of material satisfaction, was also assumed to have

[18]White and White, p. 30.
[19]For the concept of pastorals of "success" and "failure," see H. E. Toliver, *Marvell's Pastoral Vision* (New Haven, Conn.: Yale University Press, 1960), pp. 88–89.

made available an inner freedom and fulfillment such as Gatsby seeks. In the beginning of the European settlement of America, at least, there had been reason to believe that the actualizing of the ancient pastoral dream really might be feasible in such a "new" world. A palpable sense of that possibility is another distinctive quality of American pastoralism. As Nick puts it, Gatsby's dream of Daisy, represented by the green light, "must have seemed so close he could hardly fail to grasp it"—another way of saying what Hester had tried to convey to her self-hating lover by pointing to the unbounded forest: "'There thou art free! So brief a journey would bring thee from a world where thou has been most wretched, to one where thou mayest still be happy!'" But that possibility had existed a long while ago, Nick realizes, and what Gatsby did not know is that it "was already behind him, somewhere back in that vast obscurity beyond the city [before America had become an urban industrial society], where the dark fields of the republic rolled on under the night."

Gatsby's failure to grasp this historical truth is of a piece with his distorted view of certain realities before his eyes, and Nick's view of the world is only somewhat less skewed by a similar susceptibility to illusion. Nowhere is this more obvious than in Nick's account of New York itself. He sees the city from the vantage of an ambitious young man, like Gatsby, just in from the western provinces. To him, it is a ceaselessly beckoning fairyland:

> Over the great bridge, with the sunlight through the girders making a constant flicker upon the moving cars, with the city rising up across the river in white heaps and sugar lumps all built with a wish out of non-olfactory money. The city seen from the Queensboro Bridge is always the city seen for the first time, in its first wild promise of all the mystery and the beauty of the world.[20]

Nick pastoralizes the streets of Manhattan as naturally as Thoreau does the landscape at Walden Pond. "We drove over to Fifth Avenue," he says, "so warm and soft, almost pastoral, on the summer Sunday afternoon that I wouldn't have been surprised to see a great flock of white sheep turn the corner." This image occurs to Nick shortly after he has described an appalling urban wasteland—a passage that in fact gives us our first sight of the city proper in *The Great Gatsby*. It is the opening paragraph of Chapter 2. Before that, Nick has described the white palaces

[20]*The Great Gatsby*, Chapter 4.

and spectacular green lawns of Long Island suburbia, where his main characters live. But this is quite another New York:

> About half way between West Egg and New York the motor road hastily joins the railroad and runs beside it for a quarter of a mile, so as to shrink away from a certain desolate area of land. This is a valley of ashes—a fantastic farm where ashes grow like wheat into ridges and hills and grotesque gardens; where ashes take the forms of houses and chimneys and rising smoke and, finally, with a transcendent effort, of men who move dimly and already crumbling through the powdery air. Occasionally a long line of gray cars crawls along an invisible track, gives out a ghastly creak, and comes to rest, and immediately the ash-gray men swarm up with leaden spades and stir up an impenetrable cloud, which screens their operations from your sight.

This is the modern city at its worst, and it has no place in a green vision of America like Gatsby's. His inability to recognize the discrepancy between the underside of urban industrial society, as embodied in the valley of ashes, and the idealized world of his aspirations is the direct cause of his death and his failure. Every significant element of the tale, indeed—the characters and landscape and action—has discrepant meanings in accord with this duality. As Nick describes it, this other city is utterly remote and unreal. Its ashen inhabitants, who dimly go about their obscure operations, are already crumbling in that polluted air. These are people, like the auto mechanic, Wilson, whose lives are largely circumscribed by material conditions, and who share none of Gatsby's gratifying sense of a dream about to be consummated. Glimpses of this other New York, composed of the material and human detritus of industrial society, are fleeting but crucial in *The Great Gatsby*. They provide the measure by which we know that the main characters inhabit a realm shaped by myth as well as wealth. Near the end, when Nick tries to imagine how the world might have looked to Gatsby when divested of its mythic veil, he describes it hauntingly as "A new world, material without being real, where poor ghosts, breathing dreams like air, drifted fortuitously about . . . like that ashen, fantastic figure gliding toward him through the amorphous trees."[21] The ashen figure is Wilson on his way to kill Gatsby. He kills him because of Gatsby's unwillingness—or inability—to let go of his patently false conception of Daisy and, by extension, of the world.

[21]Ibid., Chapter 8.

In *The Great Gatsby* and *The Scarlet Letter,* human habitations derive their meanings from essentially the same conflict of views. At one extreme, we are shown a town or city as it exemplifies the writer's highly critical conception of the dominant culture. This is a real place represented at its worst by emblems of oppression and suffering like the valley of ashes or the scaffold. At the other ideological extreme, we are given the perception of that place by a pastoral figure like Hester or Gatsby. It is true, of course, that Hester is alienated from Puritan Boston—is eager to get away—whereas Gatsby and Nick are more-or-less enthralled by the glamour and excitement of New York. But this difference is not as significant, finally, as the similarity in their viewpoints and its ultimate implications. Gatsby and Nick (until the very end) see New York from an idealized perspective very much like the one to which Hester lends expression in the forest. ("'I'm going to fix everything just the way it was before,'" Gatsby says of his relations with Daisy.) But Fitzgerald points to Europe as the truly significant place from which the symbolic disengagement has been made, and for Gatsby, all America—urban, rural, wild— retains the attributes of that fresh green breast of the New World envisaged by arriving Europeans. This is the illusion that ashen-faced Wilson finally destroys. Thus, the outcome of the action in both works may be understood as exposing the glorious impracticality of the alternative that each has posed to urban reality.

What we have then, in our classic American literature, is not a single, fixed attitude toward the city, but a kind of semantic, or ideological, field in which a range of attitudes, some of them diametrically opposed, is generated. The field is bounded on one side by representations of the *status quo,* which is to say, by various embodiments of the dominant culture of industrial capitalism. (These are likely to be negative images like the scaffold or the valley of ashes.) On the other side, however, the field is bounded by the distinctively intense demands and expectations of a restless, journeying American self impelled by pastoral visions of possibility. Pastoralism seems to be the alternative program to the established order most attractive to Americans. It proposes not to change or resist the system as it is, but simply to withdraw in the direction of "nature" in search of alternatives. (Nature, as we have seen, refers to the presocialized resources of the self, as well as to relatively undeveloped social and political areas of the environment.) Although the illusory character of the alternative is insisted upon, and is often made to have tragic consequences, it retains a remarkably powerful hold on the imagination.

As the closing sentences of *The Great Gatsby* imply, we are prisoners of this dead dream: "So we beat on, boats against the current . . ." And in their continuing fascination with it, our greatest writers attest to its vitality even as they expose its falsity.

This fictional charting of American attitudes is far more persuasive, I submit—it captures more of historical actuality than the notion that Americans harbor some special bias against cities as such. Indeed, it casts a reasonable doubt on the validity of the abstract conception, *the city*, for it stresses the difference, rather than the similarity, between American cities and the classic preindustrial cities of Europe. Most American cities, after all, have been built since the onset of industrialization, and unlike London, Paris, or Rome, they embody relatively few features of any social order other than that of industrial capitalism. If the American city is perceived chiefly as the locus of a particular socioeconomic order, that view accords with the historical fact that millions of Americans have moved to cities, not because they preferred urban to rural life, but because of the inescapable coercion of a market economy.

The idea that the distinguishing features of the American city do not reside in its cityness becomes more evident when we consider, for example, the mass exodus of the white middle class from our cities in the recent past. Why did they leave? The usual explanation has to do with poverty and race and violence and the decline of services; our cities are close to bankruptcy because, for one thing, the social resources of the nation have had to be deflected from the satisfaction of immediate human needs to meet the ostensible imperatives of "national defense" and the overall "health" of the economy. In other words, the reason for the exodus from the city, like the reason for the influx of rural white and black southerners after World War II, has little or nothing to do with the intrinsic character of cities. Nor does it have much to do with the personal preferences of the people involved for the inherent attributes of rural or suburban as against urban life. It is a consequence, like so many of our "urban problems," of the larger socioeconomic system and its accompanying culture. All of which suggests that the bias of American intellectuals against "the city" is more apparent than real, and not a cause for puzzlement so much as a misconception.

CHAPTER 11

Slums and Skyscrapers

Urban Images, Symbols, and Ideology

SAM BASS WARNER, JR.

URBAN IMAGERY

Commonplace nineteenth-century popular imagery of the city states simultaneously that the city's streets are paved with gold and that the city is a snare and destroyer of youth. The golden image was associated with overseas immigrants, and by extension with young rural Americans who moved to the city in the hope of finding wealth. The formula of the city as a destroyer of youth flourished in popular novels and theater and was really a part of the Victorian fascination with sex and crime. The tales and dramas in this genre pandered to a rural or unsophisticated urban audience's prurient desires to hear about prostitution, gambling, and crime and to enjoy both the pleasures of views of the forbidden and the comfort of the moral ending in which evil was punished. In this sense, the voyeurism of the city-as-destroyer formula is continued today in our urban police and detective television shows.

Unfortunately for my desires to use such information about the symbolic climate of the city and the nation, I know of no system that tells me how to analyze and interpret the relationship of the one set of images to the other. Do the two reinforce each other in some way? Do they contradict each other? Or are they distinct entities held simultaneously in people's minds, without traffic between them?

Sam Bass Warner, Jr. • Department of History, Boston University, Boston, Massachusetts.

Lacking this system of symbolic analysis, I do not know how to relate my images to the nuts and bolts of urban history with any precision. I'd like to connect images to the basic descriptive social and economic data of demography, employment, housing, and so forth, which we all use in our commonplace urban work. The city was prosperous and growing rapidly when the golden image flourished, so the symbol was rooted partly in reality—but what, precisely, was being organized from reality by a phrase like "streets paved with gold"? The phrase sounds to me like an extravagance that might well have been employed by fearful people trying to summon up their courage to undertake a journey of long and unknown hardships. If this was the image's principal meaning, then it had little relationship to the city and a great deal to say about the country. Similarly, the mortality, morbidity, crime, and prostitution statistics clearly show that the nineteenth-century city was quite literally a destroyer of youth, but the stories were constructed around the moral snares and the author's fantasies of evil, not the urban environment itself. The formula tells us more about the audience than about the city, and more about their lives than about their image of any city that they knew or visited.

Some of the difficulty in linking imagery to conventional social and economic data can be overcome if we scrap the intellectual tradition that customarily rules the discussion of urban imagery. That is, we must stop considering the city a unity and being seeking an imagery that is as complex as the city's social and economic realities. After all our everyday work with the U.S. Census data consists of ordering up the city into a variety of constructs: the central business district, gray areas, industrial satellites, transportation corridors, bedroom suburbs, and so forth. Surely, the imagery of the American city must be at least as rich as the categorical imaginations of planners, architects, and social scientists.

Our major texts on urban imagery, however, are set in the molds of Judeo-Christian millennial prophecy of new worlds and new earths and the mold of the classical pastoral. Both are dyadic constructs, the former placing the city in a millennial landscape, the latter contrasting the city with the countryside.[1]

The tradition is an important one in American and English thought and letters, but its dichotomous structure of city and country was difficult

[1]M. White and L. White, *The Intellectual versus the City* (Cambridge: Harvard University Press, 1962); Raymond Williams, *The Country and the City* (New York: Oxford University Press, 1973).

to work with once cities became numerous, large, and varied. Here in the United States, sometime between 1850 and 1880, our cities began to mean many different things to many different people, and urban imagery then multiplied accordingly.[2]

At the end of the nineteenth century, the city still carried its old images of golden streets and the destruction of youth, but it had many other images as well: the Gold Coast, Fifth Avenue, and Euclid Avenue, the streets of the rich and the millionaires; the skyscrapers of New York and Chicago. Many cities in their youth, like Chicago and Los Angeles, called themselves "the garden city." Every city had suburbs of large houses, lawns, and neat sidewalks like Jamaica Plain, Brookline, and Brattle Street; every big city had its little Italy, its Lower East Side, its Germantown, its cabbage patch, its Dear Old North End, its Honkeyville and Niggertown. The class and ethnic racial imagery and vocabulary were rich and varied, some complimentary, some pejorative. The late-nine-teenth-century city was no longer a small Illinois Central Railroad town with its right and wrong side of the tracks; it was a place of multiple images, and it has been ever since.

Therefore, my first suggestion, and the only one I make with confidence, is to relax these old constraints, which required us to seek a single, or predominant, image of the city, and instead begin to collect and to ponder multiple urban images. By taking this step, the commonsense gathering of urban imagery will in some crude way begin to match the variety of social and economic data.

IMAGES, SOCIAL CONTEXT, AND HISTORICAL CHANGE

The question of how to classify, manipulate, and reason from such a multiplicity remains an unsolved problem. Clifford Geertz, however, provides some helpful suggestions.[3] From his point of view, symbols and images are units of perception that people employ when thinking. (For Geertz, there is no reason to separate cognition from feeling; both are acts

[2]Janis P. Stout, *Sodoms in Eden: The City in American Fiction before 1860* (Westport, Conn.: Greenwood, 1976); David R. Weimer, *City and Country in America* (New York: Appleton-Century Crofts, 1962), and *The City as Metaphor* (New York: Peter Smith, 1966).
[3]"Ideology as a Cultural System," in *Ideology and Discontent*, ed. D. W. Apter (New York: Free Press, 1964), 47–76.

of thinking and understanding.) Symbols and images are public, not private, entities; they are the major parts of a culture. Thinking and feeling people employ these symbols and images as models, or templates, against which they match their experience. A metaphor, or other figure of language, or a new picture, is thus an addition to the vocabulary of the society. As time passes and conditions change, the process of language formation (a not-specified activity that may add symbols by processes other than response to altered outside circumstances) adds new symbols to the culture, while old ones die out through loss of meaning and subsequent abandonment. For Geertz, if one wants to account for the appearance of a symbol, one looks first of all into the social context and historical change.

It is through the concept of ideology that Geertz has taken up the problem of multiple symbols and multiple images. Ideology, he has suggested, manages multiple images by incorporating them into a coherent (but not always logical) picture of the contemporary world. In the largest historical terms, a Geertz history of the city would say that the ancient city was conceived and built according to the cosmologies of the various ancient cultures, and that after the French Revolution, if not before, the modern city has been built according to ideology—in the American case, the ideology of secular culture, democratic politics, and liberal capitalism.

Therefore, the problem of symbolic analysis for us will be first to find the meaning of the urban symbol in the context of the times of its first appearance and active use, and then to place that symbol in an ideological structure so that its meaning and function can be interpreted as a symbol interacting with all the other active contemporary symbols that we may collect.

THE EXAMPLE OF THE SLUM

The verbal symbol *the slum* and its accompanying visual images nicely fit such an analytical process. The symbol came into common usage in a particular way. This manner of explanation, in turn, suggested a special range of public and private actions, and the symbol took an identifiable place in contemporary ideology and played an identifiable role in respect to other symbols in that ideology. Then, after about a century, conditions in American cities no longer matched the content of the symbol and its visual images, which were thus drained of their meaning and their political power, and they began to die out. Simultaneously, other symbols began to crowd into the ideology, especially concepts of social mobility, the culture of poverty, and the concept of race, and from these social changes and ideological changes, a new symbol and new visual images came into use, especially the term *ghetto*. The term *ghetto*, in its time and ideological position, suggested a new way of looking at the city, new forms of action, and an altered ideological structure. Thus, the rise and fall of the term *slum* might be thought to complete one entire Geertzian symbolic life cycle.

Slum was a cant, or journalistic word, picked up from slang. The possible origins of the slang word may have been *slime*, and one obsolete meaning was a "room." The first noted publication recorded by the OED was in an English magazine in 1825. The word appeared thereafter frequently in English reform writing, and it traveled quickly across the Atlantic. The OED records its use in the United States in 1870 and 1884.[4]

There were two distinct nineteenth-century forms of the word that should be attended to: the noun and the verb. The noun denoted a "street, alley, or court situated in a crowded district of a city inhabited by people of low class or by the very poor." The noun also referred to "a place where a number of these streets or courts formed a thickly populated neighborhood or district where the houses and the conditions of life were of a squalid or wretched character."

In England, the term was generally used in the plural and often as "back slums," thereby suggesting courts and alleys behind the main streets and squares. In America, the neighborhood or district meaning was more common. This slight variation between the two countries reflected the differing reality of the construction of the cities and towns in the two nations.

The noun (*slum*) subsumed the following items:

1. Streets, alleys, courts, and courtyards of certain kinds.
2. Particular conditions of poverty.
3. Particular conditions of housing.
4. Especially in America, the suggestion of an area of some extent, some range of space, from a few streets or courts to something as large as a whole district of the city.

Note that the noun did not include people directly. People were not a slum; people were "slum dwellers." The noun did inevitably imply something about people by directing attention to the crowded, squalid,

---

[4]*Oxford English Dictionary*, 13 vols. (New York: Oxford University Press,).

and wretched nature of the environment, but first and foremost, the word depicted an environment. The people within the environment were assumed to be like their environment in their wretchedness, but the causal links among city, slum, and slum dweller were in no way suggested by the noun. The users of the term had to supply their own explanation of causes. Thus, most slum literature, from Frederich Engels's *Condition of the Working Class in England* to Michael Harrington's *The Other America*, is a debate about slum cause.[5]

The classic American slum book, *How the Other Half Lives*, was written by a New York police reporter, Jacob Riis, and was published in 1890.[6] Riis was also a pioneer photographer, so that the symbol and the appropriate visual images diffused widely through the society as a result of his work. Riis argued that on the Lower East Side of New York there had developed a hostile environment that prevented foreign immigrants, poor people generally, and especially their children from getting a fair and decent chance to work and save and to make their way into the comfortable mainstream of American life. He especially blamed landlord greed, and he suggested adequate housing, open space, and educational reform. He believed in environmentalism, and his remedies for the slum were environmental.

The English reformers were much the same. There is, for example, the work of the journalist Henry Mayhew, who began his famous three-volume study of *London Labor and London Poor* (1864) with an article in the *Morning Chronicle* in 1849 entitled "A Visit to the Cholera Districts of Bermondsey."[7] Mayhew's work was followed by the massive studies of the merchant-philanthropist Charles Booth.[8] The appropriate and parallel visual images of slums and poverty were the etchings of Paul Gustave Doré, published in newspapers and magazines during the 1870s.

This verbal symbol and its accompanying visual images surely constituted a new way of looking at and understanding the city. As Geertz postulated in his essay, the slum was a new symbol brought into currency by altered social circumstances: social change here generated new popular vocabulary.

[5]Engels (1844; reprint, London, 1892); Harrington (New York: Macmillan, 1962).
[6]1890; reprint, New York: Dover, 1971.
[7]Mayhew (1864; reprint, New York: Dover, 1968. "A Visit to the Cholera Districts of Bermondsey," *Morning Chronicle* (London, 1849).
[8]*Life and Labour of the People of London*, 17 vols. (1902–3; reprint, New York: Kelley, 1978).

Both the absolute and the relative dimensions of poverty changed drastically during the nineteenth century. Big patches of poor appeared where before there had been few; poverty moved from the back lanes and country shacks and farms into urban prominence. Within the city, not just one well went dry or became polluted, not just a few families turned to begging, not just a few rotting houses were jammed with impoverished families. Simultaneously, the obvious wealth of the new industrialization completely redivided the social scale of the rich, the comfortable, and the poor. The noun slum encompassed all these changes.

The verb *to slum* gives important information about who used the new symbol and what social relationships its use suggested. The verb did not mean to dwell in the new environment of urban poverty. Instead, it meant to visit the slums for charitable purposes or for entertainment, "especially as a fashionable pursuit." The OED records a simultaneous use of the verb in this way in 1884 in Boston and London; in both cities in that year, fashionable parties were reported as "going slumming."

The new way of seeing thus suggested a new kind of class relationship. Slums were strange, novel, large places that people visited as a foreign territory. *Slums* were not unfortunate families to whom one went on an errand of aid. Thus, the renaming of poverty as a place, instead of a personal condition, implied a shift from the old voluntary parish visitor toward organized charity and public programs for welfare and housing.

The nasty side of the verb, the visiting of the slum by outside residents for entertainment and curiosity, suggested the growing class segregation of the modern city. No one went slumming when the poor lived on the alley behind her or his house. The nasty side of the verb also suggested the contemporary police policies, which drove prostitution, gambling, and illegal liquor into poor neighborhoods, so that the well-to-do visited such districts for specialized illicit entertainment.

It is difficult to estimate the class usage of words in the past, but it seems likely that the noun and the verb were not used by slum residents to describe their own condition or neighborhoods. In general, people at the bottom of a social hierarchy do not use terms of inferiority and oppression and failure except in anger and bitter humor—as American blacks use the word *nigger*. More particularly, the term *slum* was not employed by American urban writers who grew up in urban slums and who wrote of the condition of the poor. James Farrell, Abraham Cahan, Richard Wright, William Attaway, Alfred Kazin, and the like did not describe their poor neighborhoods as slums. In fact, one of the major purposes of this literature was to "deslum" these neighborhoods, to give dignity and respect to the poor with whom the author lived or identified. As a black school teacher recently told me, "I grew up in the New York ghetto, but I was doing fine, and I didn't know it was a ghetto until I went away to college." My suspicion is that the noun and the verb were class-specific symbols, most frequently employed by non-slum-dwellers to describe their altered relationship to the lower classes.

If by such reasoning about the relationship between the use of a word or a visual image and the contemporary social context we can account for its meaning to those who use it, then Geertz urges us to take the next step and to go on to place the symbol in its ideological structure. This is the crucial step in managing multiple images. The slum, after all, was only one urban image in a time of many. How might we interpret the relationship of the many symbols that flourished at the same moment?

Geertz would have us use ideology, a systematic body of concepts about human life and culture (concepts especially concerned with patterns of beliefs and values), as a structure that orders up the many symbols and gives them coherence as a group. (Note that the Geertzian system presupposes a cultural system and does not investigate the possibility that there are lots of loose and fragmented collections of symbols floating about in a modern culture.)

In the case of the slum symbol, its place in contemporary nineteenth-century ideology seems clear. The dominant ideology of the time when the slum symbol rose to prominence in the United States was a secular view of life that demanded democratic politics and a liberal capitalist view of economic affairs. The concept of the slum fitted nicely into such an ideology. First, it was secular. By not referring directly to people, but to places and houses, and the condition of things, it abandoned the common churchy habit of assigning moral evil to those who were impoverished. Thus, the slum symbol blurred the religious distinction between the "deserving" and the "undeserving" poor. It was democratic and equalitarian in its environmentalism.

The environmentalism of the symbol derived nourishment from ongoing developments in science and engineering, especially the new geology and biology and the growing fields of civil and sanitary engineering. By seeing organisms as interacting with their environments, the new science and engineering suggested that housing, water, sewerage vaccination, and so forth would succeed in changing individual lives in important ways.

The political success of the symbol *slum* and its accompanying visual images thus derived part of their power from environmental quality. The success was also derived from its mystifying, or obscuring, function in the overall contemporary ideological structure of secular, democratic, liberal capitalism. Neither in old-fashioned Christian terms nor in the new manner of capitalist economics did the symbol *slum* suggest any cause for the new environment it described. Slums were just there, facts of life, found objects. The symbol concentrated attention on the attributes of the new-found place as if it were like any other fact of science, something that had always been there, but that had only recently been discovered, like cholera germs. Because of the refusal to suggest any cause, to hint that the new capitalism made the new poverty, or to use the old explanation that evil people made evil places, the symbol neatly assumed a special role in contemporary ideological structure. The ideological role it took on did suggest a range of environmental action, as Geertz has suggested new symbols do. But as significantly, within the ideological structure it performed what Roland Barthes called the task of "denomination."[9] The new symbol, by separating the slums from the conditions of urban employment, told us that the slums were part of English and American cities, like smoke, or bricks, or saloons. By denomination, an historical event, something of a specific time and place, was transformed into a timeless, general fact of life. As a fact of life in the secular, democratic capitalist society, the slum could be attended to, but as a fact of life without history or cause, it need not be attended to in any way that would alter the basic values or institutions of the surrounding contemporary ideology.

The ideology of liberal capitalism remained dominant from at least 1840 to 1930, and during this time, the slum was used by left, center, and right as a symbol in the political conflict that took place within the encompassing ideological structure. In such conflict, a great deal of reform and public action was possible, and the present housing and welfare policies of the United Kingdom and the United States were in large measure derived from the symbol and its place in its nineteenth-century ideological structure.

Although Geertz did not spell out the process, it seems to me that logic requires—and his treatment of the French Revolution suggests—that a symbol might die from either of two causes: social change or ideological change. He very much believes that altered social conditions drain

---

[9]"Myth Today," in *Mythologies*, (New York: Hill and Wang, 1973), 109–158.

a symbol of its meaning, as in the case of *alembic*, which lost its currency and meaning with the invention of the retort for distilling during the seventeenth century. But a change in ideological structure might also alter the position of a symbol in the organization of related symbols, and thereby, it would become a "wrong" interpretation of a set of facts that had not in actuality changed much or at all. I think alterations in words used for people of color, like the recent shift from *colored* to *Negro* to *black*, or the shift from *girls* and *ladies* to *women*, might represent just this sort of ideological change, which alters symbol popularity and usage. It is a pity that Geertz has not given more attention to this sort of symbolic change.

In any case, in the United States, the symbol *slum* and its associated visual images passed out of fashion after World War II largely because of altered social facts. Some shifts in ideology may, as well, have contributed to its loss of meaning and currency.

The condition of the poor in the postwar American city almost totally reversed all the ingredients enumerated in the nineteenth-century slum symbol. Where the slum had been crowded with people, now it was a place of empty lots, fires, and housing abandonment. Where scrimping and saving and patching had enforced a neatness of poverty in the old slum, now the new slum was so rich that it became the graveyard for broken appliances, cars, and discarded furniture and a dumping place for local citywide trash. Morally and sexually, where the old slum had been a place of orphaned and malnourished children, child abuse, prostitution, liquor, and theft, the new urban poverty district was perceived as a place of fighting gangs of children who terrorized adults both locally and city-wide, a place where promiscuity replaced commercial sexuality, where teenagers became welfare mothers without concern about their own employment, where hard drugs replaced liquor, and crime became so widespread and random that it defied the older rules of combat between police and criminal groups. And finally, where the old slum had been immigrant and white, now it was immigrant and brown or was made up of native-born black and white migrants. Especially the brown and black poverty district challenged the symbol of the slum, a symbol that had been formed without any concept of race. The principal business of the new term *ghetto* was to fit urban poverty into the American ideology of race.

Michael Harrington's *The Other America*, an immensely popular and influential book, recorded the change from Riis's facts to the current circumstances. His book suggests some ideological changes as well. In the book, Harrington spoke of the "old slum" and the "new slum." The old slum for him had come to mean the immigrant concentration, the launching place for future social mobility; it was, for all its poverty, a place of hope and promise, which by 1962 had largely been realized. Whatever the fairness of the competition in Riis's slum, by 1960 the children and grandchildren of the immigrants had made it up and out into the larger society of the metropolis. The slum, by this reasoning, was transformed in its meaning; it became a piece of nostalgia, a token of success, a credential in a newly prominent aspect of American democratic capitalism, the ideological element of "social mobility." The rise to prominence of the concept of *social mobility* after World War II is an important event in ideological change, but this is not the place to tell that story. Its rise and its influence on the old symbol of the slum suggest the way in which ideological change can affect symbols even in the absence of changes in social conditions. In his book, Harrington summoned the concept of social mobility to make a new test of fairness: the old slum was a place of hope and success; the new slum was a place without hope and of public abandonment of its residents. Harrington also used the term "culture of poverty,"[10] adding still another new ideological element to a structure of democratic capitalism that was becoming increasingly meritocratic.

THE CONTRASTING EXAMPLE: THE SKYSCRAPER

The skyline presents a new set of problems. First, the skyline consists of a set of visual images and is not an important verbal symbol at all. The *Oxford English Dictionary* records its simple low-temperature use in both England and America. A skyline meant the place where the sky met the landform. In the examples given in the dictionary, Melville's skyline came on a desert; for another author, it was on the line of a hill. Second, the images of the skyline move in an opposite class direction from the word *slum*, the surfacing of lower class and vulgar language through the agency of journalists. Third, the skyline deals with social conditions that were located near, if not next to, the slum, but geographic proximity had no effect whatsoever on the development or the meaning of the images of the city—the slum and the skyline—which describe the same place, the modern city, but that do so without mutual recognition or interaction.

[10]*The Other America*, p. 91.

Geertz urged us to solve such problems by locating the images in contemporary ideology. Let us repeat the Geertzian steps.

Although the images of the urban skyline were very much a response to altered social facts, these images cannot be understood except through a simultaneous consideration of their social referent and their ideological setting. We cannot take the two parts one at a time, as we did in our consideration of the slum. A combined treatment is forced on us because the skyline images were part of a continuing visual tradition that was rooted in the civic pride of merchant capitalists.

Urban landscapes, street views, and city panoramas had been executed at least since the seventeenth century, and their popularity derived from public pleasure, if not direct merchant patronage, in seeing the city's buildings drawn and painted. Often, such landscape drawings or paintings appeared with keys to aid in the identification of the buildings. In the early nineteenth century, the drawing of these views was always extremely exact and detailed, so that the pictured properties could be distinguished one from another. As an element in contemporary ideology, the urban view belonged to that part of democratic capitalism that saw human works—city buildings, ships, farms, bridges—as being in harmony with God and nature. A prosperous, growing city was an ornament to God's earth and was drawn accordingly.

The camera cityscape continued the engravers' and lithographers' tradition. Its mechanical rendering often caused it to fail in its celebratory tone, but it could furnish details aplenty.

The building of skyscrapers in lower Manhattan during the building booms from 1890 to World War I constitutes the altered social facts that the later invented skyline images explained.[11] One can imagine a picture of individual or grouped buildings photographed or painted in a dramatic setting of sunlight and clouds that would have continued the earlier tradition. I can also imagine a careful drawing of numbered buildings that would have repeated the old devices. Indeed, I remember seeing an isometric rendering of Manhattan executed in the 1950s that very much represented an update of the old drawn panoramas; it did for skyscrapers what earlier artists had done for row houses and churches. But the skyline images did not emerge as traditional renderings of new social facts.

[11]See Moses King, *King's Views of New York City* (1896; reprint, New York: Arno Press, 1974) for an alternative exact rendering of the skyscraper city.

Instead, a school of photographers, a group gathered around Alfred Stieglitz and his avant-garde Fifth Avenue gallery, began photographing the city's skyscrapers in the mode suggested by the latest fashions in French painting. They concentrated on the tower itself, first rendering it in the soft tones of French impressionism, later in an interpretation of cubism that they had learned from the 1913 Armory Show and visits to Paris.[12]

As a result of these innovations, the old tradition of city landscapes was refreshed both by new objects (skyscrapers) and by the new approach (abstraction). The urban skyline thus became a modern, fashionable, exciting "new" image. The buildings were grouped and considered as silhouettes and planes. They were not stressed in their individuality or proprietorship, as formerly. In this new manner, the images of the skyline were suitable to large audiences and were ready for wide dissemination. By the 1930s, this way of seeing the city had become a commonplace of still photographers and movies.

The meaning of the new urban imagery of the skyline was twofold. On the one hand, it refreshed, and it brought up to date the old tradition of civic pride. Now, anyone could get into the car and drive over the then-new George Washington Bridge or take the Staten Island ferry and see the city in the way that the photographers—and later, *Life* magazine— saw it. At such moments, the viewer could recapture the old feeling that the hand of humankind and nature were still working in harmony.

The second meaning of the imagery has to do with the ideological problem that the skyline solved. The skyscrapers rose at a time of very active political and economic conflict over the growing prominence of the modern American corporation. The skyscraper and the Sherman Anti-Trust Act were contemporaries. The skyscraper was thus a part of a cluster of images of Wall Street, banks, corporate offices, and trusts, and agrarian, labor, and socialist agitation. Within the city itself, the tower created a problem of dominance for city residents. This problem of the giant building and the dwarfed human was explored by photographers Berenice Abbott and Paul Strand.[13]

---

[12]Bram Dijkstra, *The Hieroglyphics of a New Speech* (Princeton: Princeton University Press, 1969).

[13]Berenice Abbott, "Canyon: Broadway and Exchange Place," *New York in the Thirties* (1939; reprint Dover, 1973), picture #12.

The skyline photographers—by their special point of view, by stepping away, and by turning skyscrapers into abstract compositions—solved this political and economic conflict between the democratic and the capitalistic elements of contemporary ideology. In their hands, the skyscrapers were not corporate towers at all, they were art objects in a landscape, and therefore, these photographers moved the skyscraper image from a position of conflict in the ideology to the older position of the tradition of civic pride. So transformed, the corporate tower became the universal American symbol of the prosperous city, something every city wanted as part of its image, like a fancy railroad station, or a jazzy airport.

Therefore, the reason that the slum and the skyline can be simultaneously held as views of the same American city is that the two sets of symbols and images occupied different places in their contemporary ideological structures. The slum defined, directed, and limited public action through the device of denomination; the skyline quieted and pacified and avoided the conflict inherent in the structure of the ideology by transforming new social facts into traditional aesthetic objects, which, in turn, had a long-standing, popular, conflict-free position in the ideology. So transformed, the new urban image of the skyline was capable of mass transmission, even of commercial exploitation, as a sign of fashion, luxury, and social success.

As I conclude this survey of two sets of urban symbols and images, I find myself pleased with the Geertzian analytical steps. He gives one a good intellectual workout. By stressing the social context of symbols and images, the information he demands is very much the information that historians find relevant in their view of the processes of change.

The weakness of the Geertzian system is its fundamental vagueness.[14] If through intuition, wisdom, and luck one happens to have a deep understanding of what others might call the *structure of culture*, then one's interpretation of the history of symbolic change and social change will be rich and insightful. If, on the other hand, one has a limited and mechanical view of ideology and culture (as this paper does, with its simple democratic and capitalist categories), the results may be oversimplified and may have none of the predictive power that social science

---

[14]Note in this connection Geertz's own dismay at the disorder and confusion of Indonesian contemporary culture and his unwillingness—and acknowledged inability—to suggest what directions the culture might take next (Geertz, 65–71).

seeks. The method is suggestive—but nothing more: it underlines the problems of relationships between symbolic change and social and political change. For better or worse, it will be the historian's own sense of cultural order that will define the ideological structure, with no method, other than art and intuition, for managing multiple symbols.

CHAPTER 12

Urban Political Images in Search of a Historical Context

MICHAEL H. FRISCH

This chapter originated with a broad contemporary curiosity that led to a set of quite specific historical questions about Progressive-era urban reform. The research ended up turning on the question of urban images as a historical problem—how and why they occur as they do and how they change over time. In particular, the investigation required me to explore in detail the sources, structure, and consequences of urban imagery in the emerging academic discipline of political science.

I hope that a description of this research will illustrate, more generally, what the discipline of history has to contribute to the study of urban images. Such images are notoriously slippery at any one time, being both abstract by definition and inevitably contextual in expression. A historical perspective shows them to be both more and less slippery as they change over time. This process involves more than just a relationship between a changing social reality and disciplinary perspectives in that the disciplines themselves are historical and change in response to dynamics whose sources may lie at some distance from the urban phenomenon. I hope to demonstrate how the tools of intellectual history can help to penetrate a

This chapter is based substantially on an article previously published, in a somewhat different form, under the title "Urban Theorists, Urban Reform, and American Political Culture in the Progressive Period," *Political Science Quarterly* 97, no. 2 (Summer 1982): 295–315. Material drawn from that article is reprinted here with the kind permission of the *Political Science Quarterly*.

Michael H. Frisch • Department of History, State University of New York at Buffalo, Buffalo, New York.

complex triangular relationship whose elements are all in somewhat independent motion over time.

Finally, moving from disciplinary perspectives and history to the
larger contemporary setting of the problem, I hope that this exercise will
suggest some themes useful for understanding the role of urban symbols
in a more broadly defined American political culture.

THE URBAN CRISIS OF THE 1890s

My interest in these problems arose in part from some reflection on
the rather sudden evaporation, in the 1970s, of the "crisis of the cities"
that had so dominated the headlines and social consciousness of the previous decade. As news, as political issue, and as policy priority, the urban
crisis has seemed to fade from public view as suddenly as it had appeared
in the wake of racial violence in the streets of urban America. The near
bankruptcy of New York and other large cities prompted a brief flurry of
discussion of a generically urban fiscal crisis in the mid-1970s, and there
have been recurrences of violence, most recently in Miami. But I think it
is fair to say that the sense of a fundamental crisis in urban life and
structure, and of a fundamental urban dimension to the major social and
political problems in American society, has diminished substantially in
American public life since the late 1960s. At the same time, it would be
hard to argue that there has been any substantial alleviation of any of the
major social, economic, and political components of that period's urban
crisis; if anything, most of them have become more critical owing to
recent developments in the urban political economy and the worldwide
forces affecting it.

This contrast between a consistent reality and its swiftly diminishing
political and social visibility made it seem that, whatever objective factors
were involved, the appearance and disappearance of the "urban crisis"
was an episode in a broader kind of imagery. Perhaps, it seemed reasonable to suppose, this all had as much to do with the dynamics of American
culture and politics as it did with the "crisis" of the troubled cities themselves. These musings, in turn, suggested that it might be useful to obtain
a longer perspective on a similar phenomenon in the past, in order to
understand why manifest social facts are engaged at some times and not at
others, and why they are expressed politically in some terms but not in
other equally available ones. I decided to take a close look at an obvious
parallel: what one might call the "first urban crisis," that period of reform

ferment in the 1890s and in the first decade of the twentieth century when the condition of urban government and public service was at the center of national political debate and was a focus of tremendous organization and agitation all across the country. This involved a highly articulate and self-conscious movement, one that has received great historical attention since; as a result, urban reform bulks large in the historiography and is one of the fixtures of every survey course. Accordingly, I expected some quick answers when I turned to the literature in order to ask why the urban crisis emerged just then, why it took the forms and terms that it did, and how it was related to other dimensions of the vast social and political upheaval transforming American life in the tumultuous 15 or 20 years surrounding the birth of the twentieth century.

The first surprise was how rarely the literature, whether of the conventional or the more recently revisionist variety, addressed these concerns. The traditional approach has been to see the urban reform movement as part of the march of progress, a fundamental first step in the movement for reform, shortly to culminate in Progressivism on a national scale, and later to reach a sort of liberal apotheosis in the New Deal. But because urban reform has so often been pictured as a response to blatantly evil conditions manifestly requiring attention, there had been relatively less curiosity about the particular terms in which the reform was framed, and in what these terms might imply. The perspective on reform theory and ideology in this literature is consequently somewhat narrow and one-dimensional, focused on the urban contribution to the rise of an activist, liberal state capable of addressing the social problems arising from the rapid expansion of industrial capitalism.

So powerful was the hold of this liberal historiography that revisionist critics have tended to leave unchallenged its general reading of the content of urban reform ideology and analysis. Instead, they have sought to look behind or beneath the rhetoric of reform, to reconstruct the social structures generating reform elites, and to interpret their motivations and intentions in terms of the social and class divisions revealed in this analysis.

Both of these approaches have taught us a great deal, but neither proved very helpful for understanding why the social conflicts and problems of American society in the 1890s, which might have been conceptualized in any number of ways, came to be publicly perceived as constituting a broader *urban* crisis, one rooted in the structure and nature of the emerging industrial city. Generally, the historiography seemed either too narrow (focused on urban problems and reform responses in quite literal ways) or too broad (seeing the city as simply a backdrop or context for the social, political, and economic forces of the era).[1]

And yet, it was precisely the link between these that seemed, from my initial explorations, to require exploration. For one thing, the urban reform movement emerged in the 1890s as a consolidated national movement, with manifestations in many cities facing different circumstances and at strikingly different levels of development. This suggests dynamics not reducible to a problem–response framework and invites reflection on the possibly diverse political and cultural sources of such a phenomenon. It is not likely, for example, that the strikes, unemployment, depression, and political radicalism of 1893–1894 had no place in the consciousness of those who came to the national reform assembly in 1894 that established the National Municipal League, and yet this is exactly the impression left by most conventional historical accounts intent on tracing the development of urban reform *per se*.

Reform's sudden national dimension is not the only thing that is new and not very well understood about urban consciousness in the 1890s, for

[1]Most recent texts and general studies in urban history share the former trait to some extent. It is interesting that the more old-fashioned and narrow surveys tend to be the least faultable on these grounds. See, for example, Ernest S. Griffith, *A History of American City Government: The Conspicuous Failure, 1870–1900* (New York: Praeger, 1974), esp. 120–125. As for the latter problem, in addition to the standard interpretive surveys of this period, see the following, which are particularly relevant to this paper: Thomas Haskell, *The Emergence of Professional Social Science: The American Social Science Association and the Nineteenth Century Crisis of Authority*, (Urbana: University of Illinois Press, 1977); Morton Keller, *Affairs of State: Public Life in the Late Nineteenth Century America* (Cambridge: Belknap Press of Harvard University Press, 1977); and Jean Quandt, *From the Small Town to the Great Community: The Social Thought of Progressive Intellectuals* (New Brunswick: Rutgers University Press, 1970).

The most substantial interpretations from a left perspective are Gabriel Kolko, *Main Currents in Modern American History* (New York: Harper and Row, 1976), a recent synthesis of his well-known monographic work (see especially pp. 283–284 and 292–309); and James Weinstein, *The Corporate Ideal in the Liberal State, 1900–1918* (Boston: Beacon Press, 1968). Interestingly, Weinstein's case is probably the least well supported concerning cities, where he rested his argument on discussions of the commission and manager movements far more applicable, as he noted, to small towns and smaller cities. See Chapter 4, pp. 92–116. The most well-known and influential interpretation of reform that relates municipal reform to a broader political context is Samuel Hays, "The Politics of Reform in Municipal Government in the Progressive Period," *Pacific Northwest Quarterly* 60 (1964):157–169.

the movement that emerged was also different in having a fundamentally theoretical and social-scientific cast to it. Urban reform had been around for decades, generally expressed, at least since Tweed, in a moralistic and particularistic critique of the bosses, the political machines behind them, and the social sources of their support. In the 1890s, however, what emerged was a movement built on an analysis of urban government, an analysis self-consciously trying to move beyond the personal and anecdotal and toward a more structural understanding of the nature of cities and their place in modern society. This transformation has also been more often noticed than historically explained; the specific administrative and governmental focus that emerged, for instance, is by no means the only orientation that the reform movement might have taken, yet its centrality has been seen in the literature as more-or-less self-evident.

These developments, and the questions they raise, find expression in one further dimension quite noticeable from the vantage of intellectual history and directly relevant to the exploration of urban images. In almost every variety of writing about American cities and their governments toward the turn of the century and just after, from popular tracts to academic tomes to reform polemics, there is a dramatic alteration in the images attached to cities and their problems: the old tradition of urban pathology, which had led Jefferson to picture cities as sores on the body politic and Josiah Strong, more recently, to see them as societal cancers— this metaphorical mode was rather suddenly displaced by another. In the new framework, the city was seen as itself the political and cultural cure for its own disease. Even more, it was presented as the hope of a broader troubled society, as the crux of civilization, where modern problems must be engaged and where, through triumphant engagement, American democracy would be redeemed. This transition seems to presume important shifts in ideas, values, and assumptions. Yet it, too, has gone relatively unexplained, unless one accepts a transition from negative to positive, or pessimism to optimism, as sufficient.[2]

[2]The theme of the city as moral threat has been much discussed, but a recent study is definitive, in terms of both scope and depth of insight. See Paul Boyer, *Urban Masses and Moral Order in America, 1820–1920* (Cambridge: Harvard University Press, 1978), esp. 125–129, 170–174, and 176–179. Pathological approaches in political science are discussed in Don Martindale, "The Theory of the City," in *The City* ed. Max Weber (New York: Free Press, 1959), 16–20. The question of the city as threat or hope, as will be discussed below, is related to the question of the legal and political nature of the city as a corporate entity. For

My investigation, then, came to be centered on three linked questions: Why and in what sense did "urban" reform emerge as the defining center of so much nationwide political activity in the 1890s? Why did the structure and organization of government emerge as the defining center of that reform movement? And what significance is there, for these questions, in the simultaneous emergence of a newly minted image of the city as the "Hope of Democracy?"

A historical approach sensitive to the relation among ideas, institutions, culture, and society proved critical for engaging the problem: the limits I have mentioned in the conventional literature trace, essentially, to a cruder understanding of this relationship, one in which new urban ideas are seen as a "response" to conditions, arising as if by spontaneous generation from volatile social matter. But intellectual history helps us to understand what we grasp more intuitively in the present: that this is simply not how things work. Ideas have their own complex history and genealogy; intellectuals, broadly defined, work out of cultural roles and—in this case, especially—institutional settings equally complex and historical, and profoundly intertwined with the ideas themselves; the broader social and political context is also tightly woven into the ideas, the institutions, and the intellectuals, so as to seem both ever-present and invisible. A central task of intellectual history is to unravel this fabric and to penetrate the complex relationships among its individually complex elements.[3]

Or perhaps, the metaphor might best be archaeological, given the layers of time that have settled over the past, obscuring not only its meaning but the processes that produced it. In this respect, it is useful to

---

thorough recent discussions of this problem, see Kenneth Fox, *Better City Government: Innovation in American Urban Politics, 1850–1937* (Philadelphia: Temple University Press, 1977), 42–62. Finally, an enormously useful survey and analysis of images of cities in contemporary journals is Dana Francis White, "The Self-Conscious City: A Survey and Bibliographic Summary of Periodical Literature on American Urban Themes, 1865–1900," (Ph.D. thesis, George Washington University, 1969). I have discussed the reform literature in an essay-review of five recent titles touching on urban reform. See "Oyez, Oyez, Oyez: The Curious Case of Plunkitt v. Steffens," *Journal of Urban History* 7, no. 2 (Feb. 1981):205–218. On the National Municipal League, see Frank Mann Stewart: *A Half-Century of Municipal Reform* (Berkeley: University of California Press, 1950).

[3]For a recent overview of the current state of this field, excellent on substantive, methodological, and philosophical themes alike, see the recent collection edited by John Higham and Paul Conkin, *New Directions in American Intellectual History* (Baltimore: Johns Hopkins University Press, 1979).

distinguish between two closely related problems confronting the intellectual historian on such a dig. One is the difficulty of understanding the full meaning of unearthed artifacts whose nature and function is relatively unknown to us. For instance, in some earlier research on the Shakers, whose utopian communist communities flourished in the nineteenth century, I found my greatest challenge was to understand, from the vantage of an individualistic, skeptical world, the full social meaning and resonance of Shaker religious terminology, such as the term *afflatus*, which they regularly used to measure and express both the nature of their religious feeling and the state of their social bond. In the same sense, in teaching the survey course, I regularly have to struggle to explain what predestination meant to the early Puritans, and why—every student's question—this belief did not encourage them to succumb to every temptation of the flesh or spirit, as behavior was believed to have no determining effect whatsoever on a fate that had been fixed for them by a stern God well before their birth.

I mention this kind of familiar archaeological problem because the difficulties I encountered were of a rather different sort and require a different kind of historical imagination. In dealing with cities and historical urban imagery, the problem was not so much terms and meanings that have fallen out of our imagination and vocabulary, but precisely the opposite: concepts—such as bureaucracy, and efficiency, and administration—that remain in currency and have even become central to our understanding of the world. This very currency and centrality make them rather *too* recognizable in the historical documents. The temptation is immediately to take them at our current face-meaning and face-value, thereby obscuring the different meaning they actually may have had in their own quite different context.

In this second and, I think, more delicate and difficult sense, the job of intellectual history is to help us recover and reconstruct, through both contextual and developmental perspectives, how and why the meaning of familiar words, categories, concepts, and values has changed over time, and what these changes tell us about broader patterns of historical change. I hope this exercise in the history of urban imagery can help expose this process to view, and for an important reason: unless this is done, the very familiarity of language can—and in fact, has—tempted us into a misapprehension and misapplication of our own history in current circumstances. And in this particular instance, the fact that this reconstruction does not come easily begins to suggest how far our contemporary culture, academic and political, has traveled in the years separating

that first self-conscious urban crisis and the one that lingers today, un-
fashionable and unsolved.

POLITICAL SCIENCE AND THE PROBLEM OF THE CITY

I began by trying to understand the institutional and intellectual
landscape out of which Progressive-era urban theory emerged. The historiographical moment for such a probe seemed propitious because of a
recent outpouring of work exploring the history of academic professionalization in this same period, a literature that has generated quite lively
debate about the complex links among ideas, the institutions shaping
them, and the larger political and cultural context in which both intellectuals and institutions functioned. As so much of the Progressive literature
was written by a first generation of academic urban specialists, mostly in
what was just coming to be called political science, and as I suspected that
this professionalism might have had a lot to do with the contrast between
the urban reform of the 1890s and that of an earlier era, it seemed a
reasonable place to set out my stakes and line and begin to dig.[4]

A preliminary survey confirmed this hypothesis, but with a curious
twist that only made the problem seem more intriguing: it became almost
immediately apparent that the academic emergence of the study of politics and government is, to date, something of a problematic missing link

[4]In addition to Haskell, *Professional Social Science*, I have in mind Burton Bled-
stein, *The Culture of Professionalism: The Middle Class and the Development of
Higher Education in America* (New York: W. W. Norton, 1976); Mary Furner,
Advocacy and Objectivity (Lexington: University Press of Kentucky, 1975); and
Dorothy Ross, "Socialism and American Liberalism: Academic Social Thought in
the 1880's," *Perspectives in American History* 11 (1977–1978):5–79, and "The
Development of the Social Sciences," in *The Organization of Knowledge in
Modern America, 1860–1920*, ed. A. Oleson and J. Voss (Baltimore: Johns
Hopkins University Press, 1979), 107–130. See also an excellent review essay,
Henrika Kuklick, "The Organization of Social Science in the United States,"
American Quarterly 28 (1976), 124–141. One other study of interest, though its
argument is problematic, is Hamilton Cravens, "The Abandonment of Evolu-
tionary Social Theory in America: The Impact of Academic Professionalism upon
American Sociological Theory, 1890–1920," *American Studies* 12 (1971), 5–20.
An interesting empirical study is Al Gedicks, "American Social Scientists and the
Emerging Corporate Economy, 1885–1915," *The Insurgent Sociologists* 5 (1975),
25–47.

in this energetic new literature. Almost all the attention has been given to the professionalization of economics, which preceded that of political science, and to the golden age of sociology, which followed it. For example, Thomas Haskell's influential recent book *The Emergence of Professional Social Science*, which presumes to explain how and why new academic experts explained the world of the 1890's as they did, ignores almost totally that emerging discipline whose special concern was precisely the political institutions that were the focus of almost obsessive public discussion during the decade. Given the centrality of the study of urban government to this emerging new discipline at the time, its invisibility in the recent literature made me suspect that to understand that era's urban theory and theorists would be to begin to gauge more fully the cultural distance that has opened up between our sense of the world and theirs.[5]

Accordingly, I soon found myself digging further and further into the increasingly unfamiliar world of late-nineteenth-century political science. Finally, several levels down and at a considerable remove from urban theory, I began to find artifacts that suggest some surprising sources of that theory. In particular, I found buried there a rather substantial statue, a monument that must have cast quite a shadow in its day but that has since been all but forgotten, even by political scientists. At the base of the statue was the name John W. Burgess.

At first glance, there seem to be few reasons to recall Burgess. He has probably been most often cited, recently, in connection with discussions of ethnicity and pluralism, because he had been one of the intellectual pillars of anti-immigrant propaganda at the turn of the century and after, and one of the chief spokesmen for the "Teutonic Hypothesis" of Aryan and Anglo-Saxon racial superiority.[6] His role as an academic inno-

[5]Haskell, *Professional Social Science*, 190–191, 215, for generally sketchy treatment of political science. Furner, *Advocacy and Objectivity*, 278–291, is quite good, but her treatment of political science is somewhat peripheral to the main conceptual framework of her study. Fox, *Better City Government*, 33–41, is good on this point.

[6]See Burgess's public address, "Uncle Sam," delivered at Cologne while he was a distinguished holder of a visiting chair in Germany. Significantly, Burgess chose to have this speech included as an appendix to his very useful autobiography, *Reminiscences of an American Scholar* (New York: Columbia University Press, 1934), 380–401, esp. 396–398. William A. Dunning once remarked that Burgess stood for "The Anglo-Saxon Militant, the Teuton Rampant, and the Aryan Eter-

vator, however, though not unconnected to this, has proved far more significant, and at the time, it was certainly the basis for his enormous reputation. Burgess, at Columbia University, was to political science what Herbert Baxter Adams at Johns Hopkins was to history: the virtual creator in the American university of the research-oriented, graduate-seminar-focused professional academic discipline.[7] After several frustrating years at Amherst College, Burgess was invited to put into practice at Columbia the model he had been thinking about since his formative studies in Berlin and Göttingen. He took the ball, as they say, and ran with it. He established the School of Political Science in 1880, staffing it with former students from Amherst such as Richmond Mayo-Smith, Frank Goodnow, and Munroe Smith; he persuaded another student to publish the new *Political Science Quarterly;* in the early 1890s, he masterminded the overall transformation of Columbia into a modern, structured university. For over 30 years, Burgess's school, his journal, his students, and *their* students dominated the study of American government and politics.[8]

---

nally Triumphant," quoted in Jurgen Herbst, *The German Historical School in American Scholarship* (Ithaca, N.Y.: Cornell University Press, 1965), 126–127. See also Edward Saveth, *American Historians and European Immigrants* (New York: Russell and Russell, 1965, a reissue of the original edition, New York, 1948), 32–64. Useful as well is Barbara Miller Solomon, *Ancestors and Immigrants: A Changing New England Tradition* (Cambridge: Harvard University Press, 1956), esp. Chapter 4, "The Anglo-Saxon Complex," 59–81.

[7]See Herbst, *German Historical School,* 169–175, 177, on Burgess's role in these developments. Also, Somit and Tanenhaus, *The Development of American Political Science* (Boston: Allyn & Bacon, 1967), 16–17, 23–25; and Richard Hofstadter and Walter Metzger, *The Development of Academic Freedom in the United States* (New York: Columbia University Press, 1955), 367–382. Bernard Crick, *The American Science of Politics* (Berkeley: University of California Press, 1959), 27–29, is especially good, as is William R. Shepherd, "John W. Burgess," in *American Masters of Social Science,* ed. Howard Odum (New York: Henry Holt, 1927), 23–57.

[8]See Burgess, *Reminiscences,* 139–149, 188–244; Somit and Tanenhaus, *American Political Science,* 21–23; and Munroe Smith, "The University and the Non-Professional Graduate Schools," Book 2 of *History of Columbia University* ed. Brander Matthews et al. (New York: Columbia University Press, 1904), esp. 223–228. Exhaustive, of course, is the school's and department's own history; it is surely one of the few departments to be so served: R. Gordon Hoxie, ed., *A History of the Faculty of Political Science in Columbia University* (New York: Columbia University Press, 1955), esp. John D. Millett, "The Department of Public Law and Government," 256–283.

Burgess himself, however, managed the neat trick of dominating the field while having almost no real intellectual influence and few disciples. In fact, his own work served more as a negative reference than anything else. Because this curiosity is central to the present investigation, it must be briefly considered.

Like Herbert Baxter Adams, Burgess was deeply committed to the method of historical and comparative study, to the searching out of documents, and the study of institutional evolution. The goal was to discover how the forms of political and institutional development expressed national spirit, which Burgess took to be essentially racial in essence. While other races had their own spiritual strengths, to which he paid lip service, he argued that the special gift of Teutonic/Aryan blood was a capacity for civil government. This made the detailed tracing of Western institutions and constitutional history the appropriate concern of political science. The germ theory of historical process, to which Burgess and Adams subscribed, directed searchers back to the study of local institutions, whose evolution, it was believed, best manifested emergent Spirit.[9]

For all the scientific methodology, Burgess was an almost purely Hegelian idealist. For him the State—as the spirit of a People—was an *a priori* Idea, preceding, separable from, and frequently in conflict with the particular forms and structures of tangible government. The test of a government's legitimacy, accordingly, was the degree to which it embodied and expressed the former.[10] This philosophy both grew from and

[9]See Bernard E. Brown, *American Conservatives: The Political Thought of Francis Lieber and John W. Burgess* (New York: Columbia University Press, 1951), 131–133; Herbst, *German Historical School*, 116–117, 120–127; and Saveth, *Historians and Immigrants*, 15–21, and Solomon, *Ancestors and Immigrants*, 59–81.

[10]Burgess's major work is *Political Science and Comparative Constitutional Law* (Boston: Ginn and Co., 1890–1891). See also a concise application of his overall views to the American constitutional system in Burgess, "The American Commonwealth: Changes in its Relation to the Nation," *Political Science Quarterly* 1 (1886): 9–35. He defended his general position in *Reminiscences*, 250–253. In addition to Brown, *American Conservatives*, 113–119, 172–173, other helpful discussions of Burgess's philosophy are to be found in Bert James Loewenberg, "John William Burgess, The Scientific Method, and the Hegelian Philosophy of History," *Mississippi Valley Historical Review* 42 (1955):490–509; and Charles Gilbert, "Operative Doctrines of Representation," *American Political Science Review* 57 (1963):604–618, esp. 605. Herbst, 66–67, noted that Burgess was known to his students at Amherst as "Old Weltgeist," *German Historical School*, 66–7.

informed Burgess's life and politics. Traumatized by the agonies of living through the Civil War in the painfully divided Upper South, he emerged a passionate nationalist who thirsted for unity and order. He had nothing but contempt for the elegant balances of eighteenth-century political theory, especially the fiction of contract and the states' rights doctrine he held responsible for the war. The nation he envisioned embodied a transcendent unitary spirit based on individual rights and freedoms. This led him to distinguish between the desirability of a strong national state and the undesirability of a strong active national government. He was, in short, a *laissez-faire* nationalist.[11]

Now, for our purposes, it is not very important to trace how all this combined with the racism to make him into a notorious reactionary, disgraced by "Teutonophilia" during the next major war. It is more to the point to notice at what an early point, and in terms as much intellectual as political, he was an embattled conservative within his own profession, attacked and challenged in particular by many of his own students.

Burgess himself was quick to detect this growing generational revolt against his philosophy. Given his role as a conduit for German educational models, it is ironic that he tended to blame this revolt on the ideas that his successors were picking up in their studies abroad, especially in Germany. In a remarkable speech at the 1893 Columbian Exposition, for instance, he identified several major threats to American civilization, among them immigration, which by "polluting it with non-Aryan elements" subverted America's mission to uphold an "Aryan genius for political civilization upon the basis of a predominantly Teutonic nationality." But he reserved his major fury, in this speech, for what he held to be a less well-understood threat: the "occult and corrupting influences" of the "young professors filled with European culture," and especially filled with one part of that culture, the "vicious nonsense" of socialism.[12]

---

[11]A good discussion of the impact of the Civil War on Burgess's generation and nationalism is in Barry Karl, *Charles E. Merriam and the Study of Politics* (Chicago: University of Chicago, 1974), 32–33; on this point, also see Loewenberg, "Burgess, Scientific Method, and Hegel," 501–505; Crick, *American Science of Politics*, 97–99; Brown, *American Conservatives*, 120–131, 174–175; and Herbst, *German Historical School*, 66–67, 126–127. For an excellent discussion of the implications of this nationalist critique of divisible sovereignty for local government, which is discussed below, see a little known but very useful work, Anwar Hussain Syed, *The Political Theory of American Local Government* (New York: Random House, 1966), esp. 10–15.

[12]The speech was reprinted as "The Ideal of the American Commonwealth,"

This was not just public hyperbole. In arguing within a university committee in 1889 for the restructuring of Columbia, he had rested his case on the proposition that "nearly all the Americans who have studied abroad during the last decade have returned to this country with a more or less pronounced leaning towards state socialism." The issue, he claimed, was "whether the American point of view, now practically non-existent, shall be supplied." This supply he held to be the "paramount duty which Columbia College owes the American people."[13]

The threat of socialism, state or otherwise, was not really the source of Burgess's discomfort, of course. Even more to the point, Columbia University was not part of the solution. As Burgess surely must already have sensed from the work of his protégés there, it was part of the problem: by the late 1880s, the first generation to come through American graduate training was already turning the comparative method against the idealism of Burgess and Adams. Nothing was more central to this revolt than the emerging study of public law and administration. And at the heart of that study, for reasons we need to understand, was the problem of the place and meaning of urban government.[14]

The form that this revolt took at Columbia, led by Frank Goodnow,

---

Political Science Quarterly 10 (1895), 404–425; quoted passages, 406–407, 410–412. See also, Shepherd, "Burgess," in Odum, *Masters of Social Science*, 54–55, on Burgess's resentment of the younger generation around him. On the context of German education to which Burgess referred, see Herbst, 1–10.

[13]Burgess, "Report of the Several Faculties to the Special Committee of the Trustees on the Elevation of the Courses of Instruction" (New York, 1889), printed in Hoxie, *Faculty of Political Science*, 51.

[14]On the generational conflict, see Crick, *American Science of Politics*, 95–96, 101; and Somit and Tanenhaus, *American Political Science*, 61–63, which puts it in the broader context of a general attempt to "Americanize" a new field, which still, in the mid-1890s, found almost half the reviews in the *Political Science Quarterly* covering foreign volumes, mostly German. For the atmosphere at Columbia, and the presence of Burgess for younger colleagues and students, see Richard Hofstadter, *The Progressive Historians: Turner, Beard, Parrington* (New York: Knopf, 1968), 179–181, on Beard; see also Max Lerner, "Charles Beard's Political Theory," in Howard K. Beale, ed., *Charles A. Beard: An Appraisal* (Lexington: University of Kentucky Press, 1954), 28–32, on Burgess as negative reference. A scathing review of Burgess's magnum opus by Woodrow Wilson can be found in *The Atlantic Monthly* 67 (1891): 694–699, reprinted in Arthur Link, ed., *The Papers of Woodrow Wilson*, vol. 7 (39 vols.; Princeton, N.J.: Princeton University Press, 1966 to date), 195–203. Finally, for a sense of the changing of the guard, see Frank Goodnow's address as the first president of the new American Political Science Association, "The Work of the American

will be clearer if we turn for a moment to parallel developments at Johns
Hopkins, where the young Woodrow Wilson was forging an original and
widely noted critique of American politics, a critique with administrative
theory at its center. As Morton White noted decades ago, Wilson and his
generation were almost obsessed with getting at what seemed to them
real life—with getting beyond the abstract formalism of the orthodox
thought surrounding them.[15] In politics, this meant getting beyond the
reification of constitutions and institutions, historically or in the present.
It meant describing how things actually worked or didn't, and it meant
measuring the distance between government on paper and government
in action. The term Wilson used to describe this latter pole—the pole of
government in action, real government—was *administration*.[16]

The critique had more at its base, of course, than just philosophy. It

---

Political Science Association," *Proceedings of the American Political Science
Association* (1904):35–46. It should be noted that most of these conflicts were
intellectual; for the most part, Burgess was a genial colleague and an enormously
imposing and successful teacher; see the memoir by one more disposed to
appreciate his virtues, Nicholas Murray Butler, *Across the Busy Years: Recollec-
tions and Reflections* (New York: Scribner's, 1939), 68–69.

[15]Morton White, *Social Thought in America: The Revolt against Formalism* (New
York: Oxford University Press, 1976, orig. edition, 1949), 3–7. See also Cushing
Strout, *The Pragmatic Revolt in American History: Carl Becker and Charles
Beard* (New Haven, Conn.: Yale University Press, 1958), 90; Edward Purcell,
*The Crisis of Democratic Theory: Scientific Naturalism and the Problem of
Value* (Lexington: University Press of Kentucky, 1973), 5–10, 17. There is an
excellent discussion of the Burgess legacy-to-be-overthrown in Hofstadter, *Pro-
gressive Historians*, 182–186, and in Lerner, "Beard," 30–32. See also Brown,
American Conservatives, 156–258. So total has been the defeat, that Burgess's
contributions are easily overlooked; for a sensitive discussion placing them in
context, see Martin Landau, "The Myth of Hyperfactualism in the Study of
American Politics," *Political Science Quarterly* 83 (1968):378–399, esp.
378–382.

[16]See, of course, Wilson's classic essay, "The Study of Administration," *Political
Science Quarterly* 56 (1941, a reprint of the original 1887 article, *PSQ* 1):481–
506. On Wilson's thought generally in this period, see Henry Wilkinson Bragdon, *Woodrow Wilson: The Academic Years* (Cambridge: Belknap Press of Harvard University Press, 1967), 101–106. On the particular point of reaching a
"real" level, see in addition to the citations in Footnote 15, Crick, *American
Science of Politics*, 106, and Dwight Waldo, *The Administrative State: A Study
of the Political Theory of American Public Administration* (New York: Ronald
Press, 1948), 3–7. See Frederic C. Howe, *Confessions of a Reformer* (New
York: Scribner's, 1925), for the 'famous first pages' paean to Wilson and the
others at Hopkins, where, Howe says, "my life really began."

was not coincidental that Burgess's credo grew so directly out of the experience of his generation in a nation first shattered by civil war, and then battered by the seeming impossibility of achieving a postwar unity and national harmony. As Wilson's generation came of age, the agenda had changed: now the major fixation was on what Henry George popularized as the unstable and occasionally explosive tension between the twin products of the industrial age, progress and poverty. The challenge to American democracy was to show itself capable of defusing this bomb, a job seemingly made more difficult by the rise of corporate power, the swelling of a diverse, aggressive labor movement, the collapse of government into corruption and incompetence, and a radical specter assuming corporeal form in both domestic and imported varieties. Wilson and many of his young colleagues eagerly took up this challenge, acknowledging its high stakes: if American government could not prove equal to the task, then the socialist critique would have to be admitted, together with its belief that a socialist reconstruction of society and its institutions was as necessary and natural to the world of industrial capitalism as bourgeois republicanism had been while capitalism emerged out of feudalism.[17]

Here Burgess and Adams were turned on their heads. Where, to them, eighteenth-century theory inhibited the expression of the State-as-Spirit, to Wilson it represented a more simple anachronism in the modern world, and an impediment, more importantly, to the development of the more positive governmental capacity necessary for dealing with a transformed social and economic order. Nowhere were progress and poverty on a more ominous collision course than in modern cities, of course, and nowhere was the gap between the forms and realities of power more incapacitating. Given the silence of the U.S. Constitution on urban government, cities were, by definition, invisible in orthodox theory. Their palpable reality, then, and their highly problematic politics, stood for Wilson as a proof of the irrelevance of the received orthodox approaches in political science: this made dramatically manifest the need for a reformulated theory capable of first seeing the cities, and then dealing with them.[18] We shall consider this theory in detail shortly; for now it is

[17]See especially Ross, "Socialism and American Liberalism."
[18]For an excellent discussion of the relationship between administrative thought and the municipal question, see Fox, *Better City Government*, 33–39, 42–62. On Wilson, see Bragdon, *Wilson: Academic Years*, 196–198. Also useful is Keller, *Affairs of State*, 289–297. For an illustration of Wilson's approach, see Link, *Wilson Papers*, Vol. 5, 559–563, notes for a lecture on municipal government within a series on administration.

important to appreciate how municipal affairs functioned as an almost
inevitable crux of the assault on the idealist orthodoxy, an assault that
Wilson and the others mounted with the very weapons of historical and
comparative analysis that Burgess and Adams had handed them.

Although he never published most of the writings and notes on
administrative law and history that fill the volumes of his collected papers
for these years, this study was Wilson's major intellectual preoccupation
throughout the early 1890s. As the decade's tempo of political and social
strife quickened, Wilson was insistent on interrupting his own speedy
climb up the academic ladder—from Bryn Mawr to Wesleyan to Princeton—to return for six weeks or so every winter to Johns Hopkins, where
he delivered a lecture series on public law and administration that culmi-
nated in an elaborate comparative study of municipal government in the
United States, England, France, and Germany.[19] As it happened, in 1896
these lectures coincided with an intense political standoff between Baltimore's new reform mayor and its unreconstructed council. Wilson, already widely known as a public speaker, found his Hopkins lectures
suddenly a public sensation. Shortly thereafter, he made his maiden
political speech—at a giant municipal reform rally where he shared the
platform with Teddy Roosevelt.[20]

It is hard to say which was a more significant development in the
1890s, the centrality of municipal questions to an emerging new political
science or the authority of academic social scientists in urban reform
movements, as Wilson's debut indicates. For the first, it is interesting to
note that the earlier American Social Science Association, Haskell's subject, divided its labors into categories that allowed no room for a particular focus on urban concerns, especially governmental. By the 1890s, however, municipal government had come to dominate the quasi-academic–
quasi-professional periodical press that reached that same audience. And

[19]See, for example, Wilson's lecture notes, Link, *Wilson Papers*, Vol. 6, 484–521.
These are introduced with a helpful editorial note on the lectures, 482–484. See
also Bragdon, *Wilson: The Academic Years*, 183–201, on these lectures. Wilson
also made the same points repeatedly in public lectures through the period. "I
am loaded to the muzzle on municipal reform," he noted (Link, Vol. 6, 675).
The lecture cycle is repeated in different forms. See Link, Vol. 7, 112–114, for
an editorial comment on the 1891–1893 lectures, with notes, 114–158.
[20]See Wilson's notes, and newspaper accounts, in Link, *Wilson Papers*, Vol. 9,
411–414, 437, 449–454, 461–465, 468–473, 477–480, 482–483. The March 4,
1896, rally is discussed and reported, 483–484.

this dominance was even more true in academic political science: by mid-decade, over 20% of the articles in Columbia's *Political Science Quarterly* were on municipal themes.[21]

As to the second point—reform activism—there is little need for extensive demonstration. Goodnow and most of his younger Columbia colleagues worked hard in the mayoral campaigns of their president, Seth Low. But far more visible and important was their hugely influential role, joined by colleagues elsewhere, in shaping the agenda of the national reform movement. Present at the creation of the National Municipal League in 1894, these academics succeeded gradually in shifting its focus from reportage to prescriptive analysis. When the League's *Municipal Program* was unveiled in 1899, it bore the clear stamp of the new political science: its drafting had been dominated by Goodnow, his students John Fairlie and Delos Wilcox, Wilson's classmate Albert Shaw, and Leo Rowe of the University of Pennsylvania. Lawyer Horace Deming, who chaired the committee, was the rule-proving exception, as his contribution reflected the academic theory far more than it did the tradition of mugwump moralism from which he came.[22]

There is one more point to be made before turning to a closer analy-

[21]Haskell, *Professional Social Science*, 104–106, noted that the divisions followed the lines of the *old* professions: education, health, jurisprudence, and social economy, replaced teaching, medicine, law, and the ministry. See also Dana White, 606–607, who noted that the urban themes of the early period were tangential to other foci and tended to be, when focused on government, reportorial and sensationalist, rather than analytical in any sense. This unique thesis is somewhat mechanical, but it produces an extraordinary overview: White has surveyed everything published in a group of selected journals and has analyzed the total contents by theme, as well as providing profiles of the contents of each individual magazine, 37 in all, ranging from semipopular to academic journals. The rise of a quasi-profession of urbanism experts is, he argued, revealed by the trend in both subject matter and approach in the late 1880s and the 1890s. See also Fox, *Better City Government*, 42–58, and Griffith, *American City Government*, 266–269, for a discussion of this theme.

[22]See *A Municipal Program, Report of the Committee of the National Municipal League, Adopted by the League, November 17, 1899, Together with Explanatory and Other Papers* (New York: Macmillan, 1900). This report includes the program itself and articles by Goodnow, Shaw, Fairlie, Wilcox, and Deming. See also Goodnow's presidential address, "Work of the American Political Science Association," for an explicit argument that activism was the heart of the new group's mission, 43–45. For background, see Stewart, *A Half-Century of Municipal Reform*, 23–30, 40–49.

sis of this theory, and that is to observe that this activism was as integral to the intellectual assumptions of the new discipline as the urban focus was their logical consequence. In fact, activism lay close to the heart of what these scholars understood by the very term *science*. To them, as Dwight Waldo noted, "one became scientific by studying 'nature not books;' the scientific method was thought of as the natural partner of a practical reformism." They would have agreed with Marx, or rather he was expressing a broader assumption in social science, when he declared that "the point is to change the world."[23] Needless to say, they had a rather narrower sense than he of what kind of change that world needed, and their activism was restricted to the "practical," reflecting an already advanced retreat in American academia from the more fundamental examination of the assumptions of capitalism that marked social thought in the 1880's.[24] Burgess's fear of socialism, as we shall see, was not something that his students discarded with his Hegelianism. All this is still to say, however, that active engagement with the broader context of politics was a central dimension of the newer urban theory fashioned by political scientists, and it was seen as appropriately so. With this in mind, we are in a position to see how and why they made the city "the hope of democracy" and what this meant at the time, both in terms of municipal government and in terms of the broader political concerns to which urban theory was essentially addressed.

[23]Waldo, *Political Science in the United States of America* (Paris: A UNESCO Booklet, 1956), 12. Karl Marx, "Theses on Feuerbach," in Robert C. Tucker, ed., *The Marx-Engels Reader* (New York: 1972), 107–109. On the general "scientific" justification for activism, see Crick, *American Science of Politics*, 107; Somit and Tanenhaus, *American Political Science*, 42–47; and Haskell, *Professional Social Science*, 73. Karl, *Merriam*, 12, 25, noted that Merriam chose Columbia over Hopkins because of its relatively deeper commitment to involvement in the "real world." On the background of this notion in earlier doctrines of the whole man and public service, especially in the New England colleges from which Burgess and so many of the political scientists came, see George Peterson, *The New England College in the Age of the University* (Amherst, Mass.: Amherst College Press, 1963), 25–28, 172–195.

[24]On the academic retreat from socialism, see Ross, "Socialism and American Liberalism;" Bledstein, *Culture of Professionalism*, 372; and the debate between Mary Furner, *Advocacy and Objectivity*, and Thomas Haskell, *Professional Social Science*, over whether this is to be understood in sociopolitical or intellectual terms. See Furner, 41, 98, 106–117, 143–162; and Haskell, 154, 163, 175–187.

THE "CULTURAL ORGANICIST" APPROACH

To try to understand this theory by reading what has been written about it recently is a little like trying to navigate a tricky channel by relying on a map rather than a nautical chart: we can see the major outlines, but the underlying defining configurations remain hidden. Many of the vessels of recent scholarship, accordingly, end up on the rocks of confusion and contradiction. In them, reform theory is misjudged in a variety of ways: usually, it is wrapped in one blanket and labeled a theory of "administrative efficiency." Sometimes, there is a conservative/progressive dichotomy, like Holli's structural versus social reform. Sometimes there is a spectrum. But whatever the typology, the literature rarely gets much beyond labeling because it rarely takes the content of urban reform theory very seriously, a failure that the current interest in social history has unfortunately and unnecessarily reinforced.[25] Once the ideas are studied closely, however—one can almost say once the books are actually read—it is possible to make a lot more sense out of them, and to see how their light illumines the surrounding context.

The central problem confronting these theorists was the American city's powerlessness—both formally, in terms of constitutional interpreta-

---

[25]For some representative examples of what I am talking about, though hardly an exhaustive list, see Melvin Holli, *Reform in Detroit, Hazen Pingree and Urban Politics* (New York: Oxford University Press, 1969), especially the influential chapter "Social and Structural Reform," 157–178, esp. 174–175. John Buenker, *Urban Liberalism and Progressive Reform* (New York: Norton & Co., 1973), 119–120, 211, 221, tries to escape but is trapped by "two strains" of reform, mislabeled. The political science literature is equally uneven, sometimes making acute observations on one page, and then throwing the blanket over important distinctions on the next. See, for instance, Waldo, *Administrative State*, 43, and Hoxie, *Faculty of Political Science*, 262. The only recent works that show real clarity and depth in dealing with reform thought are, unfortunately, limited by seeing only the urban dimension of its applicability. See Fox, *Better City Government*, 42–48, and Martin Schiesl, *The Politics of Efficiency, Municipal Administration and Reform in America, 1830–1920* (Berkeley: University of California Press, 1977), 169–170, and my discussion of these recent works in "Oyez, Oyez, Oyez." For otherwise good treatments, which fail because the authors see the writings only as evidence of nostalgia for community, see Quandt, *Small Town to Great Community*, 137–159, which is exceptionally weak concerning cities, a curiosity considering the book's strengths in dealing with other social issues and social sciences.

tion, and actually, in terms of the real distribution of power among economic interests, the parties, and the state governments. As Gerald Frug has shown in an important recent article, the city, as a kind of corporation, had previously occupied a niche not very distinct from that of private corporations: both were bodies intermediate between the individual and the State, with distinctly defined powers and obligations. By the end of the nineteenth century, however, this intermediate ground was collapsing, propelling its occupants in opposite directions. Business corporations moved toward the sphere of the individual, claiming and more-or-less obtaining the unlimited rights accorded individuals under a liberal constitution. Municipal corporations, meanwhile, found themselves captured within the orbit of the State, subordinated to the legislatures, and losing most of their rights and powers because of the U.S. Constitution's resistance to the dangerous principle of divisible sovereignty. The challenge, therefore, was to find a way out of this dilemma and to empower the cities to engage the challenges before them: the new political scientists felt compelled, in effect, to save democracy from its inhibiting legal and formal self.[26]

The turn-of-the-century writers who took on this challenge tended to cluster around two distinct poles, one of which, revealingly, stood a good bit closer to the new academic political science than the other. Each grouping also—and this, too, is significant—sprawled across any left–right distinctions that one could draw, whether these concerned assumptions about the need for radical reform or about the nature of the emerging capitalist order.

Borrowing a phrase that Morton White used in a somewhat different context, the first position could be called that of the *cultural organicist.* This approach assumes that the American city variously was, is, or ought to be a corporate organism, a cultural core of civic spirit. Drawing heavily on aspects of the Burgess–Adams Germanic tradition, writers close to this pole adopted the distinction between polity and government, locating the germ of the nation in an organic local civic community distinguishable from its governmental institutions. This approach presumed autonomous local communities and, accordingly, prescribed virtually autonomous local governments as best suited to them. Its architects turned to compara-

[26]Frug, "The City as a Legal Concept," *Harvard Law Review* 93 (Apr. 1980): 1059–1154. Chapter 13 of this volume is an edited version of Frug's article.

tive study to demonstrate the value of the autonomy seemingly found in Europe, past and present.[27]

Albert Shaw best illustrated this approach. Very much in the modern idiom, he professed to care little about issues of form and structure, in contrast to functions: he saw his encyclopedic study of English and continental muncipalities as simply detailing, for instructive purposes, a governmental approach that seemed effective and popular in actual practice. But his thick volumes also projected a consistent if somewhat implicit theory. The ability to make expedient choices proceeds only from a capacity rooted, he felt, in practical self-government. And this, in turn, he tended to justify less by an appeal to necessity than by a claim that the city existed as a free-standing political community, morally if not quite legally prior to the claims of the State.[28]

In content, Shaw's vision was modern-dress mugwumpery. He dreamed of what might be called a dairy democracy—one that was pasteurized, that was freed from racial and ethnic civic impurities, yet not homogenized, in that the cream would still rise to the top. He held immigrants primarily responsible for the mess of urban affairs, and he felt that only accountable, service-delivery-efficient government on the business-corporation model would succeed in facilitating the larger civic mission of the urban community.[29]

Shaw's smug and stuffy reformism, however, is far less central to our concerns than the fact that these assumptions—the moral autonomy of the urban community, the utility of the business analogy, and the sense of an immigrant threat to the polity—are detectable at the base of a substantial and diverse group of theoretical studies from this period. This is even

---

[27]White, *Social Thought in America*, 11–15; see also Dana White, "Self-Conscious City," 98–101, on this group and approach. There is sensitive discussion in Boyer, *Urban Masses and Moral Order*, 252–256; Waldo, *Administrative State*, 73; and Fox, *Better City Government*, 42–62.

[28]See Shaw's major works, *Municipal Government in Great Britain* (New York: Century, 1895) and *Municipal Government in Continental Europe* (New York: Century, 1895). See also useful reviews by Frank Goodnow, in *Political Science Quarterly* 10 (1895):171–175, and 11 (1896):158–162. There is a solid recent biography, Lloyd Graybar, *Albert Shaw of the Review of Reviews: An Intellectual Biography* (Lexington: University Press of Kentucky, 1974). See Howe, *Confessions*, 556, for an eloquent testimonial to Shaw's personal impact.

[29]Graybar, *Shaw*, 64–66, 70–90, esp. 81–86, on immigrants.

true—in fact, it is especially true—of many works raising more fundamental questions about the larger capitalist system in which American cities existed. Here, the best example is Frank Parsons and his book *The City for the People*. Parsons was an idiosyncratic free-lance intellectual who never quite fit into the academic mold, except for a few years when he joined Edward Bemis and other radical refugees finding sanctuary at the then-Populist-controlled Kansas State University. His book is an ungainly but passionately powerful hymn to municipal socialism, one that begins on the title page by defiantly renouncing bourgeois copyright privileges and never lets up after that. Behind the passion was exhaustive study and documentation, a definitive case against the private mismanagement of utilities, and a careful case for both public ownership and complete home rule.[30]

The theoretical ground for these claims was uncertain, a sort of mushy cooperativism that lay closer to Albert Shaw than to socialism. For Parsons, the People's City would be morally sovereign, representing, as it did, "the condensation of the ages." It would be protected against the State only insofar as it claimed, he argued, the same autonomy in government that corporations claimed in private business. And within this thus-justified autonomy, civic patriotism would raise the best people to power, on the one hand, and, on the other, protect the city from the polluting effect of "that foul admixture of serfhood pouring in from Europe."[31]

In these terms then, the range of theorists being called *organicist* defined an approach to regenerated municipal government that was far more consistent than their politics might indicate. When we ask what kind of writers tended to embrace it, as a group, we also come up with a pattern politically eclectic but otherwise consistent. They tended to be generally quite tangential to the circle of professional academic disciplin-

---

[30]See Arthur Mann, "Frank Parsons, The Professor as Radical," in *Yankee Reformers in the Urban Age* (Cambridge: Harvard University Press, 1954), 126–144, esp. 126–135 on his biography, 139–141 on political thought. Frank Parsons, *The City for the People* (Philadelphia, n.d., but 1900), title page, 5, 9–13. The book is really three book-length chapters, one on public ownership, 17–254; one on direct legislation, 255–386; and one on home rule, 387–469.

[31]Parsons, *City for the People*, 5–7, 9, 156, 321–357, 405, 411, 391–392. Mann, *Yankee Reformers*, 9, 137, 141. Mann was unsure how to deal with Parsons's combination of radicalism and racism, so he attributed the racial ideas to his roots in "social engineering." As the text makes clear, my interpretation differs substantially.

ary study, like Frank Parsons. Some, like Albert Shaw, who had been trained in these newer modes, were no longer active in the universities. Those who were, and who represented the new social science, tended, to the extent that they shared the organicist approach, to represent the new sociology, like Edward Ross, or economics, like Ely and Bemis (to an extent) and Columbia's Richmond Mayo-Smith, who carried the racism of Burgess and Francis Amasa Walker to new heights of social pseudo-science.[32] But as a group, they were not, pointedly, close to the new political science. For in the mainstream of that emerging discipline, at Hopkins and Columbia, we see a very different theoretical baptism taking place. And this brings us back to Woodrow Wilson and especially to Frank Johnson Goodnow.

THE ADMINISTRATIVE THEORY OF THE CITY

"At the present moment," Goodnow wrote in an 1895 review of Albert Shaw, "we are probably more at sea, so far as the municipal problem is concerned, than at any other time in our history."[33] Given what we have already learned about the view from Columbia and Johns Hopkins, this assessment of the largely organicist literature comes as no surprise. Beyond the fact that it was heavily descriptive and comparative, it failed to engage two dimensions that Goodnow, Wilson, and their colleagues all held to be central requirements of the new political science: the recent literature failed, first, to locate cities in a larger legal and constitutional framework, and it therefore failed, second, to approach an adequate description of the real forces at work in and on municipal government. On each level—form and fact—Goodnow, Wilson, and the others argued repeatedly that there was a cardinal error: the isolation of city government and of the very notion of the city more generally from the political society in which these were inevitably imbedded, and which was

[32]See, for instance, Barbara Solomon, *Ancestors and Immigrants*, 77–81, on Mayo-Smith, who is also quoted at length in Dana White, "Self-Conscious City," 394–399. Many critics have noted the organicist dimension but have been unclear about its relation to other dimensions of political thought and theory. See, for example, Roy Lubove, "Frederick C. Howe and the Quest for Community," *The Historian* 39 (1977):270–291, which links Howe with Shaw and Parsons on superficial grounds, 274–275.

[33]Goodnow, "Review" of Albert Shaw, *Municipal Government in Continental Europe, Political Science Quarterly*, 11 (1896):160.

just as inevitably imbedded in them. This error the newer political scientists labored mightily to correct.[34]

From their vantage, at least the dilemma if not the solution was easily stated. Modern cities were by definition "organizations for the satisfaction of local needs." At the same time, they were also agents of the state, responsible for those interests that the citizens held as participants in a larger civic society. This dual character meant that cities were in some respects independent but had no real claim on more formal sovereignty, because this could and did attach only to the State, in which, by law, their nature was subsumed. Goodnow observed that this was clear enough in theory, but it had become even more compelling in point of historical fact: the accelerating interdependence of a nationalizing industrial economy made the claims of that larger system ever stronger, and rendered the already dubious claim to local sovereignty anachronistic in real terms as well.[35]

Given all this, the political scientists held the impulses for home rule, in the almost medieval sense frequently invoked, to be self-indulgent fantasies, pernicious because of their capacity to absorb the energies needed for dealing with the real questions of the real political world.[36]

---

[34]See Frank Goodnow, *City Government in the United States* (New York: Century, 1904), 302–304, for a good statement of this point. See also Goodnow, "Powers of the Municipal Corporation," in *Proceedings of the Louisville Conference for Good City Government and of the Third Annual Meeting of the National Municipal League* (Philadelphia, 1897), 63–66. In contrast, it is interesting to note (cf. comment in Footnote 1) that Hays's "Politics of Reform" never mentions the relationship of the city and state governments in his discussion of both the theory and the actuality of politics in urban progressivism. For background on Goodnow, see Millett, "Department of Public Law and Government," in Hoxie, *Faculty of Political Science*, 256–283, esp. 262; Crick, *American Science of Politics*, 107; Gilbert, "Doctrines of Representation," 609–611; Waldo, *Administrative State*, 77–80; and Haskell, *Professional Social Science*, 252 on the textual point raised here.

[35]Frank Goodnow, *Politics and Administration* (New York: Russell & Russell, 1967, reprint of 1900 edition), 47–52; "Powers of Municipal Corporation," 67–71; *City Government in the United States*, 69–88. This theme is well discussed by Fox, *Better City Government*, 42–62, 80–89; and especially by Syed, *Political Theory of Local Government*, 95–99, 155–156. See also Keller, *Affairs of State*, 332–336.

[36]Syed, *Political Theory of Local Government*, 87–95, 96–99. See Howe, who was generally for home rule in a less careful sense of the term, come closer to this position in his more theoretical writing, as in *The Modern City and Its Problems* (New York: Scribner's, 1915), 73–75, 85.

Wilson was very forceful on this point. Delusions of autonomy, he argued, could only produce a net loss in civic capacity, sending effective
power sliding into the hands of a local business elite or the state legislature, and most likely both, in corrupt tandem. In opposition, he argued
the need to see the city as neither "an economic corporation" nor "a
political unit, or society, or state on a small scale." Rather, it must be seen
as a unique combination requiring a unique approach, as a "humane
economic society" that would not "create checks and balances," but generate "communal feeling and energy."[37]

As this unhelpful term suggests, Wilson had only vaguely worked out
the notion of the "humane economic society" by the time he turned to the
Princeton presidency. But his analysis of existing municipal law and administration, a direct extension of his earlier approach to government-in-
action, was clear and thorough. In the hands of Frank Goodnow, almost
identical insights were fashioned into a far more complete and coherent
theory.

Most modern readers readily associate Goodnow with the famous
politics–administration dichotomy, and the general consensus seems to
be that he offered the latter as a substitute for the former, seeking to
isolate a value-free sphere of efficient government from the turmoil of
politics. He is often regarded as having been, therefore, the leader of a
sort of conservative revolution in democratic theory, one who, to the
extent his impulses were other than narrowly elitist, was misled through a
naive concentration on legal form and structure.[38]

This image makes me think that we should say about Goodnow what
a recent student observed about Burgess—that he is generally discussed
"with the respectful vagueness as to what were his actual views that well
demonstrates his unshakeable position in prehistory."[39] Actually, one
could go somewhat further and say that, if for some unhappy reason Frank

[37]These points are to be found throughout Wilson's administrative and municipal
   writings in the late 1880s and the 1890s. See, for a good statement, his lecture
   notes in Link, Vol. 6, 484–492. Other related arguments are in Vol. 6, 52–57,
   both of these from 1889.
[38]Holli, *Reform in Detroit*, 171–179, argued the "conservative revolution." Other
   writers who tend to misread Goodnow in one or more particulars include
   Schiesl, *Politics of Efficiency*, 73–74, 169–170; Robert Wiebe, *The Search for
   Order* (New York: Hill and Wang, 1967), 166–170; and Keller, *Affairs of State*,
   342. See Landau, 384–387, 398–399, "Myth of Hyperfactualism" for a perceptive discussion of why it has proved so easy to miss the point in such writings.
   Also helpful is Gilbert, "Doctrines of Representation," 609–614.
[39]Crick, *American Science of Politics*, 97.

Goodnow has been consigned to hell, his particular eternal torment probably consists entirely of reading the hopelessly garbled versions, in almost any discussion one can cite, of his own lucid and explicit writings. The context being developed here, however, should prove helpful in stripping the image down to its textual base, and in making use of what we find there.

What we find, in the first place, is that for Goodnow the famous distinction between politics and administration has meaning *only* in the context of the state–city relationship. Far from being a linear either/or between two abstract qualities, the distinction is one that Goodnow offered as a way of mapping the different possibilities of distributing real and formal power in a complex constitutional system. The dichotomy, that is, functions as more a descriptive than a normative tool in this context, and it is applied primarily to explicating the state–city relationship. This produced an argument along the following lines:

Given the fact of state law and the circumstance of interdependence, it is unsurprising that in the United States' real political power had gravitated to the legislatures. And because the cities were increasingly active as agents of more active state governments, their retained authority was only superficially their own—actually, they enjoyed real latitude only for carrying out the instructions of the detailed special legislation issuing from the legislatures. The situation was thus one of centralized legislative authority and decentralized administrative authority.[40]

Now, the dominance of the legislatures, and the party machines running them, had been faulted by just about everybody. Where Goodnow was different, and influential, was in criticizing in similiarly functional terms the mechanical, formal solutions that others found so attractive. The hold of the eighteenth-century formalism, he argued, offered reformers only two ways to combat excessive legislative power: they could limit it by constitutional change in the balance and separation of powers, or they could rely on judicial interpretation. But the tide of history made the first approach hopeless, and the power of the reigning "Dillion Rule"

[40]Probably the clearest and most concise statement is in Goodnow, "Powers of the Municipal Corporation," 67–71. See also Syed, *Political Theory of Local Government*, 155–156; Keller, *Affairs of State*, 294–297; and Fox, *Better City Government*, 9–12, all of which understand the basic relationships but fail to see their political implications in terms of the larger system, as opposed to their administrative implications within the city in the narrow and conventional sense of that term.

in jurisprudence—which strictly denied any local claims to sovereignty—foreclosed the second.[41]

Goodnow offered administration as a practical way out of this formal cul-de-sac. Neither constitutional nor judicial, administrative changes could redefine the nature of legislative power in the interest of more meaningful local autonomy, while refining the state's powers for the realization of its broader public-interest responsibilities. Because the state had to have some control of its agents, he said, let it be through centralizing overall administrative authority, which could be flexibly defined and distributed for action, rather than through the straitjacket of detailed special legislation. Instead of the legislature's telling the cities what to do (because it could not really delegate to them law-making power), a central administration could more simply ensure that the general mandate of the legislature would be met by supervising the actions that the cities could be granted a broad freedom to devise in meeting it. The result would be, in other words, administrative centralization and decentralized local decision-making, if not quite law-making. Rather than the state's gathering power, as it had done, and parcelling out responsibility, Goodnow demanded that the state gather the responsibility so that real, effective power could legally and practically be given to the municipalities to handle their own affairs more flexibly. This was the model that Goodnow and others thought they saw in the much-admired and generally popular governments of European cities.[42]

---

[41]Goodnow, *City Government in the United States*, 90–96, 102–103. On the legal tradition and the impact of the Dillon Rule, see Syed, *Political Theory*, 53–56; Keller, *Affairs of State*, 346–347; and Fox, *Better City Government*, 23. For an interesting example of how such ideas were being developed in ancillary fields, see William C. Chase, "The Influence of the American Law School: University Legal Scholarship and the Rise of Modern Administrative Government, 1870–1978," (Ph.D. thesis, Harvard University, 1978.) The title does not convey the degree to which the thesis focuses on administrative law and theory. See pp. 16–19, 28–33, especially. Chase devoted a chapter to Ernst Freund, a student of Goodnow who generally failed in efforts to bring some of the same insights to the teaching of law in the changing law schools—especially at Chicago, 157–208, esp. 157–164. See also, on law, Bledstein, *Culture of Professionalism*, 188–189.

[42]Goodnow, *Politics and Administration*, 47–54. See also Waldo, *Administrative State*, 108–110. A useful but uninspired study of Goodnow, helpful on this point, is Lurton W. Blassingame, "Frank J. Goodnow: Progressive Urban Reformer," *North Dakota Quarterly* 40 (1972):22–30, esp. 28–30. Also, Stewart,

Without understanding the central/local dimension of the politics–administration dichotomy, it is almost impossible to understand what these latter terms mean in Goodnow's work. This is even more apparent when we consider their application to municipal government itself. Goodnow held that urban government was essentially administrative in nature, and this has commonly been taken to mean that he sought to turn power over to administrators while denying it to politicians. This has often been read to mean, further, that he sought to divide the executive from the legislative, allowing the former to run the city with the aid of an efficiency-minded bureaucracy on the business-corporation model. By this point in our discussion, perhaps it will come as less of a surprise to discover that he meant precisely the opposite and endorsed, in fact, an opposite solution.[43]

Here is a perfect illustration of the need to understand the antiformalist critique in its own terms, not in their later meaning. Where orthodox classical theory divided powers formally to inhibit action, Goodnow and his colleagues sought to combine powers in real terms, in order to liberate the capacity for action. Politics and administration, he argued again and again, were not forms to be separated by levels of government, and certainly not by branches: rather, they were functional distinctions visible in different proportions throughout government. In fact, it was precisely the capacity of these functions to join levels, and to help merge formally separated legislative and executive powers, that appealed to Goodnow. He hoped that clearer distinction—not literal separation— would make possible the necessary consolidation for generating new civic

---

Half Century of Reform, 40–41, is good on this point, and on Goodnow. See also Fox, *Better City Government*, 82–83, and my critique of his argument in "Oyez, Oyez, Oyez."

[43]See Lawrence J. R. Herson, "The Lost World of Municipal Government," *American Political Science Review* 51 (1957):330–345, esp. 333, on how Goodnow's terms have been read. See Wiebe, *Search for Order*, 149–150 on this. Also, for contrary texts, see Goodnow, *Politics and Administration*, 18–22. Goodnow himself left little room for confusion, especially as regards the "business model," in "Powers of the Municipal Corporation," where he said (66), "It has become the fashion in this country of late years to speak of the city as a business corporation, and to regard the work of the city as rather business than governmental in character. This view of the city's position is, however, an incorrect one, and if followed it is believed, it will lead to disastrous results."

capacity. It would lead to cooperation between state and local government, as well as a consolidated, effective government in the city itself.[44]

This point, finally, helps to explain why he argued that in the constitutional sense cities must be thought of as administrative in character. By this argument, he sought to claim for municipal government a more realistic autonomy and power. By accepting this definition, one gave up only what was indefensible anyway: politics in the sense of sovereignty. But because ordinances and other city actions were technically regulations, not laws, the definition sacrificed nothing in effective terms. And what was retained was a broad area granted by the state administrative authority within which a consolidated polity—Goodnow, image notwithstanding, favored an all-powerful council, elected in large cities on a ward basis—could function in an uninhibited way.[45] The administrative definition, in other words, was functionally political in the sense that we commonly understand: its aim was to invigorate, enlarge, and liberate the local decision-making process, and it saw this as something reachable by structural change, rather than through the mystical, idealistic, and commonly racist notions relied on by the organicists.

Goodnow worked hard to distinguish his theory from the conservative business-corporation model, to which it was almost immediately connected by many observers. The distortion came up so often that he joked in his inaugural address as the first president of the new American Political Science Association in 1904 that he had "come to regard its use as evidence of an absolutely hopeless condition of mind in the one who uses

[44]Goodnow, *Politics and Administration*, 23–25, 38, 44, 87–90, 148–149, 158; Herson, "Lost World of Municipal Government," 333–336; Keller, 294–297. Wilson made a similar point in his Hopkins Lectures; see Link, *Wilson Papers*, Vol. 8, 86 (1893). Robert Daland, "Political Science and the Study of Urbanism," *Political Science Quarterly*, 51 (1957):494, is clear on the point that Goodnow *never* sought a rigid separation, nor was he as naive about the nature of politics as many have assumed. Waldo, *Administrative State*, 19–20, 80–84, is good on this point.

[45]Goodnow, *City Government in the U.S.*, 156–160, 189–184, 200–202. Wilson also made a similar argument about the need to generate civic capacity, and he offered this as the main goal of administrative approaches. See Link, *Wilson Papers*, Vol. 6, 52–57; Vol. 7, 344–368; and Vol. 11, 74–84, for a sense of the consistency with which he advanced this theme throughout the 1890s. See also Blassingame, "Goodnow," 28–30, and Karl, *Merriam*, 48, on these points.

it."[46] But the misunderstanding was understandable, especially once finely argued ideas left the texts and entered the lists, where a theorist could not control how the ideas were appropriated and applied.

Given this elusive quality, therefore, it is impressive testimony to the vigor and effectiveness with which Goodnow and his followers advanced their new framework that, by the turn of the century, and through the new century's first decade, it was precisely their assumptions that dominated not only urban theory, but the urban reform movement itself. This can be seen in almost every provision of the *Municipal Program* of the National Municipal League, as well as in most of the major books that brought municipal thought to a wide and attentive audience—books by Goodnow's students Wilcox and Fairlie and later Charles Beard, by the Chicago sociologist Charles Zueblin, and, of course, by Frederick C. Howe, especially the classic *The City: The Hope of Democracy*.[47]

These books, it must be said, do not fit neatly under the headings used here, partly because our labels represent emergent positions not always consistently held, and partly because the more popular literature was addressed to a wider audience for a wider range of purposes than Goodnow and other scholars needed to engage. These works thus tend toward the evangelical, with civic revival painted in the familiar colors of home rule and localized spiritual rebirth. Nevertheless, at their analytic heart, the popularized works show consistently how the new municipal

[46]Goodnow, "The Work of the American Political Science Association," 43. Chase, "The Influence of the American Law School," 161–164, describes Goodnow's frustration, even within his teaching environment, over the way in which his approach to law was dismissed as formalistic and remote, when actually it was intended to bring the dilemmas of the real-world nature of public law to the far more remote professionalism of the usual legal curriculum. See also Stewart, *Half-Century of Reform*, 40–42.

[47]*Municipal Program*, passim. See Howe, *The City: The Hope of Democracy* (New York: Scribner's, 1905), and Delos Wilcox, *The American City: A Problem in Democracy* (New York: Century, 1904), for example; also Charles Beard, *American City Government* (New York: Macmillan, 1912), and Charles Zeublin, *American Municipal Progress* (New York: Macmillan, 1902, revised 1916). These books were all semipopular and journalistic, devoting most of their space to summing up recent American experiences in government, and usually organized by topical area, rather than by the more abstract and theoretical comparisons of the earlier treatises. Nevertheless, the concern was still focused on larger questions of the nature of government and administration. See also, Griffith, *American City Government*, 258–262, 271–275.

theory was coming to transform the old. They concede the impossibility of autonomous community, and they seek to construct, through administrative autonomy, a definition of the city as an effective, pluralistic polity, one that is effective in serving its own needs and also, by virtue of its integration in a larger political and administrative system, capable of providing a modern democratic example of wider applicability.[48]

This redemptive mission, in fact, is perhaps the most distinctive characteristic of the newer model texts in comparison with the older organicist treatments. This suggests the significance of Howe's revealing title. It is not so much the point that progressive democracy will help efficiently to solve city problems; he did not call his book *Democracy: The Hope of the City*. Rather, the central focus is on how a new approach to government can be a means to the end of generating, by political involvement, a new, unmystical civic capacity, which could meet the general challenge to democracy posed by industrialization, immigration, and class division.[49]

Such a theory could easily be embraced at various points of the political spectrum, and so it was. Left progressives like Howe and Beard saw the hope as a genuine chance to restructure a faltering society almost overwhelmed by the contradictions of change. Those more in the center were also hopeful, though they identified the threat with the society's

[48]See, for example, Howe, *Hope of Democracy*, 1–7, 24–28, and *Modern City*, 61–75. Howe has been difficult for critics to understand, partly because his books are uneven and not always well controlled; partly because readers are misled by the ironic tone of his later autobiography and read this tone back into his earlier work, where it does not, I think, apply; and because, most importantly, they do not appreciate the real questions that Howe addressed, or the framework within which his writing fit. The result is a vision of Howe, and the others, as sort of "nostalgia-seeking romantics" fixed on small-town values. I find little in the record to support this conclusion. See, especially, Quandt, *Small Town to Great Community*, 24–25, 148–150, and Lubove, "Howe," 270–275, where Howe is lumped with Parsons and Shaw. See the murky discussion of Howe in Wiebe, *Search for Order*, 140–144, 156, for another illustration of this problem.

[49]Howe, *Hope of Democracy*, 24–28. See *Confessions of a Reformer*, 236–237, where Howe indicated that the *City* book was only the first of a series on the various levels of government, all devoted to a general democratic revival. See Lubove, 236–237, for an interpretation that, missing this orientation outward, can see little but hopeless romanticism and nostalgia in Howe's vision. See, for another illustration of the consciousness that my reading detects, Beard, *American City Government*, 386.

severest critics, and their optimisim was tinged with the anxiety of this political conflict. With regularity, reform theorists acknowledged the validity of the broader socialist indictment of capitalism's democracy, especially at the municipal level, where defense of the actual record was impossible. If the critique were not to be held more generally valid, and if socialist solutions were not to become legitimate, then the critique would have to be answered where it was most telling, and this became the weighty burden of the revived cities. As Charles Merriam suggested, they had a vital "androclean function" to perform in addressing the thorny contradictions of capitalism so evident in municipal affairs.[50]

On this point, as on so many others, nobody expressed more eloquently than Jane Addams the tension between an admissable socialist critique and its inadmissable consequences. Her speech before the Congress of the 1904 St. Louis World's Fair shows how directly this fear was connected to municipal theory. It suggests as well how thoroughly the framework we have been studying had, by then, become assimilated within the progressive reform outlook.[51]

---

[50]See Beard, *American City Government*, 386. Howe, *Hope of Democracy*, 9–23 repeatedly offers the city as a way to deal with the acknowledged social problem, by generating class harmony, rather than class conflict. The awareness of the socialist critique, and a similar contrast of class harmony versus class conflict approaches, can be found widely in the literature. See Woodrow Wilson, who lectured frequently on "democracy," contrasting it with socialism and using administration and municipal government as his focal points. Link, *Wilson Papers*, Vol. 7, 80–81, 344–368, for example; and Vol. 11, 74–84, a few years later. Wiebe, 154–156, was correct, I think, in pointing to the "deceptive optimism" of the approach described. See also Boyer, *Moral Order*, 279–280; Gilbert, "Doctrines of Representation, 611–612; and Hoxie, *Faculty of Political Science*, 29–31, for a discussion of tensions over socialism dating back to the 1880s, when a student-prize winner named Daniel DeLeon scandalized the school by making a radical speech at a public meeting. The Merriam quote is from Karl, 54. Actually, Merriam mentioned Androcles in the wider context of university and business cooperation, but as he saw, at the time and in his career, a reformed municipal context as the form and ground for that cooperation, the usage here seems supportable.

[51]Jane Addams, "Problems of Municipal Administration," *American Journal of Sociology* 10 (1905):425–444. This paper is also printed in the publications of the International Congress of Arts and Sciences of the Fair. This elaborate congress is discussed by Quandt, *Small Town to Great Community*, 102–103, and is mentioned by Herbst, *German Historical School*, 203, as marking one of the high points, in terms of visibility and legitimacy, of the new social science.

Most city governments, Addams charged in terms familiar to us by now, were hopelessly out of touch with the spiritual and material needs of modern society. They were blind to the ways in which those needs were better understood by some—by bosses, machines, ethnic organizations, and radical movements in particular. She saw reformers as befuddled by the appeal of all these, and she likened the helpless mugwump governments to the "religious revivalist [who] looks with longing on the fervor of a single-tax meeting, or the orthodox Jew who sees his son ignoring Yom Kippur and pouring all his religious fervor . . . into the Socialist Labor Party." She went on more seriously:

> There is no doubt that the rapid growth of the socialist party in all crowded cities is largely due to the recognition of those primary human needs which the well established governments so stupidly ignore. . . . They are practicing industrial government for an industrial age. . . . All that devotion, all of that speculative philosophy . . . concerning the real issues of life could, of course, easily be turned into a passion for self-government and the development of a natural life, if we were truly democratic from the modern evolutionary standpoint.[52]

That standpoint, she went on to outline in great detail, was precisely the one whose assumptions we have been reconstructing here. She looked to a government on the Goodnow model to help cast off those eighteenth-century notions "that repress rather than release the power of the people." She sought a new force in the largest cities, wellsprings of "the human dynamic character of progress."[53] And she looked to the practical dynamics of political involvement, released into action by structural reforms "from the modern evolutionary standpoint," as the agent that would regenerate the city and save democracy from all that threatened it. The city was not simply its hope—it was perhaps American democracy's last hope.

THE CITY AND AMERICAN POLITICAL CULTURE

In this necessarily quick tour through a partially completed archaeological dig, we have seen that the shift from the city as political cancer to the city as democratic hope involved fundamental changes in the legal,

[52]Addams, 437–438.
[53]Addams, 444.

constitutional, and political image of the city. Although this transformation had obvious roots and consequences within the urban context—real
responses to real and proximate urban problems—I have argued that it
can be understood only by moving outside that context in two senses: we
must recognize its sources in the institutional and intellectual emergence
of academic political science, and we must appreciate how that political
science functioned as a link to the broader concerns about societal
changes and conflict.

These conclusions stand at quite a remove in tone, as well as substance, from the conventional image of Progressive-era urban theory.
Even among its historiographical friends, the image of city government
held by Goodnow and others like him has been treated patronizingly, as a
nostalgic reminder of an earlier day when naive reformers supposedly
believed that mechanical tinkering alone, in the interests of more efficient
administrative machinery, could produce better city government. Less
sympathetic critics have held these reformers responsible for introducing
into American politics a set of far more pernicious administrative blind-
ers, which denied the necessity for and the possibility of fundamental
political change. These reformers are, in short, held responsible for drain-
ing the politics out of urban political science. I hope that I have made it
clear, through a demonstration of some of the tools of intellectual history,
how fundamentally these assessments miss the mark, and how they do so
by a fundamental misreading of the historical context that gives meaning
and point to this urban theory.

There is a powerful irony in all this, because we have discovered that
these earlier theorists held, in the broadest terms, precisely the image of
the city that they are accused of lacking: the city as a polity with a crucial
responsibility for engaging the largest, most deeply political challenges
facing American society. I also hope it is clear that my point has hardly
been to endorse the political content of this particular perspective, nor to
argue that its concrete prescriptions ought to have been adopted more
broadly in its own time, much less ours. I do believe, however, that this
story has a point to make about our own images of the city, of this society,
and of the relationship between them, one that is almost too obvious to
notice. This is the point, if I may push a tired metaphor one more time
around the ring: to the extent that it has been important to dig out these
old artifacts and dust them off, the main significance may lie less in the
treasure than in the dirt we have scraped away. It seems to me that the
real value of recovering the lost meaning of these urban images lies in

their power to make us think about why they have been so covered over, and to reflect on the transformations in values and ideas that have filled in the ground over them.

At this stage of my research, without having yet done more than preliminary work at other levels of the dig site, I can offer only some highly tentative comments about how this transformation came about. For one thing, it is clear that Goodnow's theory was, in terms of cities, almost self-destructive in its logic of national consolidation. Charles Beard was a loyal disciple of Goodnow, and he remained interested in municipal questions in practical terms for many years. But in his 1912 text on municipal government, he conceded that "strictly speaking there can be no such thing as municipal science, because the most fundamental concerns of cities, the underlying economic foundations, are primarily matters of state and national control."[54] Goodnow's effort to retain for local government a genuinely democratic dimension, in terms of real political process, was by this view ultimately doomed. Its demise immobilized much of the progressive left, caught as it was between a municipal socialism that had nowhere to go and a nationalized radicalism that inevitably lost touch with the concrete communities so important, as Jane Addams saw, to its appeal and integrity. And as the democratic content drained out of municipal governmental reform, some of it siphoned over to the federal government during the New Deal, and much of it simply soaked up by an emerging, middle-class consensus, left behind was the shell of bureaucratic structure and functional administration. This, perhaps, begins to explain why administrative reform became so sterile, why municipal radicalism disappeared so quickly, and why the corporate liberalism described by James Weinstein was so successful in obliterating our images of what both had meant.[55]

However tentative these judgments, I think we are on safe ground in finding in the curtain of invisibility that has fallen on the political thought of that earlier era a significance beyond ordinary obscurity or obsoles-

---

[54]Beard, *American City Government*, Vol. 9, 386. Beard remained a disciple of Goodnow, and a loyal friend. He later traced his resignation from Columbia in 1917, over a famous academic-freedom case, to a less well-known incident: the university's caving in to the wishes of an aging John Burgess, who successfully vetoed Goodnow when he sought to be named the successor to Burgess's about-to-be-vacated chair. See Hoxie, *Faculty of Political Science*, 104–108, 264–266; and see Hofstadter, *Progressive Historians*, 170–185 on Beard more generally.

[55]Weinstein, *Corporate Ideal and the Liberal State*, passim.

cence. This significance is well captured and readily expressed through contrasting the images of the city—especially as a part of a larger democratic society—held then and now. Then, it was deemed the province of politics—and political science—to engage the most fundamental questions about the nature and legitimacy of our political institutions, and urban government was seen as the most appropriate locale for this engagement. Then, the literature of urbanism centered on the relation of formal government—politics and administration—to the real structures of power and class throughout American society. These questions animated the generation of Wilson and Goodnow, whatever we may think of its formulaic answers or larger ideological intent. None of this can be claimed for the present one, whose own "urban crisis" has routinely been conceived of in terms of "problems" needing largely administrative "solutions," rather than as rumblings along the manifestly unstable fault lines of race and class that run beneath our entire society. The distinction between a society and its political institutions, a distinction traceable to Burgess and one that his successors sought so strenuously to retain while redefining—this distinction can barely be expressed, much less engaged, in our current political language. To come back to the exact point from which we departed, I do not think that it is too much to suggest that whereas the urban imagery of our first "urban crisis" encouraged an engagement with the far broader political and social issues confronting American society, the urban imagery of our more recent version served to deflect and even to finesse such larger political questions.

A comparative, historical approach to urban images and how they change, in this respect, helps to expose and explore this narrowing of our political culture, our ability to perceive the reality around us and to express it in political terms. If this narrowing represents a loss, and if it is one that scholars can help to remedy, then the story traced here has a corollary lesson as well. In contrast to the emergent professionalism of the 1880s and 1890s, our academic culture is substantially without the sense of obligation to engage and transform the political reality it studies. Yet this is an obligation, Frank Goodnow would be quick to point out, that he and his generation held to be central to the very nature and mission of social science.

CHAPTER 13

The City as a Legal Concept

GERALD E. FRUG

CITY POWERLESSNESS

The Current Status of Cities

American cities today do not have the power to solve their current problems or to control their future development. Their impotence is expressed in their legal status. Under current law, cities have no "natural" or "inherent" power to do anything simply because they decide to do it. Cities have only those powers delegated to them by state government, and traditionally those delegated powers have been rigorously limited by judicial interpretation. Moreover, city authority exercised pursuant to unquestionably delegated powers is itself subject to absolute state control. In an attempt to curb this unrestrained power, most state constitutions have been amended to grant cities "home rule," but local self-determination free of state control is still limited, even in those jurisdictions, to matters "purely local" in nature. These days, little, if anything, is sufficiently "local" to fall within such a definition of autonomy. State law, in short, treats cities as mere "creatures of the state."

Firm state control of city decision-making is supplemented by federal restrictions on city power. The U.S. Constitution, through the Fourteenth Amendment and the commerce clause, has been construed to limit city power. In addition, the federal government is today taking an

A longer version of this chapter was previously published in the *Harvard Law Review* 93, no. 6 (Apr. 1980):1059–1154.

Gerald E. Frug • Harvard Law School, Cambridge, Massachusetts.

increasing part in determining city policy, sometimes by mandating city action but more often by attaching strings to the federal grants-in-aid on which the cities have become dependent.

The growing importance of grants-in-aid illustrates another source of city powerlessness, a declining ability to generate income. City income is largely dependent on something cities cannot control: the willingness of taxpayers to locate or to do business within city boundaries. The problem of the increasing exodus of the wealthier taxpayers, including businesses, from the nation's major cities is notorious. Even if the cities could ensure that taxpayers would remain within their borders, however, current law does not allow the cities to tax them. Generally, every city decision to increase taxes must be expressly approved by the state, and some states even have a constitutional limitation on the amount of taxing permitted. The U.S. Constitution, particularly through the commerce clause, also restricts the kinds of taxes that cities can impose.

Even more stringent restraints curb the cities' ability to borrow money. State law imposes on cities detailed restrictions that supplement the normal market restraints applicable to other borrowers. Thus, the city's borrowing authority is generally limited to a fixed percentage of its property base, and even borrowing within that amount often requires a popular referendum to authorize the debt. Moreover, the use of borrowed money is restricted to "capital" as opposed to "operating" expenses. Given these limits on cities' taxing and borrowing ability, city dependence on state and federal financial aid is not surprising.

City power is limited in other ways as well. Cities, unlike states, are not general law-making bodies. Because of their dependence on a legitimate delegation of state power, their ability to regulate private activity is more like that of an administrative agency than of the state itself.[1] Moreover, state constitutions have generally been interpreted as authorizing cities to perform only a "welfare-improving regulatory service" and as denying them "a general authority to define rights or alter the basic legal structure of civil society . . . [by making] 'private' or 'civil' law."[2]

Not only are cities unable to exercise general governmental power, but they also cannot exercise the economic power of private corporations.

---

[1]See F. Michelman, "States' Rights and States' Roles: Permutations of 'Sovereignty' in *National League of Cities v. Usery*," *Yale Law Journal* 86 (1977): 1165, 1170 n.21.
[2]Ibid.

Municipalities may not engage in any "business" activity unless it "falls properly under the heading of a "public utility" and is not for profit.[3] Thus, both "public" and "private" city functions are largely reduced to the provision of certain municipal services. Yet today, even many of these services, such as education, transportation, and health care, are provided not by cities but by special districts or public authorities that are organized to cut across city boundaries and over which cities have no control.

The limits on city power described above usually seem natural and uncontroversial. They appear simply to follow from the status of cities as junior members of the governmental hierarchy. This sense of naturalness keeps us from questioning these limits or trying to think of ways to change them. Indeed, it is difficult even to imagine what another legal status for cities would look like.

Sharply different legal power is of course imaginable for private corporations. The restriction of city powers to those delegated by the state is clearly inapplicable; private corporate power can be exercised for any legal purpose merely by filing papers in whatever state the incorporators choose. The limitations imposed on cities by the Fourteenth Amendment or the commerce clause do not apply to private corporations; indeed, whereas cities are restrained by these provisions of the Constitution, corporations are protected by them. Similarly, the absolute limits on city taxing and borrowing power and on city business opportunities have no analogue for private corporations, whose revenue-raising capacities are instead governed by the market.

Federal and state governments, of course, have extensive constitutional authority to regulate private corporations, and in fact, they have exercised this power to a considerable degree. Yet, our conception that private corporations ought to remain independent of state power substantially restrains the actual exercise of that power. Moreover, corporate property rights, unlike city "rights," are not fully subject to state control; rather, their protection from governmental control is the cornerstone of the "free-enterprise" system.

The point of this comparison between the law for cities—municipal corporations—and the law for private corporations is that we never even think to make it. The differences between the two types of entities are simply too obvious: one is public, the other private; one governed by

[3]F. Michelman and T. Sandalow, *Government in Urban Areas*, (St. Paul, Minn.: West Publishing Co., 1970), p. 103.

politics, the other by the market; one a subdivision of the state, the other a part of civil society. In the modern development of the law for the cities, the historical connection between public and private corporations has been forgotten in favor of an automatic incantation of the distinction between them: city discretion is the application of coercive power to liberty and must be restrained, whereas corporate discretion is the exercise of that liberty and must be protected. Thus, our conceptual framework, based on the public/private distinction, helps to confirm the current powerlessness of cities.

City powerlessness, moreover, appears to be both an inevitable and a desirable feature of modern life. It seems a necessary result of a national economy and the increasing centralization and bureaucratization of all aspects of American society. The idea of real local power conveys a picture of the strangulation of nationwide businesses by a maze of conflicting local regulations and the frustration of national political objectives by local selfishness and protectionism. Far from seeming a political choice, the rejection of local power seems to be implied by the needs of modern large-scale organizations, both public and private.

In addition, there is a widespread belief that although cities are supposed to protect the public interest, they cannot really be trusted to do so. This distrust engenders support for the state and federal control of cities to prevent local abuse of power, to curb local selfishness, or to correct the inefficiencies resulting from "balkanized" local decision-making. City discretion of any kind evokes images of corruption, patronage, and even foolishness. This sense of necessity and desirability has made local powerlessness part of our definition of modern society, so that decentralization of power appears to be a nostalgic memory of an era gone forever or a dream of romantics who fail to understand the world as it really is.

Why City Powerlessness Matters

Our ideas about the powerlessness of cities are so well settled that it is difficult for us to see why city powerlessness matters. It is tempting to relate the cities' lack of power to the so-called crisis of the cities. But exactly what this crisis is, or why we should care about it, is uncertain. It may be the need to improve the quality of life for those—often poor, often black or Hispanic—who live in the nation's major cities, or the need to encourage greater concentrations of people because of the energy shortage and the environmental damage caused by the suburbanization of the countryside, or the need to preserve city institutions important to the nation as a whole, such as trade or cultural centers.

Yet, if the "crisis of the cities" means no more than these kinds of problems, an increase in city power does not seem necessary for their solution. Indeed, many of these problems might be solved more quickly if local autonomy were prohibited altogether, and cities were administered by federal officials authorized to implement a national urban policy. The need for city power does not rest on the view that local autonomy is the only, or even the most efficient, way to solve local problems.

In fact, if we focus on cities as they are currently organized and managed, we will not see the argument for city power. Cities as they currently exist should not simply be made more powerful. Rather, the argument for city power rests on what cities have been and what they could become. Cities have served—and might again serve—as vehicles to achieve purposes that have been frustrated in modern American life. They could respond to what Hannah Arendt has called the need for "public freedom"[4]—the ability to participate actively in the basic societal decisions that affect one's life. This conception of freedom—a positive activity designed to create one's way of life—differs markedly from the currently popular idea of freedom as merely "an inner realm into which men might escape at will from the pressures of the world," of a "*liberum arbitrium* which makes the will choose between alternatives."[5]

It is not that cities are the only form in which the exercise of public freedom is possible in American society. The Populist movement can be viewed as an experiment in popular participation. In addition, some writers have suggested that private corporations are vehicles for creating new forms of human association based on the communal tie created by the pursuit of common goals.[6] Such an idea has many possible meanings, ranging from socialism, on the one hand, to business management based on the infusion of communal values, on the other. But surely a more likely source of public freedom has always been the cities, in part because of the

[4]H. Arendt, *On Revolution*, (New York: Pelican Books, 1962), pp. 114–115, 119–120.

[5]Ibid. The concept of public freedom was the definition of freedom in the Greek *polis*. It rests on the ideal of *isonomy*, the notion that equality of political decision-making will eliminate the division between government and society, between ruler and ruled.

[6]See, for example, E. Durkheim, *The Division of Labor in Society*, trans. G. Simpson (New York: Free Press, 1933), pp. 1–31.

tradition of local participatory democracy from the colonial era to as recently as de Tocqueville's time.

Why are cities today governed as bureaucracies, rather than as experiments in participatory democracy? The answer cannot simply be that they are too large, because when city powerlessness first became a legal principle, there were only two cities in the United States with over 100,000 people. Moreover, many cities are as small today as Athens was in classical times.

Instead, the answer must be sought in the development of our liberal ideology, which makes the idea of participatory democracy seem so bizarre, so dangerous, and so unworkable that most state constitutions prohibit its emergence.[7] Complementing this ideology is the relationship between participation and powerlessness. Because significant powers have been withheld from cities, the idea of cities' becoming experiments in popular democracy is unattractive. Individual participation in powerless institutions fails to provide individuals with the opportunity to shape their lives in a meaningful manner. Thus, state control has prevented cities from becoming experiments in participatory democracy while simultaneously making them unlikely targets for attempts at popular control.

City powerlessness, then, diminishes the possibility of developing a form of human association based on participation in public power. City power would not ensure the success of such a form of association, but it could be an important ingredient of it. Indeed, a powerful city is desirable only if it becomes transformed, modifying its functions and organization and, perhaps, its boundaries to engender greater participation in its decision making.

THE ROLE OF LAW IN CITY POWERLESSNESS

Even if the powerlessness of cities and its consequences are recognized, the question remains how the law has contributed to that status of cities. What role am I claiming for law in the development within liberal

---

[7]State constitutions contain a wide variety of restrictions on local government activity and organization which, cumulatively, would make a system based on mass participation impossible. See, for example, *Pennsylvania Constitution*, Article 9.

theory of the status of cities, and what role am I claiming for liberalism itself in the development of the city?

For some, liberalism is characterized by its emphasis on the belief that the passions can be subordinated to reason, that the world can be rationalized both in terms of thought and by the organization of social life, and that the way to do so is by a scientific dissection of all aspects of life, thereby rendering them orderly and controllable.[8] For our purposes, liberalism is based on the more fundamental proposition that the world is divided into spheres of reason and of desire, of fact and of subjective values, of freedom and of necessity, of the development of the self and of the need for communal relationships, of the free interaction of civil society and of the demands of the state, of the controlling importance of empirical fact and the controlling importance of ideas. Liberalism is not a single formula for interpreting the world; it is, instead, a view based on seeing the world as a series of complex dualities.[9]

Liberalism, however, provides no method for deciding how any particular feature of life should be allocated between its dualities. There was nothing, for example, in the early development of liberal thought that determined the place of cities within liberal society.

Over time, liberals have adopted changing, often contradictory, solutions to this persistent problem. Cities have sometimes been seen as the essence of freedom ("The air of the city makes one free," says a German proverb) and sometimes as a danger to freedom; cities have been touted as the source of individual development and fulfillment and as the source of atrophy of individualism and of the blasé attitude; cities have been characterized as the expression of bourgeois rationalism and as the threat of the passions, or politics, to that rationalism; cities have been classified as part of society and as part of the state; cities have been analyzed as purely empirical phenomena and as pure creations of the mind.

The principal puzzle confronted by liberal theorists concerning city status was that cities seemed to be entities intermediate between the state and the individual. Cities could be understood as vehicles useful for the exercise of the coercive power of the state; they could also be under-

---

[8]K. Mannheim, *Ideology and Utopia*, trans. L. Wirth and E. Shils (New York: Harcourt Brace Jovanovich, 1936), pp. 122–23.
[9]See generally, Mannheim, pp. 3–33, 122–123, 164–191; R. Unger, *Knowledge and Politics*, (New York: Free Press, 1975); D. Kennedy, "The Structure of Blackstone's Commentaries," *Buffalo Law Review* 28 (1979):258–61, 294–300, 354–362.

stood, like voluntary associations, as groups of individuals that sought to control their own lives free of state domination. Cities were partly creations of the state, yet they were also partly creations of the individuals who lived within them. Thus, cities failed to fit neatly into liberal theory, which sought to allocate all aspects of social life to one of the poles of its dualities, in this case either to the sphere of the state or to that of the free interaction of individuals within civil society.

But gradually, there has developed a process of slowly working out a solution to the status of cities within liberal theory, a process still going on despite our settled feeling that we have arrived at a "natural" status for cities. My claim is that this process has, to a large extent, been carried on by the development of legal doctrine. The results of this process are our current perceptions that cities represent state rather than individual interests and that city powerlessness is necessary and desirable.

This process of defining a status for cities within liberal theory is simply an example of the general development of liberal ideas. Liberalism, like any general theory, is useful only to the extent that it can help people to understand their lives and the world around them. Thus, liberal thinkers have tried to explain all the puzzles of human nature and social life by making concrete the meaning of the liberal dualities. The development of legal doctrine has generally been one form that this effort has taken. Thus, law has been part of the definition of liberal thought. It has sometimes been influenced by ideas arising elsewhere in liberal theory, while at times influencing those areas by its own development. But it cannot properly be understood apart from its role within the development of liberal theory.

Law has been a special way of articulating the meaning of liberal theory. The legal system serves an important legitimating function, providing a moral force so that attempts to go outside it come to be viewed as attacks against "the entire legal system and therefore the consensual framework of the body politic."[10] Whenever the legal process is adopted as a mode of analysis, it fuels the notion that the results of application are natural, apolitical, and deductive. In addition, the law has its internal demands, such as those for consistency and generality, and

[10]E. Genovese, *Roll, Jordan, Roll,* (New York: Vintage Books, 1974), p. 28. See also, D. Hay, "Property, Authority and the Criminal Law," in *Albion's Fatal Tree: Crime and Society in Eighteenth Century England,* Douglas Hay et al. (New York: Pantheon Books, 1975), pp. 17–33.

these demands themselves have influenced the development of liberal theory.

In working out a legal status for cities, the courts have for centuries wrestled with the question, which has perplexed liberal theorists, whether to classify cities as an exercise of freedom by individuals or as a threat to freedom analogous to that posed by the state. English courts, for example, were asked to decide whether city charters once awarded could be revoked by the king, by Parliament, or not at all. To resolve this question, the courts, in effect, had to decide whether cities, like the state, were a threat to freedom, thus justifying central control of their charters, or whether cities protected individual rights and thus needed protection from the state.

The city was regarded as being like the state in that context, and as we have seen, the answer that has generally been developed by the legal system in such situations has been to identify the city with the state and to conceive of the city as a threat to freedom. Yet, legal theory is still working out the exact relationship of the city, on the one hand, and the state and the individual, on the other, within the liberal idea of society. In 1978, for example, the U.S. Supreme Court considered whether the federal antitrust laws should be applied to cities, as they are to individuals and private corporations, or whether cities should be exempt from these laws, as are state governments.[11] In deciding the case, four Justices associated the city within the state, four associated it with individuals, and the final, deciding Justice said that sometimes the city acts like an individual and sometimes like the state. As this case demonstrates, in every case involving city power, courts must classify the city within liberal theory.

The empirical world—the economic, demographic, and political activities that affect city life—has been the source of people's understanding of cities and has affected their ideas of and actions regarding city power. But their frames of reference, their liberal ideology, have organized the mass of empirical data and experience in a way that has channeled their perceptions and actions and that therefore has influenced the development of the cities. To put it another way, there has been a continual process of accommodation of people's ideas about cities to the empirical world as they saw it, and at the same time, what was seen has been affected by selecting out, or assimilating, possible perceptions of the world and of the city to conform to preexisting ideas. The combined

---

[11]*City of Lafayette v. Louisiana Power and Light Co.*, 435 U.S. 389 (1978).

process of the accommodation of ideas to experience and the assimilation of experience to ideas means that, to some extent, the world has been made to conform to our ideas and, to some extent, the ideas have been made to conform to the world.

THE DEVELOPMENT OF THE LEGAL STATUS OF CITIES

The best way of understanding a legal concept is to analyze it in the way a geologist looks at the landscape. For a geologist, any portion of land at any given time is "the condensed history of the ages of the Earth and . . . a nexus of relationships."[12] Our current legal conception of cities is similarly the remnant of a historical process, so that its meaning cannot be grasped until the elements of that process, and their relationships, are understood. Thus, this section should be understood as an effort to describe how liberal thinkers at different points in history have interpreted the question of city power—the proper relationship of the city, the individual, and the state. Each attempt to resolve the question has had a cumulative effect on our current understanding of how to think about the issue; each stage in the process should be understood as adding to, and not replacing, its predecessor.

The Medieval Town

Its Status as an Association

The medieval town was not an artificial entity separate from its inhabitants; it was a group of people seeking protection against outsiders for the interests of the group as a whole. The town was an economic association of merchants who created the town as a means of seeking relief from the multiplicity of jurisdictional claims to which they, and their land, were subject. These merchants gained their autonomy by using their growing economic power to make political settlements with others in the society, specifically the king and the nobility. They achieved a freedom from outside control that was made possible by, and that allowed to be enforced, a strong sense of community within the town. This autonomy

---

[12]O. Paz, *Claude Lévi-Strauss: An Introduction*, trans. J. Bernstein and M. Bernstein (New York: Dell Publishing, 1970), p. 6.

for the merchants and their ability to establish their own communal rules were recognized in the legal status of the town.

City autonomy meant the autonomy of the merchant class as a group with distinct privileges within society. Yet, it should be emphasized that the medieval town established the rights of a group that could not be distinguished from the rights of the individuals within the group. The status of the individual merchant was defined by the rights of the group to which he belonged, namely, the medieval town. As a result, the medieval town had some features that for us are unrecognizable: a strict identity established between individual interests and the town's interest as a whole, a lack of separation of individual property rights and town sovereignty rights, and a mixed political and economic character.

The interests of the merchants were not only the goal of town autonomy; they also provided the basis for the functions of the medieval town. The town association controlled individual commercial conduct with a thoroughness unmatched in history. It protected the worker from competition and exploitation; regulated labor conditions, wages, prices, and apprenticeships; punished fraud; and asserted the town's interests against neighboring competitors. It is therefore important to understand the aspect of "freedom" that was achieved by the autonomy of the medieval town.

It was, in essence, the ability of a group of people to be governed, at least to some extent, by their own rules, free of outside interference. As Fernand Braudel described it, with some exaggeration:

> The medieval city was the classic type of the closed town, a self-sufficient unit, an exclusive Lilliputian native land. Crossing its ramparts was like crossing one of the still serious frontiers in the world today. You were free to thumb your nose at your neighbour from the other side of the barrier. He could not touch you. The peasant who uprooted himself from his land and arrived in the town was immediately another man. He was free—or rather he had abandoned a known and hated servitude for another, not always guessing the extent of it beforehand. But this mattered little. If the town had adopted him, he could snap his fingers when his lord called for him.[13]

In some areas, particularly Italy, Flanders, and Germany, this autonomy allowed the towns to lead a fully separate life for a long time. But even where such a separate life was not achieved, as in England, the structure

[13]F. Braudel, "Towns," in *Capitalism and Material Life 1400–1800*, trans. M. Kochan (New York: Harper & Row, 1967), pp. 402–403.

of the town provided its inhabitants the shelter to pursue, largely on terms defined within the town, their own economic interests.

This autonomy by no means created the medieval town as an idyllic oasis of freedom in a world of feudal bondage. Internally, often from the outset, the towns were not democratic but hierarchical; they operated under the strict control of an oligarchic elite. Far from the achievement of communal bliss within the towns, the exercise of hierarchic power

> quickly set in motion their class struggles. Because if the towns were "communities" as has been said, they were also "societies" in the modern sense of the word, with their pressures and civil wars: nobles against bourgeois, poor against rich ("thin people," *popolo magro,* against "fat people," *popolo grasso).*[14]

But we must try to understand how even those subjected to the power of others within the town could look at their town, describe it as a community, and defend the importance of its autonomy.

The identification of the individual with the town as a whole was, first of all, based on the place of the town in the life of its inhabitants. The town defined their place in society, defended them from outsiders, and enabled them to pursue their livelihood. Protection of town autonomy was necessary for the protection of their way of life. Patriotism and loyalty to the town resulted; thus, some have characterized medieval towns as "the West's first 'fatherlands.'"[15]

In addition, the idea of community was maintained by the complex idea of "city peace":

> (C)ity peace was a law of exception, more severe, more harsh, than that of the country districts. It was prodigal of corporal punishments: hangings, decapitation, castration, amputation of limbs. It applied in all its rigor the *lex talionis:* an eye for an eye, a tooth for a tooth. Its evident purpose was to repress derelictions, through terror. All who entered the gates of the city, whether nobles, freemen or burghers, were equally subject to it. Under it the city was, so to speak, in a permanent state of siege. But in it the city found a potent instrument of unification, because it was superimposed upon the jurisdictions and seigniories which shared the soil; it forced its pitiless regulation on all. More than community of interests and residence, it contrib- uted to make uniform the status of all the inhabitants located within

---

[14]Ibid., p. 399.
[15]Ibid. Braudel emphasized that the patriotism of the townspeople "was for a long time to be more coherent and much more conscious than territorial patriotism, which was slow to appear in the first states," p. 399.

the city walls and to create the middle class . . . . (T)he peace created, among all its members, a permanent solidarity.[16]

Most important, the hierarchic organization of the town did not undermine the value of the association but was itself legitimized by the
medieval concept of society. The legitimacy of the autonomy of the town
or any other group did not depend on the protection of individuals from
the group. To comprehend how individuals could think that they benefited simply by the freedom of the town as a whole requires an understanding of the medieval conception of the role of the individual in
society.

Medieval political thought did not seek to distinguish the separate
interests within the town or between the town and the rest of society;
rather, it sought to analyze their harmonious unity. Neither the idea of an
individual identity separate from the town nor that of town autonomy
separate from others in society implied a notion of opposition between the
parts and the whole. The individual contributed to town functions and the
town contributed to society's functioning.

Because preserving the integrity of the parts was necessary to preserve the whole, preservation of town autonomy was necessary to preserve the ability of town inhabitants to contribute their part to the operation of society. Thus, the autonomy of the medieval town cannot be
understood from our modern perspective of separating the individual
interests from the town interests, and then the town interests from the
"state" interests. The idea of the autonomy of the town and of its citizens
merged; as Frederick Maitland saw in the English medieval borough,
there were absent the distinctions that we recognize as fundamental:
between personal property rights and town sovereignty rights, between
the town as a collection of individuals and the town as a collective
whole.[17]

The Liberal Attack on Group Identity

Slowly, however, an entity separate from its membership—the town
with a capital T[18]—"struggles into life."[19] This emergence of the town as

[16]H. Pirenne, *Medieval Cities*, trans. F. Halsey (Princeton: Princeton University
Press, 1925), pp. 199–201.
[17]F. Maitland, *Township and Borough* (Cambridge, Mass.: University Press,
1898), pp. 11–12.
[18]Ibid., p. 85.
[19]Ibid., p. 80.

an entity with rights and duties independent of, even opposed to, its inhabitants, this creation of the town as "a person," occurred long before the first corporate charter was granted in England by Henry VI in 1439.[20] It grew with the idea that "(T)he 'all' that is unity will not coincide with, may stand apart from, the 'all' of inhabitants."[21] Only once this was established could the effect of the king's actions with respect to the towns become distinguishable from its effect on the towns' citizens. Only then was it possible to conceive of the king's attempt to control the towns as liberating, and not restricting, the individual. Thus, the separation of the individual's interest from the town unity and the increase of the king's power over the town were part of the same process.

The dissolution of the medieval town as an organic association and the accompanying increase in the power of the king over the town were part of the general liberal undermining of medieval society itself. A similar process has been traced within medieval rural society.[22] Indeed, the progress of liberalism can be understood, as Otto Gierke saw it,[23] as a progressive dissolution of all unified structures within medieval society: the feudal manor, the medieval town, and even the king himself. Instead of seeking to understand the harmonious working of the whole, liberalism separated out from each aspect of life an individual interest as contrasted with a group interest and, at the same time, consolidated all elements of social cohesion into the idea of the nation-state. With the development of liberalism, the "Sovereignty of the State and the Sovereignty of the Individual were steadily on their way towards becoming the two central axioms from which all theories of social structure would proceed, and whose relationship to each other would be the focus of all theoretical controversy."[24]

The evolution of liberalism can thus be understood as an undermin-

---

[20]Ibid., p. 18.

[21]Ibid., p. 85.

[22]See generally, F. Braudel; B. Moore, *Social Origins of Dictatorship and Democracy* (Boston: Beacon Press, 1966), pp. 3–110, 413–508. On feudal society outside the towns, see generally, M. Bloch, *Feudal Society*, trans. C. A. Manyon (Chicago: University of Chicago Press, 1961).

[23]Gierke referred to liberalism as the "theory of natural law"; see O. Gierke, *Natural Law and the Theory of Society 1500–1800*, trans. E. Barker (Boston: Beacon Press, 1935), p. 35.

[24]O. Gierke, *Political Theories of the Middle Ages*, trans. F. W. Maitland (Boston: Beacon Press, 1958), p. 87.

ing of the vitality of all groups that had held an intermediate position between what we now think of as the sphere of the individual and that of the state. The unity of the church, the feudal manor, and the medieval town dissolved into entities separate from, and opposed to, the interests of their members, and each of them established separate relationships with the emerging nation-state. Even the king himself became divided into his "individual" and "State" parts, a division "between his private property and the State's property which was under his care."[25]

It should be remembered that the king, the church, the university, and the medieval town were the principal examples of medieval corporations and that many of these institutions were, together with the feudal manor, the principal objects of liberal attack. For Gierke, the changing of the conception of the corporation was the vehicle by which liberalism undermined the status of those groups.

To show how this was done, Gierke contrasted two conceptions of the corporation, the Germanic and the "antique-modern."[26] In the Germanic conception, the corporation is an organic unity that is not reducible to a collection of individuals or to an artificial creation of the state. Rather, its existence is seen as "real in itself." The "antique-modern" conception, however, views the corporation as merely the sum of its individual members and, simultaneously, a "fictional person" created by, and therefore subject to, the state. This contrast is hard for us to grasp unless we recall the powerful conception of unity in medieval thought and the fracturing of that unity by liberal thought, which came to focus instead on the individual and the state. The movement from the Germanic to the antique-modern conception of the corporation facilitated the undermining of the corporate entity by the development of individual freedom from corporate unity and of state power over corporate unity. Entities like the medieval town, "formed and interpreted as a fraternal association,"[27] with autonomous power for the unity as a whole, could gradually become mere locations for individual effort and mere "creatures of the state."

For early liberal thinkers, the attack on the autonomy of medieval corporations, including the medieval town, was necessary to protect what

[25]Ibid., p. 63. See generally E. Kantorowicz, *The King's Two Bodies* (Princeton: Princeton University Press, 1957).

[26]O. Gierke, *Natural Law*, pp. 162–165, 180–195.

[27]M. Weber, *The City*, trans. D. Martindale and G. Neuwirth (New York: Free Press, 1958), p. 96.

they considered the vital interests of individual liberty and of the emerging nation-state. Their perspective, then, was the predecessor of our own; they sought to eliminate the domination of individuals within the town by the town oligarchy and to establish the rule of law over all centers of power. So important was the need to restrict the towns' control of individual activity and their irresponsible local protectionism that the increase in the power of the nation-state necessary to achieve these objectives seemed benign. In other contexts, liberal thinkers viewed increasing the power of the state as necessarily a threat to individuals—one interest advances only at the expense of the other. But increasing the power of the state over the towns was understood as simultaneously advancing both state and individual interests. This viewpoint encouraged early liberal thinkers, as it encourages us, to see the eradication of the power of the towns as a step forward in the progress of freedom.

Yet, the defense of the power of the town was itself based on the notion of freedom. In fact, as we have seen, it was the idea of freedom from feudal restrictions that was the basis for the creation of the town. Elimination of the town as an entity intermediate between the state and the individual could, therefore, threaten the way of life—the freedom—of those protected by town autonomy. Thus, both the liberal efforts to destroy the town and the efforts to preserve it were made in the interest of freedom.

The Early Modern Town

Its Relationship to the King

In spite of the liberal attack, the towns retained much of their autonomy and power, at least until the beginning of the nineteenth century. The primary explanation for this fact in the case of English cities, the models for the American law of cities, was the retention of a major aspect of their medieval identity; the towns remained "economic corporations"[28] whose franchises provided protection against control by the king and fracturing by individuals. Commerce was the basic activity of municipal corporations, and the power of the economic elite, who played an increasingly dominant role in the towns, was both the force behind, and the result of, the protection afforded by the corporate charters. An under-

[28]Ibid., p. 133.

standing of the nature of city autonomy in England prior to the nineteenth century therefore requires an examination of the relationship between this economic elite and the king.

The king's relationship to the economic elite in the towns was one of
mutual dependence as well as mutual suspicion. The assumption of control of the cities by this largely self-perpetuating oligarchy created a conflict with the craftsmen and the proletariat within the towns, a conflict
that dominated the towns' political life. The elite were thus forced to seek
outside support for their privileges, particularly from the king. In addition, the elite increasingly looked to the king for social advantages and
legal protection. The king, for his part, favored control by a small group
on whom he could depend for financial and administrative support. This
mutuality of interest became a centerpiece of mercantilism.

Yet, the king remained suspicious of the independent power wielded
by the members of economic oligarchy and persistently sought to bring
them under his control. They, in turn, resisted royal interference as an
inroad on the basic rights of Englishmen, because the liberty of the towns
and the protection of freehold interests, such as the corporators' freehold
interest in the corporate franchise, had been established by the Magna
Carta.

The issue of royal power and of corporate freedom was entangled
with another central issue of the time, the relationship of the king and the
Parliament. From the fourteenth century, municipal corporations were
represented in Parliament, where they became a dominant influence.
This parliamentary role provided an alternative forum for protecting city
interests and obviated the need to seek the kind of political autonomy
asserted by cities elsewhere in Europe. Moreover, because the rural
upper classes were themselves developing commercial interests, they
tended to align with city interests against the king rather than, as elsewhere, with the king against the cities. Thus, the issues of the limitation
of the king's power with respect to Parliament and with respect to the
cities were two aspects of protecting the same interest: that of the commercial class.

The Attack on City Charters

The uneasy alliance between the king and the commercial oligarchy
broke down in the late seventeenth century, thereby precipitating royal
conflicts with both the cities and the Parliament. The dispute with the

cities took the form of an attack by the king on their corporate charters, because the charters defined both the power of the corporate elite over ordinary citizens and their relationship to the king. As far back as the thirteenth century, the king had asserted the power to revoke these charters for wrongdoing. The issue became increasingly sensitive, however, because city officials had begun to determine both the identity of city representatives in Parliament and the identity of the juries on which the king depended to enforce the laws.

The question of the status of corporate charters became the focus of what has been called the "most important case in English history,"[29] the *quo warranto* brought in 1682 by Charles II, in which he challenged the legitimacy of the corporate status of the City of London. The arguments made in the case[30] are significant because they illustrate how liberal thinkers conceived of the issue of city autonomy near the close of the seventeenth century.

The king, believing the issue to be one of needing central control to prevent societal conflict, asserted the right to revoke the charters of cities and other economic corporations later formed on the model of the cities, such as the East India Company, the Hudson Bay Company, and some of the American colonies. If their charters could not be forfeited for wrongdoing, they would become "so many commonwealths by themselves, independent of the Crown and in defiance of it."[31]

For the cities, however, corporate power was liberty itself, the corporate charter being evidence of rights vested in the corporation by the king. If the wrongdoing of an individual could be treated as if it were that of the corporation and could thus result in the forfeiture of the corporate charter, the vested rights on which the members of the corporation relied would be rendered valueless. In short, the vested rights acquired by the corporate franchise were rights of property and must be protected to ensure the liberty of all Englishmen.

Thus, the conflict over whether the city charter was a revocable franchise or a vested right represented, in microcosm, the fundamental split in liberal political theory between positivism, the Hobbesian view that individual interests are subordinate to the command of the state, and

---

[29]J. Levin, *The Charter Controversy in the City of London 1660–1688, and Its Consequences* (London: Athlone Press, University of London, 1969), p. 80.
[30]Ibid., pp. 29–49.
[31]Ibid., p. 48.

natural rights theory, the Lockean view that the state reaffirmed, and was limited by, natural human rights.

The king's victory in the London case represented a victory for the positivist position and established the legal principle of royal control of the cities for a time. Many other city charters, as well as the charters of some American colonies, were surrendered to Charles II and James II under the threat of further *quo warranto* proceedings. Yet, the royal conflict with the commercial class merely shifted its location to Parliament. Finally, in 1688, the Glorious Revolution ended the Stuart reign. As a result, the London case was reversed, the surrender of other city charters was undone, and the immunity of corporate charters from royal abrogation was reestablished.

The Glorious Revolution, however, did not lead to the adoption of a Lockean protection of corporate rights as we would understand it today. Although the revolution protected corporate charters from the only source then thought to threaten them—the king—it did not resolve the extent of Parliament's power over those charters. The revolution was a victory for both Parliament and the cities; increasing the power of one secured the interests of the other. Hence, one could support the victory of both Parliament and the cities without conceiving of Parliament as the "state" that could invade corporate "rights." Even almost a century later, Blackstone shared the same view. He did not see the Parliament as a threat to corporate freedom, even though it had absolute power to dissolve corporations, because Parliament itself considered corporate charters inviolate.

At the time of the American Revolution, then, corporate liberty was protected against royal attack, but the extent of its vulnerability if Parliament became hostile remained unresolved. The resolution of this issue—the confrontation of legislative power and corporate rights—produced for the first time a legal distinction between public and private corporations. Until the early nineteenth century, no such distinction between cities and other mercantile entities chartered by the king existed either in America or in England, because all such corporations possessed similar legal powers and protections. Indeed, neither Blackstone nor Stuart Kyd, who authored the first treatise on corporations in 1793, even mentioned the concepts of public and private corporations. We must therefore turn to the question of how, in America, the public/private distinction became decisive in resolving the issue of legislative control over corporations, a resolution that left public corporations in the Hobbesian sphere of com-

mand and private corporations in the Lockean sphere of rights. Before
this question may be answered, however, a preliminary issue must be
explored: Why were American cities even viewed as corporations for
purposes of determining the scope of their rights against the state?

The Early American City

Its Corporate Status

Prior to the revolution, there were only about 20 incorporated cities
in America. In New England, where local autonomy was most fully established, no city possessed a corporate franchise; instead, the power of the
New England towns was based on their role as the vital organizing unit in
social life. Although originally subordinate to the colonial government,
the towns increasingly established their power on the basis of the direct
popular sovereignty exercised in town meetings. By the late eighteenth
century, colonial legislatures were far from being considered a threat to
town liberty—a role assigned to the English king and his colonial representatives—because these legislatures were composed of representatives
of the towns who were under explicit instructions to represent the towns'
interests. Moreover, proposals to turn New England towns into corporations were denounced as attempts to weaken the towns by substituting
elitist English boroughs for direct democracy.

In the South, Charles Town, South Carolina, was the only major city.
Although it had "many of the characteristics of a city-state,"[32] it, too, was
not a corporation. Its power was based not on town meetings as in New
England but on the influence of its merchants. These merchants dominated both the colonial legislature and the complex of organizations that
ran the town. In 1723, Charles Town successfully resisted attempts to
transform the city into a corporation.

Even in the Middle-Atlantic region, in which incorporated cities
were most numerous, the corporation was not always the basis of a town's
governance. For example, in Philadelphia, one of the two major corporate
cities in colonial America, special-purpose commissions and voluntary
associations progressively assumed duties previously entrusted to the corporation, which was considered archaic and aristocratic. By the late eigh-

[32]Waterhouse, "The Responsible Gentry of Colonial South Carolina: A Study in
Local Government 1670–1770," in *Town and Country*, ed. B. Daniels (Middletown, Ct.: Wesleyan University Press, 1978), p. 160.

teenth century, the Philadelphia corporation was "a club of wealthy merchants, without much purse, power or popularity."[33]

In general, then, colonial towns did not have the formal corporate
structure of the English cities. Instead, they could be viewed as bearing a
resemblance to the kind of associations that created the medieval towns,
and thus, their power could have been perceived as based on the freedom
of association rather than on corporate rights. Both medieval and colonial
towns were established by people who broke away from existing social
restraints and who formed relatively closed societies with new social
structures. Moreover, the relationship in colonial America between the
aspects of association represented by the town and the aspects of association represented by the family and by religion was often quite close.
Conceiving of colonial towns as associations was therefore by no means
impossible. Nevertheless, despite the evidence that the towns were associations, they were treated by the courts as if they were corporations.

We can only speculate why towns were viewed in this manner. One
possible explanation is that, at the time, many people saw no radical
distinction between a corporation and an association. Even colonial religious bodies often considered themselves corporations, their corporate
nature seen as affirming and strengthening their associational ties.
Whereas from a lawyer's point of view a corporation could be formed only
by a grant of a corporate charter from the Crown, an alternative conception was that a corporation existed whenever a group possessed and exercised power. It was thus not dispositive to say that the towns had no
charters, because medieval cities had also been considered corporations
long before they had in fact received corporate charters. Indeed, many
medieval cities—London being the most prominent—became corporations by prescription rather than by grant because they had existed as
corporations "time whereof the memory of man runneth not to the
contrary."[34]

The important point about colonial towns and cities was that they

---

[33]S. Warner, *The Private City* (Philadelphia: University of Pennsylvania Press,
1968), p. 9. Other sources on the development of Philadelphia local government
include E. Allison and B. Penrose, *The City Government of Philadelphia* (Baltimore: Johns Hopkins University, 1887); R. Brunhouse, *The Counter-Revolu-
tion in Pennsylvania 1776–1790* (Harrisburg: Pennsylvania Historical Commission, 1942); J. Diamondstone, "The Government of Eighteenth Century
Philadelphia," in *Town and Country* ed. B. Daniels (Middletown, Ct.:
Wesleyan University Press, 1978).
[34]W. Blackstone, *Commentaries* (New York: Arno Press, 1972), p. 473.

exercised power as a group; as a group they had rights, as a group they had powers. Such an association would be a corporation, or "quasi corporation," because the corporation was the dominant way of asserting group authority and protecting group rights. The towns were "bodies politic," and all bodies politic—English cities, colonial towns, churches, the states themselves—seemed to be corporations.

The City's Relationship to the Legislature

The question of the appropriate extent of legislative power over the cities was therefore decided as part of the larger issue of the desired extent of legislative power over all corporations, whether cities or other mercantile bodies. In late-eighteenth-century America, the larger issue was deeply troubling. On the one hand, corporate rights had been protected from the king by the Glorious Revolution; these rights, once recognized, seemed to deserve protection from legislative infringement as well. America had rejected the English notion of legislative supremacy in favor of the Lockean concept of a legislative power limited by natural rights. Legislative denial of these rights could be tolerated no more than could executive denial. On the other hand, corporations exercised a power in society that seemed to limit the rights of individuals to earn their livelihood, and this power, wielded by an aristocratic elite to protect their monopolistic privileges, needed to be controlled by popular—that is, legislative—action. Thus, although the exercise of legislative power was perceived as a threat to corporate rights, the exercise of corporate rights risked the curtailment of legislative power thought necessary to protect the welfare of the people.

On a deeper level, the corporation represented an anomaly to liberal thinkers who envisioned the world as sharply divided between individual right-holders and state power, the ruled in conflict with the ruler. The corporation exhibited traits of both poles: it was part ruled and part ruler, both an association of individuals and an entity with state-granted power. The continued existence of the corporation demonstrated that the liberal effort to destroy the intermediate forms of medieval social life—to re-create the world as one populated solely by the individual and the state—had not yet succeeded. The corporation was thus a feudal remnant, a vestige of the medieval town.

Even more troublesome was the fact that the corporation was in some aspects a protector of, and in other ways a threat to, both individual rights and state power. The corporation not only protected individual property rights but it also served as a miniature republic, impervious to state power. The dilemma created by the corporation, then, could be solved neither by the retention of its present form nor by abolition in favor of individual rights as urged by Adam Smith, or in favor of the state, as advocated by Hobbes.

The Adoption of the Public/Private Distinction

The Development of the Distinction

To solve the problem created by the intermediate status of the corporation, early-nineteenth-century legal doctrine divided the corporation into two different entities, one assimilated to the role of an individual in society and the other assimilated to the role of the state. The corporation as an entity that was simultaneously a right-holder and a power wielder thus disappeared. In its place emerged the private corporation, which was an individual right-holder, and the public corporation, an entity that was identified with the state. The very purpose of the distinction was to ensure that some corporations, called *private*, would be protected against domination by the state and that others, called *public*, would be subject to such domination. In this way, the corporate anomaly was resolved so that corporations, like the rest of society, were divided into individuals and the state.

This public/private distinction for corporations was not purely a legal invention. The distinction had been generally emerging since the American Revolution, and both the newly created public and private identities were the product of a pervasive liberal attack on the exclusive privileges and oligarchic power wielded by corporations.

The attack that established the "private" character of business corporations developed as their number expanded, rising from only eight in 1780 to several hundred by the time of the critical *Dartmouth College* opinion in 1819.[35] Even though these business corporations were public service enterprises, such as canals, bridges, water supply companies, and banking enterprises, their creation raised troubling questions concerning the amount of protection afforded their investors and participants. As the courts gradually developed protections for the investors' property, pres-

---

[35]*Trustees of Dartmouth College v. Woodward*, 17 U.S. (4 Wheat.) 518 (1819); see M. Horwitz, *The Transformation of American Law 1780–1860* (Cambridge: Harvard University Press, 1977), pp. 111–114.

sure mounted on the legislature to expand the opportunities for incorporation from a favored few to the more general population.

Yet, as the legislature yielded to this drive for more incorporations,
the demand for the protection of property rights for those involved itself
increased. As one commentary noted,

> The process which multiplied the institution [of the corporation] and
> the unfoldment of its private character reacted upon each other in a
> reciprocal, accumulative fashion. Every new grant strengthened the
> grounds for considering it private; every new affirmation of private-
> ness strengthened the hands of those who demanded new grants.[36]

This process gathered momentum, culminating in the middle of the nineteenth century in the Jacksonian effort to pass general incorporation laws,
thus allowing the "privilege" of incorporation to be exercised by all.

The attack on the exclusiveness of city corporations worked in another direction. Although the number of city corporations could not be
expanded, participation in their operation could be enlarged. With the
sovereignty of the people as the emerging basis of republican politics, and
with the need created by population growth to add new functions to city
corporations, the pressure for state legislation to end aristocratic corporate governance mounted. The most important closed corporation in
America, that of Philadelphia, was abolished by radical republican legisla-
tors in 1776, and it was replaced several years later with a modified, more
broadly based, corporation.

This attack on the privileged control of city corporations and the
concomitant expansion of participation in corporate governance made it
increasingly difficult to separate the city corporation from the people as a
whole, that is, to view city corporate rights as distinct from the rights of
the public at large. The movement toward what was then considered
universal suffrage, in the 1820s and 1830s, helped confirm the emerging
public character of city corporations, thus setting them in contrast to the
"private" business corporations.

The Protection of Property

Despite these developments, American courts in the early nineteenth century had great difficult in establishing the public/private distinction for corporations. All corporations continued to have similar
characteristics. Corporations, whether cities or mercantile entities, were

[36]O. Handlin and M. Handlin, *Commonwealth* (New York: New York University
Press, 1947), p. 173.

chartered only to further public purposes, and many of their functions overlapped. All corporations were, in one sense, created by individuals and, in another sense, created by the state through the award of the franchise. Many mercantile corporations wielded the same powers as cities, such as eminent domain, and many cities received their income from the same sources as mercantile corporations, primarily commerce and trade. Both cities and mercantile corporations served to protect the private investments of individual founders and allowed those active in their governance a large degree of self-determination. Many cities and mercantile corporations were controlled by an elite, and consequently, both were subject to popular attack. Finally, cities and mercantile corporations alike could be viewed as associations of individuals organized to achieve commercial ends. In short, all corporations wielded power and all corporations protected rights. The concepts of power and rights, so fully merged in the medieval town, had not yet been segregated into their public and private indentities.

In determining where to draw the public/private distinction for corporations, the courts first decided what was it important to protect against state power. In *Trustees of Dartmouth College* v. *Woodward*, decided in 1819, the U.S. Supreme Court gave its response to this question, an answer that came straight from Locke: what needed protection was property. The scope of property rights thus divided private from public corporations, private corporations being those founded by individual contributions of property, and public corporations being those founded by the government without such individual contributions.

Having decided the importance of property rights, the court then sought to determine the status of cities under the public/private distinction. Although three major opinions were delivered in the case, Justice Story, who had four years earlier first made the public/private distinction for corporations in a U.S. Supreme Court opinion, presented the most complete discussion of the issue:

> Another division of corporations is into public and private. Public corporations are generally esteemed such as exist for public political purposes only, such as towns, cities, parishes, and counties; and in many respects they are so, although they involve some private interests; but strictly speaking, public corporations are such only as are founded by the government for public purposes, where the whole interests belong also to the government.[37]

[37]*Trustees of Dartmouth* v. *Woodward*, 17 U.S. (4 Wheat.) 668–669 (Story, J., concurring).

This passage, however, is ambiguous. Justice Story may have been arguing that the critical distinction between private and public corporations was whether they were founded by individuals or "founded *by the government* for public purposes, where the *whole interests* belong to the government."[38] Yet, if that were the definition of public corporations, most cities could not be public corporations: most were not founded by the government, nor did they belong wholly to the government. Alternatively, Justice Story may have accepted what was "generally esteemed" at the time if not "strictly speaking" true: that all cities were public corporations.

Seventeen years later, in his *Commentaries on American Law*, Chancellor Kent offered his own view of the status of cities within the public/private distinction:

> Public corporations are such as are created by the government for political purposes, as counties, cities, towns and villages; they are invested with subordinate legislative powers to be exercised for local purposes connected with the public good, and such powers are subject to the control of the legislature of the state. They may also be empowered to take or hold private property for municipal uses, and such property is invested with the security of other private rights.[39]

In this passage, Chancellor Kent apparently rejected the notion that, in order for an entity to constitute a public corporation, the "whole interest" must belong to the government. He simply asserted that cities were "created by the government," thus denying their actual history both in England and in America. Having taken that step, Kent then divided city authority into two parts: legislation for the public good, and the possession of property for municipal uses. Of these, only city property received protection from state control. Just as public and private corporations are distinguished by the need to protect private property, cities themselves became bifurcated by the same need—self-determination was retained only for the protection of their private property. It is this view that became, and remains, the law concerning the status of cities in the United States.

The Subordination of the City to the State

It is by no means self-explanatory why, once corporate property rights were protected, early-nineteenth-century writers like Chancellor

[38]Ibid., (emphasis added).
[39]C. Kent, *Commentaries on American Law* (New York: Author, 1836).

Kent seemed to think it obvious that the other functions of cities would be subordinate to state power. Cities, like other corporations, had never based their resistance to state control simply on the protection of property. Freedom of association and the exercise of self-government had always been values sought to be protected by the defense of the corporation. It did not, therefore, follow from the need to protect property that property alone needed protection and that these other values could be sacrificed to state domination. Indeed, even at the time, these other values were seen as part of the definition of liberty, their defense being most clearly articulated in the defense of state power against federal control encapsulated in the doctrine of federalism.

In addition, such a notion of subordination would turn the political world as it then existed upside down. New England towns had controlled state legislatures since before the American Revolution, and the move in other sections of the country to end aristocratic city governance in favor of democracy was not made with the intention of establishing state control over cities. Nor could subservience to the state be considered an inevitable product of liberal thought. The proper relationship of city to state was instead a hotly contested political issue. Some argued that the sovereignty of the people required control at the local level, but others feared the power of democratic cities over the allocation of property in America. Aristotle, Montesquieu, and Rousseau could be invoked in favor of power at the local level, whereas Madison and Hume could be cited to show the danger of local self-government. Thus, it is necessary to explain how legal theorists could classify cities as public corporations and thereby subject them to state control.

Once the cities became synonymous with the people within them, one could acknowledge city rights only if one were willing to recognize the right of association and self-determination for any group of people, however large. Such a recognition would threaten many other important values. It would limit the nation's ability to establish a unified political system under the Federal Constitution, preventing the needed centralization of authority and perpetuating the idea that the nation was merely a loose federation of localities. Moreover, these groups, particularly small groups, could be seen as "factions" dangerous to the individuals within them, inhibiting the individuals' free development and threatening their property rights. In other words, recognizing the rights of the city as an exercise of the freedom of association would frustrate the interests of both the state and the individual and would defy the liberal attempt to dissolve the power of groups in favor of the state and the individual. Recognizing the rights of the city as an association would thus bring to the surface what was sought to be denied: that corporations were the continuation of the group rights of the medieval town, protecting both the associational and the property rights of its members.

Recognition of city rights would also bring to the surface the conflict between the values of association and of property rights themselves, a conflict that had been hidden by the fact that both values had traditionally been protected by the corporate form. Prior to the emergence of the public/private distinction, there was no difference between a corporation's property rights and its rights of group self-government. But now group self-government—or popular sovereignty—seemed a threat to property rights, and property rights seemed a necessary limit to popular sovereignty. Thus, any recognition of the rights of the city would require the courts to choose between associational rights and property rights in particular cases, rather than simply protecting property rights against the power of "governmental" collective action. All these problems seemed to disappear, however, if recognition of the rights of cities were avoided.

The amount of emphasis to put on the fear of democratic power in explaining the judicial decision to limit the power of cities is, of course, a matter of conjecture. Such fear plainly existed, however, even in the minds of such champions of local power as Jefferson and de Tocqueville. Although Jefferson saw towns as the "elementary republics" of the nation, which must be preserved so that "the voice of the whole people would be fairly, fully, and peaceably expressed . . . by the common reason" of all citizens,[40] he also saw them as objects to be feared: "The mobs of great cities add just so much to the support of pure government, as sores do to the strength of the human body."[41] For de Tocqueville, "the strength of free peoples resides in the local community," giving them both the "spirit of liberty" and the ability to withstand the "tyranny of the majority,"[42] but the size of American cities and the nature of their inhabitants were also so threatening to the future of the republic that they required "an armed force which, while remaining subject to the wishes of the national majority, is independent of the people of the towns and capable of sup-

[40]Quoted in Arendt, p. 253.
[41]T. Jefferson, *The Writings of Thomas Jefferson* Vol. 4 ed. P. Ford (New York: G. P. Putnam, 1904), p. 86.
[42]A. de Tocqueville, *Democracy in America*, trans. George Lawrence, ed. J. P. Payer (Garden City, N.Y.: Doubleday, 1969), pp. 62, 68–70, 262–263.

pressing their excesses."[43] Indeed, the vision of cities as being the home of "mobs," the working class, immigrants, and, finally, racial minorities is a theme that runs through much of nineteenth- and twentieth-century thought. Chancellor Kent's own fears of the democratic cities were surely no secret.

Yet, one need not rely on the assertion that the subordination of cities was the product of the unwillingness to protect the cities' rights of association and the fear of democratic power. Because the issue of city power was decided as part of the issue of corporate power, the threatening ideas associated with the rights of association did not need to be brought to consciousness. It is for this reason that the classification of American cities as corporations mattered; it can be understood as helping to repress the notion that associational rights were being affected in defining the laws governing city rights. No rights of association needed to be articulated when discussing the rights of "private" corporations, because property rights were sufficient to protect them against state power, and there was nothing that required rights of association to be imagined in discussing the subordination of "public" corporations. Yet, if no rights of association were recognized, cities, increasingly deprived of their economic character—the basis of their power for hundreds of years—had little defense against the reallocation of their power to the individual and to the state. There was nothing left that seemed to demand protection; therefore, nothing could prevent the control of the cities by the state.

The developments in legal doctrine that led to the public/private distinction for corporations did not immediately alter the allocation of power between American states and cities. In fact, prior to the 1850s, local autonomy remained largely intact. The impetus for the assertion of state political power to curb local autonomy finally came when the desire to restrict city activity in favor of private activity increased. In light of the new conception of public and private activities, the investment by cities in business enterprises no longer seemed an appropriate "public" function, and local regulation of a city's business community seemed to invade the "private sphere." Hence, state control over these city activities was invoked. State control of cities during this period, however, was by no means limited to the assurance of a *"laissez-faire"* policy designed to prevent both cities and states, as governments, from intervening in the private sector. Much state legislation compelled the cities to raise and

[43]Ibid., p. 278 n.l.

spend money for state-supported causes, including the promotion of economic enterprise. Other state legislation—so-called ripper legislation—simply sought to transfer control of the city government to state-appointed officials. For a wide variety of purposes, then, state power to control cities could now be exercised—and was being exercised—as a matter of law.

The Modern Law of Municipal Corporations

Dillon's Treatise

The legal doctrine that cities were subject to state authority was enthusiastically endorsed by John Dillon, who in 1872 wrote the first and most important American treatise on municipal corporations.[44] Dillon did not seek to disguise the values that he thought important in framing the law for municipal corporations. In speeches, law review articles, and books, Dillon eloquently defended the need to protect private property from attack and indicated his reservations about the kind of democracy then practiced in the cities.

It would be a mistake, however, to read Dillon's defense of strict state control of cities as simply a crude effort to advance the interests of the rich or of private corporations at the expense of the poor inhabitants of cities. Instead, it is more plausible to interpret Dillon as a forerunner of the Progressive tradition; he sought to protect private property not only against abuse by democracy but also against abuse by private economic power. To do so, he advocated an objective, rational government, staffed by the nation's elite—a government strong enough to curb the excesses of corporate power and at the same time to help those who deserved help. It is important to understand how Dillon could consider state control of the cities as a major ingredient in accomplishing these objectives.

According to Dillon, a critical impediment to the development of a government dedicated to the public good was the intermingling of the public and the private sectors. Strict enforcement of a public/private distinction was essential both to protect government from the threat of domination by private interests and to protect the activities of the private economy from being unfairly influenced by government intervention. Moreover, to ensure its fully "public" nature, government had to be

[44]J. Dillon, *Treatise on the Law of Municipal Corporations* (Chicago: J. Cockcroft, 1872).

organized so that it could attract to power those in the community best able to govern. Class legislation in favor of either the rich or the poor had to be avoided—neither a government of private greed nor one of mass ignorance could be tolerated. Instead, it was the role of the best people to assume responsibility by recognizing and fulfilling their communal obligations: "It is a duty of perpetual obligation on the part of the strong to take care of the weak, of the rich to take care of the poor."[45]

This vision pervades Dillon's work on municipal corporations. From his perspective, cities presented problems that seemed almost "inherent" in their nature. By merging the public and private spheres, cities had extravagantly invested in private businesses, performing functions "better left to private enterprise."[46] As both a state and a federal judge, Dillon saw firsthand the problems engendered by the municipal financing of railroads. He therefore advocated constitutional limitations and restriction of the franchise to taxpayers whenever any expenditure of money was at stake in order to prevent cities from engaging further in such transactions.

At the same time, Dillon believed that all of the functions properly undertaken by cities should be considered "public." He therefore criticized the courts for contributing to the division of city activities into public and private spheres. For half a century, the courts had distinguished the city's governmental functions, which were subject to absolute state power, from its proprietary functions, which received the constitutional protection afforded to rights of private property. Although conceding that such a distinction was "highly important" in municipal corporation law,[47] Dillon found a city's retention of any private identity "difficult exactly to comprehend."[48] Because a city was by definition created by the state, "which breathed into it the breath of life,"[49] there seemed nothing private about cities at all.

Most troubling of all to Dillon, cities were not managed by those "*best fitted* by their intelligence, business experience, capacity and moral character."[50] Their management was "too often both *unwise* and *extrava-*

---

[45]J. Dillon, "Property—Its Rights and Duties in our Legal and Social Systems," *American Law Review* 29 (1895):173.
[46]Dillon, *Treatise*, p. 22.
[47]Ibid., p. 82.
[48]Ibid., §39, p. 83.
[49]Ibid.
[50]Ibid., Chapter 1, §9, p. 21 (emphasis in original).

gant.[51] A major change in city government was therefore needed to achieve a fully public city government dedicated to the common good.

But how could this be achieved? To Dillon, the answer seemed to lie in state control of cities and in judicial supervision of that control. State control, though political, was purely public, and the "best fitted" could more likely be attracted to its government. Moreover, enforcement of the rule of law could play a role, because law was "the beneficence of civil society acting by rule, in its nature . . . opposed to all that [was] fitful, capricious, unjust, partial or destructive."[52] The state and the law working together could thus curb municipal abuse by rigorously enforcing the public/private distinction.

In his treatise, Dillon could not have more broadly phrased the extent of state power over city functions. State power "is supreme and transcendent: it may erect, change, divide, and even abolish, at pleasure, as it deems the public good to require."[53] In addition to legislative control, he argued for a major role for the courts:

> The courts, too, have duties, the most important of which is to require these corporations, in all cases, to show a plain and clear grant for the authority they assume to exercise; to *lean against constructive powers*, and, with firm hands, to hold them and their officers within chartered limits.[54]

Once all these steps were taken, Dillon argued, the cities' governance could properly be left to democratic control. Although Dillon's vision of society may be gone forever, Dillon's statement of the law of municipal corporations, stripped of its ideological underpinnings, largely remains intact today.

Attempts to Establish a "Right to Local Self-Government."

The most extensive rebuttal to Dillon was published in 1911 by Eugene McQuillin in his multivolume treatise, *The Law of Municpal Corporations.*[55] In an exhaustive survey, McQuillin traced the historical devel-

[51]Ibid., p. 22 (emphasis in original).
[52]J. Dillon, *The Laws and Jurisprudence of England and America* (Boston: Little, Brown, 1894), p. 16. Dillon here was paraphrasing, although not citing, Edmund Burke: "[L]aw itself is only beneficence acting by a rule," *Reflections on the Revolution in France* (New York: Dutton, 1967), p. 56.
[53]Dillon, *Treatise*, §30, p. 72.
[54]Ibid., Chapter 1, §9, pp. 25–26 (emphasis in original).
[55]E. McQuillin, *A Treatise on the Law of Municipal Corporations*, 1st ed. (Chicago: Callaghan, 1911).

opment of municipal corporations and found the essential theme to be a
right to local self-government. He rejected the suggestion that cities were
created by the state, arguing that "(s)uch (a) position ignores well-established, historical facts easily ascertainable."[56] McQuillin strongly criticized courts that failed to uphold the right of local self-government.

McQuillin also sought to buttress his argument by inventing a new
rationale for the public/private distinction within municipal corporation
law, the distinction that had so confused other writers. There was a
general consensus, McQuillin noted, that absolute state power could be
exerted only over a city's "public functions." Those functions, he argued,
were those that in fact had been given the city by the state. Because the
justification for state supremacy depends on the idea of state creation,
state control must be limited to those things so created. Powers not
derived from legislative action must therefore be "private" and subject to
the same constitutional protection as other private rights. The power of
the locality that historically was exercised prior to a state charter—the
right to local self-government—is, then, a "private" right and cannot be
subject to state supremacy.[57]

In 1923, William Munro, in his classic work, *The Government of
American Cities*, stated that Dillon's position on state control of cities was
"so well recognized that it is not nowadays open to question."[58] Mc-
Quillin's thesis, on the other hand, has been substantially revised even in
his own treatise by its current editor:

> (T)he municipal corporation is a creature of the legislature, from
> which, within constitutional limits, it derives all its rights and
> powers. Distinction should be made between the right of local self-
> government as inherent in the people, and the right as inherent in a
> municipal corporation; while as to the people, the right has quite
> commonly been assumed to exist, but as to the municipal corporation
> the right must be derived, either from the people through the con-
> stitution or from the legislature.[59]

No other serious academic challenge to the Dillon thesis has ever been
made.

There was in the late nineteenth century, however, a political challenge to state control of cities launched under the rallying cry of "home

[56]Ibid., 2nd ed. (Chicago: Callaghan, 1928), §268 (246), p. 679.
[57]Ibid., §190 (169), pp. 514–516.
[58]W. Munro, *The Government of American Cities* (New York: Macmillan, 1923),
    p. 53.
[59]McQuillin, 3rd rev. ed. (Chicago: Callaghan, 1979), §4.82, p. 137.

rule." Once state invasion of city authority became a common occurrence, it became apparent that cities were not faring well under the doctrine that purported to give private enterprises rights and public bodies power. Although by 1886 private corporations had fully become "persons" whose rights were constitutionally protected,[60] public corporations no longer had the sovereign power they had once exercised. Moreover, their remaining power derived only from specific state authorizations that were strictly construed by the courts. The solution offered to correct the cities' absence of rights and loss of self-government was the amendment of state constitutions.

Late-nineteenth- and early twentieth-century reformers, in fact, achieved the enactment of a bewildering variety of constitutional amendments designed to protect city autonomy. These constitutional amendments, however, failed to achieve their objective of local autonomy. The reason for their failure lies in the continuing liberal unwillingness to tolerate an intermediate entity that appears to threaten the interests of both the state and the individual.

One of the most common constitutional amendments was a restriction on state power that gave a state authority to pass only "general" and not "special" or local legislation. This restriction was designed to curb state efforts to control detailed city decision-making by specific legislation. Yet, if the state's ability to deal with substate, or local, problems were prohibited altogether, individuals would be subject to irresponsible local action or neglect. Accordingly, these constitutional restrictions have not been interpreted as prohibiting "general" legislation aimed at a class of cities, even if the "class" is really only one city, for example, a class of cities with a population of 29,946–29,975.[61] Restrictions on special legislation, then, have become merely weak equal-protection clauses limiting the state legislature's ability to classify cities. They are ineffective because there is nothing "suspect" about state restrictions and nothing "fundamental" about the invasion of local autonomy.

Another important state constitutional restriction was designed to grant cities "home rule," meaning both the ability to enact legislation without specific state permission and the ability to prevent certain state invasions of local autonomy. Where permitted, home rule has been useful in expanding the cities' ability to exercise their powers without seeking

[60]*Santa Clara County v. Southern Pacific Railroad*, 118 U.S. 394 (1886).
[61]See *Ponder v. State*, 141 Tenn. 481, 212 S.W. 417 (1919), dealing with counties.

detailed state authorization. However, it has not successfully created an area of local autonomy protected from state control. Because some state control of city action is, of course, necessary to protect both state interests and individual liberties, the courts have grappled with determining what matters are of "state concern" and what matters are "purely local" in nature. Given the fact that any local action can be seen as frustrating state objectives and that any governmental action restricts individual liberty, protection of cities under home rule is possible only if there is some strong sense that the values being protected "outweigh" the risks involved. Such a sense, however, has all but disappeared under the liberal attack on city autonomy. As a result, very little that is "purely local" can be found, and state control of cities has not been affected significantly by state constitutional protection of home rule. Thus, in accord with the liberal view, the interests of the state and the individual have been upheld at the expense of city power, even in the face of supposedly restrictive constitutional amendments.

Cities Become Businesses Again

In 1890, Dillon referred to the need to make city governments more businesslike:

> In many of its more important aspects a modern American city is not so much a miniature State as it is a business corporation,—its business being wisely to administer the local affairs and economically to expend the revenues of the incorporated community. As we learn this lesson and apply business methods to the scheme of municipal government and to the conduct of municipal affairs, we are on the right road to better and more satisfactory results.[62]

McQuillin, however, resisted this reformulation of city status, insisting that cities should retain their identity as miniature states.[63] To understand this dispute, we must analyze the nature of the reformers' attack against city corruption.

In the popular American mythology, the history of cities in the late nineteenth century is aptly reflected by the chapter headings of Samuel

[62]J. Dillon, *Commentaries on the Law of Municipal Corporations*, 4th ed. (Boston: Little, Brown, 1890), p. 34.
[63]E. McQuillin, *The Law of Municipal Corporations*, 2d ed. (Chicago: Callaghan, 1928), §106, pp. 302–306.

Orth's book *The Boss and the Machine:* "The Rise of the Machine," "Tammany Hall," "The Awakening," and "The Expert at Last."[64] Recent historians have sought to revise this image of history, substituting a more complex version of what was at stake in the movement to replace city machines with more "businesslike" forms of city government.[65] For the immigrant, the machines responded to vital needs for jobs and services in a manner that was corrupt but humane. For the "reformer-individualist-Anglo-Saxon," whose goals were "citizenship, responsibility, efficiency, good government, economy, and businesslike management,"[66] the machine represented an evil that had to be curbed.

Despite the reformers' rhetoric, it was city corruption and not its eradication that transformed the cities into businesses. What corruption meant was the mingling of the private sector's profit motive with the business of the state. As Max Weber's brilliant portrayal of the boss in his essay "Politics as a Vocation" suggests, the boss was much more a late-nineteenth-century businessman than was his successor in the reform city governments.[67] Although the nature of the invasion of the profit motive into the public sphere was undesirable, the reformers, in their "search for order"[68] in political chaos, dealt with corruption in a way that, while transforming city governments into a less political form, by no means transformed them into businesses. Instead, further controls over city operations were added, controls—such as civil service requirements for employees and the appointment of managers not removable by the chief executive officer—that would be unthinkable for any American business.

By the steps they took to reinforce the public/private distinction, the reformers reinforced the powerlessness of cities. Their efforts to transform the cities helped to erode further the sense of the city as a center of political autonomy or of direct democracy. Today, almost half of American

[64]S. Orth, *The Boss and the Machine* (New Haven: Yale University Press, 1919), p. vii.

[65]See, for example, R. Hofstader, *The Age of Reform* (New York: Vintage Books, 1955), pp. 173–184; J. Weinstein, *The Corporate Ideal in the Liberal State: 1900–1918* (Boston: Beacon Press, 1968), 92–116; R. Wiebe, *Business and Reform* (Cambridge: Harvard University Press, 1962). For a general review and critique of the literature, see J. Buenker, *Urban Liberalism and Progressive Reform* (New York: Norton, 1973), pp. 198–239.

[66]Hofstader, p. 183.

[67]*From Max Weber*, ed. H. Gerth and C. W. Mills (New York: Oxford University Press, 1957), pp. 77, 109–110.

[68]See, generally, Wiebe.

cities have "nonpartisan" elections, commission governments, or city managers. In the place of democracy are the ideas of expertise, objective decision-making, and government by rational rules.

The reforms, however, did have one curious side effect: if cities were to be considered businesses, some argued, they should own and operate some vital city services, such as utilities. This concept of the city as a business is far from Judge Dillon's, but it was the centerpiece of the solutions to city corruption offered by other reformers (such as Frederick Howe).[69] Eliminate the corrupt businessman seeking city contracts, they argued, and you eliminate the principal source of corruption; with municipal ownership, no such corrupt contracts would exist. The reformers did achieve some, but only a limited amount of, municipal ownership as part of transforming the city into "a business."

Conclusion

Reviewing the history of the city as an institution, we can see that a complex transformation of the city has occurred, a transformation that has increasingly narrowed the definition of its nature to that of an entity authorized by the state to solve purely local political problems. The city has changed from an association promoted by a powerful sense of community and an identification with the defense of property to a unit that threatens both the members of the community and their property. Ideas and experience have altered the city completely, and it is this alteration that I have sought to convey by referring to the increasing powerlessness of cities. It is not simply that cities have become totally subject to state control—although that itself demonstrates their powerlessness—but also that cities have lost the elements of association and economic strength that had formerly enabled them to play an important part in the development of Western society.

It should not be overlooked that the form of social organization that the cities represented became undermined just at the time that popular participation in city affairs had at last become generally possible. Moreover, there is some irony in the fact that this process reached completion during the last few decades of the nineteenth century, the period de-

---

[69]See F. Howe, *The City: The Hope of Democracy*, ed. Robert E. Burke, (Seattle: University of Washington Press, 1905). See also C. Beard, *American City Government* (New York: Century, 1912), pp. 128–241.

scribed in Arthur Schlesinger's seminal history of cities entitled *The Rise of the City*.[70] In this work, Schlesinger argued that urbanization caused the "rise" in city importance. Yet urbanization did not curb the declining role of the city as an institution; on the contrary, urbanization simply reinforced the controls exercised over cities. The fear of the changing nature of the city population led to additional political support for these controls, and that support could not be countered with any effective notion of a right of local self-determination. .

The current status of cities is now an unstated assumption in most of the recent literature. Sociological work like that of the so-called Chicago school[71] and historical work by those who followed Schlesinger[72] have focused on the city as a place to live. Most political scientists who have written on the city as an institution have limited their inquiry to its internal governmental structure, accepting as a given the extent of its power and the amount of state control.[73] Thus, our current image of cities has become an established part of liberal social thought.

THE POSSIBILITY OF CITY POWER

The Problem of Decentralizing Power

Decentralization as a Dilemma within Liberalism

The problem raised by the current status of cities is not simply one of deciding how much power we want to allocate to certain minor political subdivisions. The issue involves, instead, the fundamental question of whether any decentralization of power is possible in a liberal society. The

[70]A. Schlesinger, *The Rise of the City 1878–1898* (New York: Macmillan, 1933). This was the pioneering work that led to the now burgeoning interest in urban history. See S. Warner, "If All the World Were Philadelphia: A Scaffolding for Urban History, 1774–1930," *American Historical Review* 74 (1968):26.

[71]The central work is R. Park, E. Burgess, and R. McKenzie, *The City* (Chicago: University of Chicago Press, 1967). See also, *Classic Essays on the Culture of Cities*, ed. R. Sennett (New York: Meredith, 1969), pp. 13–19, 91–233.

[72]See works cited in Warner.

[73]See, for example, E. Banfield and J. Q. Wilson, *City Politics* (Cambridge: Harvard University and M.I.T. Press, 1963); R. Dahl, *Who Governs?*, (New Haven: Yale University Press, 1981); N. Polsby, *Community Power and Political Theory* (New Haven: Yale University Press, 1963).

liberal attack against the city, traced in the previous section, can be understood as illustrating the precariousness of establishing within liberalism any form of group power intermediate between a centralized state and the individual. Every example of group power—whether political or economic, public or private—permits the power wielder to invade the spheres of both the individual and the state and is thus subject to the same liberal attack as has been waged against the cities. This attack may help explain the diminishing position in our society of forms of decentralized power as diverse as the family and the American states.

At the same time, the need to decentralize power is not widely questioned. Indeed, the history of the city repeatedly illustrates the idea that the protection of entities intermediate between the state and the individual can be regarded as a defense of freedom, not simply as a danger to it. The creation of the medieval town as a protection for the merchants' way of life, the defense of the English corporation against the king in the name of rights of property, the vitality of the colonial town as an association, the defense of a "right of local self-government" against Dillon's support of state control of the cities, and the effort to gain "home rule" can all be seen as attempts to preserve intermediate entities in order to protect individuals from the power of a centralized state. Moreover, all these examples of the idea of group autonomy can contribute to the attempt to define the concept of "public freedom" discussed in the first section of this chapter: the ability of a group of people, working together, to control actively the basic societal decisions that affect their lives.

Indeed, it is a paradox that although liberalism can be understood as an attempt to eradicate group power in favor of that of the individual and the state, most liberal thinkers seem convinced that the creation of a world without any intermediate bodies—a world in which the state is the only power-wielder other than individuals themselves[74]—would leave individuals powerless to prevent a centralized state from threatening their liberty. Liberal thinkers have sought to avoid this problem, prin-

---

[74]This is the liberal vision of society expressed by Rousseau. See J. Rousseau, "The Social Contract," in *The Essential Rousseau*, trans. Lowell Bair (New York: Mentor Book, 1974). The critique of Rousseau's vision is a mainstay of the literature on political theory. For an interesting evaluation of Rousseau's theory, see A. Levine, *The Politics of Autonomy*, (Amherst: University of Massachusetts Press, 1976); for an attempt to place it in the context of democratic theory generally, see C. Pateman, *Participation and Democratic Theory* (Cambridge: Cambridge University Press, 1970), pp. 1–44.

cipally by imagining that power can be allocated solely to individuals, with the state all but withering away. An example is the pretense that a *laissez-faire* society could do away with a powerful state when, of course, such a state would be indispensable in creating, construing, and enforcing "private rights." These days, however, the continued existence of a powerful state is too obvious for most liberal thinkers to ignore. They, too, therefore, seek safety in the power of intermediate entities that can protect them from the power of the state.

Liberals, then, have been caught in a perilous contradiction: they have sought to destroy intermediate forms of power, but they also want to preserve them. Until recently, this contradiction had escaped the notice of many liberal thinkers. This was possible because private corporations, the principal remaining source of decentralized power in America, were portrayed as individuals—as persons—rather than as bodies exercising group power intermediate between the individual and the state.

But the image of major American corporations as individuals has become increasingly less convincing. The threats that such corporations pose to real individuals are now being curbed, for example, by labor laws and civil rights legislation, as are the threats that they pose to the state, by regulation and planning. Private corporations once again appear to be examples of the original meaning of "corporate" power: group power. As a result, they are now being subjected to the very attack already successfully waged against public corporations.[75] Indeed, it is in the defense of private corporate power that the need for entities intermediate between the state and the individual is now most often expressed.

Those who now defend the need for some form of decentralized power do so, as did their predecessors, because of its connection with "freedom." As noted earlier, "public freedom" can be achieved only by preserving the authority of a group small enough to allow active participation by group members. Other definitions of freedom, such as "freedom of choice" and the maintenance of civil liberties, have also been tied to some form of independent corporate life. Yet immunizing, even to a limited extent, any definition of freedom is dangerous.

In supporting the need for decentralized power, one should not make the mistake of denying the force of the liberal attack against it.

[75]See, for example, A. Berle, *Power without Property*, (New York: Harcourt Brace, 1959); R. Dahl, *After the Revolution*, (New Haven: Yale University Press, 1970), pp. 115–140; J. Galbraith, *Economics and the Public Purpose*, (Boston: Houghton Mifflin, 1973); J. Galbraith, *The New Industrial State*, (New York: New American Library, 1967).

Independent corporate power of any kind does threaten individuals. We have seen examples of these threats in the history of the city outlined in the previous section, and similar examples can be drawn from the more recent history of private corporations or even from the history of the family, which in ancient times itself "was a Corporation."[76]

Our choice, then, whether or not to have strong intermediate bodies is not a choice between vulnerability and protection. The exercise of state power infringes individual rights protected by independent corporations, yet the exercise of corporate power infringes individual rights protected by the state. Every time we seek state help to protect us from a corporate invasion of our rights, we strengthen one threat to liberty at the expense of another; yet, every time we prevent the state from protecting us against corporate power, we accomplish the same result. Our only option is to choose which danger to liberty seems more tolerable, more controllable, or more worth defending.

Decentralization as an Option within Liberal Society

We can, of course, decentralize power if we decide to do so. We are not prisoners of our liberal ideology, forced by a mechanistic idealism to deny the preservation of group power. We can create any powerful entity that we want to create. But if we wish to create powerful intermediate bodies, we must find a way to enable them to retain their power when challenged by individuals or by the state.

Any kind of absolute corporate immunity from state control, such as nineteenth-century thinkers might have imagined in terms of home rule for cities or property rights for corporations, is, of course, a fantasy, as would be ceding to corporations absolute power over individuals. Yet, corporations, once subjected to state power to some extent, cannot be defended against that power by seeking, in classic liberal terms, protection of corporate "rights."[77] There will always be a good argument in favor of greater individual liberty from corporate power or greater state restriction of corporate power. And if the state decides the conflict between these values and corporate rights (who else could?), the destruction of corporate power cannot be prevented. We know this not only because of the process of subordination that has already been completed in the case of cities but also from the history of the attempt to protect private corpo-

[76]H. Maine, *Ancient Law*, (London: J. Murray, 1861), p. 184.
[77]See Kennedy, "Blackstone's Commentaries," pp. 261–264, 354–362.

rate power through substantive due process.[78] Independent group power is simply not an idea, whether clothed in the name of rights or sovereignty, that can be defended within a liberal legal system against liberal attack. The power of these intermediate entities must, therefore, be based on more than mere rights; it must rest on their actual ability to exercise power within society.

In fact, the power of intermediate groups, where it has occurred, has always been based on more than the protection of their legal rights. Two examples can illustrate this point. The current power of private corporations rests in part on their importance to the nation's economic system, so that any political or legal attempt to destroy their power would create what would seem to most people to be frightening instability. This degree of power can be self-protecting. When cities possessed real economic power in this sense, their ability to resist state control was much greater than it is today (notwithstanding the fact that their current "political" power to tax is the "power to destroy").

Second, as we have seen, cities, when they did not base their power merely on economic strength, rested it on their role in the daily lives of their citizens. Medieval towns were powerful because they represented an economic-political-communal unit that allowed their citizens to achieve a new status within feudal society. New England towns, at the height of their power, were religious and fraternal communities, and their ability to represent what seemed to be the fundamental interests of their citizens enabled the towns to control the state, rather than the other way around. The role of the *polis* in Greek life was so central that Aristotle could describe the human being as a political animal. Thus, the former power of cities depended, as the current power of corporations depends, on their actual place in social life. If any form of group power is to be protected, therefore, such power must be based not simply on a legal status empty of an underlying rationale but on its importance—both as a matter of experience and as a matter of thought—to our lives.

Cities as Possibilities for Decentralized Power

We seem, however, unable to conceive of a way in which cities could resume such importance. Our inability to imagine cities exercising real

---

[78]See generally L. Tribe, *American Constitutional Law* (New York: Foundation Press, 1978) §8–1 to §8–7.

decentralized power stems in part from our tendency to reduce that possibility to the concept of political decentralization.[79] There is, however, no meaningful possibility of purely political decentralization. To begin with, there has never been a concept of purely political local autonomy in Western thought. As we have just noted, all powerful local units, whether Greek cities, medieval towns, or New England towns, combined their "political" identity with other forms of religious or fraternal cohesion or economic power.

Second, the liberal undermining of intermediate entities has nowhere been so effective as in presenting the danger involved in genuine decentralization of power to a purely political, purely governmental body. Decentralization of power to such an entity would make it, to the extent of its independence from state power, a sovereign political body. But to permit two sovereigns to function within the same state would create what is called *imperium in imperio,* "the greatest of all political solecisms."[80] No area of political power can be left to the uncontrolled discretion of local authorities: every local action affects other localities; there must be a body to resolve local political conflict. Thus, the need for a single unified sovereign has become a fundamental premise of Western political thought.[81]

Third, small units can be seen—as Madison saw them[82]—as the greatest governmental danger to individual liberty. Indeed, it may not be enough merely to apply the U.S. Constitution to restrain the political power exercised by cities or to reform city power by making it more "rational." The mere delegation to cities of broad political power, even though leaving that power fully subject to state legislative control, can be considered an impermissible threat to individual liberties.

[79]Much of the current literature proposing decentralization of power to cities or neighborhoods assumes that what is simply political decentralization. See, for example, W. Farr, L. Liebman, and J. Wood, *Decentralizing City Government* (New York: Praeger, 1972); M. Kotler, *Neighborhood Government,* (Indianapolis: Bobbs-Merrill, 1969). Political decentralization was also the goal of the federal government's efforts to achieve community control through the Office of Economic Opportunity program, the Model Cities program, and the State and Local Fiscal Assistance program (revenue sharing) in the 1970s.

[80]B. Bailyn, *The Ideological Origins of the American Revolution* (Cambridge: Belknap Press, 1967), p. 206.

[81]The classic statement is that of Thomas Hobbes, see *Leviathan* (Oxford: Clarendon Press, 1909), Chapter 17, pp. 131–132.

[82]*The Federalist,* no. 10 (J. Madison).

Finally, even if cities could exercise the amount of political power for their own jurisdiction that state legislatures exercise for the state as a whole, their ability to control effectively the future of their communities would be sharply limited by the independent exercise of economic power by private corporations. Not only would city power continue to be limited by the constitutional protections afforded private corporations (such as the commerce clause), but as a practical matter, cities would still have to depend for their survival on the goodwill of the private corporations that did business within their boundaries. The influence on national political decision-making of the need to protect the economy is well recognized in modern political analysis, but that influence is vastly greater if private-sector decision-makers can readily move their businesses across city boundaries to avoid the political decisions that they oppose. The very split between political and economic power, with political authorities dependent on their ability to tax economic entities in order to pay for government services, would thus determine much of the agenda of even a powerful local government.

The decentralization of power to cities need not, however, be limited to the transfer of purely political power. Cities could be given the kind of power that we are willing to decentralize in our society, the kind of power wielded by those entities that still exercise genuine decentralized power: private corporations. A start could be made, as some have suggested,[83] by transferring a portion of the banking and insurance industries to city control. In having cities perform these functions, we need neither accept the current structure of American cities nor re-create a modern version of a hierarchical medieval town. We could create any form of city organization that seemed worth having.

If we can decentralize power despite the liberal undermining of intermediate groups, why have we chosen to rely on private corporations rather than cities as our principal means of doing so? The answer must be attributed in part to the continuing power of our liberal ideas, which suggest that the kind of organizations that wield economic power in this country are radically different from cities—a difference summarized by their being "private" and cities' being "public"—and that this difference legitimates the *status quo* against any genuine transfer of power to cities.

---

[83]See, for example, Case, Goldbert, and Shearer, "State Business," *Working Papers for a New Society* (Spring 1967): p. 67.

The Erosion of the Public/Private Distinction as a Justification for City Powerlessness and Corporate Power

The public/private distinction generally serves as the explanation for city powerlessness and the justification for corporate power. To attempt to construct powerful cities, we must first examine the legitimacy of this way of distinguishing cities and corporations. Indeed, the public/private distinction so powerfully affects the city/corporation comparison that, until we can put it aside, we will not be able to analyze these entities in any other way.

The Bases of the Distinction between Public and Private Corporations.

The Need to Protect Private Property. The original basis for the public/private distinction was the need to protect private property. Yet, at least since the appearance in 1932 of Berle and Means's celebrated work, *The Modern Corporation and Private Property*,[84] the "private property" status of the assets of major American corporations has been seriously questioned. Berle and Means argued that the separation of ownership and control in the modern, "publicly held" corporation has placed the control of corporate assets in the hands of a relatively small number of corporate managers, with shareholders so widely dispersed that they cannot exercise meaningful influence on corporate policy. Corporate assets can no longer be considered the private property of shareholders, not only because shareholders cannot effectively obtain their *pro rata* share of the assets or control their use, but because, as Berle's later studies showed, most corporate property is not derived from the shareholders' investment at all, but from business savings and corporate borrowing. In addition, individual shareholders have allowed much of what remains of their voting control to be exercised by institutional investors.[85]

The shareholders' property interest has thus been reduced to the market value of their stock and has thereby become detached from corporate assets themselves. Except for their ability to sell their corporate investment, shareholders who contribute part of a private corporation's

---

[84]A. Berle and G. Means, *The Modern Corporation and Private Property* (New York: Commerce Clearing House, 1932).
[85]Berle, *Power*, pp. 41–58.

assets have begun to resemble taxpayers who contribute part of a public corporation's assets. Neither controls the use of the assets but each elects managers who do.[86]

But if corporate assets are not the shareholders' private property, they are certainly not the property of corporate executives or directors. Because no human owner can be found, the corporation itself seems the only possible candidate to be the owner of corporate property. And if that is true, all corporations, including "public" corporations, can be seen as owners of private property.

Corporate property has thus become separated from the concept of individual possession; it has become group, not private, property. This "dissolution of the atom of property," Berle and Means argued, "destroys the very foundation on which the economic order of the past three centuries rested."[87] The message was well recognized by the conservative economist Joseph Schumpeter, who saw the "Evaporation of the Substance of Property" as facilitating the transition from capitalism to socialism.[88]

"Public" and "Private" Managers.   It might also be said that corporate executives are private individuals and that city executives are public individuals. We classify corporate and city executives in this way in order to impose obligations on public employees that are not imposed on private ones. As Karl Marx suggested in his essay "On the Jewish Question," to label the individual in civil society (such as in a private corporation) "private" and a state employee "public" is to divide those who can lead an earthly life of economic gain from those who must regard themselves as communal beings and must act in a heavenly fashion.[89] This vision still retains a powerful influence on our thinking. It delegitimizes political activity, as political behavior, of necessity, falls far short of a heavenly standard.

In the twentieth century, however, the dichotomy between public

---

[86]For an analysis of the role of shareholders in corporate management, reviewing the extensive relevant literature, see, M. Eisenberg, "The Legal Roles of Shareholders and management in Modern Corporate Decisionmaking," *California Law Review* 57 (1969):1.

[87]Berle and Means, *The Modern Corporation*. See also Berle, *Power.*

[88]J. Schumpeter, *Capitalism, Socialism and Democracy* (New York: Harper Torchbooks, 1942), p. 156.

[89]*The Marx-Engels Reader*, ed. Robert C. Tucker (New York: W. W. Norton, 1972), pp. 31–32.

and private behavioral ideals has been greatly eroded. Increasingly, we see the need for both public and private officials to meet a standard of communal behavior. Modern corporate managers present themselves as having "public" obligations; indeed, it is this "corporate conscience" that, for Berle, partly provided the continuing legitimacy of private corporate power. Indicia of this growing ideal of the public responsibility of private corporations include their expanding role in supporting artistic endeavors and recent proposals to add so-called public members to corporate boards of directors. It is true that the demand for legislation restricting corporate activity demonstrates our skepticism that corporate officials will achieve a communal standard of behavior. But the same is true of public officials, for whom our insistence on "heavenly" rather than "earthly" behavior has also become largely a matter of statutory obligation, with a maze of conflict-of-interest legislation, open-meeting laws, competitive-bidding requirements, and other restrictions all seeking to curb their expected earthly misconduct.

Coercive Power. Another traditional distinction between public and private corporations is that only governmental corporations exercise power over private individuals. This distinction has been attacked in a variety of ways. An examination of the power that property rights afford those to whom they are allocated has led some, notably Morris Cohen, to identify the close relationship that still exists between property and sovereignty.[90] Economists, such as John Kenneth Galbraith,[91] have emphasized the power that large corporations exercise in controlling market decisions. Others have analyzed the pervasive influence of corporate officials on the exercise of political power.[92]

The evidence of private corporate power is overwhelming enough for Abram Chayes to accept it as a premise:

> Professor Adolph Berle, in a contemporary summary note, tells us: "Some of these corporations are units which can be thought of only in somewhat the way we have heretofore thought of nations." All the instruments agree: the modern corporation wields economic and so-

---

[90]Cohen, "Property and Sovereignty," *Cornell Law Quarterly* 13 (1927):8. The closeness of that relationship is demonstrated by the history of the city outlined in Part 3, S. Sato and A. Van Alstyne, *State and Local Government Law*, 2nd ed. (New York: Little, Brown, 1977).

[91]J. Galbraith, *The New Industrial State*, 2nd rev. ed. (New York: New American Library, 1971).

[92]See C. Lindblom, *Politics and Markets* (New York: Basic Books, 1977).

cial power of the highest consequence for the condition of our polity.
Let us accept it as our first premise.[93]

In recognition of this power, two Supreme Court Justices have argued
that corporations should no longer be recognized as "persons" protected
by the Fourteenth Amendment from government control.[94] For the same
reason, Berle has argued that corporate action should be considered
"state action" to be restrained by the Fourteenth Amendment.[95]

Voluntary Participation. Another argument for distinguishing public from private corporations, one closely related to the issue of exercise of
power, is that participation in a public corporation's activities is involuntary, whereas participation in those of private corporations is voluntary.
There are two basic lines of rebuttal to this position. The first seeks to
demonstrate the involuntary aspect of submission to economic power,
thus suggesting that both political and economic power lie toward the
involuntary end of the voluntary/involuntary spectrum; the second seeks
to demonstrate the voluntary aspect of participation in city affairs, thus
suggesting that both powers lie toward the voluntary end of the spectrum.
For our purposes, it does not matter which of the two characterizations is
more convincing. The point instead is to demonstrate that the volun-
tary/involuntary distinction does not by itself neatly separate private from
public corporations.

The argument that seeks to demonstrate the involuntary aspects of
economic power focuses on two related ingredients: first, that economic
activity depends for its survival on political and legal coercion, and second, that the exercise of economic power, when applied to people who
need work and food to live, is itself coercive. The role of legal coercion in
the maintenance of private power has been widely recognized.[96] Indeed,
legal remedies are so important to the maintenance of economic power

[93]A. Chayes, "The Modern Corporation and the Rule of Law," in *The Corporation in Modern Society,* ed. Edward Mason (Cambridge: Harvard University
Press, 1970), p. 28.

[94]See *Wheeling Steel Corp. v. Glander,* 337 U.S. 562, 576 (1949) (J. Douglas
dissenting, joined by J. Black).

[95]A. Berle, "Constitutional Limitations on Corporate Activity: Protection of Personal Rights from Invasion by Economic Power," *University of Pennsylvania
Law Review* 100 (1952):933.

[96]See, for example, Cohen; Hale, "Force and the State: Comparison of 'Political'
and 'Economic' Compulsion," *Columbia Law Review* 35 (1935):149; L. Jaffe,
"Lawmaking by Private Groups," *Harvard Law Review* 51 (1937):201.

that "if a statute undertook to take from property owners all legal remedies against trespass and conversion, it would most likely be regarded as an act of force (against the owners) though the only affirmative force to which it subjects the owners is that exerted by private trespassers."[97] Such a statute illustrates the dependence of property owners on legal rights without which the owners would be rendered defenseless against the will of others.

Second, the example also reminds us that state action may be coercive even if it does not involve a threat of imprisonment. Yet, the broad range of coercive state activity can also be performed by economic entities:

> (S)uppose a state, without imposing any duty on a person, and without imprisoning him or seizing his property in a sheriff's execution, simply destroys an opportunity he had to obtain employment or to sell his property; and does it, not by imposing any duty on him, but by forbidding other persons to employ him or to buy from him. In such cases, he has no option in the matter. But the state is threatening him with no harm which private persons are not at liberty to inflict upon him. Yet he has been held to have constitutional rights which are infringed by such state action. The action must be regarded as an exertion of force, not merely on his potential employer or buyer, but on *him;* otherwise it would scarcely be held to invade his rights. But the only force that reaches him is the supposed non-action of private individuals.[98]

The actions described are coercive because any denial of money can be coercive, whether by an exaction of a tax or a penalty, a denial of a job, or an exclusion from the ability to buy the necessities of life. Economic power allows its possessor to profit from the mutual dependence necessary in a modern, integrated economy and to enforce its will through state action; it is, in this sense, grounded in the element of coercion.

The argument that city action, like economic activity, can be considered voluntary, proceeds in a very different fashion. It requires us to focus on the city itself rather than the abstract idea of "the state." Once we do, it becomes clear that no one is forced to live in a particular city any more than she or he is forced to work for, buy from, or invest in a particular corporation. Leaving a city once it is selected may be hard, but that difficulty must be attributed, in part, to the difficulty of finding a new

[97]Hale, "Force and the State," p. 179.
[98]Ibid., p. 176.

job in another locality. The substantial shift of the American population over the last 30 years dramatizes the fact that moving out of a city without changing jobs is a genuine choice. Of course, we must live in some "city"—some political society—but in modern society, we must, in the same way, transact with *some* commercial entity. In both cases, we can select which entity we prefer, but neither an exit from the capitalist system nor one from a given political system can be made easily.

Moreover, city taxes need not be considered involuntary, whereas payments to private corporations are considered voluntary. City taxes are imposed by elected officials and often by a vote of the people themselves. Indeed, it is their very susceptibility to change that makes local property taxes targets for mass action (such as California's Proposition 13). At a more basic level, political activity, like economic activity, can be understood to be the result of a consensual agreement made by competing groups. Of course, no individual gets his or her way in every political transaction; but he or she is understood to consent not to every particular result but to the rules of the process that determines the results.

The same can be said of economic activity. The individual in economic life cannot, in every transaction, reopen the nature of the contract and the property rights on which the transaction is based, although changes in those rights would affect the results of the bargain. For economic transactions to be possible, each actor must impliedly consent to certain rules regulating political activity. Such a theory of consent does not undermine the voluntary nature of the process, for the rules can be changed by group decisions (which themselves will be based on certain rules). Political activity, then, like economic activity, is grounded in the "morality of consent" expressed within the framework of existing rules[99]; indeed, consent is the justification for both the democratic process and the market economy.

Functions and Controls.   A final distinction between public and private corporations is said to rest on the functions that they now perform and on whether these functions are governed by "political" or "market" forces. But even if this is true today, it is only because we have decided, on political grounds, to allocate to each type of corporation different functions and different controls. At the time of the *Dartmouth College* decision, public and private corporations could not be differentiated by

[99]See A. Bickel, *The Morality of Consent* (New Haven: Yale University Press, 1975).

function. The decision in the nineteenth century to transfer some functions (such as railroads) from public to private control, like the twentieth-century decision to transfer functions (railroads again) the opposite way, cannot create their public or private nature, unless we mean no more than to label the entity now performing them.

Nor is the existence of market or political controls decisive. If we allowed cities to operate banks, cities could be subject to the market, just as railroad executives could be popularly elected. Allocating functions and types of controls is simply a matter of deciding who ought to perform a service and who ought to control it. There is no value-free way of making these decisions.

Even today, however, the functions of public and private corporations are largely indistinguishable. This can be made clear by playing the "game" of trying to identify a government activity without a private counterpart:

> The judiciary? Mediation and arbitration play a widespread and increasing role. Police? Pinkertons are famous in our history; today every large company and school has its own security force, and private eyes continue to be hired for peephole duty; many highly innovating industries have their own secret service working in the world of industrial espionage. Welfare? Any listing of private, highly bureaucratized and authoritative welfare systems would be as long as it is unnecessary.[100]

For local governments, the game could continue indefinitely: Sanitation? Health care? Parking? Utilities? Housing? The results of this game will reveal the virtual impossibility of a meaningful, nonpolitical distinction between functions "naturally" performed by public or by private corporations, between "public goods" and "private goods." Only our judgment about the extent to which the state ought to control the exercise of the function determines who performs it.

The Modernist Attempt to Merge Public and Private

The erosion of the private nature of corporate power as the basis for describing and justifying that power has not been simply an accident. It is the result of the increased growth and concentration of corporate power after the Civil War and of the conscious effort of modernists—from the

---

[100]T. Lowi, *The End of Liberalism* (New York: Norton, 1969), p. 44.

Progressives to Berle, Laski, and Galbraith—to emphasize the effect of these developments on the private status of corporate power.[101] The modernists have strenuously sought to undermine the public/private distinction both as the basis for corporate power and elsewhere in modern society.

The modernist effort can be viewed as an attack on the dominant position of major private corporations in late-nineteenth- and twentieth-century America. According to this view, the modernists sought to curb the concentration of private power because they recognized its growing ability to control the lives of the public at large. They therefore denied that corporate power was truly private. But they did not seek to transfer private power to a purely public substitute. Instead, they sought to create entities that were neither public nor private or (amounting to the same thing) that were both public and private.

The creation of federal administrative agencies was the modernists' first major achievement in this regard. These agencies were designed not only to curb the abuse of private power but also to take some of the public or "political" element out of governmental decisions—to put them on a more rational, businesslike basis. Decisions would not be based on private interests, but they would not be political, either; they would be based instead on the "public interest." Administrative agencies thus represented the merging of the concepts of public and private into the idea of expertise.

There are other ways to interpret the rise of administrative agencies—and of the Progressive movement itself—than as part of a search for neutral expertise. Revisionist historians[102] argue that the creation of these agencies can be interpreted as an attempt by major corporations to gain public power in order to advance their own private ends. According to this view, the merger of public and private has not meant an expansion of

[101]For an analysis of the Progressives, see, generally, L. Hartz, *The Liberal Tradition in America* (New York: Harcourt Brace Jovanich, 1955), pp. 203–255; Richard Hofstadter, *The Age of Reform* (New York: Vintage Books, 1955); Robert Wiebe, *The Search for Order 1877–1920* (New York: Hill & Wang, 1967). For recent modernist works, see, for example, Berle and Means, *The Modern Corporation;* Galbraith, *The New Industrial State;* H. Laski, *Liberty in the Modern State* (London: Farber & Faber, 1930).

[102]See, for example, G. Kolko, *The Triumph of Conservatism* Chicago: Quadrangle Books, 1963); Weinstein, *The Corporate Ideal.*

the public sector at the expense of the private but the reverse: an invasion of the public sector by private interests.

We need not enter into the debate over the nature of the merger of public and private. By whatever definition one accepts, the growth of mixed public/private entities in modern times is enormous. Public/private entities of all kinds have been created on the state and local as well as the federal level. Public service corporations, special districts, and public authorities have been designed to take over major functions, including transporation, development, housing, health, and education, and to manage them in a "nonpolitical" fashion. Until recently, all these innovations were clearly intended to be public, rather than private. But now, corporations are openly being created as mixed public/private entities; the Communications Satellite Corporation, the National Railroad Passenger Corporation, and the Corporation for Public Broadcasting are current examples. More and more functions are being absorbed into a model expressing the abolition of the public/private distinction.

Thus, the breakdown of the public/private distinction, far from expanding city power, has simply created new competitors for it. But why did those who recognized the need to break down the public/private distinction rely on the creation of new kinds of "public" bodies to exercise power rather than on the city, which had historically bridged the public/private distinction? It is not that cities are fully and irreversibly public and political and therefore distinguishable from the public/private entities that the modernists have created. Indeed, part of the modernist effort has been to create "businesslike" cities through the innovations of city commissions, city managers, and other attempts to ensure "rational" decision-making. Perhaps the image of the cities as areas filled with immigrants, the working class, the poor, and later, blacks and Hispanics has made reformers suspect that they could never establish for long a reign of rational expertise (or of private power) on such a foundation.

But to this idea must be added another: the reformers sought centralization as well as the creation of mixed public/private entities. It was primarily to the federal government that they turned for solutions. To the extent that local entities were created, they were regional, multicity entities (for example, the Port Authority of New York and New Jersey). If we accept the position that Progressivism was an attempt by major corporations to exercise public power, such an effort to achieve centralization would not be surprising. And even if the reformers were truly looking for expertise and rationality, they would be likely to seek it in centralized federal agencies, because centralization would be thought necessary to check the power of those giant entities that needed to be brought under control.

The Choice between City and Corporate Power

As we have seen, the public/private distinction allowed nineteenth-century thinkers to deal with the anomaly that corporations protected individual rights and facilitated state power while simultaneously threatening those rights and frustrating that power. The public/private distinction seemed to make the problem go away by splitting corporations into their harmless, right-bearing private identities and their threatening and therefore limited public identities. However, the undermining of the private nature of business corporations and the growth of new forms of public/private power have caused the reappearance of the problem of the combined right-threatening and right-protecting nature of all corporations, but this time without a convincing public/private escape hatch.

This undermining of the public/private distinction allows us at last to compare directly the desirability of the city and the business corporation as forms of decentralized power. In my view, the current preference for the corporate over the city form can be understood as a choice for a certain model of organizing human activity, for a specific model of human association.

Although the socialist and syndicalist traditions suggest the possibility of democratic business corporations, the likelihood of transforming the modern business corporation into a vehicle for mass participation seems frustrated by size, geographic dispersion, and the variety of groups—contributors, workers, and customers—who would compete for rights to participate. At the same time, although professional management, commission government, and nonpartisan elections have been at the heart of the modernist attempt to transform cities into businesses, there seems to be an ineradicable element of democracy in city affairs. It is hard for us to imagine a geographic association without *some* degree of participation by its members or a business corporation without *some* kind of hierarchical chain of command. Thus, although continued reliance on business corporations could lead to more democracy, and although a shift of power to the cities could lead to more technical hierarchy, it seems more likely that a shift of power to the cities would mean a shift of emphasis from hierarchical associations to more democratic ones.

Indeed, a restructuring of city power to promote a greater degree of "public freedom" is the rationale for an increase in city power. If so, the continued preference for the modern business corporation, as well as the modernist attempts to legitimate the corporation by adding "public" rather than "private" individuals to its boards of directors, by advocating federal rather than state chartering, and by creating centralized public/private entities based on the corporate model, must be understood as a preference for technical hierarchy over democratic control.

Paradoxically, however, as this process has unfolded, there has been increasing disillusionment with the hierarchical form of association, whether public or private, and increasing suspicion that government by neutral expertise is a chimera. Simultaneously, there has been a growing awareness that the fact that city power might lead to more participatory democracy cannot justify a preference for business corporations over cities in a country in which the notion of legitimacy is so closely tied to the democratic ideal. Thus, on the question of a choice between models of human association, there seems at least as much justification for preferring cities to the business corporations as the other way around.

Yet, reformers historically have been stymied in their effort to achieve real, local political power; they have not wanted to abandon community power, but there has seemed to be no way to achieve it.

What explains the unwillingness to give up the idea of city autonomy and the inability to achieve it? In my view, the idea of local autonomy recreates in political terms the subject/object dichotomy in social life. A good description of the subject/object dichotomy—the relationship of self to others—is by Duncan Kennedy:

> Others (family, friends, bureaucrats, cultural figures, the state) are necessary if we are to become persons at all—they provide us the stuff of our selves and protect us in crucial ways against destruction. Even when we seem to ourselves to be most alone, others are with us, incorporated in us through processes of language, cognition and feeling that are, simply as a matter of biology, collective aspects of our individuality. Moreover, we are not always alone. We sometimes experience fusion with others, in groups of two or even two million, and it is a good rather than a bad experience.
>
> But at the same time that it forms and protects us, the universe of others (family, friendships, bureaucracy, culture, the state) threatens us with annihilation and urges upon us forms of fusion that are

quite plainly bad rather than good. A friend can reduce me to misery
with a single look. Numberless conformities, large and small aban-
donments of self to others, are the price of what freedom we experience in society. And the price is a high one. Through our existence as
members of collectives, we impose on others and have imposed on us
hierarchical structures of power, welfare, and access to enlighten-
ment that are illegitimate, whether based on birth into a particular
social class or on the accident of genetic endowment.[103]

This "fundamental contradiction—that relations with others are both
necessary to and incompatible with our freedom"[104] appears in two forms
in the attempt to create city autonomy. First, at times, we identify ourselves with our local community, recognizing that joint action with others
is essential for us to achieve our own objectives, that alone we can do
nothing. The community becomes a form of the "self" and outsiders and
the central government take on the role of "others." These others then
appear as threats to our capacity for self-determination, and we seek
against them a "right of local self-government" or "home rule." But these
others are not only threats; they are also necessary to our community's
survival. Our local life depends on and cannot be disentangled from
them. Although we do not want to sacrifice ourselves to outsiders, we
cannot separate ourselves from them. Thus, whereas the absence of local
autonomy implies our submission to the domination of others, the actual
achievement of local autonomy seems impossible.

Second, we sometimes see our local community as itself the embodi-
ment of the threat of others to our individual lives. This threat seems so
intense that we are willing to seek the help of outsiders who are themselves threatening—the state—to protect us from local domination. Yet, if
the state's attempt to save us is too pervasive, we immediately switch to
the first mode of understanding the local community, in which we identify it with ourselves, and then, we seek to prevent further outside domination in the name of local autonomy.

In the search for local autonomy, then, we move relentlessly from
one of these visions to the other. We cannot tolerate the absence of local
autonomy because of our first vision, and we cannot tolerate genuine
autonomy because of our second. As we oscillate between the poles of this
contradiction, we seek one or the other as the stable basis for understanding the role of the city in our lives. But both visions are true.

[103]*Blackstone's Commentaries*, pp. 211–212.
[104]Ibid., p. 213.

We need not, however, overcome this version of the subject/object dichotomy to create a basis for local autonomy. We need only establish a *modus vivendi* that accepts, with all its dangers, a form of city power. But to do this, we need a basic rethinking of liberalism and then a restructuring of our society itself.

ACKNOWLEDGMENTS

The principal sources on which I relied for this article include D. Kennedy, "The Structure of Blackstone's Commentaries," *Buffalo Law Review* 28 (1979):205; D. Kennedy, "Form and Substance in Private Law Adjudication," *Harvard Law Review* 89, no. 8 (1976):1685; D. Kennedy, "The Rise and Fall of Classical Legal Thought" (Manuscript on file at the Harvard Law School Library, Oct., 1976); M. Horwitz, *The Transformation of American Law 1780–1860* (Cambridge: Harvard University Press, 1977); R. Unger, *Knowledge and Politics* (New York: Free Press, 1975); R. Unger, *Law in Modern Society* (New York: Free Press, 1976); F. Michelman, "Political Markets and Community Self-Determination: Competing Judicial Models of Local Government Legitimacy," *Indiana Law Journal* 53, no. 2 (1977–1978):145; K. Marx, "On the Jewish Question," in *The Marx-Engels Reader*, ed. R. Tucker (New York: W. W. Norton, 1972); E. Durkheim, *The Division of Labor in Society*, trans. G. Simpson (New York: Free Press, 1933); M. Weber, *The City*, trans. D. Martindale and G. Neuwirth (New York: Free Press, 1958); O. Gierke, *Political Theories of the Middle Ages*, trans. F. W. Maitland (Boston: Beacon Press, 1958); O. Gierke, *Natural Law and the Theory of Society 1500–1800*, trans. E. Barker (Beacon Press, Boston 1934); O. Gierke, *Associations and the Law*, trans. G. Heiman (Boston: Beacon Press, 1977); F. Maitland *Township and Borough*, (Cambridge, Mass.: University Press, 1898); F. Braudel, "Towns," in *Capitalism and Material Life 1400–1800*, trans. M. Kochan (New York: Harper Colophon, 1967); L. Hartz, *Economic Policy and Democratic Thought: Pennsylvania 1776–1806* (Cambridge: Harvard University Press, 1948); O. Handlin and M. Handlin, *Commonwealth* (New York: New York University Press, 1947); A. De Tocqueville, *Democracy in America*, trans. G. Lawrence (Garden City, N.Y.: Doubleday, 1969); K. Mannheim, *Ideology and Utopia*, trans. L. Wirth and E. Shils (New York: Harcourt Brace Jovanovich, 1936); H. Arendt, *On Revolution* (New York: Pelican Books, 1962); J. Dewey, *The Public and Its Problems*

(Chicago: Swallow Press, 1972); W. Kohler, *Gestalt Psychology* (New York: Liveright, 1947).

In addition, unpublished works by and conversations with Duncan Kennedy, Morton Horwitz, Roberto Unger, Richard Parker, Lloyd Weinreb, Charles Donahue, Henry Steiner, Lewis Sargentich, and Frank Michelman have been especially helpful. The errors are mine alone.

CHAPTER 14

Cities and Countryside in Anthropology

ANTHONY LEEDS

MISCONCEPTIONS ABOUT THE URBAN—BROADER PERSPECTIVES

Most current discussion of "urbanism" and "urbanization" can be shown to be ethno- and temporocentric and based on a historically particular class of urban phenomena and urban forms of integration. Exegesis of text after text—whether produced by persons ostensibly doing "pure," "objective," descriptive, or "basic" science, or engaged in some form of application—shows systematic orientations whose axiomatic presuppositions and logical consequences can be clearly laid out as emanations of a specific world view.

Briefly, to summarize the world view underlying this ethnocentrism, the fact that some form or another or urban society has existed for between 8,000 and 10,000 years in the Old World and in the New World for some 3,000 years or more is forgotten entirely. Generalizations are then made about "urbanism" and "urban society" based essentially on the urban experience of the past few hundred years, apparently without the realization that all urban phenomena of the past 500 years have been ineluctably affected by the expansion of the capitalist system, in short by

A longer version of this chapter was published in *Urban Anthropology* 8 (Winter 1979): 227–247.

Anthony Leeds. • Department of Anthropology, Boston University, Boston, Massachusetts.

the development of what Wallerstein calls the "World System."[1] The generalizations are, then, in fact, not about "urbanization" in general but about a single form of "urbanism" or "urbanization," its evolution, and its acculturational by-products.

That there are other forms of urban structure, or urban phenomena, of urban society is practically universally forgotten, except perhaps by persons, mostly anthropologists, involved with broad understandings of societal evolution,[2] or historians concerned with comparisons of urban civilizations, and architects or art historians concerned with comparisons of urban form.[3] The fact of such variants of "the urban experience" is

[1]See Emmanuel Wallerstein, *The Modern World-System: Capitalist Agriculture and the Origins of the European World-Economy in the Sixteenth Century* (New York: Academic Press, 1974).

[2]See R. McC. Adams, *The Evolution of Urban Society* (Chicago: Aldine, 1966); R. J. Braidwood and G. R. Willey, *Courses towards Urban Life: Archeological Considerations of Some Cultural Alternates* (New York: Wenner-Gren Foundation, 1962); V. G. Childe, *Man Makes Himself* (London: Watts, 1948); *What Happened in History* (Harmondsworth: Penguin, 1942); "The Urban Revolution," *Town Planning Review* 21 (1950): 3–17; R. G. Fox, *Urban Anthropology: Cities in Their Cultural Settings* (Englewood Cliffs, N.J.: Prentice-Hall, 1977); J. E. Hardoy and R. P. Schaedel, eds. *El proceso de urbanización en América Latina diesde sus orígens hasta nuestros días* (Buenas Aires: Instituto Torcuato Di Tella, 1969); *Las ciudades de América Latina y sus áreas de influencia a través de la historia* (Buenos Aires: SIAP, 1975); A. Leeds, "Towns and Villages in Society: Hierarchies of Order and Cause," in *Cities in a Larger Context*, ed. T. W. Collins, Proceedings of the Southern Anthropological Society, No. 14 (Athens: University of Georgia Press, 1980), pp. 6–33; H. Nutini, "The Latin American City: A Cultural-Historical Approach," in *The Anthropology of Urban Environments*, ed. T. Weaver and D. White (Boulder, Colo.: Society for Applied Anthropology, Monograph 11, 1972), pp. 89–96; R. Redfield, "The Folk Society," *American Journal of Sociology* 52 (1947): 293–308; *The Little Community: Viewpoints for the Study of the Human Whole* (Chicago: University of Chicago Press, 1955); *Peasant Society and Culture* (Chicago: University of Chicago Press, 1955); R. P. Schaedel, *Urbanización y proceso social en America* (Lima: Instituto de Estudios Peruanos, 1972); R. P. Schaedel, J. Hardoy, and N. S. Kinzer, eds., *Urbanization in the Americas from the Beginnings to the Present* (The Hague: Mouton, 1978).

[3]See P. Hall, *The World Cities* (New York, Toronto: World University Library, McGraw-Hill, 1966); J. E. Hardoy, *Pre-Columbian Cities* (New York: Walker, 1973, 1964); *Urban Planning in Pre-Columbian America* (New York: George Braziller, 1968); C. H. Kraeling and R. McC. Adams, eds., *City Invincible* (Chicago: University of Chicago Press, 1960); R. M. Morse, "Las ciudades latinoamericanas. 1. Antecedentes," (México, D. F.: Secretaría de Educación Púb-

uniformly obliterated by persons concerned with "development" and "modernization." Their programs and plans are invariably built on premises derived from the single, historically recent form of urban experience—the capitalist city in urban capitalist society. As will be seen, this is not entirely surprising since much of such developmentalism is rooted in the discipline of economics, itself a specific Western and capitalist form of thought and ideology.

Even anthropologists, however, have failed to view specific urban forms in the wider perspective. Doing so would have permitted them to sort out what was generic to urban structures and what was specific to only a class of such structures. The properties of the latter have often been taken as properties of the former, with the result that erroneous generalizations are drawn about urban form and process. Failure to see the temporal and spatial specificity of these properties is failure to see immensely broader alternatives of organization of urban societies, failure to see the relationship between, on one hand, a specific historical sequence and, on the other, general evolutionary aspects of the progression of urban societies, and the failure to see drastically different possible "solutions" to the "problems" of urban societies through policy, plans, and political action. A problem derived from seeing urban phenomena in terms of only a single class of urban societies is that of getting bogged down in conceptualizations formulated in terms of that single experience. Such conceptualizations, as I have shown elsewhere,[4] have produced

lica, *Ediciones SepSetentas*, No. 96, 1973); "Las ciudades latinoamericanas. 2. Desarrollo histórico," (*Ediciones SepSentas*, No. 97, 1973); "Trends and Patterns of Latin American Urbanization, 1750–1920." *Comparative Studies in Society and History* 16 (No. 4, 1974): 416–447; L. Mumford, *The Culture of Cities* (New York: Harcourt, Brace, 1938); *The City in History: Its Origins, Its Transformations, and Its Prospects* (New York: Harcourt, Brace, and World, 1961); G. Sjoberg, *The Preindustrial City* (New York: Free Press 1960); M. Weber, *The City* (Glencoe, Ill.: Free Press, 1958; originally published, 1921).

[4]See A. Leeds, "The Anthropology of Cities: Some Methodological Issues," in *Urban Anthropology: Research Perspectives and Strategies*, ed. E. M. Eddy (Athens: University of Georgia Press, 1968), pp. 31–47; "Comment" on D. P. Bwy's "Instability in Latin America: The Cross-Cultural Test of a Causal Model," *Latin American Research Review* 3 (No. 2, 1968): 79–87; "Informal Author's Summary," in *City and Country in the Third World*, ed. A. J. Field (Cambridge: Schenkman, 1970), pp. 273–276; "The Concept of the "Culture of Poverty:" Conceptual, Logical, and Empirical Problems, with Perspectives from Brazil and Perú," in *The Culture of Poverty: A Critique*, ed. E. B. Leacock (New York:

systematic distortions of understanding, systematic omissions in description (e.g., of urban agriculture),[5] and systematic imposition of misbegotten policies and plans.[6]

The major misconceptualizations involved are those which oppose "urban" to "rural" and "urban society" to "rural society" or "peasant society"; those which identify "urban" with "city"; those which conceive of "communities" as some sort of largely closed, localized nucleation of persons, houses, and institutions; or those that conceive of localities as communities.[7]

At a most general level, *all* human nucleations, from the smallest "tribal" villages to the largest megalopolises, have the same functions

---

Simon and Schuster), pp. 222–284; "Urban Society Subsumes Rural: Specialties, Nucleations, Countryside, and Networks: Metatheory, Theory, and Method," in *Atti del XL Congresso Internazionale degli Americanisti* (Rome, 1972), Vol. 4 (Genoa: Tilgher, 1976), pp. 171–182; "Review" of *Anthropologists in Cities*, ed. George M. Foster and R. V. Kemper (Boston: Little, Brown, 1974), in *American Anthropologist* 78 (No. 2, 1976): 448–449; "Towns and Villages in Society: Hierarchies of Order and Cause," in *Cities in a Larger Context*, ed. T. W. Collins, Proceedings of the Southern Anthropological Society, No. 14 (Athens: University of Georgia, 1980), pp. 6–33; "Lower-Income Urban Settlement Types: Processes, Structures, Policies," in United Nations, *The Residential Circumstances of the Urban Poor in Developing Countries* (New York: Praeger, 1981), pp. 21–61; A. Leeds and E. Leeds, "Brazil and the Myth of Urban Rurality: Urban Experience, Work, and Values in 'Squatments' of Rio de Janeiro and Lima," in *City and Country in the Third World*, ed. A. J. Field (Cambridge: Schenkman, 1970), pp. 229–272, 277–285; "Accounting for Behavioral Differences: Three Political Systems and the Responses of Squatters to Them in Brazil, Perú, and Chile," in *The City in Comparative Perspective: Cross-National Research*, ed. John Walton and L. H. Masotti (Beverly Hills, Calif.: Sage, 1976), pp. 193–248.
[5]See A. Leeds, "Political, Economic, and Social Effects of Producer and Consumer Orientations Towards Housing in Brazil and Peru: A Systems Analysis," in F. Rabinovitz and F. Trueblood, eds., *Latin American Urban Research*, Vol. 3 (Beverly Hills: Sage), pp. 181–215; "Locality Power in Relation to Supra-Local Power Institutions," in *Urban Anthropology: Cross-Cultural Studies of Urbanization*, ed. Aidan Southall (New York: Oxford, 1974), pp. 15–41 (written 1964); "Housing-Settlement Types, Arrangements for Living, Proletarianization, and the Social Structure of the City," in W. Cornelius and F. Trueblood, eds., *Latin American Urban Research*, Vol. 4 (Beverly Hills: Sage), pp. 67–99; A. Leeds and E. Leeds, "Brazil and the Myth of Urban Reality".
[6]See the last section of A. Leeds, "Housing-Settlement Types."
[7]See A. Leeds, "Political, Economic, and Social Effects"; "Towns and Villages in Society."

with respect to an inclusive society: facilitation of all forms of exchange, transfer, and communications, while linking the nucleation or locality both with other localities and with the society at large.

Within that generality, at some point in societal-cultural evolution, an interrelated, threefold specialization appeared in society. One form of specialization is that of localities—sometimes for ecological reasons, sometimes for sociocultural reasons, sometimes for both. Such specialization, even without the other two described below, is found incipiently in simple societies. The result of such specialization is that the societal system, as such, comes to be characterized by the internal *differentiation of functions* of localities, superimposed on the *universal functions* of all localities just mentioned.

Another form of specialization is that of the components of technology—tools, materials, techniques, housings, tasks, activities, labor/skills, and knowledge[8]—whose result is differentiation in the structure of labor and of the ecological determinants of its ordering.

The third form of specialization is that of institutions—the separating out by function of more-or-less autonomously ordered and chartered ways of doing things,[9] ranging from large-scale orders such as government, church, and education, to small-scale institutions such as roles.

Each of these forms of specialization is in some measure independent and in some measure a resultant of the other. Thus, a certain degree of locality specialization can occur—minimally, to be sure—in the absence of any significant technological or institutional specialization, while the development of these latter forms of specialization tends to generate an increase in locality specialization. Considerable technological specialization may occur without significant locality specialization. However, further increases of specialization, especially in the domain of materials, necessarily governed by the ecological variation of resource location, induces locality differentiation, for example, by generating production activities of one sort in one locality and of a different sort in another, with

[8]See A. Leeds, "Some Preliminary Considerations Regarding the Analysis of Technologies," *Kroeber Anthropological Society Papers* (Spring 1965); 1–9; and "Technology," "Technology and Subsistence," in *Encyclopedia of Anthropology*, ed. D. E. Hunter and P. Whitten (New York: Harper & Row, 1976).

[9]See A. Leeds, "Some Problems in the Analysis of Class and the Social Order," in *Social Structure, Stratification, and Mobility* ed. A. Leeds (Washington: Pan American Union, 1967), 327–361; and "Institutions," in Hunter and Whitten, *Encyclopedia of Anthropology*.

specialized trade activities of different kinds within each and between
them.

I define *urban* as the interacting confluence of all three of these
specializations, a definition quite in line with *implicitly* presupposed attributes in most standard definitions of *the urban*.[10] By definition, then,
that which is urban is *always* a matter of degree, and degree of urbanness
is measured not by the size of nucleations (which may be profoundly
affected by ecology, institutional structures, and policies), nor by density
(which may be profoundly affected by locality and technical specializations, as well as by policy), nor, *generally*, by the classical measures of
"urbanization" effectively derived from recent Western experience, but,
rather, by an interaction index of the three forms of specialization (to a
large extent, these govern size and density).

Justification for such a definition is worth presenting. First, in anthropology, despite a long-standing tradition of studying so-called communities in isolation, everyone except the most gung-ho ideologist of
community studies knows that any given locality chosen for such a study
is variously linked with other localities. This is quite as true for "simple"
primitives as for modern states, as for example, Birdsell has shown.[11]
When one looks beyond the anthropologists' model of the self-sufficient
isolated community into the actual data of description in the monographs,
such ties are always evident, if unsystematically described. Systematic
attention would clearly have shown the network relations of localities to,
and in, larger systems as well as identified the types of flows, however
intermittent, among them. It would also have helped define societal

[10]See V. G. Childe, *Man Makes Himself* and "The Urban Revolution." The
endings *-ism* and *-ization*, added to the root *urban*, both have specific sets of
connotations, none of which mean precisely "having the properties of being
urban." *Urbanism* sometimes seems to mean that, but it also means rather
unclearly defined things such as "attitudes about cities," "policies with respect
to cities," etc. *Urbanization* means, usually, "the process of city population
growth" or, sometimes, much more widely, "the process of becoming citylike or
graced with towns and cities." I use *the Urban* here to indicate "that which is
urban, having the properties of being an urban society,") borrowed from the
Spanish *el Urbano*, which is fairly commonly used with the meaning I define.
[11]J. B. Birdsell, "Some Environmental and Cultural Factors Influencing the
Structuring of Australian Aboriginal Populations," *American Naturalist* 87
(1953): 169–207; see also !Kung Bushmen material or A. Leeds, "Some Problems in Yaruro Ethnohistory," in *Actas y Memorias del 35° Congreso Internacio-
nal de Americanistas*, Mexico, 1962 (México, D. F.; 1964): 157–175.

boundary conditions, to which we have given almost no attention in anthropology—a serious problem since network ties exist over these boundaries as well as internally, though, I would propose, with markedly less density over the boundaries than internally.

By extension, any city or town is part of a total system—a *societal* system of localities, each of which has some function in the total system. Where localities are specialized and as locality-specialization increases, their functions are differentiated and the linking ties become more critical or more tightly coupled and also more hierarchic. They also *tend* to become more multistranded, although this is not a necessary consequence.

Second, all anthropologists know that one specialty requires another. Specialization means, necessarily, a *structure* of interrelated differentiations. Indeed, one cannot properly describe one specialty by itself— whether that specialty be a technological one, a role, or an institution. They come in sets. Most descriptions tend, or have tended, to focus on one or a reduced number of specialties, but a more-or-less discomforting awareness of their relation to others not being described is almost always nagging us. The implication of these considerations may be summarized in the assertion that the greater the degree of either or both of these forms of specialization (aside from their interaction effect), the more complex and differentiated the total societal order, including nonchartered—that is, noninstitutional—forms of organization such as networks, rank, and class.

The interaction of the three forms of specialization—seen as an evolutionary process creating ever-greater differentiation—involves ever-greater complexity of order characterized by, on one hand, translocal, differentiated structures (e.g., the classes of a class system), represented also in localities, and, on the other, specialization of localities as such, all linked to each other. It may further be noted that the internal specialization of localities subtends such derivative properties as density and population size, properties standardly given as criteria of "urban."

The interaction effect of the three forms of specialization is a very complex problem involving all sorts of ecological dimensions. Suffice it to say, here, that once they start interacting, the degree and rate of differentiation increase. More important is the ultimate comprehensive inclusion of all aspects of society in the total structure of specialization: all people, all action, all culture, all social organization, all technology become specialized. Hence, insofar as such systems display those properties conventionally designated as "urban" we are *obliged* to regard the *entire* society as urban and cities merely as concentrations of more-or-less large ranges and arrays of certain types of specialties.[12]

Elsewhere, I have pointed to the utility of looking at agriculture, mining, lumbering, fishing, and the like as specialty sets subordinate to the total structure of specialization in a society.[13] They are linked into the latter by complex systems of exchange moving in all directions among all kinds and levels of locality and all kinds and levels of institutional structure.

Given the general proposition presented above—the general model—and this intimate linkage of these particular specialty categories and sets with the total specialty system, it is evident that "a peasant is an urban "man," as is also a miner, a lumberjack, and a fisherman. They are all operators or actors within systems of locality, of labor, of technical, institutional, and informal social organizational specialties. Further, they *comprehend* such complex specializations with a cognitive *model* of society which recognizes its complexity, including the structure of its urban centers and their hierarchical relations.

It is no accident that we have numberless descriptions of "successful" "adaptations" of supposedly "unskilled" and "unspecialized" "peasants" to cities. My argument, represented in all the quotation marks, is that social scientists have consistently misread the *meaning* of this phenomenon. They have failed to see that the participants are *already* urban people because the observing anthropologists have interpreted the "rural" as *tribal*, that is, as nonspecialized in any significant degree in any of the senses I have defined, and as largely isolated from the "urban" (i.e., city) society as a result of some inherent property of rurality (see comments on Redfield below), while sociologists have treated the "rural" as some sort of converse of the city—the opposite of density, large size, anonymity, secondary relationships.

All of these conceptions are demonstrably and drastically false. Put another way, once a significant interaction of the three kinds of specialty develops, all rural people are urban people. It is necessary to understand

---

[12]A. Leeds, "Towns and Villages in Society: Hierarchies of Order and Cause," in *Cities in a Larger Context,* ed. T. W. Collins, Proceedings of the Southern Anthropological Society No. 14 (Athens: University of Georgia Press, 1980), pp. 6–33.

[13]A Leeds, "Towns and Villages."

rural as referring simply to a subset of specialties of an urban society and *rural people* as referring to part or sub-societies of urban societies, as in effect, Kroeber, speaking of peasants, said 35 years ago.[14]

So far, the discussion has delineated two subclasses of all human societies: primitive and urban societies. Doing so has already posed a dilemma for those holding the ethnocentric view of the Urban, or at least for me, in that the idea of the "social urbanization" of agricultural personnel must necessarily also apply to *all* urban societies if agriculture is to be regarded as urban, as I propose. It is logically wrong to see "social urbanization" as a historically recent phenomenon if we hold any *generic* theory about the nature of urban society.

The conception of "social urbanization" as being recent and as being a property of a certain subclass—I would say subsubclass (see below)—of societies is itself a product of a certain intellectual history, chiefly of anthropology. Not only did this intellectual approach tribalize "peasants," reify "peasant societies," and hermetically seal off "peasants," "peasant societies," and even "peasant economics" from the larger societies of which they were parts, but it even reformulated the supposed trajectory of sociocultural evolution either to place "peasants" at a "stage" of evolution intermediate between "tribal" or "folk," on one hand, and "urban," on the other, or practically to assimilate them to "folk" culture.

The chief offender (and offender he was) was Robert Redfield, building out of his Mexican experience. In publications between 1930 and 1956, he created a thoroughly formalistic model of the trajectory of sociocultural evolution. This model was constructed on an idealized conception[15] of a moral tribal society (practically devoid of pragmatics, choice, or strategy), a reified and idealized "peasant society" operating as a closed system, and a misapprehended and ethnocentric conception of city life derived from Robert E. Park, Ernest W. Burgess, and especially Louis Wirth, who generalized the Chicago of the 1910s or 1920s as a world model not only of cities but of the urban in general.[16] Fortunately, most of this sorry metaphysics has not stood the test of time and criticism;

---

[14]A. L. Kroeber, *Anthropology* (New York: Harcourt Brace, 1948), p. 284.

[15]See R. Redfield, "The Folk Society."

[16]R. Redfield, *Tepotzlan, A Mexican Village: A Study of Folklife* (Chicago: University of Chicago Press, 1930); *The Folk Culture of Yucatan* (Chicago: University of Chicago Press, 1941); *The Primitive World and Its Transformations* (Ithaca, N.Y.: Cornell University Press, 1953); *The Little Community; Peasant Society and Culture.*

most of it has disappeared. However, some still lingers, especially in conceptions, still prevalent in anthropology, about "peasants." The reformulated way of looking at this evolutionary problem appearing in the following pages fits into a general theory of the Urban, thereby permitting, or better, *requiring*, us to look at several different kinds of society at once. That is, it forces us to do the theoretical work of comparison, differentiation, structural and processual analysis, and generalization at one and the same time.

DIFFERENTIAL INTEGRATION OF URBAN SOCIETIES THROUGH THE CLASS SYSTEM

As the three forms of specialization interlock and interact, social orders themselves differentiate. Such differentiation *inherently* leads to class differentiation in society—using any of the currently standard social science usages of the term *class*, but most especially one form or another of the Marxian conception of class. In oversimplified form, all urban society and all urban societies are class societies, as V . Gordon Childe pointed out long ago.[17] This follows, too, from the general theory proposed above. That they are also state societies likewise follows but need not be pursued in detail here, except to say that the theory of specialization requires the emergence of specialized coordinative and administrative functions, hence government.

What is critical is our universal recognition that these specialized, urban, state societies present a great array of drastically different forms of organization; that, within this variety of expression, rather similar forms often appeared which we tend to classify together. We therefore speak of feudal Europe, of feudal Japan, possibly of feudal early China, of a possibly feudal-like phase in early Indian history, and, as we get confused about the critical criteria, we slither off into argument whether this or that African state or chiefdom was feudal or not, and even whether the first centuries after the Iberian conquest of South America were feudal or not.

What are the critical criteria? They are the criteria that we, as analysts—historians, anthropologists, political scientists, etc.—consider most relevant in analyzing what holds the society together, what links its spe-

[17]Childe, *Man Makes Himself* and "The Urban Revolution" and *What Happened in History.*

cialized pieces, or "parts," into a "whole," providing the routes of exchange, transmission, and transfer. One common way of talking about the question of linkage—or of what holds society together—in practically all the social science disciplines is the idea of *integration*. This term, however, has also come to take on an ethnocentric sense in the context of the temporo- and ethnocentric development models which have infused all the social sciences, especially the essentially noncomparativist ones like economics and political science. It is this latter, ethnocentric sense of *integration* which carried over into the formulation of the problem of "social urbanization" which I am using as example here.

The general proposition that I wish to forward is: Different forms of urban society involve different forms of societal integration. These forms of integration are expressed through the structures of class relations. The structures of these class relations determine what the forms of integration of the "rural" specialty sets with those of the urban centers—that is, with the "towns," "cities," *and other nodal points*—will be. In fact, they also determine what the very characteristics of all the urban centers will be. Thus, medieval European urban centers—towns, abbeys, castles, manors[18]—not only were quite different from capitalist ones but lay out for us major features of the class organization and the societal specialization to which it was attached. The urban centers themselves were specialized according to major institutional features and class orders of the society. This feature of medieval urbanism led that great ethnocentric,

---

[18]These are clearly urban centers, at least in the sense of this chapter. Each is a central place, with a central administration. Each has a remarkable array of specializations and specialists. Each is itself a specialized nucleation with a specialized function in the larger society, and a nodal point for exchange and transfer, as of taxes and foodstuffs. Each is hierarchic, class-divided, and institutionally complex. Each has its literate system of complex record keeping, ranging from censuses to production and tax figures. Each is a substate of a more inclusive state. See, in this connection, Abbot Irminon (ca. 800 A.D.), "The Polyptich of Saint Germain des Prés" (trans. from A. Longnon, *Polyptique de l'Abbaye Saint-Germain des Prés*, II) (Paris, 1892), in *Introduction to Contemporary Civilization in the West*, Vol. 1 ed. Contemporary Civilization Staff, Columbia College (New York: Columbia, 1946), 34–38; Louis the Pious (ca. 795 A.D.), "Capitulare de Villis," from *Monumenta Germaniae Historica*, Leges II, 1 (1883) (trans. in *Introduction to Contemporary Civilization in the West*), Vol. 1, 25–33; J. Mundy and P. Riseneberg, *The Medieval Town* (Princeton, N.J.: Van Nostrand, 1948); H. Pirenne, *Medieval Cities* (Garden City, N.Y.: Doubleday, Anchor, 1956 originally published, 1925).

comparative historian and sociologist Max Weber to say that medieval society did not yet have "true" cities—that is, they were not like those he knew from capitalist society which provided his model of Truth not only for cities but for bureaucracies as well.[19] Put another way, using our everyday terms in the way I have redefined them here, the characteristics of both rural and urban ("country" and city) areas of an urban society and the relation between them are defined by the interaction of the structure of specialties of the society and its class relations. The major implication, for present purposes, is that *every* urban society has its characteristic form of "social urbanization." We can even *predict the properties* of the social urbanization and its processes, actions, and events from the form of integration of the society.

CAPITALIST INTEGRATION OF URBAN SOCIETY

For this purpose, it suffices here to compare and contrast two equally "valid" forms of societal integration, say, feudal and capitalist. I turn to the latter first because it is the most familiar and, simply by putting the key properties in the context of the discussion, immediately illuminates the contrasting type of social urbanization in feudal society. These sketches are brief and incomplete, dealing only with a few relevant, illustrative variables.

Capitalist society revolves about the centralization of the productive process ("integration," in the popular ethnocentric jargon of the social sciences). Even under the putting-out system, there was a centralization of management and handling. The centralization, on one hand, involves concentrating numbers of specialties and specialists and, on the other, developing new forms of flow of wealth (i.e., capital), as well as organizing its concentration. Such tasks can be and have been carried out in a number of different ways, but in the West, a specific form of so doing was invented beginning 500 or more years ago and became the integrating form not only for the West but, more recently, largely for the world. This form we call *capitalist accumulation.* One of its chief properties is capital accumulation in private or quasi-private hands, controlled largely by individual or small-group entrepreneurial decision-making, all with the goal of making not merely recompensatory but cumulative profits. These prof-

[19]M. Weber, *The City* (Glencoe, Ill.: Free Press, 1958, 1921).

its are not directed chiefly to consumption ends but to continuous reinvestment in order to make more profits.

Although primitive capital accumulation can be carried out in other ways (although this is not recognized in Western economics because it is overwhelmingly concerned with raising capital within the framework of *preserving* the capitalist system), the chief means used in capitalist development have been, on one hand, the appropriation of the means of production, as in the enclosures in sixteenth-century England and in the expropriations of common lands (*baldios*) in twentieth-century Portugal and, on the other hand, the generating of a cheap wage-labor supply. *Cheap* means "paid much less than the value of its product," that is, exploited. Since the capital accumulation, primitive or otherwise, in great measure excludes the producer of the value concerned from its use, two exclusive categories of persons are generated, that is, two major classes.

It is in the interest of one of these two classes to make sure that the capital keeps flowing to it, but not back, in any significant proportion, to the other. This requirement, over time, leads to the generation of forms of control to preserve such a system of flows. Accordingly, we find emerging the typical forms of the capitalist state and the correlated informal structure characterized by invidious individualism even where, later in this development, corporate structures are developed. We see the emergence of what comes to be known as "liberalism" both as a structure and an ideology: minimum intervention of a state which acts as a handmaiden to the economy, and so on.

It should be noted that primitive capital accumulation could have been or could be carried out by the state or by private and public corporations while still not being integrated around some major participation by the value producers in the value produced, nor around a major redistributional system (i.e., some form of socialist integration). Such societies have been organized around continuous private and quasi-private accumulation operating *through* the state, as in several Latin American countries at various times and as in Portugal and the various fascist states of Europe in this century.[20]

Neither concentration of productive resources and the means of production nor continuous private accumulation of profits and wealth, nor even a labor paid in money wages, exists in nature or society by necessity.

---

[20]See N. Poutlantzas, *The Crisis of Dictatorships* (London: New Left Books, 1976).

It is not the case that increasing specialization requires geographical concentration of multiple specialties and specialty sets on a grand and increasing scale. My argument is that that process which our current temporo-ethnocentric literature calls "urbanization" is a product of a historically particular orientation toward the means of production, labor, and value produced by labor; one which eventually produced its characteristic ideology, even its characteristic science—called neoclassical economics—and, even more, its diagnostic catch-phrase to summarize all this, namely, "cost–benefit analysis." This phrase can be translated as "a procedure for reducing costs of inputs (e.g., labor and raw materials) and increasing profits"—the general program of capitalists and capitalism. It is interesting to note that materialist anthropologists living in capitalist societies have widely adapted the use of this (folk) concept to the analysis of primitive societies and how they handle, say, their gardens, cows, and pigs.

Let us turn briefly to labor needs under such a system. As the properties of the system become increasingly defined and increasingly dominant, a labor supply is needed which is increasingly detachable from geographical contexts. It must be movable from localities of origin to points of concentration of capital. It must also be detachable from social contexts of origin, specifically from community and family, and, later, also from associations (e.g., unions), for at least two reasons. The first is to detach it from any sort of social group which might act in a corporate way against the interests of capitalist encroachment (e.g., in England of the sixteenth century, the struggles against enclosures; in the nineteenth century, the Luddites; in the twentieth century, various community resistances to being wiped out by the encroachment of the European economic community's 40-ton trucks and the roads to carry them). The second is to create a free-flowing supply of the minimal labor unit, the single person, especially men, in order to create maximal adjustability of the labor force needed in any given enterprise at a minimal cost. The cost is reduced by having to support only the individual worker. Where one has, in addition, to support, say a family group—as, for example, by providing housing or other services—costs go up in proportion to benefits. That is, profits decrease. The maximal adjustability is achieved, of course, by hiring or firing the minimal possible labor unit, that is, just one person at a time.

By the same token, the characteristic "cost–benefit analysis," as a social process operating in the context of private property for private profits, generates a much greater degree of geographical concentration of specialties than in other forms of societal integration with similar levels of specialization. Note the geographical redistribution of specialties and the population stabilization of Havana in postrevolutionary Cuba.[21] In cases such as the latter, the development of transportation systems is directed at the relative *dispersion* of clusters of specialties instead of their continuous concentration. Note the Red Chinese effort to develop backyard steel production in the earlier years. What is involved, here, using the sloganistic capitalist metaphor, is a drastic redefinition of what is costly and what is beneficial, especially the widening of what is referred to by both terms to far vaster ranges of human interest, endeavor, and personnel.

The capitalist cost–benefit concentration of specialties generates the characteristic structure and process of urban centers (of villages, towns, cities, mine heads, farmsteads, lumber camps, etc.) which we are so familiar with from our daily lives and which so many take to be paradigmatic of the Urban and hence label with such terms as *urbanization*. We are, in fact, continuously living in, experiencing, and looking at *capitalist* forms of urbanization. Some of the chief features of capitalist urban structure and process have already been adverted to: concentration, including that of labor, as a necessary capitalist consequence of specialty and capital concentration, and labor detachment from geographic and social contexts of origin. Great density, large population agglomerations, and increasing population size are necessary symptomatic results but, as diagnostic traits of the Urban in general, are of limited value since they describe only the cities—and then chiefly capitalist cities—of urban society and not urban societies as wholes, especially noncapitalist ones.

Given these basic conditions of capitalist urban structure and process—a historically particular set of phenomena—the *particular* phenomena of "social urbanization" *necessarily* follow. They follow whether encountered in Latin America or, for that matter, in the United States, internally, and, at the turn of the century, between the United States and the rural areas of half of Europe and parts of Asia, especially China, as well. It is necessarily the case that capitalist interests generate models of connecting "peasant" areas more tightly to the areas of concentrated capital resources (i.e., cities) and the corresponding systems of control in order to generate flows of labor and capital, as well as at least part of the

[21]M. Acosta and J. E. Hardoy, "Urbanization Policies in Revolutionary Cuba," in *Latin American Urban Research*, Vol. 2 (1972): 167–178.

markets on which profits depend. The capitalist interests establish the structural channels by which labor concentration, capital flow, and marketing can be facilitated. The whole procedure is justified by science— specifically the capitalist science of economics, which today endlessly discusses the relative merits of "generalized development" as against "growth poles" and "trickle down," most commonly opting for the latter two, not surprisingly. It even has a label for the entire procedure just described: *integration*. It will be noted that *integration* here means the capitalist form of linking agricultural hinterlands to cities and labor to capital, and only that form.

FEUDAL INTEGRATION OF CLASS SOCIETY

To turn now to another form of society: feudalism clearly did not look like this at all. Profits, as a structural and institutional aspect of the political economy, as in capitalism, simply did not exist. The capitalist form and process of profit making should *not* be confused with making some amount over cost and value (in medieval public discourse, the problem of "just price"), which is *hoarded* as personal wealth or some portion of which is paid in taxes or tribute to an overlord in a personalized payment for public functions.[22] The hoarding of wealth is not carried out in a competitive market with N players striving to get into the profit and reinvestment system but by a largely jurally restricted set of players to accumulate hoards for sumptuary and other consumptional purposes *and* for utilization in *public* duties and functions.

Such a system required relatively *fixed* labor, including a very large range of specialists both in the agrarian sector and in the production of sumptuary goods and the goods needed for maintaining the whole system, especially relatively personalized military equipment.[23] The whole structure of feudal society was institutionally directed at nonmobility of a geographical or social sort. (This nonmobility was strengthened by serfly rights to land and their jural tie with it—drastically different from the detachability by sale of slaves in a capitalist system.) Monetarization was deliberately suppressed (e.g., "peasants" were not allowed to hold gold and silver or their money forms). Note, in this connection, "peasant" awareness of the problem reflected in any number of, say, the Grimms'

---

[22]F. W. Maitland and F. Pollock, *History of English Law* (1895).
[23]See footnote 18.

fairy tales about finding lumps or hoards of gold or, in the opera *Boris Godunoff*, the symbol of the idiot who finds a kopek. Put another way, demonetarization of agrarian producers is a deliberate *class* policy of control and wealth accumulation. It is one which has persisted even in certain capitalist contexts until quite recently (e.g., in parts of Portugal until the 1950s and 1960s). In this case, the contradiction between a coexisting wealth accumulation based on a nonmonetarized fixed labor force and capitalist accumulation based on a mobile labor force reflected itself in a very striking form of internal migration, at least from the 1930s until the end of the 1960s, referred to as *ranchos*, followed by an equally striking explosion of emigration from the same area of origin as the *ranchos*, which immediately disappeared as the area in question monetarized by means of migrant remittances sent from abroad. The suppression of monetarization is itself directed at making mobility difficult, hence at its suppression or control.

But the structure and process of urban centers are also shaped by this entire order. Labor needs inside the medieval urban center (city, town, castle, abbey, manor) are very much restricted by the class interests themselves—largely to specialists who can handle the sumptuary, housing, and subsistence needs of the controlling class. It is a major interest to keep others than these *out* of the towns, fixed in their own agrarian, mining, or other extractive areas. There is no *labor* need for masses of "unskilled" and "semiskilled" workers, to use the capitalist classifications serving to categorize large numbers of people and to cheapen their labor. At the same time, there was every *political* reason not to want restless masses of people right in the locales of the public display of pomp and wealth. In fact, jural restrictions on residing in towns and penal sanctions for doing so illicitly existed throughout medieval society. The urban centers, therefore, tended to remain small. They tended to be fairly sharply separated in social and functional terms from the agrarian hinterlands. The connection between urban centers and country was intermediated by the taxation system and its administrators—church, military, royalty, nobility—and largely (and sometimes formally, as historically particular forms of integration) by socially and jurally restricted subclasses of persons, the merchants (a special caste in India and an almost castelike order in China and Japan before capitalist encroachment).

Another feature of medieval society which it is of utmost importance to recognize is that the societywide specialized institutions of church, military, public administration, commerce, and agrarian production—the very separation and specialization of which are themselves diagnostic of urban society generally—were geographically segregated into distinct and distinctive urban centers: the abbey, the castle town, the commercial town, and the manor, respectively, although the first two also had their own agrarian bases. The abbey, like the castle town and the manor, aside from its religious specialization, was also a very complex, internally differentiated, hierarchic, and specialized system of quasi-public administration, labor allocation, production, and social and political controls—in short, a statelike order with an administrative center, the abbey itself. Abbey records much resemble those of a state or a very large industrial corporation.[24] In a nonethnocentric view, such a description of an abbey indicates an urban place or center (quite corresponding to Mayan temple communities or Cambodian Angkor Wats and Thoms, and many other examples, as well as to forms of urban place more familiar to us), one treatable by central place theory. In a parallel manner, the castle town was the urban central place for the military aspect of public administration and the manor for large-scale agrarian production.[25] (To generalize this last piece of the argument, *any* farmstead is an urban central place, characterized by a minimum range of specializations of a certain type, but including production, exchange, and managerial functions.)

Just like in "capitalist" or "Asiatic" societies, in medieval society "peasants" learned models of town life. They learned jural norms about their relation to urban places and experienced specific institutional relations to representatives of and from urban places, for example, taxation and the rights of the first night (*jus primae noctis*). All of these constituted aspects of one kind of social urbanization—or urban socialization.

The medieval European system, just like the capitalist system, had its characteristic ideology and science. Medieval people lived in a world of fixed species, created in the beginning by God for *all* generations. Species existed in a fixed hierarchy, the *scala naturae* or Great Chain of Being,[26] which, of course, applied not only to interspecies ranking but also to intraspecies ranking. Accordingly, human society had its fixed ranks as well as "species" differences, that is, class differences (e.g., the estates or castes or castelike orders). Each of the classes or estates had its

---

[24]See Irminon, "The Polyptich," and Louis the Pious, "Capitulare de Villis."
[25]See Louis the Pious, "Capitulare de Villis."
[26]A. O. Lovejoy, *The Great Chain of Being: A Study in the History of an Idea* (Cambridge: Harvard University Press, 1937).

species characteristics, that is, its own proper societal functions, not to be aspired to by members of other classes. Since these societal tasks came, *ab origine*, from God, they were also Good. This entire science and ideology was broadly reflected, in Western medieval society, in Catholic ideology (and brought to a peak by a Catholic theologian-scientist, Saint Thomas Aquinas), which consistently reinforced the idea that it was God's will for each type of person to fulfill his proper calling, to live in his proper station in life, to do Good by accepting the Good of what he was by God's Providence. Further, the ideology was even encapsulated in an image of society as body[27]: the prince was the head; the heart was the senate; the eyes, ears, and tongue were the judges and governors of provinces; the hands ("arms"!) were the officials and soldiers; stomach and guts were the financial officers (!!); and the feet (of clay, presumably!) were, of course, the husbandmen or "peasants."[28] The model is one of fixity and immutability of relationships, though the parts might go through the cycle of birth, growth, and aging (i.e., the reproduction of labor in its proper place).

CONCLUSION

Several critical conclusions are to be drawn from the above discussion. First, *clearly*, all the "pieces" of feudal society were tied together, or in current terminology, the "variables" were "tightly coupled." In short, *medieval society was highly integrated*, just as "integrated" as capitalist society. The point is that the medieval form of integration was drastically different from the capitalist form of integration. It was built on the fixity of labor, fixity of class membership, restricted uses of the forms of competition, the geographical as well as social *distancing* of classes, and separation physically of their functions in the productive and sociopolitical processes.

Second, correspondingly, the structures and processes of urban places look quite different from those of capitalist society: in one instance,

[27]See residues of this conception in the idea of 'the body politic' and in British functionalism's organicism; cf. A. R. Radcliffe-Brown, "On the Concept of Function in Social Science," in *Structure and Function in Primitive Society: Essays and Addresses* (Glencoe, Ill.: Free Press, 1952).

[28]John of Salisbury, "The Body Social," in *The Portable Medieval Reader* [12th century], ed. J. B. Ross and M. M. McLaughlin (New York: Viking, 1949), pp. 47–48.

practically fixed sizes of rather small urban centers differentiated by major societal functions; in the other, Weber's "true"—no more "true" than any other—city, in which occurs the superposition of all societal functions in single urban places characterized by continual and virtually uncontrollable growth to create, ultimately, "world cities,"[29] metropolises (and "metropolitan sprawl"), "megalopolises,"[30] and so on. Each has its characteristic local and regional land use and internal ordering, for example, in capitalist cities, substantial confusion and contradiction between formal and informal ordering and enormous stress over zoning, community versus private interests, residential location and process, etc., and in capitalist circum-city regions, decline of agrarian uses to be replaced by abandoned areas, wastelands, reforestation, or industrial uses, as in the New Jersey area around New York and in the environs of Boston. The breaking of the boundaries of medieval urban places can be seen in any city over 400 years old in Europe, while the accompanying, capitalism-induced landscapes just described are also immediately recognizable (perhaps its most recent and most visually striking symptom is the car mortuary on the edges of towns).

Third, the different forms of integration and the different systems—structures and process—of urban centers entail different forms of "social urbanization." Medieval societies had their characteristic forms, just as capitalist societies—or, better, each of the rather different structures of evolving capitalist society[31]—have theirs. The contemporary Latin American case of "social urbanization" is one characteristic of a relatively late or recent phase of capitalist evolution, undoubtedly a special subcategory of the latter rooted in the structures of neocolonial dependency.

Fourth, bits and pieces of modifications of late medieval forms of "social urbanization" were integrated into the colonial mercantile- or commodity-capitalist organization of Latin American society from 1500 on. As capitalism itself evolved, both the forms of social urbanization attached to mercantilist-commodity capitalism and the still older, epifeudal forms became increasingly less useful and more poorly adapted to the needs of the new forms of industrial, finance, monopoly, and transna-

[29]See P. Hall, *The World Cities.*

[30]J. Gottman, *Megalopolis: The Urbanized Northeastern Seaboard of the United States* (New York: Twentieth Century Fund, 1961).

[31]See A. Leeds, "Capitalism, Colonialism, and War—An Evolutionary Perspective," in *War: Its Causes and Correlates,* ed. M. A. Nettleship and D. Givens (The Hague: Mouton, 1975): pp. 483–513.

tional capitalism. Also, the fixity of labor had to be broken down by formal and informal means: by legislation, military action, institutional reorganization, indirect economic penetration, encouragement of intra- and international migration, planning (especially by economists), elite revolutions, invention of new forms of organization, and the utilization of social networks. The older forms of social urbanization have been caused largely to disappear, to be replaced by the kind of social urbanization discussed by Margolies *et al.*[32]

Placing the ethnocentric version of "social urbanization" in a general theoretical framework of urban societies leads to the recognition that there is nothing inherent or inevitable about the form of social urbanization in question. The *theory* implies that other choices and alternatives are possible. Contrary to the implicit position of nineteenth-century evolutionism and to practically all Western developmentalist thought today, societies need not inevitably become capitalist. Not only are alternative models actually present, enjoying essentially like degrees and forms of specialization, but others are both thinkable and, at least in principle, institutionally feasible. Alternative models of societal integration mean alternative models of social urbanization.

With alternative models of societal integration and social urbanization at hand, questions of choice become critical. At such a juncture, we can no longer be mere analysts and theorists but necessarily must also be citizens and creatures of values since we are forced to decide on action (including inaction). We must decide on what our values are, collectively and individually, and, accordingly, make choices, that is, plans and programs at all levels of societal organization from international to personal.

Finally, I wish to urge that we should always formulate our problems in terms of more general, comparative, and contrastive theory. If we do not, we always run the danger of the ethnocentric formulation of problems. Just as strong theory—at least, societal theory, if not also theory in the physical sciences—has political implications, so, too, does an ethnocentric formulation of a theoretical problem. Inevitably, it serves certain interests. Just as ethnocentric economics and ethnocentric economists almost universally serve certain interests, social urbanization, as somehow inevitable or in the nature of things, serves certain interests, especially when translated into various forms of ameliorative and cooptative planning and policy.

---

[32]See Special Issue: "Social Urbanization in Latin America," ed. Luise Margolies and R. H. Lavenda, *Urban Anthropology* 8 (Nos. 3 and 4; Winter, 1979).

CHAPTER 15

Ex Uno Plures

A Walk through Marxist Urban Studies

PAOLO CECCARELLI

Marxist studies of urban problems often remind me of a children's game I used to play with friends in the summer. We lay on the beach looking at the big, lazy clouds in the sky. We had to give them names, according to the images they evoked in each one of us. "It is a lion's head." "Nooo . . . they are two interlaced giants." "Come on. It is a beautiful woman—the sleeping beauty." All of us saw different things and argued very strongly in favor of the image we thought was the right one. We usually were bitterly divided over interpretations, and skillfully dialectic in defending them. At the same time, and this is what I remember best, our imagery developed according to a common paradigm. Images were taken mostly from the animal world, either human beings or beasts. We stuck to these very rigidly. While we were bitterly divided over interpretations, and very smart in pointing out how wrong others were, all of us were very loyal to our common standard. A cloud never was a big walnut tree, a medieval castle, or a Spanish galleon.

Marxist urban students often accuse each other of the most nefarious errors and deviations, and one wonders why they pretend to belong to the same camp. But at the same time, they have a few basic things in common that characterize them very different from other students of urban processes. Their and my cities are unlike those of others, and belong to the same and very peculiar family of creatures.

Paolo Ceccarelli • Department of Social and Economic Analysis of the Territory, Istituto Universitario di Architettura, Venice, Italy.

I start my analysis from this image because I want first to correct the conventional assumption that the Marxist approach to urban and regional problems is a kind of rigidly defined doctrine in which there is little room for differences of judgment and for dissent. From Marx and Engel's very first analysis of the dichotomy between town and country, this has never been true. In their works, one can easily trace substantial methodological differences in the way phenomena are analyzed, as well as different evaluations of the role that social and economic variables play in shaping urban environments. However, it would be equally wrong to assume that Marxists are at present mostly *chiens sans collier*, who follow divergent paths of analysis, and who suggest explanations that are inconsistent with one another. Common and cohesive traits still exist even though it is anything but easy to enumerate the variety of differences that have developed among the followers of Marx and Engels.

In the following pages, I shall first suggest a few things that urban Marxist students do have in common. I shall later try to explain why their views on many important issues differ so much.

CENTRAL TENETS OF MARXIST URBAN ANALYSIS

Some of the things that Marxists have in common are a methodology, a general theory of society and history, and some common subject matter. The original source was the Hegelian dialectic, which was reworked by Marx on the basis of his principles of historical materialism. Since then, Marx's progeny have produced numerous families and, often, opposed tribes of theories. Let us consider some of these important common traits more specifically.

First is the dialectic relation that exists between theory and praxis. Marxists cannot conceive of a theory that cannot be used to change or improve the society in which they live. Thus, they are forced to be very attentive to the historical component of problems—the way in which different processes originate, change, and interfere over time. Marxists do not—or at least they are not supposed to—think of social and economic phenomena as universals, which are fixed forever and are absolute in character. Social events are always seen as being the result of specific processes and relations among social classes and economic variables at a certain moment in time. Situations that are studied can be changed, and the very way in which they are studied can imply how to change them. Within these general guidelines, substantial differences can be found. There are students who are very close to a historically deterministic approach, whereas others are almost structural functionalists. And there are Marxists who are attracted by historicism, as there are others who have a voluntaristic view of social processes, and who are from time to time seduced by anarchism.

The same variety can be found in the political objectives that are pursued. Whereas some students lean toward social democracy, others believe in a "permanent revolution." After all the "renegades" Kautsky, Bukharin, Trotsky, Stalin, Liu Shao Chi, Chin Chin, and Dubçek were all Marxist theorists with divergent views on politics.

A second common trait traceable in urban analysis by Marxists is that they regard the different components of a city and a territory as products of large-scale economic and social forces that have developed over a long span of time. These forces always interact dialectically and are frequently in conflict with each other. The components of a territory are never regarded as individual and isolated elements. They are thought of as parts of a network of events, which can possibly be inconsistent with one another but nevertheless are tightly intertwined and mutually explicable. All of the Marxist students, including the revisionist ones who believe that Marxism is at present little more than a useful heuristic device, think that the components of a system can be explained only when the whole system is taken into consideration, and that this whole is, in turn, the result of a permanent dialectical confrontation among its individual components. The way in which a territory is structured and organized results from broad social and economic processes. It also results from the resistance of individuals—minority groups and lower classes—to the strategies of the classes in power. This common approach helps to explain why academics such as Harvey and Lefebvre[1] and most of the Italian students of urban problems relate equally to Marxism.[2]

[1]D. Harvey, *Social Justice and the City* (London: Edward Arnold, 1973); H. Lefebvre, *Du rural à l'urbain* (Paris: Éditions Anthropos, 1970; *La révolution urbaine* (Paris: Gallimard, 1970); *Le droit à la ville* (Paris: Éditions Anthropos, 1972); *La production de l'espace* (Paris: Éditions Anthropos, 1974).
[2]J. Borja, *Movimentos sociales urbanos* (Buenos Aires: Ediciones SIAP-Planteos, 1975); J. Benington, *Local Government Becomes Big Business* (London: CDP Information and Intelligence Unit, 1976).

I have purposely left to the end of my list the common traits that are generally regarded as the very core of a Marxist analysis of spatial organizations: the largely shared view that the organization of territory is the result of the social relations of production. The way in which settlements are located, land is used, functions are distributed, and work is organized changes according to the prevailing mode of production; and therefore, capitalism, the mode of production that is now dominant in several regions of the world, modifies the territorial organization that had resulted from previous modes of production. In effect, the territory becomes an exchangeable commodity. It loses the use value that other societies had given it in the past, and that present-day socialist societies pretend to attribute at least partly to it.[3] This is a central assumption in the Marxist theory of the city and the organization of space. But it has more than a merely theoretical importance. The Marxist interest in urban social struggle, political action, and innovation in planning policies and methods originates from the effort to challenge and eventually to overturn the subjugation of space and its elements to the market.

In addition, what Marxists seem to have most in common is the need to differ from one another in the way they approach issues: a difference that stems from the historical context and the economic, social, and political situations of each Marxist student. Thus, the prevailing interest that Marx had in the value theory and rent has for a long time been less central in other Marxist students' thought. Engels, for instance, centered interest less on the problem of the town and country relationship and more on the reproduction of the labor force, whereas the role of town and country relationships was crucial in the debate among Lenin, Trotsky, Bukharin, and Stalin after the Russian Revolution. Also, the emphasis in the post–World War II years on the concept of the state and the relationship between structure and superstructure corresponds to a change in problems and interests. Similarly, the emphasis has shifted in recent years when the causes and the nature of new radical movements in welfare societies had to be explained. The present critique of structural-functional analysis, the determinist expectation of the rapid collapse of capitalism, and the belief in the "inevitability" of socialism are still other examples. Each of these different efforts dealt with presumed errors and misinterpretations that other Marxist analyses had previously developed.

[3]The process of "commodification" of the space and the theoretical problems related to it are analyzed by Harvey, *Social Justice*, chap. 5.

FUNDAMENTAL THEMES AND ISSUES

These points may be all the clearer if we consider a group of important issues in Marxist research in the historical and socioeconomic setting in which they have been analyzed and elaborated. For this purpose, I shall first examine a number of theoretical problems faced by Marx and Engels that are directly connected with the organization of space: the problem of the relationship between town and country in a capitalist society, rent theory, and the housing question. A second area of interest is the debate that developed in the aftermath of the Russian Revolution on the relationship between town and country—the class relationship between blue-collar workers and peasants that ought to take place in the making of a socialist society. In addition, I shall also examine another important problem: economic and regional planning.

A third important focus in Marxist studies relates to the analysis of the state and the capitalist economy in Western welfare societies. Capitalism has introduced planning and equalization policies, the working class has been partially integrated into the economic system, and the public sector has continuously grown. These changes have not turned capitalist societies into socialist ones, but at the same time, the original forms of overexploitation of workers, strict dependence of the state on a few private interests, etc., no longer exist. There is a need to reinterpret the nature of capitalist economy and the new form that the state takes in welfare societies. This, in turn, requires Marxists to explain the character of the newly emerging class structure, to redefine the concept of the working class, and to clarify the role it actually plays in advanced societies.

Another group of contributions refers to the development of a Marxist theory and praxis that does not focus on Western capitalist countries and the conditions of the "metropolitan" proletariat. Imperialism (including the soviet imperialism), dependence, unequal exchange, and the contradictions that have developed between the interests of the working class in developed countries are the center of analysis. Marxist students from former Western European colonies and countries dependent on the United States have reversed the binoculars that Marxism had traditionally used to study the mechanics of capitalism.

The last section of my analysis takes into consideration recent efforts to go beyond a number of explanatory and prescriptive models used in the 1960s and 1970s. The crisis of the so-called "actually existing socialism" in

Eastern Europe, some regions of Asia, and Latin America and the emergence of new actors in social struggles in advanced capitalist countries compel a critical reassessment of several well-established Marxist assumptions. The debate focuses again on theoretical developments and methodology.[4]

MARX AND ENGELS: URBAN PROBLEMS AND SPATIAL ORGANIZATION

Marx and Engels examined the problems of cities and of the organization of space in a number of their works: *The Condition of the Working Class in Britain* (1845), *The German Ideology* (1845–46), *The Manifesto of the Communist Party* (1848), *Grundrisse* (1857–1858), *Capital* (1867–1894), *The Housing Question* (1872), *Anti-Dhüring* (1878), etc. Their most direct contribution to the study of urban processes is the analysis of the antagonistic, long-term relationship between town and country in capitalist societies. The antagonism between urban and rural social organizations is the result of the division of labor and private property, which reached their extreme and most advanced form in western Europe in the nineteenth century. Thus, Marx and Engels stated:

> The bourgeoisie has subjected the country to the rule of the towns. It has created enormous cities, has greatly increased the urban population as compared with rural, and has rescued a considerable part of the population from the idiocy of rural life. Just as it has made the country dependent on the towns, so it has made barbarian and semi-barbarian countries dependent on the civilized ones, nations of peasants on nations of bourgeois, the East and West. The bourgeoisie keeps more and more doing away with the scattered state of the population, of the means of production, and of property. It has ag-

---

[4]It is impossible, of course, to summarize in a few pages the intellectual processes that have mobilized vast human resources, have generated many theoretical debates, and have produced great, and often tragic, political confrontations. I also leave out several important aspects of Marxist research on territorial problems, for example, Mao Zedong's and the Chinese views on the town–country problem—(L. Hoa, *Reconstruire la Chine: Trente ans d'urbanisme, 1949–1979* (Paris: Éditions du Moniteur, 1981); the extremist Cambodian theories about deurbanization; and the more pragmatic approaches by the Vietnamese— (Nguyen Duc Nhuan, "Désurbanisation du développement régional au Viet Nam International," *Journal of Urban and Regional Research* 2 (1978): 330–350.

glomerated population, centralized means of production, and has concentrated property in a few hands.[5]

In the *Condition of the Working Class in England* (1844), Engels focused his attention on the economic and social implications of the fracture between urban and rural societies in the most industrialized country of his time.

Marx's analysis of rent dealt with still another aspect of land and space in a capitalist society. In capitalist systems, the land has become less and less a collective good, as it frequently was in precapitalist societies. It is privately owned, and its value is increasingly defined on the basis of its market value more than on its potential collective use. In a capitalist economy land becomes an exchangeable commodity.

Marx developed his analysis mostly with reference to the agricultural land, but it is on the grounds of this theory that recent conceptualizations of urban rent and the urban real-estate market have been developed.

Marx and Engels were interested in these problems because they wanted to understand better the internal mechanics of the growing capitalist process. They also worked out a broad political strategy to attack the very origins of the proleterian condition. Problems such as the town and country relationship, and rent are analyzed in the *Manifesto* and in other political writings.[6] Changes in towns, rural areas and the problems of the urbanized working class are approached with a critical view of bourgeois theories and of the utopian socialism of Owen, Fourier, and Proudhon. Marx and Engels argued that the social reforms proposed by the utopians missed the true meaning (and the actual importance) of capitalism. They had mistaken the outcomes of the capitalist process for its causes and had suggested unrealistic solutions to problems that were evolving in an opposite direction.

Neither Marx nor Engels produced an alternative policy—they assumed that their first political responsibility was to analyze the ongoing processes and to criticize the policies being proposed. A good example is

[5]K. Marx and F. Engels, *Manifesto of the Communist Party* (London: Lawrence and Wishart [1848] 1943), p. 8.
[6]Marx and Engels, *Manifesto;* Marx, *Capital, A Critical Analysis of Capitalist Production*, 3 vols. (Moscow: Foreign Languages Publishing House [1867–1894] 1961); Marx, *Grundrisse, Foundations of the Critique of Political Economy* (Harmondsworth, England: Penguin [1857–1858, 1953] 1973); Engels, *The Condition of the Working Class in England* (Oxford: Basil Blackwell [1845] 1958); Engels, *The Housing Question* (Moscow: Progress Publishers [1872] 1975).

the three articles that Engels wrote in 1872 in the *Volksstaat*, the German Social Democratic Party newspaper, on the housing question. In those articles, later collected in a booklet entitled *The Housing Question*,[7] Engels criticized Proudhon's idea of giving workers their houses as private property. He warned that home ownership potentially tied the worker to a specific place, and eventually to a specific job, and that this restrictiveness was a severe constraint in a historical period when mobility to a large city was for immigrant workers the strongest guarantee of improvement in their social condition. Besides, the opportunity to have an almost free house and possibly to produce staple foods in its backyard would result in lower wages. In fact, a worker would continue to pay for the rent, not in the form of a payment to the landlord, but in the form of unpaid labor; that is, a share of the worker's wage would be kept by the capitalist employer: "In this way savings invested by a worker in his house would become, at least partly, capital: not to him, but to his employer."

According to Engels, the dream of utopian thinkers and bourgeois reformers of turning industrial workers into homeowners in order to free them from the horrendous housing conditions in industrial cities (which, among other things, were a source of social and political instability) was at the very end consistent with the rationale of capitalist exploitation. The housing scarcity that reformers fought against had been produced by the same capitalist growth that had concentrated workers in large cities at a faster rate than new houses could be supplied—and by the same capitalism whose recurrent crises from time to time left the workers jobless and without means of subsistence. Consequently, the housing problem could be solved only through a radical economic and social change. Only when capitalist systems are overturned is there a chance to overcome the town–country antagonism and its consequences.

LENIN AND THE PROBLEM OF TOWN–COUNTRY RELATIONSHIPS

Lenin tackled the problem of town–country relationships in the *Development of Capitalism in Russia*,[8] one of his early works, written in the years 1896–1899, when he was in his 20s. He believed that, even after a

[7]Engels, *The Housing Question*.
[8]V. I. Lenin, *The Development of Capitalism in Russia* (London: Martin Lawrence, 1936–1938).

thorough social overthrow, precapitalist relationships of production in agriculture would continue to survive in Russia:

> . . . the situation is entirely different in a territory in which not all the land is occupied and which has not been entirely populated. The inhabitants of such a territory, who are forced out of agriculture in a populated district, may migrate to an uninhabited part of that territory and "take new land into cultivation." The result will be an increase in the agricultural population, and this increase may be (for a certain time) not less, if not more, rapid than the increase in the industrial population.[9]

Lenin's work intertwines with a revolutionary political project and with the real problems that a revolutionary political elite in power will have to face. In *The Theory of the Agrarian Question*,[10] Lenin specifically examined the problem of how to eliminate the conflict between town and country. In his opinion, the task ahead for socialism was not to get rid of big cities but to produce a different and more balanced territorial organization:

> The fact that we openly acknowledge that large cities are an element of progress in the capitalist society does not prevent us from including the abolition of the antagonism between town and country among our ideals (and in our program of action . . .). . . . On the contrary: the end of the town-country antagonism is a necessary step to ensure that every one has access to these treasures, and to eliminate the segregation from civilization of millions of country people that Marx has rightly defined "the idiocy of rural life."[11]

Lenin extended this point:

> If nothing precludes the abolition of the antagonism between town and country (an act which is not isolated, but a part of a more complex set of actions) this is not the consequence of the "esthetic" feeling. As Engels suggests, in large cities men live in the stench of their excrements, and as soon as they can, they escape in search of clean air and fresh water. The industry also disperses everywhere in the country—they too need clean water. The exploitation of waterfalls, canals, and rivers for producing electric power further supports this trend towards "industrial dispersion."[12]

---

[9]Lenin, *Selected Works*, 12 vols. (London: Martin Lawrence, 1936–1938), p. 56.
[10]Lenin, *Die Agrarfrage und die "Marxkritiker" in Werke*, 5 vols. (Berlin: Dietz Verlag, 1955).
[11]Ibid., p. 149.
[12]Ibid.

In the aftermath of the October Revolution, the improvement of town and country relationships became an urgent imperative. The structural causes of the conflict presumably did not exist anymore, and the time had arrived to build the new socialist society in all of its different components. Lenin's view was that it was worthless to reorganize the Russian system of towns and rural regions that had been inherited from czarism. New, large-scale territorial organization had to be developed. The preconditions to overcoming the town–country antagonism lay in the division of the Soviet Union into a number of different economic regions and in a policy of regional development. The problem was faced within the Goelro plan for the rapid electrification of the country. On February 2, 1920, at the first session of the Panrussian Central Executive Committee (VCIK), Lenin declared, "We must show the peasants that the industrial organization based on the most advanced technology, i.e. the electrification . . . ends the conflict between town and country."[13] The town and country relationships were consequently connected to other problems: centralization and decentralization, the reorganization of a modern transportation system, planning, interregional relationships, industrial locations, and the crucial problem of the existence of equal and different nationalities in the Soviet society.

Lenin also believed that it was convenient to "maintain for some time ahead the mercantile form of production (exchange through purchase and sale) as the *sole* form of economic relationship with the town which peasants can accept, in order to foster the economic junction between town and country."[14] Those were the years of the Novaya Ekonomicheskaya Politika (the NEP), which Lenin himself defined as an economy "of state capitalism in a proletarian state" moving toward socialism. The theoretical debate on the role that the minuscule urban working class and the immense world of Russian peasants would have in the new Socialist Russia also influenced more specific areas of analysis and research, for example, the efforts to work out new theories of the organization of space, and of models for new cities and neighborhoods;[15] the debate between "urbanists" and "disurba-

---

[13]Quoted in *La costruzione della citta sovietica, 1929–31* ed. P. Ceccarelli (Venezia: Marsilio, 1970), 20.

[14]Quoted in J. S. Stalin, *Les problèmes économiques du socialisme en URSS* (Moscow: Éditions en Langues Étrangères, 1952), p. 7.

[15]H. Chambre, *L'aménagement du territoire en URSS* (Paris: Mouton, 1959).

nists" at the end of the 1920s; the planning of new linear cities; and the Moscow Master Plan of 1935.[16]

The discussion about the new "modes of life," which involved Sabsovic, Strumilin, and others,[17] had already made clear in the mid-1920s the problems of developing a socialist society by means of changes in only the economic structure. Social behavior, individual attitudes, and interpersonal relationships had to be thoroughly changed if a new and more advanced system of social relationships was expected to take place.

To give rise to new relationships between the urban and the rural world, the state had to be totally different from the czarist one. It had to be a state able to efficiently carry on a process of true modernization. Lenin's famous catchword "Soviet plus electrification equals Socialism" expresses the basic difficulties and contradictions that the new Marxist leadership of the old and holy Russia had to face and would hopefully solve in the years ahead.

STATE AND SOCIAL MOVEMENTS IN POST–WORLD WAR II EUROPE

Amazing changes had taken place by the end of World War II. Fascism and Nazism had been defeated. Capitalism, as an economic and political system, had expanded further and, thanks to new forms of imperialism, still dominated old and new colonies. The Soviet Union had become a big power that controlled many regions of the world and threatened several others. In this totally new international picture, Western Europe no longer played the political role that it had before the war. Deep social and political changes had taken place in the United Kingdom, France, and Germany. Europe was split in two, and most of the tradi-

---

[16]H. A. Miliutin, *Sotsgorod: The Problem of Building Socialist Cities* (Cambridge: M.I.T. Press [1930] 1974); A. Kopp, "Changer la vie, changer la ville," *De la vie nouvelle aux problèmes urbains—URSS 1977–1952* (Paris: Union Générale d'Éditions, 1975); Kopp, *Town and Revolution: Soviet Architecture and City Planning 1917–1935* (Cambridge: M.I.T. Press, 1970); M. De Michelis and E. Pasini, *La città sovietica 1925–1937* (Venezia: Marsilio, 1976).

[17]L. M. Sabsovic, *L'URSS dans dix ans* (Paris: Bureau d'Éditions [1929] n.d.); S. G. "Problema Socialisticeskich Gorodov Planovoe Khoziaistvo," in Ceccarelli, *La Costruzione della Città Sovietica.*

tional political and cultural ties with Eastern Europe were broken off. Countries like Italy and Spain emerged from a long sleep.

European capitalist societies of the postwar years were different from the ones of the nineteenth century and the first decades of this century. Capitalism had changed and had become a much more fragmented system of power. The capitalist state had become a highly articulated system that often made decisions autonomously from big economic interest groups. It had been able to successfully manage its recurrent crises, and to recover from the violent social and political contradictions that had afflicted it from time to time. In several countries, the state acted as an arbiter of the economy and as an entrepreneur. It was often the biggest employer and supplier of income. Working-class parties had changed, too, and had reorganized according to the changes in their constituency. Large numbers of workers behaved as moderates to defend their newly acquired income levels and social status.

It was in this context, marked by the years of reconstruction, Cold War, economic growth, and detente, that European Marxists were forced to elaborate new conceptual tools. Marxists, not surprisingly, started an effort to reanalyze the reality of advanced capitalism, and to reconstruct their instruments for political action. This effort partly corresponded to the crisis of the most orthodox Communist parties (as in France) and the success of the ones that were more articulated and flexible (the PCI in Italy). It was also related to the increase in strength of "modern" Social Democratic parties in Scandinavia, the United Kingdom, and, later, Germany and France.

During the postwar period, territorial problems became very important. Western Europe experienced large-scale changes in the distribution patterns of population and activities. Cities became metropolises, the country was increasingly abandoned, and entire regions either boomed or sharply declined. The amount and features of fixed capital also changed. Governments in European countries implemented large-scale programs of social housing; transportation infrastructure and services were improved; and national states not only invested large amounts of funds in these programs but had to find a balance between equity (i.e., the social objectives of these policies), and efficiency (i.e., the ability of the state and of the public sector at large, to implement them successfully).

Cities were the loci of most of these policies. Most of the processes of redistribution, mobility, and social integration were, in fact, taking place in cities. To understand the new capitalist state, it was therefore important to study cities, to understand how they worked as social, economic, and political systems. The French Marxist sociologist Henri Lefebvre, for instance, convinced of the centrality of urban problems in modern society, argued that the industrial society was not an end in itself but a preparatory stage for urbanism. As he stated:

> When we use the words "urban revolution" we designate the total ensemble of transformations which run throughout contemporary society and which serve to bring about the change from a period in which questions of economic growth and industrialization predominate to the period in which the urban problematic becomes decisive, when research into the solutions and forms appropriate to urban society takes precedence.[18]

If it is to be combated effectively, the "multiform Proteus" that is capitalism must be carefully studied in the wide variety of its aspects. And this task was as difficult in the 1960s as it was in Marx's time.

In the 1960s, when the development of capitalism in Europe and the world was at its peak, a number of Marxist students began to work out new concepts, new analytical tools and methods.[19] Louis Althusser had

---

[18]*La révolution urbaine*, p. 56.

[19]P. Baran and P. Sweezy, *Monopoly Capital* (New York: Monthly Review Press, 1966), studied the new form of monopoly capital; M. Kalecki, *Theory of Economic Dynamics* (London: Allen & Unwin, 1954), explained recent economic trends in advanced capitalism and how they related to politics; and P. Sraffa, *Production of Commodities by Means of Commodities* (Cambridge: Cambridge University Press, 1961), reformulated crucial concepts in the Marxist economic theory. New approaches to the problems of the capitalist state were suggested by R. Miliband, *The State in Capitalist Society* (London: Weidenfeld and Nicholson, 1969); and new explanations of the origins and the development of capitalism were provided by the historical studies of K. Polanyi, *The Great Transformation, The Political and Economic Origins of Our Time* (Boston: Beacon Press, 1957); E. P. Thompson, *The Making of the English Working Class* (London: Victor Gollancz, 1963), and E. J. Hobsbawm, *The Age of Revolution, Europe 1789–1848* (London: Weidenfeld and Nicholson, 1962). "Unorthodox" Marxist thinkers were also rediscovered: K. Korsch, *Marxism and Philosophy* (London: New Left Review [1923] 1970); G. Lukacs, *History and Class Consciousness* (Cambridge: M.I.T. Press, 1923); E. Pashukanis, *General Theory of Law and Marxism in Soviet Legal Philosophy by V. I. Lenin et al.* (Cambridge: Harvard University Press [1929] 1951), and *Allgemeine Rechslehre und Marxismus* (Frankfurt: Suhrkamp [1929] 1966); and especially A. Gramsci, *Selections from the Prison Notebooks*, ed. Q. Hoare and G. N. Smith (New York: International Publishers, 1971), whose contributions to the analysis of the modern state, power coalitions, and class relationships opened a wide debate.

the strongest impact on the studies of social and political processes related to this territory in those years.

Central in Althusser's analysis are the relationships between economic and political-ideological components. These relations give rise to a structural whole that is at the same time unified and highly complex, and whose different levels are distinct and relatively autonomous. Each element of the complex can develop in a different way, and contradictions between and within each element are not produced by a single factor—for instance, economics—but by all of the effects of the structural whole. Each element of the whole is consequently structurally determined. This situation changes over time, and in different historical periods, dominant instances change as a result of how the major contradictions play out. At the very end, it is the economic determinant that has a crucial influence; in fact, it "determines which of the instances in the social structure occupies the determinant place," including itself. A typical case is the model that Althusser worked out to explain the relationship between structures and individuals:

> The structure of the relations of production determines the *places* and *functions* occupied and adopted by the agents of production. . . . The true subjects (in the sense of constitutive subjects of the process) are . . . the relations of production (and political and ideological social relations). . . . These are irreducible to any anthropological inter-subjectivity—since they only combine agents and objects in a specific structure of the distribution of relations, places and functions, occupied and "supported" by objects and agents of production.[20]

In different ways, Althusser influenced first contributions by both Castells and Lojkine, two of the leading figures of the new French Marxist urban sociology. In his major book *The Urban Question*,[21] Castells defined space as an expression of the social structure, produced by the elements of the economic, political, and ideological systems, by their combination, and by the social practices from which they proceed. The three instances (economic, political, and ideological) are broken down into a series of subelements at different levels. Each one of them is the object of detailed empirical research. Production is, for instance, analyzed through the elements that are internal to the work process (the

[20]L. Althusser and E. Balibar, *Reading Capital* (New York: Pantheon, [1965] 1972), p. 180.
[21]Cambridge: M.I.T. Press [1972] 1977.

factories), the relationship between the work process and the instances as
a whole (the industrial environment), and, finally, the relationships between the work process and other instances (the administrative system).
As Castells said:

> The relationship which the different sub-elements of the urban sys-
> tem, their role and levels, have among themselves and with the social
> structure defines the conjuncture of the urban system. The insertion
> of the support agents in the structural backcloth thus constituted, will
> define urban social practices, the only significant realities for our
> research.[22]

There is no social structure without contradictions, and consequently, the analysis of the urban system leads necessarily to the study of
urban politics. According to such a theory, the study of the state and its
system of policies becomes crucial to an understanding of late capitalism.
They are the devices by means of which the reproduction of the dominant
mode of production is guaranteed. Also, urban social movements must be
studied. They are "systems of practices" that cause structural changes in
the urban system, as well as substantial shifts in the balance of forces
involved in class struggle.

In the 1970s, empirical research systematically focused on planning
processes, as an expression of the role that the state plays to reinforce the
interests of the economic elites on one side, and to contain pressures by
social movements on the other. An empirical study such as the one by
Castells and Godard on Dunkerque[23] is representative of these new approaches and interests. The same applies to the theoretical model that
Lojkine has developed in *Le marxisme, l'état et la question urbaine*.[24]
Several other students have analyzed other aspects of the state machinery
and the urban policies which have been implemented in the post–World
War II years. Tapalov has studied French housing policies,[25] Preteceille
social services,[26] and Cherki and Mehl transportation.[27] In these studies,

[22]Ibid., p. 166.

[23]M. Castells and F. Godard, *Monopolville, l'entreprise, l'état, l'urbain* (Paris:
Mouton, 1974).

[24]Paris: PUF, 1977.

[25]*Les promoteurs immobiliers: Contribution à l'analyse de la production cap-
italiste du logement en France* (Paris: Mouton, 1974).

[26]E. Preteceille, M. Pencon, P. Renda, and M. Chantrein, *Équipements collec-
tifs. Structures urbaines et consommation sociale* (Paris: CSU, 1975).

[27]*Les nouveaux embarras de Paris* (Paris: Maspero, 1978).

the influence of the analysis of Poulantzas[29] on the structure of political systems in advanced capitalist countries and their relationship with the state and the economy[28] often joins the influence of the Althusserian methodology.

Urban social movements have been carefully studied with reference both to their internal structure and mechanics (who are the participants, when and how the movements have begun, how they have developed, and so forth) and to their objectives, methods of action, and actual outcomes. The relation between social movements and the state and between social movements and political elites is central in the research work by Castells, Godard, Cherki, and Dominique Mehl in France;[29] by Spanish students like Borja;[30] and by a score of Italian students.[31] The problem of the state from the viewpoint of its relations to social and economic forces and its functioning has been faced by Marxist analysts in the same year in different countries. Johannes Agnoli and Claus Offe have studied the problem of legitimization of the German state,[32] and Altvater has concentrated on state interventionism as a way to secure the reproduction of a capital that is increasingly unable to provide its own basic necessities.[33] Hirsch has explored the nature of the state in late capitalism, that is, the form and function that it has taken at the present historical juncture.[34] Analyses by Agnoli, Altvater, Hirsch, and Offe are often highly theoretical and abstract and do not have a direct reference to urban

[28]*Political Power and Social Class* (London: New Left Books, 1973), and *Classes in Contemporary Capitalism* (London: New Left Books, 1975).

[29]*Sociologie des mouvements sociaux urbains: Enquête sur la région Parisienne* (Paris: École des Hautes Études en Sciences Sociales, 1974).

[30]*Movimentos sociales urbanos.*

[31]A. Daolio, *Le lotte per la casa in Italia* (Milan: Feltrinelli, 1974); G. Della Pergola, *Città e conflitto sociale, Inchiesta al Garibaldi-Isola e in altri quartieri periferici di Milano* (Milano: Feltrinelli, 1973); P. Ceccarelli, "Venice: Urban Renewal, Community Power Structure and Social Conflict," in *The Conservation of European Cities*, ed. D. Appleyard (Cambridge: M.I.T. Press, 1979), pp. 52–64.

[32]Agnoli, *Überlegung zum burgerlichen Staat* (Berlin: Verlag Klaus Wagenbach, 1975); Offe, *Strukturprobleme des Kapitalistischen Staates* (Frankfurt: Suhrkamp, 1975).

[33]"Some Problems of State Interventionism," in *State and Capital*, ed. J. Holloway and S. Picciotto (London: Edward Arnold, 1978).

[34]"The State Apparatus and Social Reproduction: Elements of a Theory of the Bourgeois State," in Holloway and Picciotto.

problems, but their methodological contribution to a better understanding of planning processes and urban politics is as important as those by French Marxists.

Important analyses of the problems faced by the state in advanced capitalist countries have also been carried on by American Marxists. *The Fiscal Crisis of the State* by O'Connor[35] provides useful tools to explain the economic and fiscal problems faced by large cities in welfare societies.

Several key problems and notions have been dealt with by structuralists. Among them are the relations between space as a social formation and modes of production in advanced capitalism; the process by which space is created by elements of the economic, political, and ideological systems; criticism of the ideological content of the notions of "urban" and "urbanism"; and the role that the state plays in space through policies oriented toward "collective consumption." A less important contribution has been the effort to build neat and well organized taxonomies of urban phenomena and processes.

Also, substantial criticisms have appeared. The inability of "structuralist" theory to take adequate account of the contradictions between social practice and its explanatory models is a major weakness that partly accounts for the gross political mistakes that the Left has made in recent years. The fact that social formations are in reality more complex than is assumed by theory has been emphasized by several critics. They have pointed out that structuralists have often achieved positive results in spite of the methods they have used. Harloe doubts if it is possible to maintain the "structuralist" approach and method of procedure of *La Question Urbaine* because it "ultimately obstructs the analysis of real situations rather than aiding it."[36] Structuralism is also accused of being a 'circular' theory: once certain assumptions are given, the results are already determined, and in a way, they always confirm the initial hypotheses.[37]

The weaknesses of the "structuralist" approach and the effort to overcome them are examined by Castells in the afterword to the English

---

[35]New York: St. Martin's Press, 1973.

[36]*Captive Cities. Studies in the Political Economy of Cities and Regions*, ed. M. Harloe (New York: Wiley, 1977), p. 20.

[37]Szelenyi, "Regional Management and the Changing Class Content of the Urban–Rural Dichotomy in the 'Transition to Socialism.' The Case of pre- and post-Revolutionary Eastern Europe (Flinders University of Southern Australia, 1980; mimeo), footnote 17.

translation of *La Question Urbaine,* published five years after the original
French book. His self-critique concludes:

> The problem is not so much that of its correctness as that of its
> usefulness. . . . The most important task, from the point of view of
> the present phase of theoretical work, is not . . . to define elements
> and to formalize their structure, but to detect the historical laws at
> work, in the so-called "urban contradictions and practices." It is
> premature at the moment to try to reach the level of structural for-
> malization proposed, for historical laws determine the forms of the
> structure rather than the reverse.[38]

SZELENYI AND THE RELEVANCE OF "URBAN"

Two events already mentioned, which in the 1960s and 1970s influenced Marxist research and theory, were, first, the development of new
political experiences in less developed countries and the sequence of
conflicts that they have started and, second, the crisis of the "actually
existing socialism" in several countries. It is partly the confrontation between these new problems and the Althusser-derived approaches that
have opened new research directions in Marxist urban studies. Many
events have occurred since 1916, when Lenin wrote *Imperialism: The
Highest Stage of Capitalism,*[39] and even since the seminal book *The
Political Economy of Growth* by Paul Baran.[40] Theoretical research and
broad comparative studies on dependence and underdevelopment[41] have
thrown new light on colonialism and postcolonialism and their historical
evolution. Also, massive empirical research on individual countries and
specific situations in different socioeconomic settings has been carried
on—work exemplified by the studies by Stavenhagen on the Mexican
agrarian movements and by the researches by Santos, Quijano, and sever-

[38]Castells, *The Urban Question,* p. 438.
[39]London: Martin Lawrence, [1916] 1936–1938.
[40]New York: Monthly Review Press, (1948) 1957.
[41]See S. Amin, *Unequal Development* (New York: Monthly Review Press, 1976);
   A. Emmanuel, *Unequal Exchange* (New York: Monthly Review Press, 1972); A.
   G. Frank, *Capitalism and Underdevelopment in Latin America* (New York:
   Monthly Review Press, 1967); C. Furtado, *Economic Development of Latin
   America* (Cambridge: Cambridge University Press, 1970); I. Wallerstein, *The
   Capitalist World-Economy* (Cambridge: Cambridge University Press, 1979).

al others on urban problems in Latin American countries.[42] New concepts to explain economic and social situations have also been formulated—in part, to make new policies, to start processes of change, and even to ignite revolutionary movements. Such is the case of the notion of center-periphery, the critical analysis of marginality, the reassessment of the role of peasants in the process of development, and the new models of state organization and of political systems for developing societies.[43]

Three contributions were of particular importance: first were the contributions of an historical approach to the analysis of social systems, and more specifically the contributions of the comparative historical research on growth processes.[44] Second were the models of development that dependent societies tend to follow. Empirical research has frequently suggested that they tend neither toward a capitalist mode of production nor toward an "orthodox" socialist model. They evolve into heterogeneous and complex social formations, where different modes of production coexist. The state has a very peculiar role in these systems, and social classes interrelate in unusual ways. This change has stimulated important questions on the nature of the political systems of Western

[42]Santos, *Aspects de la géographie et de l'économie urbaines des pays sous-développés* (Paris: Centre de Documentation Universitaire, 1969), and "L'urbanizzazione dipendente in Venezuela," in *L'urbanizzazione dipendente in Venezuela*, ed. M. Castells *et al.* (Milan: Mazzotta, 1972); Quijano, "Dependencia, cambio social y urbanizacion en America Latina," in *Urbanizacion y Dependencia en America Latina*, ed. N. Schteingart (Buenos Aires: SIAP, 1973); P. Singer, *Economia politica de urbanizacao* (São Paulo: Editora Brasiliense, 1975).

[43]References to different contributions by Latin American Marxists to the study of urban problems can be found in J. L. Coraggio, T. Noyelle, and M. Schteingart, "Spatial Organization, Social Processes and Community Struggles in Capitalist Socio-economic Formations," in *Reading List in Radical Political Economics* (New York: Union for Radical Political Economics, 1977).

[44]Dependent countries continue to be strongly differentiated, despite their forced integration into the capitalist system. This phenomenon is the result of substantial original differences and of differences in the domination that colonial and postcolonial powers have imposed on them. Strongly different national and regional histories, societies, and economies result from these original differences. In turn, equally differentiated political systems emerge. When differences and inconsistencies in developing countries are examined, one must also take into consideration the specific circumstances that differentiate metropolitan countries. The existence of discontinuity and fragmentation in the developing world brings into question the use of "pure" paradigms to explain advanced societies.

capitalism and in "actually existing socialist" societies. It is not accidental
that the neocorporatist theory by Schmitter and other students, which has
proved to be fruitful in the analysis of recent political trends in Western
societies originated partly from the study of a number of Latin American
political systems.[45] Third are the studies of social and economic marginality—the analysis of all of the components of the social and economic
structure that have an informal character and that do not integrate into
the existing system, yet have an important role in the society.[46]

An overall evaluation of Marxist studies on developing societies, by
scholars from those countries would undoubtedly be positive. So far, their
impact on both theory and praxis has been important. The more independent scholars have even inherited the "heretical" spirit of Lukacs, which
they use to analyze the present problems of socialism.

Thus, Ivan Szelenyi criticized the widely shared belief among Marxist students in Western countries that a specifically *urban* social relation
does not exist. He denied that "there are only class relations determined
by contradictions between capital and labor,"[47] that is, that there is only
an abstract and pure capitalist mode of production that corresponds to the
one of late capitalism. And he refuted the view that all of the problems,
including the urban ones, can be reduced from the "pure" model as a
contradiction of capitalist reproduction. According to Szelenyi, it is on
these grounds that some authors, including Castells and Harvey, have
eventually suggested that the urban-rural dichotomy does not exist anymore, and that "urban" and "urbanism" are sheer ideology. Szelenyi's
argument is that the theory advanced by Castells and Harvey may seem
true when the analysis is centered only on advanced capitalist countries.

---

[45]Schmitter, *Interest Conflict and Political Change in Brazil* (Stanford, Calif.:
Stanford University Press, 1971), and "Still the Century of Corporatism?" *The
Review of Politics* 36 (1974): pp. 85–131.

[46]What is more, the study of marginality in less developed societies has also led to
the examination from a different viewpoint of the existence of similar facts in
more advanced societies. Analyses of the labor market structure in developing
countries have, for instance, been helpful in formulating recent theories of the
dual and segmented labor market in mature capitalist societies. It has under-
lined the need for a more careful, problem-oriented approach to social movements and forms of the economy. There is no need to remember how important
the contributions by U.S. social scientists who have worked in developing countries have been in the study of unemployment and poverty in North American
cities.

When the problems of capitalist countries are taken into consideration, one can see that the urban-rural dichotomy has been reproduced on a world scale. The fiscal crisis of the large cities in industrialized countries, too, can be fully explained only when the role of the multinational capital and its exploitation of the rural regions of the world are considered. Szelenyi also argued that

> The legitimation crisis of the state in late capitalism—so closely linked to the contradictions between the socialized nature of the "means of collective consumption" and the private expropriation of productive capital—is not so much the expression of a "pure" capitalist mode of production but rather the very end of this pure form.[48]

One conclusion drawn from Szelenyi's argument is that "urban" is not just a reflection of capitalist relations of production: the urban question cannot be deduced from the contradiction of reproduction within any abstract model of the capitalist mode of production. "Urban" is not only a relatively distinct phenomenon analytically; it is as much a producer of capitalism as it is its product."[49] The reference to Lefebvre's approach in opposition to Althusser's is evident.

According to Szelenyi, urban autonomy and self-regulating urban management, which had a crucial role in the formation of Western European capitalism, were suppressed in Eastern Europe in the sixteenth and seventeenth centuries before they could fully develop. And, as he stated, "It is probably less the weakness of rural class struggle, but the early failure of burghers to maintain their urban autonomy which prevents capitalist accumulation and the generalization of capital–wage labour relationships."[50] This event is not only interesting for a better understanding of history, it is important in explaining the present nature of "actually existing Socialist" societies.

Must the incomplete transition from feudalism to capitalism still be interpreted (as it has frequently been) as a process that put eastern Europe in a backward and peripheral position? Or has it rather been a process that set the prerequisites for a different type of development?

---

[47]Quoted by F. Lamarche, "Property Development and the Economic Foundations of the Urban Question," in *Urban Sociology, Critical Essays*, ed. C. Pickvance (London: Tavistock Publications, 1976), p. 86.
[48]Szelenyi, "Regional Management."
[49]Ibid., p. 12.
[50]Ibid., p. 13.

Szelenyi asked the question "Are these deviations from the Western model signs of backwardness or rather the first step on the road in 'transition to socialism'."[51] In his answer he demonstrated that there is a continuity between the prerevolutionary models of managing urban and regional development and what he called the present "socialist redistributive system of regional management." The "actually existing Socialism" is a specific system, with its own characteristics, and it is very deeply rooted in history. The ways in which it works and looks for legitimization are unique in character; and it cannot be applied elsewhere.

A second inference is that the urban-rural opposition has not become progressively marginal to capitalism. Instead, this opposition is still one of capitalism's major contradictions. The problem is that "urban" and "rural" do not at present have the connotations that they had in the past. They have become more complex and extended phenomena. Szelenyi's method refers to the one that E. P. Thompson used in his analysis of class and in his criticism of the structuralist theory of class. Szelenyi says:

> Urbanization is a historical process, it is the process of making the urban form from the non-urban at the scale of a national state or at a world scale and this historical process is interrelated to the expansion of capitalism, presupposes it, facilitates it, and follows from it. If this process comes to an end, then we have to rethink which social formation are we confronted with. Let me again refer to the question of the *Grundrisse* to illustrate the meaning of this inter-relationship: ancient classical history—Marx is probably right—is indeed the "ruralization of the city" which is a historical process, a continuous struggle as well. But when this ruralization of the city succeeds, then it is at the same time the end of antiquity and it indicates the beginning of a new epoch.[52]

To define the role of the "urban" in transition is an important problem. When the transition from feudalism into capitalism is examined, a controversial issue is whether the process of transition was started by forces inherent in feudalism or rather by exogenous factors, such as urban autonomy.

But capitalist countries show substantial differences among themselves, some of which are strongly connected with their different histories. Does Szelenyi's argument also apply to the study of urban processes

[51]Ibid., p. 13
[52]Ibid., p. 14.

in those countries? The answer is yes, as several studies of atypical cases of capitalist development in Western Europe show. "Eurocommunism" in southern European countries is largely based on this assumption.

Marxist urban studies are still at the beginning of a long, and often hard, march, a march whose route has become increasingly winding and ramified.

Note on Sociological Images
of the City

NATHAN GLAZER

There is no accepted sociological image of the city—but there are a number of different sociological images of the city. The images I discuss here are not dealt with—or not dealt with in quite this way—by Peter Langer; but these images, too, are far from being the full gamut.

By way of preface, one kind of study that might be neglected when we talk about sociological images of the city is the work of demographers. Most closely bound to data, they are least imagistic, if you will, in their work. And yet the demographic work on cities also presents an "image," or a series of images. There is first the crowding of people into cities, with the rise of centralized political systems, the onset of industrialization, and the service-producing society. Second, there is the emptying out of the inner city, a process that began quite some time ago in the advanced industrial countries. Third, there is the increasing wave pattern, moving outward, of urban population. First, the inner cities lose population, then the older parts of cities, then the inner suburbs, and most recently entire metropolitan areas, and the most rapidly growing areas become the "exurban" ones or the hardly populated (or urbanized) wilderness areas: northern New England, the northern Great Lakes, the Ozarks, the Mountain States.

This seems like a simple image indeed, and yet it is very powerful, particularly if we begin to see this pulsing outward movement in the light of the varying responses of different population groups. For example, one major subject of concern in dealing with urban problems has been the

---

Nathan Glazer • Graduate School of Education, Harvard University, Cambridge, Massachusetts.

337

future of American blacks. They were a small-town and rural population 70 years ago, to be found in only small numbers in large cities. In World War I, in the 1920s, in World War II, and during post–World War II prosperity, they flowed into the large cities, concentrating in the oldest and most central parts of them. We have seen the same waves as have affected urban population generally affecting them in recent decades: they, too, flow to the suburbs and the peripheries.

What, then, happens to the centers? In part, new immigrants to the cities flow into them—immigrants from overseas, and perhaps returning, gentrifying suburbanites. But waves of immigration outward do mean a permanent thinning out of population in the center.

One can apply the demographic pattern that seems so common—a flow into the center, followed by flows outward to ever-more-distant suburbia and exurbia—to other racial and ethnic groups. One can see how it affects families and individuals in different stages of the life cycle: the young unmarried, the young married, those who are divorced, those whose children have left the home, and those who can no longer maintain themselves in their own homes.

Demography, in its application to the geography of the city, gives us, perhaps, our most solid base for creating valid images of the city, but it is true that these images do not cover other elements—culture, attitude, outlook, style of life—that contribute to a denser sense of image. It is with these kinds of images that I am most concerned here. And here we can see an interesting divergence and conflict in the way that sociologists have seen cities.

Like Langer, my starting point is Louis Wirth's essay.[1] Wirth was a member of the Chicago school of urban sociologists, still the most distinctive (and influential) of all American sociologists dealing with cities. Robert E. Park was the dominant figure. One of his major books on cities was *The Immigrant Press and Its Control*—and that gives an idea of what they were doing.[2] A second major figure was W. I. Thomas, and his major work is *The Polish Peasant in Europe and America*.[3] They were studying the city as it filled up with immigrants from abroad and with rural emi-

[1] L. Wirth, "Urbanism as a Way of Life," *American Journal of Sociology* 44 (July 1938):1–24.

[2] R. E. Park, *The Immigrant Press and Its Control* (New York and London: Harper & Bros., 1922).

[3] W. I. Thomas and F. Znanieki, *The Polish Peasant in Europe and America* (New York: Alfred A. Knopf, 1927).

grants. If one means by *image* a picture, they created the most influential actual image of the city. Ernest W. Burgess, in a very influential book edited by Park, Burgess, and Roderick McKenzie,[4] drew up a crude map of Chicago and drew concentric circles around the central business district. He numbered the resultant circles. Zone I was the central business district, II the zone of transition, III the zone of independent working-class homes, IV the zone of better residences, and V the commuter's zone. You can't do much better than that with a simple image. It has been very influential.

Wirth, one of the group, whose doctoral thesis is The *Ghetto*,[5] a study of the Jewish area of first settlement in Chicago, described in his influential essay, "Urbanism as a Way of Life," what the content of urban life was to the Chicago sociologists. He said urbanism was defined by three elements: size of population, density of population, and heterogeneity of population. And these characteristics had consequences for social life. Size meant many different kinds of people, segregated in their own districts, nevertheless competing with others (for space, housing, and jobs, though I don't think he specifically mentions the latter), subject to formal control rather than informal and organic solidarity, as in the countryside or the small town. People played highly segmented roles; that is, they presented one specialized side of themselves at a time—worker, tenant, customer—rather than acting as complete people. Their social relations were characterized by superficiality and anonymity, and they made their social contacts more on the basis of utility, less on the basis of kinship and ethnicity. (Again, I may be extending Wirth's argument a bit.)

Density meant all this but in particular the specialization of parts of cities for given functions, determined by the highest rate of economic return.

Heterogeneity meant that old-fashioned caste relationships broke down, class relationships became more complicated, that people's statuses fluctuated, were unstable, and created insecurity. Heterogeneity led to commercialized recreation, which appealed to varied groups and leveled distinctions. The family weakened, as people found their amusements outside it; kinship ties became less important; the neighborhood

[4]R. E. Park, E. Burgess, and R. D. McKenzie, *The City* (Chicago: University of Chicago Press, 1967).

[5]L. Wirth, *The Ghetto* (Chicago: University of Chicago Press, 1928).

and its ties weakened; and we had a commercialized society "catering to thrills." Everything in the city, in this image, tends to weaken old, traditional, primary-group cultures, in favor of commercial judgments, the search for the new and the contemporary, and the dominance of mass media and mass culture. It's a grim picture, and it also has a related image—the expressionistic image of the city in German movies of the 1920s. American movies don't do quite as good a job in evoking this image of the city, but perhaps one can get the idea from *The Maltese Falcon*, *The Big Sleep*, and their imitators.

However, Herbert Gans's "Urbanism and Suburbanism as Ways of Life" modifies this image severely.[6] Gans is best known for two books: *The Urban Villagers* and *The Levittowners*,[7] an inner-city study and a suburban study, respectively, and in both he found that Wirth had grossly exaggerated the effects of size, density, and heterogeneity. The village still lives, Gans tells us, in the inner city as well as in the outer city and the suburb. There are still important primary ties; that is, family and kinship remain important. The disintegrating messages of the commercial and cosmopolitan worlds are filtered out to serve the objectives of family and neighborhood and ethnic group. Wirth's description is limited radically and concerns only a part of the city: the inner city with its cosmopolites, unmarried young people, and couples without children; its ethnic villages; its deprived; and its downwardly mobile and trapped people. And even these escape most of the consequences that Wirth projected. Each segregated group interacts with another only superficially, and it is only the deprived and the downwardly mobile for whom the full impact of what Wirth described as urbanism is unleashed.

What is the image here? A collection of villages. Gans attacked not only the view of the disintegrating effect of the inner city, but the popular postwar view of the suburb as a place of conformity and homogeneity. He agreed that there was conformity and homogeneity but insisted that they resulted not because people were forced to live in suburbs, but because this was the way they wanted to live. They had lived that way, if they could, in the inner and outer city, and the suburb only made it possible

[6]H. Gans, "Urbanism and Suburbanism as Ways of Life: A Re-evaluation of Definitions," in *People and Plans: Essays on Urban Problems and Solutions* (New York: Basic Books, 1968).

[7]Gans, *The Urban Villagers: Group and Class in the Life of Italian-Americans* (New York: Free Press, 1962); and *The Levittowners: Ways of Life and Politics in a New Suburban Community* (New York: Pantheon Books, 1967).

for them to extend the style of life that they preferred. In contrast to Wirth, he called it a "quasi-primary" style of life. It was not as tight and immune to outer influences as the primary group of the tradition society or village, but firm enough in its standards.

This more or less defines the two major conflicting views of the city. It disintegrates and destroys, says one. Not so, or not so fast, says the other. Thus, Wirth emphasized the acculturation and assimilation of Jews in his study of the ghetto in the early 1920s. The ghetto was gone or going, said Wirth. But notice that in the 1970s a lot of people were telling us that the ghetto is still here—even if it is now called the "gilded ghetto." The urban village of new arrivals is re-created by their children in the suburbs.

Unfortunately, that doesn't complete our catalog. Gans wrote perceptively at the end of his essay:

> Many of the descriptive comments made here are as time bound as Wirth's. In the 1940's, Wirth concluded that some form of urbanism would eventually predominate in all settlement types. He was, however, writing during a time of immigrant acculturation and at the end of a serious depression, an era of minimal choice. Today, it is apparent that high-density heterogeneous surroundings are for most people a temporary place of residence: other than for Park Avenue or Greenwich Village cosmopolites, they are a result of necessity rather than choice. As soon as they can afford to do so, most Americans head for the single-family house and the quasi-primary way of life of the low-density neighborhood, in the outer city or the suburbs.[8]

Gans was aware that his point of view about what kind of cities people wanted or made was equally time-bound: "However, changes in the national economy, society, and culture can affect people's characteristics—family size, educational level, and various other concomitants of life-cycle change and style. . . . The rising number of college graduates, for example, is likely to increase the cosmopolite ranks."[9]

In other words, things could and would change. But I would emphasize in particular that things would change because of political interventions. To the Chicago school the city was very much a "natural" growth. Consider the concentric circles. These, in the Chicago sociologists' view, were not dominated by political intervention and political action. They were the result of almost primal or primordial forces. One had to assume,

[8]Gans, "Urbanism and Suburbanism," pp. 47–48.
[9]Ibid., p. 48.

of course, a certain distribution of income, changes in that distribution, property rights, and the like—but these were all taken for granted. Once we set the stage, a natural process or natural processes begin to operate— segregation, succession, conflict—and out of this process the Chicago image of the city emerges. The degree to which they thought it natural is emphasized by the term they used for their approach to the city: *social ecology*. *Ecology* is a much more familiar word in the environmentalist 1970s and 1980s than when Chicago sociologists picked it up from biologists in the 1930s.

The social ecology viewpoint emerged when government played very little role in shaping the city—or so it was believed. In the 1950s, we began to have urban renewal, rebuilding the older parts of city central business districts; we had expanded subsidized housing for the poor; in the 1960s, we had efforts to spread this housing into middle-class and suburban areas—specifically affecting the "natural" pattern of American cities, whereby the poor lived in the center, the better off further out; and we even had an abortive and disastrously unsuccessful "new town" effort. In this enterprise, government attempted to realize an image of the city that emerged from the thinking of city planners. One would have to go back to Ebenezer Howard and his *Garden Cities of Tomorrow* to find the chief influence in creating this image.[10] But my point in discussing governmental intervention is to emphasize to how large a degree both Wirth and Gans saw the city and the suburb as the products of governmentally unaffected economic and cultural forces. Even though Levittown was helped by government-guaranteed mortgages and required some political effort to implement, to Gans it was not these that pushed people, against their desires, to move into Levittowns—they truly preferred it to the living quarters available in the older parts of the city.

When government intervenes, it is clear that an image is guiding it. It wants to see more business, commercial, and residential activity in the old centers. It wants to mix the income classes and the racial groups. One would have to conclude, however, that government has been at best only partially successful in realizing its images. The classes are still for the most part residentially separated, as are the races, and the central cities, even after all the investment that has been poured into them, compete only weakly with the new suburban developments.

[10]E. Howard, *Garden Cities of Tomorrow* (London: Faber and Faber, 1960, originally published 1898).

Government, Gans seems to say, if we take together *The Urban Villagers* and *The Levittowners*, can destroy (as it destroyed the ethnic West End area of Boston described in the first book), but it cannot create—it is the entrepreneurs, responding to what they think people want, who create the new suburban development.

Two other images of the city merit brief notice, and in at least one of these, government as well as the large-scale entrepreneur is the destroyer. One is the image of the city as kaleidoscope. This is a variation of the view of the city as Jane Jacobs sees it, in *The Death and Life of Great American Cities*.[11] This has also been characterized as "the view from Greenwich Village," where she once lived. Thus, William H. Whyte celebrated urban congestion and variety.[12] Narrower sidewalks and smaller parks than any formal planner thinks people can tolerate will bring people closer together, and they will manage fine, Whyte argued. Whyte lives in and takes many of his examples from crowded midtown Manhattan.

Both Jacobs and Whyte celebrate the small-scale, the diverse, the mixed, and thus have to be antagonistic to the large-scale, whether government imposing its huge housing projects or equally huge downtown redevelopments, or the big developers who respond to the incentives that government gives to create such homogeneous developments. There is a logic—a planning or commercial logic—to the large-scale, but to Jacobs and Whyte, it destroys the essential quality of the city, its diversity. Who can arrange to have artisans' shops or struggling art galleries or sandal makers in the expensive commercial space of any new, large-scale development (or small one, for that matter)? Better to retain the old, for its advantages in creating a diverse social environment. Jane Jacobs also argued that there are other benefits to small-scale diversity, such as the watching eyes in mixed neighborhoods restraining crime.

This is perhaps the most attractive image of the city. Although its chief protagonists are not sociologists, they have a sociological imagination, and sociologists respond to that kind of city pattern, as do tourists, if it is not too dangerous. And when it is, developers now create an artificial (and expensive) diversity, using the small-scale structures of the past (as

[11] J. Jacobs, *The Death and Life of Great American Cities* (New York: Random House, 1961).
[12] W. H. Whyte, *The Social Life of Small Urban Spaces* (Washington, D.C.: Conservation Foundation, 1980).

in Quincy Market in Boston) to assist them or literally building at small scale for the purpose of re-creating the image of the old, diverse city, as in the South Street Seaport development in New York. But this is a limited image, if we look back to Wirth and Gans. Attractive as it is to sociologists, and when sanitized, to tourists, most people don't want to live in it or raise their children in it.

The last sociological image that I will comment on is the relatively new Marxist urban sociology—which in a sense is the community-power-structure view writ large. The bourgeoisie, or the capitalists, not only dominate on the local scale, they represent larger national and extranational—indeed, "world system"—forces. These neo-Marxist writers are very attached to the notion of a world system. It is the concentric-circle image of Park and Burgess expanded, over the nation, and the world. In the center are the metropolis and the metropolitan country. They exploit the rest of the world. Thus, they suck in labor for their needs, determine where it is to be placed to interfere least with the opportunity to make profits. The small concentric system and the large concentric system merge. These writers also emphasize class conflict. But there is conflict in every sociological image, and the only difference one sees in neo-Marxism is (1) that the neo-Marxists emphasize class conflict as basic, against other kinds such as ethnic, cultural, between organized groups, and the like, and (2) once again, the conflict is writ large: the local conflicts reflect national and world class conflict.

I would argue not with the facts but with the interpretation. Of course, we see in Paris the North Africans; in London the Indians, Pakistanis, and West Indians; in New York and Chicago and Los Angeles the Puerto Ricans, Mexican-Americans, blacks, and now Vietnamese, Indians, and others. But should we call it capitalist exploitation, or immigration in search of opportunity? Do these movements serve only the dominant social strata, the capitalists? And are the interests of the dominant social strata always the same?

All images have their purposes—which is not to say that they do not connect with some reality of the city. And which image we find useful (as in much of sociology, one can hardly say "true" or "false"—it depends) will depend on what uses we plan to make of it.

Notes on Contributors

PAOLO CECCARELLI, Dean of the Istituto Universitario di Architettura di Venezia, has been Visiting Professor at the Massachusetts Institute of Technology and the University of California, Santa Cruz, and Visiting Associate at the Center for European Studies, Harvard University. In recent years he has been working on local government politics of communist and socialist parties in Southern Europe. He is the author of *La costruzione della città sovietica* (The Making of the Soviet City), 1970; *Risanamento e speculazione nei Centri Storici* (Urban Renewal and Land Speculation in Inner Cities), 1974; and *La crisi del governo urbano* (The Crisis of Urban Government), 1978.

MICHAEL H. FRISCH teaches History and American Studies at SUNY-Buffalo. He is co-editor of the recently published *Working-Class America: Essays on Labor, Community, and American Society* (1983) as well as the author of *Town into City: Springfield, Massachusetts and the Meaning of Community* (1972) and numerous essays in urban social history, the theory and practice of oral history, and historiography.

GERALD E. FRUG is a Professor of Law at Harvard University and a specialist in local government law. Before joining the Harvard faculty, he served in a number of governmental positions, including that of Health Services Administrator of the City of New York, and was Professor of Law at the University of Pennsylvania. He is the author of numerous articles dealing with questions of both public and private law.

NATHAN GLAZER is Professor of Education and Sociology at Harvard University and a co-editor of *The Public Interest*. His books include *The Lonely Crowd* (with David Riesman and R. Denney, 1973), *American Judaism* (1972), *Beyond the Melting Pot* (with D. P. Moynihan, 1975), *Affirmative Discrimination* (1976), and *Ethnic Dilemmas, 1964–1982* (1983).

PETER HALL is an economic geographer who is especially interested in the geography of planning. Presently he is Professor of Geography and

City & Regional Planning at the University of California and Professor of
Geography at the University of Reading, England. His books include
World Cities (1966), *The Containment of Urban Britain* (1973), *Planning
and Urban Growth: An Anglo-American Comparison* (with M. Clawson,
1973), *Urban and Regional Planning* (1975), and *Great Planning
Disasters.*

JOHN R. HARRIS is Professor of Economics and Director of the African Studies Center at Boston University. He has held research and
teaching appointments in Nigeria and Kenya, has served as an advisor to
the Economic Planning Ministry (BAPPENAS) of Indonesia, and has con-
sulted for the World Bank, United Nations, USAID, and a number of
other developmental organizations. He has published widely in professional journals and is best known for his work on rural-urban migration in
developing countries.

MICHAEL HINDERY, a doctoral candidate in American Civilization at
the University of Pennsylvania, has also taught in the Urban Studies
Program. He did graduate work in Urban Planning at the University of
Washington and is the author of several monographs on neighborhood
development in Seattle. His dissertation topic is citizen participation in
the 1960s and 1970s.

ROBERT M. HOLLISTER is Associate Professor and Chairman of the
Department of Urban and Environmental Policy, Tufts University. For-
merly Associate Professor in the MIT Department of Urban Studies and
Planning, Professor Hollister is coauthor (with Tunney Lee) of *Develop-
ment Politics: Private Development and the Public Interest* (1979), co-
editor (with Seymour Bellin and Bernard Kramer) of *Neighborhood
Health Centers* (1974); and co-editor (with Philip Clay) of *Neighborhood
Policy and Planning* (1983).

PETER LANGER is Assistant Professor of Sociology at Boston University. His research has included studies of suburban social organization,
the social networks of urban men, and the social consequences of downtown revitalization efforts. Current interests are a study of sentiment and
symbolism in gentrifying neighborhoods and an evaluation of policies for
the control of adult-entertainment businesses.

ANTHONY LEEDS, Professor of Anthropology, Boston University, has
done urban field work in Brazil, Portugal, Peru, and Texas, with briefer
experiences and visits in Colombia, Venezuela, Spain, Argentina, and

Chile. He is author (with Elizabeth Leeds) of *A Sociologia do Brasil Urbano* (1978) and of *Minha Terra: Portugal, Poems of Celebration and Lamentation* (1984) and editor (with A. P. Vayda) of *Man, Culture, and Animals: The Role of Animals in Human Subsistence* (1965) and of *Social Structure, Stratification, and Mobility* (1967).

KEVIN LYNCH is a planner and city designer, the author of *Image of the City* (1960), *Site Planning* (1962), *Managing the Sense of a Region* (1976), *What Time is This Place?* (1976), *A Theory of Good City Form* (1981), and a number of other books in the field. For many years Professor of City Design at MIT, he is now a principal in Carr, Lynch Associates. His principal interests center around the large-scale physical environment, its design, its meaning for those who inhabit it, and how they can come to control it effectively.

LEO MARX is the William R. Kenan, Jr., Professor of American Cultural History at MIT. He teaches in the Program in Science, Technology, and Society, and is the author of *The Machine in the Garden: Technology and the Pastoral Ideal in America* (1964). Other of his essays relevant to this subject are: "Pastoral Ideals and City Troubles," in *The Fitness of Man's Environment* (1968); "American Institutions and Ecological Ideals," in *Science* (1970); "The American Revolution and the American Landscape," in *America's Continuing Revolution* (1975).

LISA REDFIELD PEATTIE was trained as a social anthropologist at the University of Chicago where her father, Robert Redfield, and grandfather, Robert Park had both developed images of the city. She has studied American Indians, public schools and public housing in the United States, and housing and planning projects and small enterprises in developing countries. Her books include *The View from the Barrio* (1968), *Thinking about Development* (1981), *Making Work* (with William Ronco) 1983, and *Women's Claims* (with Martin Rein).

THOMAS REINER, a city and regional planner (MCP-MIT), worked in this field in New England and Puerto Rico. He subsequently obtained his Ph.D. from the University of Pennsylvania where he teaches in the Regional Science Department. He is the author of *The Place of the Ideal Community in Urban Planning*, and of articles on planning theory and related topics.

EDWARD ROBBINS is currently Assistant Professor of Anthropology-in-Architecture at MIT. He has done research and written about class and ethnicity in a Canadian mining town, private streets in St. Louis, and the spatial implications of telecommunications technology. Presently he is working on the relationship between culture and architectural form and practice.

LLOYD RODWIN, Director of the (MIT) Special Program for Urban and Regional Studies of Developing Areas (SPURS), was a founder (with M. Meyerson) of the Joint Center for Urban Studies of MIT and Harvard University. Currently a Ford International Professor at MIT, his books include *The British New Towns Policy, Housing and Economic Progress, Nations & Cities* (1970), and *Cities and City Planning* (1981).

MARTIN SHEFTER has taught at Harvard University and the University of Chicago, has been a member of the School of Social Science at the Institute for Advanced Study in Princeton, N.J., and currently is an Associate Professor in the Department of Government at Cornell University. He has written extensively on patronage and machine politics, the fiscal politics of American cities, and the development of American political parties and party systems.

CHARLES TILLY teaches history and sociology at the University of Michigan, where he also directs the Center for Research on Social Organization. His books, both individual and collaborative, include *The Vendee* (1964), *Race and Residence in Wilmington* (1965), *Subsidizing the Poor* (1972), *An Urban World* (1974), *The Formation of National States in Western Europe* (1975), *Strikes in France, 1830–1968* (1974), *The Rebellious Century* (1975), *From Mobilization to Revolution* (1978), *Class Conflict* and *As Sociology Meets History* (1981). His next books will be *The Contentious French, 1600–1980* and *Big Structures, Large Processes, Huge Comparisons*.

SAM BASS WARNER, Jr., is a Williams Edwards Huntington Professor of History and Social Science at Boston University. His books include *Streetcar Suburbs* (1962), *The Urban Wilderness* (1972), *The Way We Really Live, Social Change in Metropolitan Boston Since 1920* (1978).

Index